Praise for

Homemade for Sale

Having spoken with thousands of cottage food entrepreneurs, I can confirm that this book is exactly what someone needs when starting a cottage food business. I've seen many new entrepreneurs making tasty products with bland profits, and *Homemade for Sale* correctly focuses on the missing ingredient—marketing. It will give your new business an edge in a crowded marketplace. Well-researched, loaded with examples, and perfectly tailored to the home cook, this book will point you in the right direction and set you up for success!

—David Crabill, founder, Forrager.com and The Forrager Podcast

Homemade for Sale is the most comprehensive resource for anyone wanting to start a home-based business in the fast-growing cottage food and food freedom movement. This book is for any home-based food entrepreneur, regardless of your background or level of experience with running your own enterprise. It will help you jumpstart your dream home business, whether you want to sell cookies and jams or whether you live in a food freedom state where you can sell cheesecakes and meals or even run a restaurant out of your own home. Kivirist and Ivanko are two of the most important leaders in the cottage food movement and have been instrumental and absolutely indispensable to the movement's rapid progress over the last few years. We are all grateful to have them.

—Erica Smith Ewing, senior attorney, Institute for Justice

By the time you finish reading *Homemade for Sale,* you'll be wearing your farmers-market-John / jam-n-jelly-Jane hat in total confidence.

—MaryJane Butters, author, *Milk Cow Kitchen*, MaryJanesFarm.org

Lisa and John are leaders in this community and *Homemade for Sale* is a must-read for anyone considering or already running a cottage food business.

—Mark Josephson, founder and CEO, Castiron

Homemade For Sale is an inspiring guide for anyone interested in starting a home-based food business. Lisa and John have been through the fire themselves and scoured the cottage food industry to find the best resources to help you get off the ground and succeed. From understanding your state's laws to incorporating your business to choosing the right products customers to market to, they take you step-by-step through everything you should be doing and thinking about. Their profiles on other cottage food entrepreneurs bring everything a little closer to home and might be just the motivation we all need to take part in the movement ourselves.

—Lev Berlin, founder, ReciPal

Homemade FOR SALE

UPDATED AND EXPANDED EDITION

HOW TO Set Up AND MARKET A Food Business FROM YOUR HOME KITCHEN

Lisa Kivirist & John D. Ivanko

Cover design by Diane McIntosh.

Cover images: Front top image; third from top; forth from top; fifth from top; back cover image © John D. Invanko Photography.
Illustration — Cooking Utensils © iStock ma_rish.
Chapter vector graphics © MJ Jessen

Printed in Canada. First printing October 2022.

Inquiries regarding requests to reprint all or part of *Homemade for Sale* should be addressed to New Society Publishers at the address below.

To order directly from the publishers, please call 250-247-9737, or order online at www.newsociety.com

Any other inquiries can be directed by mail to:

New Society Publishers
P.O. Box 189, Gabriola Island, BC V0R 1X0, Canada
(250) 247-9737

LIBRARY AND ARCHIVES CANADA CATALOGUING IN PUBLICATION

Title: Homemade for sale : how to set up and market a food business from your home kitchen / Lisa Kivirist & John D. Ivanko.

Names: Kivirist, Lisa, author. | Ivanko, John D. (John Duane), 1966- author.

Description: Updated and expanded edition. | Includes index.

Identifiers: Canadiana (print) 20220394725 | Canadiana (ebook) 20220394733 | ISBN 9780865719699 (softcover) | ISBN 9781550927634 (PDF) | ISBN 9781771423595 (EPUB)

Subjects: LCSH: Home-based businesses—Management. | LCSH: Food industry and trade—Management. | LCSH: New business enterprises—Management. | LCSH: Home-based businesses—Marketing. | LCSH: Food industry and trade—Marketing. | LCSH: New business enterprises—Marketing.

Classification: LCC HD62.38 .K49 2022 | DDC 664.0068/1—dc23

Funded by the Government of Canada | Financé par le gouvernement du Canada

To food entrepreneurs across the country, who have been pickling, baking, preserving, and blending some of the most delicious food products we've ever savored. Thanks to laws around food freedom and microenterprise home kitchen operations, some of you are even grilling, sautéing, barbequing, frying, or freezing some amazing prepared meals or treats. Your home kitchens rock!

Disclaimer

THIS BOOK IS DESIGNED to and makes every effort to provide accurate information. It's sold with the understanding that neither the publisher nor the authors are engaged in rendering legal, accounting, or other professional services. Each person's legal or financial situation is unique, as is the application of the law to the facts with the fair and reasonable interpretation of them. Any action pursued related to the contents of this book should be undertaken with the counsel and advice of a trained legal, tax, investment, and accounting professional. Because of the risk involved with an investment of any kind, neither the publisher nor the authors assume liability for any losses that may be sustained by the use of the advice described in this book, and any such liability is hereby expressly disclaimed. If legal or other professional assistance is required, the services of a professional should be sought, especially since some of the information could, and likely will, change because it relates to governmental tax law and its interpretation thereof.

Resources from the North Central Region SARE

A new addition in *Homemade for Sale*'s second edition is the range of cottage food resources and recipes developed through support from North Central Region SARE (Sustainable Agriculture Research and Education). The North Central Region SARE Farmer Rancher Grant Program supports farmers in projects that help grow sustainable agriculture production in the USA. This includes value-added products, ways farmers can use what they raise in foods that will then bring in a higher price and increase farm viability.

Lisa Kivirist led three SARE Farmer Rancher projects, creating resources for both farmers and anyone wanting to use more locally grown products in their cottage food products and sell more effectively. A variety of new resources and materials are found throughout this book resulting from these SARE projects, work that is supported by the National Institute of Food and Agriculture, U.S. Department of Agriculture, through the North Central

North Central SARE logo

CREDIT: NORTH CENTRAL SARE

Region SARE program. It includes the following projects: FNC21-1282—Resources & Recipes to Support Farmers to Diversify Income through Value-added Bakery Product Sales (Agreement Number 2020-38640-31522); FNC18-1130—Increasing Value-added Product Sales through Cottage Food Bakery Products Produced in Home Kitchens (Agreement Number 2017-38640-26916); FNC15-998—Increasing Value-added Product Sales through Improved Labeling—Packaging (Agreement Number 2014-38640-22156).

Support from North Central SARE brings these resources to life, including tested non-hazardous recipes, packaging and labeling ideas, and creating attractive displays. For more information on North Central SARE, see https://northcentral.sare.org.

Chapters 5, 7, 8, and 9 contain resources developed through these projects. This information is only a guide, however, and should be used in conjunction with other sources on the subject. The authors and publisher disclaim any liability, loss, or risk, personal or otherwise, that is incurred as a consequence, directly or indirectly, of the use and application of any of the contents of this product. Mention, visual representation, or inferred reference of a product, service, manufacturer, or organization in this information product does not imply endorsement by USDA, NIFA, or the SARE program. Exclusion does not imply a negative evaluation. The U.S. Department of Agriculture is an equal opportunity provider and employer.

Contents

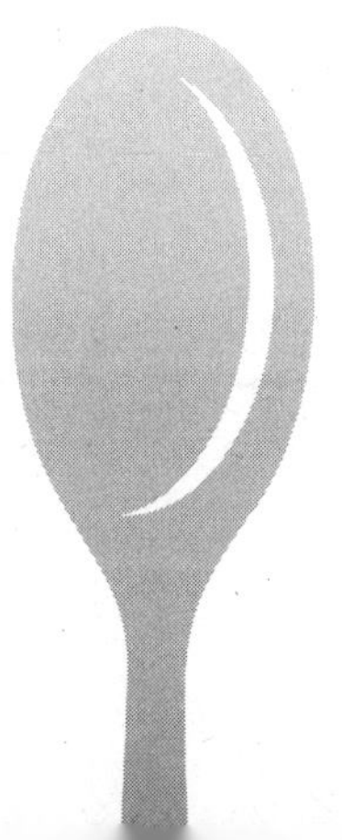

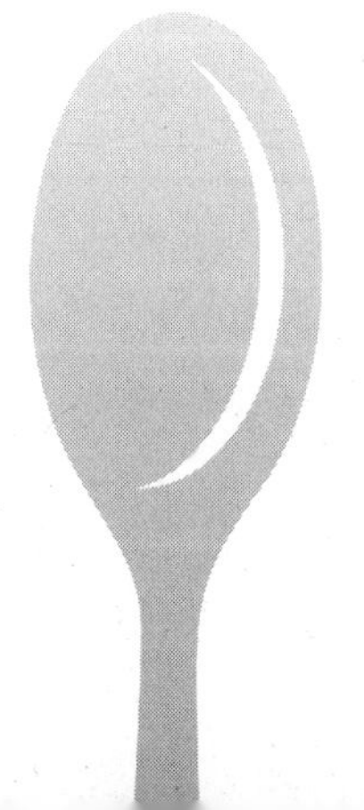

Acknowledgments

FOOD IS SYNONYMOUS with community. We enjoy sharing every jar of pickles or loaf of zucchini bread with friends, family, and our bed and breakfast guests. We love the land, the delicious treats that can be created from our harvest of it, and the grins that accompany every bite.

This book champions community too. Without the amazing creativity, passion, and talents of home cooks everywhere, our sense of taste would go dormant. The food you create in your home kitchens is what this book both celebrates and inspires. Special thanks to those cottage food entrepreneurs who graciously shared their stories for this book: Dawn M. Belisle (Delights by Dawn), Elizabeth Berman (Small Oven Pastries), Lauren Cortesi (Bella's Desserts), Mynhan Hoang (My Fair Kitchen), Tamsin Perfect (Tamsin's Cakes), Dave "Poppy" Sanders (Poppy and Sweetpea's Cookies), and Madhavi Tandon (Maia Foods LLC).

Thanks, also, to David Crabill of Forrager.com and *The Forrager Podcast*, who helped put cottage foods on the map and continues to guide the movement by providing a podcast, a directory, a forum for discussion, and a quick reference guide to what's happening in every state. Appreciation goes out to Alexia Kulweic, executive director for Farm to Consumer Legal Defense Fund; Sophia Kruszewski, clinic director with the Center for Agriculture & Food Systems at the Vermont Law School; and Rachel Armstrong, founder and executive director of Farm Commons, for their legal insight and their organizations' support for small-scale farmers looking to diversify into value-added products.

Deep gratitude to Erica Smith Ewing and all the legal visionaries at the Institute for Justice who fight for our rights in Wisconsin and way beyond, including Suranjan Sen, Justin Pearson, Meagan Forbes, Connor Beck, and Michael Bindas. Thanks to Corrie and Heather Miracle, of Sugar Cookie Marketing, for sharing insights and expertise related to Facebook, Instagram, website SEO, and other technical opportunities. To Renee Pottle, thanks for sharing tips on canning success.

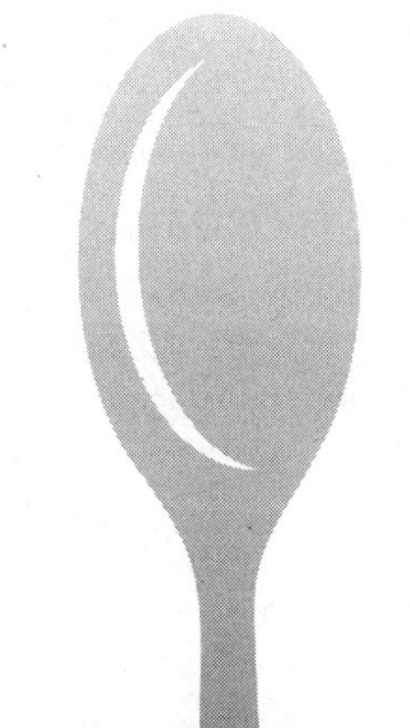

Appreciation to Jan Joannides and Brett Olson, founders of Renewing the Countryside, for championing our work and the voices of rural food and farm businesses and for hosting the first-ever Home-based Food Entrepreneur Virtual National Conference, and to Eli Goodwell, Elena Byrne, and Jody Padgham for their support.

This new edition gratefully reflects the efforts resulting from three North Central SARE Farmer Rancher grants, with deep appreciation to the woman-powered farmer team behind the recipe testing and development: Dela Ends, Ashley Wegmueller, Linda Dee Derrickson, Danielle Matson, Kalena Riemer, Anastasia Wolf-Flash, and Jen Riemer. Special thanks to Dan Harrigan at Blackhawk Technical College (Monroe Campus) for his support with local water activity testing and insight. Deep thanks to the North Central SARE staff for making this possible and for cooking up so many resources for farmers in sustainable agriculture, including Beth Nelson, Joan Benjamin, Jean Andreasen, and Marie Flanagan.

We're indebted to the many experts who have shared their knowledge both in these pages and continually as we expand this movement. Special thanks to Pratik Banerjee at the University of Illinois at Urbana-Champaign, Jane Jewett at the Minnesota Institute for Sustainable Agriculture, Alyssa Hartman and Amy Halloran of the Artisan Grains Collaborative, and Laura Gosewisch of Vital Ground Farm.

Our Wisconsin story exemplifies the cottage food collaborative spirit that ripples throughout these pages. Lisa draws so much inspiration and positive mojo from the friends she shares this journey with and who have been instrumental in our fight for opportunity in our state. Warm cookies to Kriss Marion and Dela Ends, fellow plaintiffs that exemplify how shaking up democracy is much better when shared with friends. Hat tip to Jobea Murray for her support growing the Wisconsin Cottage Food Association and our amazing Wisconsin Cottage Food Ambassadors. Gratitude to the Wisconsin Farmers Union

Taking a break from recipe testing and baking for the North Central SARE-funded project. They nailed it: A great-tasting non-hazardous frosting recipe to top muffins made with fresh local produce.
CREDIT: JOHN D. IVANKO PHOTOGRAPHY

for collaboratively supporting our original efforts to expand the cottage food legislation in our state to include baked goods.

Thanks to open cooperation with other state associations and a special-kindred spirited shout-out to Shelley Erickson and Jennifer Carriveau of the Minnesota Cottage Food Producer's Association, Kathy Zeman at the Minnesota Farmers' Market Association, Martha Rabello of the New Jersey Home Bakers Association, and Molly Pickering of the Illinois Stewardship Alliance. Recognition goes to the numerous and enthusiastic Facebook group members—the cookiers, cottage food bakers, and state groups—from whom we've learned so much and been inspired by your collaborative spirit to help everyone's business thrive.

Lisa draws deep daily energy from a rich and diverse network of women who cheer her on and keep her rolling, through pandemics and beyond. Big thanks to Rose Hayden Smith, Melinda Hemmelgarn, Angie Tagtow, Gabriele Marewski and her local Green County Soil Sisters network, with a special shout-out to Betty Anderson, Erica Roth, Cara Carper, Pat Skogen, FL Morris, Brenda Carus, and so many more.

Without the talents of our editor, Rob West, and the visionary guidance of New Society Publishers—Ingrid Witvoet, Judith Brand, Greg Green, Sue Custance, and all the marketing folks—our book would be nothing more than a half-baked idea. And once again, Diane McIntosh designed the perfect cover.

Finally, to our son, Liam, we cannot thank you more for your patience as Mom and Dad pecked away at the keyboard—and your never-ending sense of humor. You kept us laughing, buzzed on coffee, and well-nourished with your home-cooked gourmet meals for our family suppers. While our parents, Aelita and Valdek Kivirist and Susan Ivanko, may never have created a product in their own kitchens for market, their skills behind the counter provided the foundation for our culinary career today. They say you learn most by example, repeated over and over again.

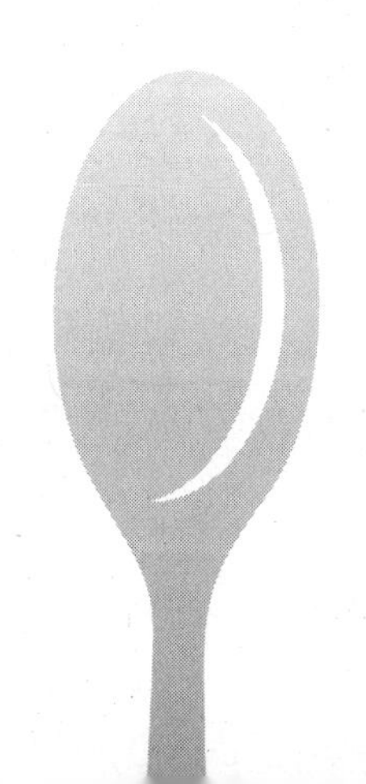

Introduction: Cottage Food, Food Freedom, and Growing a Movement

WELCOME TO THE SECOND EDITION of *Homemade for Sale!* First and foremost, thank you—our growing and collaborative cottage food community—for being an integral ingredient in this expanding national movement of home-based food entrepreneurs. Since this book first came out in 2015, *Homemade for Sale* has served as the leading national guide to help you go from a hobbyist giving away those tasty treats to real-life business owner.

We knew something important was baking and bubbling when *Homemade for Sale* was first released. Sure enough, the cottage food industry has grown in multiple ways since then, from expanding state laws to the blooming food freedom movement. We kept the key bread-and-butter elements of business start-up and marketing in this edition but added whole new sections to help you navigate today's evolving cottage food and food freedom scene.

"There's nothing I love to do more than making decorated sugar cookies, and I bring them to parties, and my friends keep saying you should sell these, but I don't know where to start."

"I'm always growing more than I need in my garden and started canning and love making items like jams, salsa, and pickles, and I don't see anyone selling these at my local farmers' market. I wonder if I could do that?"

"Going through the COVID-19 pandemic, I really thought about what I wanted out of my life and my values. I realized I no longer want to work for someone else, sit in an office, behind a computer. It's time to be my own boss and work from home. I want to call the shots."

"Like clockwork every Christmas, my family loves my special gingerbread cookies and tells me I could make money selling them, but I've never run my own business and feel overwhelmed."

"I love baking, but I really have no interest in starting a full-time bakery, especially being a stay-at-home mom with young kids. But doing something part-time from home from my home kitchen. That's something for me. It's also important to me to be a role model for my kids by being a mom while running my own business."

"I got laid off from my food service job during the pandemic. Honestly, I'm so not interested in going back to that industry because of the low pay and long hours. I love food and creating beautiful edibles. Now I want to reinvent myself and build something of my own."

"There's nothing more satisfying than making and sharing my fruit jams and jellies with others. I keep giving everything away, but my friends tell me they'd be happy to buy from me. But I don't have big bucks to start a full-blown commercial operation. I heard I could do this from home, but I'm nervous about it being legal."

"I run an organic farm and always have excess seasonal produce that I bring home from the farmers' market that doesn't sell. I'd love to diversify my income base and add canned items and baked goods that showcase these local ingredients."

"My husband keeps telling me that I need a project. We're retired, but I don't like playing golf or fishing. I feel at home in the kitchen and have a knack for creating yummy treats for my husband and his friends. Starting a food business sounds like it might be fun and rewarding."

Can you relate to any of these enthusiastic home cooks? If so, you're not alone. You could be part of a growing movement of people starting small food businesses from their homes. No capital needed, just good recipes, enthusiasm, and commitment, plus enough know-how to turn ingredients into sought-after treats for your local community. Everything you require is probably already in your home kitchen. Best of all, you can start your journey right away!

Thanks to new laws, regulations, or successful legal action currently on the books, small-scale food businesses can be operated from home kitchens

in all 50 states. These state laws, most often referred to as "cottage food laws," allow you to sell certain food products to your neighbors and community. By "certain foods," the laws generally mean various shelf-stable "non-hazardous" food items, often defined as those that are high-acid, like pickles, or low-moisture, like breads. Because of this definition, some of the state cottage food laws have been nicknamed Pickle Bills, Cookie Bills, or Bakery Bills on their journey to becoming laws where you live.

Cottage Food Surge

The tremendous surge of cottage food businesses since 2015 has been driven by the following factors.

Expansion of State Cottage Food Laws

It is now legal to sell from your home kitchen in every state. These expanded laws mean a more diversified range of products can be sold, more gross revenue can be earned, and greater flexibility in terms how you can sell.

For example, the first edition of *Homemade for Sale* reflected that most state laws prevented you from selling wholesale out of your home kitchen. You won't read that in this new edition because wonderfully it isn't true anymore. Several states, like California and Iowa, now allow wholesale to retailers. Over half of states have either no gross sales caps or sales caps so high—like $250,000—that there really is no limit to what you can earn from your home kitchen.

Launch of Food Freedom Laws

This edition features a whole new section devoted to food freedom! These so-called food freedom laws enable you to sell more than non-hazardous, shelf-stable food products out of your home. Food freedom laws allow food entrepreneurs to sell what are considered hazardous foods, from live fermented foods to fully prepared ready-to-eat meals. California led this important evolution with the 2018 passage of AB-626, the California Homemade Food Act. Other states are moving in this direction. While the food freedom laws are distinctly different than a state's non-hazardous cottage food law, consider them "cousin legislation." The huge uptick in food freedom initiatives is a win for anyone who wants the freedom to earn.

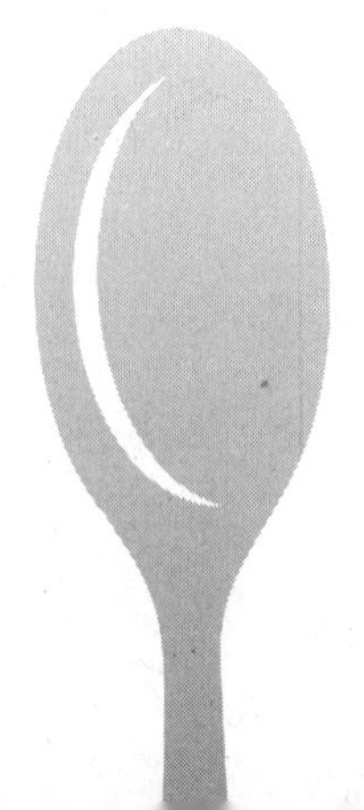

The Pandemic Pivot

The COVID-19 pandemic resulted in a perfect storm of opportunity for the number of new cottage food businesses to surge, with people left scrambling after being laid off from a job in the food and restaurant sector, or finding themselves needing to work from home while caring for young children. States like New York reported an over 50% increase in new cottage food producers during the early days of pandemic. During this challenging time, we worked with Renewing the Countryside to host the first-ever Home-Based Food Entrepreneur Virtual National Conference in April, 2021, drawing over 900 attendees.

"Shocks to the labor market created by COVID-19 accelerated the [cottage foods] trend, as legislatures have sought to give entrepreneurs the opportunity to start or expand successful businesses from home. These expansions enable individual entrepreneurs and small enterprises to operate without being subject to the same level of scrutiny as full-scale restaurants and food manufacturers, which in turn reduces start-up costs and barriers to entry."

— Harvard Law School Food Law and Policy Clinic,
Cottage Foods and Home Kitchens:
2021 State Policy Trends (January 2022).

Continued Growth of Local Food Movement

Underlying cottage food and food freedom laws are a continued increase of customers wanting to know their producer, their farmer, and their local food artisan and to support and prioritize a locally based food economy. The pandemic only increased this interest when supply chains were severely disrupted in our industrial food system.

As the first comprehensive and authoritative guide to launching a successful food enterprise operated from your home kitchen, the second edition of *Homemade for Sale* provides a clear road map to go from idea and recipe to final product. The book continues to offer specific strategies and resources for people running home-based food businesses, unlike other books that

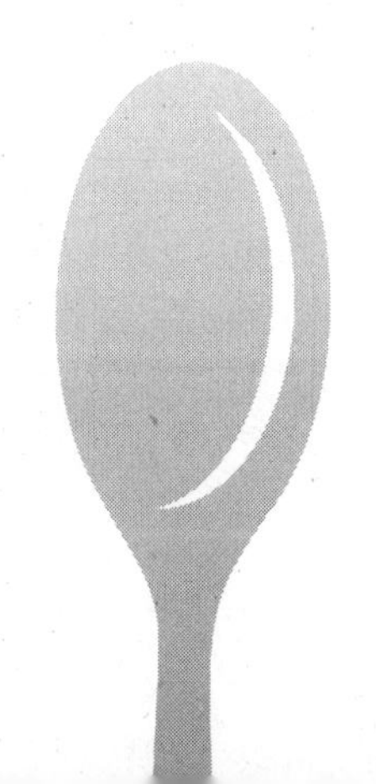

Canada's "Cottage Food" Conundrum

At the time of writing, there are no general national or provincial "cottage food laws" (or pending bills) in Canada. Generally speaking, if you live in Canada, under no circumstances can you produce food in your kitchen and sell it to the public—unless you are a farmer or selling certain home-baked products at a farmers' market in certain provinces that allow for it.

"The Canadian Food Inspection Agency provides regulatory oversight with respect to many aspects of food and related products in Canada, including, for example, labeling and packaging requirements for these products," explains Carly Dunster (carlydunsterlaw.com), a food lawyer based in Ontario, Canada. "The federal government has also passed legislation entitled the Safe Food for Canadians Act, which came into force in 2019, that consolidates a number of federal food laws and demonstrates an increased emphasis on food safety at the federal level.

"It is conceivable that someone could create a commercial kitchen in their home, but the requirements are onerous, both in terms of just the physical infrastructure you would need and in terms of the zoning," continues Dunster. "For example, you can't operate a commercial kitchen out of your home unless your house is zoned commercially, which isn't typical. The federal organization that regulates food is the Canadian Food Inspection Agency (inspection.gc.ca), but the operation of a commercial kitchen would, in many ways, be governed by provincial and municipal regulations and public health agencies."

Another source of further information related to food preparation is Restaurants Canada, restaurantscanada.org.

However, in specific cases—if you operate a farm, for example, and want to sell specific non-hazardous food items made in your home kitchen at a farmers' market, community market, charity fair, or similar "temporary food market"—your province may allow you to do so. Consult with your local health authority.

According to the *Guideline for the Sale of Foods at Temporary Food Markets*, August 2020, from the BC Centre for Disease Control (bccdc.ca), an agency of the Provincial Health Services Authority, lower-risk foods prepared in home kitchens are allowed to be sold to the public at temporary markets, like farmers' markets. Additional requirements include, but are not limited to, the following:

- Lower-risk food means food in a form or state that is not capable of supporting the growth of disease-causing organisms or the production of toxins. One or more of the following factors usually apply to these foods:
  - Water activity (Aw) of 0.85 or less, or
  - A pH (hydrogen ion concentration) value of 4.6 or less.
- Vendors of home-prepared foods at temporary food markets must only sell foods that are considered to be lower risk. Vendors are allowed to sell home-prepared lower-risk foods at temporary food markets without contacting or receiving approval by the local Health Authority.
- Vendors of lower-risk foods are not required to submit an application before commencement of sales. It is the vendor's ☛

and the market manager's responsibility to ensure that all lower-risk foods meet the definition of a lower-risk food.

- Public health is protected by ensuring that food prepared at home that is offered for sale at temporary food markets is limited to lower-risk foods.
- A sign is displayed that is clearly visible to the consumer at the point of sale stating that "This food has been prepared in a kitchen that is not inspected by a regulatory authority," or equivalent wording.
- Pets should be excluded from kitchens during the time food is being prepared.
- Home-prepared/packaged food may be subject to Canadian Food Inspection Agency (CFIA) and Health Canada requirements for allergens, labeling, weights, and measures. Vendors are advised to check with their local CFIA office to ensure their packages/labels comply with applicable federal requirements.
- The following list contains examples of lower-risk foods that may be acceptable for home preparation and sale at a temporary food market:
  - applesauce
  - brownies
  - bread and buns (no dairy or cheese fillings)
  - butter tarts
  - pies (fruit-filled only, no cream-filled or cream-based)
  - cakes (icing sugar only, no dairy or synthetic whipped cream)
  - dry cereal products
  - chocolate (provided it is used for re-melted or re-molded products only and (1) not purchased from bulk bins; (2) sourced from a chocolate manufacturer that can provide a certificate of assurance that chocolate is free from *Salmonella*).
  - cinnamon buns (sugar icing only)
  - cookies
  - dried fruits
  - fresh fruits and vegetables
  - fudge
  - hard candy
  - honey
  - jam and jelly (pH 4.6 or less or aw of 0.85 or less)
  - muffins (no dairy fillings)
  - popcorn
  - noodles (dry flour and water only, no egg based)
  - pickled vegetables (vinegar base, pH 4.6 or less)
  - relish (vinegar base, pH 4.6 or less)
  - wine and herb vinegar
  - syrup
  - toffee
  - salsa (contains no animal protein); pH 4.6 or less if the product is made with fresh tomatoes and is thermally processed; pH 4.2 or less if the product is made with fresh tomatoes and is NOT thermally processed.

"We sell wood-fire-baked sourdough bread, plus syrups, sauces, salsa, both pressure and water ☛

bath-canned, all produced from our vegetables and fruits," says Denise Cross of Mountain Valley Farm (mountainvalleyproduce.com) located in West Kelowna, British Columbia. She operates the "beyond organic" farm with her husband, Tom, and son, Brandon, making all their products in their farmhouse kitchen. "We sell all of the products at both our Farmgate Market and the local farmers' market."

"We've determined to take it one step at a time, practice what we preach, and share our belief in respecting ourselves and our environment with the next generation, our neighbors, our customers, and our community," adds Tom Cross. "Our goal is to invite, support and share with all who believe there is importance in real food."

A similar exemption for farmers to sell value-added, non-hazardous foods at a farmers' market exists for Ontario as well. According to the Niagara Region Public Health (regional.niagara.on.ca), "A special exemption is provided at farmers' markets to allow vendors to sell non-hazardous home prepared products. This exemption is not applicable to any other commercial facilities or events. The purpose of this exemption was to allow farmers at a farmers' market to sell a variety of products made from their own produce or fruit (i.e., jams, jellies, pies)."

focus on commercial baking or food product businesses. As defined by the law, your business, at least when you start, will be a part-time, small-scale operation operated by you.

"Starting a food-oriented small business can be more than just a dream. If you want to package and sell your soup, jam, candy or grandma's salsa, you'll find many customers willing to try your new taste sensation, plenty of places such as farmers' markets to sell your product, and believe it or not, you can have low start-up costs."

— Rhonda Abrams, *USA Today* (November 29, 2013)

With most of the cottage food laws passed since 2008, states make it possible for anyone to earn income, follow a culinary passion or dream, and have some fun. How? By selling specific food items made in your home kitchen. From pies to pickles, wedding cakes to granola, preserves to decorated cookies, fledgling food entrepreneurs no longer need to sink more than $50,000 into a commercial kitchen or fork over $50 an hour to rent a licensed facility to turn Aunt Emma's biscotti recipe into a money-making dream business. We now have the freedom to earn.

These expanding cottage food laws make home kitchen enterprises the next hot small-business trend, accessible to anyone with a passion for food. Turn your ribbon-winning state fair strawberry rhubarb pie or "famous within your family" fudge into an enjoyable business that can earn you some money to pay off those credit card balances or save for a rainy day. With millions of Americans living paycheck to paycheck, never has it been easier to moonlight out of your kitchen to make ends meet. Perhaps you'll even sell enough goodies to cover that family vacation you always wanted but could never afford.

"If you've been spending the holiday season whipping up goodies to share with family and friends, you might have caught yourself wondering whether you could turn your prize-winning peppermint bark or mouthwatering marmalade into a tasty sideline business or retirement income. Maybe so. In fact, this is a great time to savor the increasing opportunities for food entrepreneurs. Consumers are embracing specialty and artisanal foods like never before."

— Nancy Collamer, *Forbes* (December 21, 2012).

Work Your Passion for Food

What do Paula Dean, Martha Stewart, and Mrs. Fields have in common? They all started their business from their home. Like you, they share a passion for food and chose careers in the kitchen that they love.

Flash forward to today. All 50 states have some form of a cottage food law passed or equivalent legal ruling in place since the Great Recession of 2007. These laws were viewed as a relatively low-cost option to spur

"Allowing for cottage food operations is an easy way that states can support the development of small businesses and increase the availability of local products within their borders. As more consumers become interested in supporting local food economies and more producers begin starting their own food businesses, states need to make sure that those local businesses can survive and thrive. Although many states have cottage food or home-based food processing laws on their books, there are still a number of ways in which states can update and improve their cottage food regimes to match the growing demand and opportunity for cottage food operations."

— Harvard Food Law and Policy Clinic, A Division of the Center for Health Law and Policy Innovation.

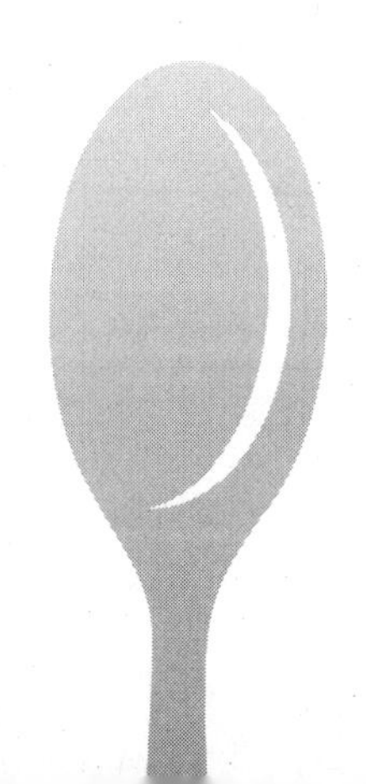

entrepreneurial start-ups. With minimal, if any, inspections or registration processes, cottage food laws can be administered by state agencies for much less than the costly inspections required of full commercial operations.

While many of these laws have been around for over a decade, little information is still available regarding the number of cottage food start-ups and their sales. For reasons not clear to us, few states are tracking the growth or impacts of these home-based food entrepreneurs other than counting the number of paid registrations collected for those states that even have them. During the first year that California's law was in place, more than 1,200 new businesses registered. Arizona is home to more than 2,400 cottage food operators. In Pennsylvania, 2,500 licenses for a limited food establishment—their term used for home-based food product operations—were issued in 2021. Data on other states remains elusive. Ranging in size, sales, and product offerings, these businesses would not have legitimately existed be it not for the cottage food laws passed.

"Nine out of ten respondents started their ventures to be their own boss and do something they enjoy. Eight out of ten did so to have better work-life balance."

— Entrepreneur from Home study completed 2020–2021, by the Institute for Justice (ij.org)

Many food entrepreneurs are drawn to the cottage food industry because they love cooking and love the autonomy that comes with minding their own business and being their own boss. Perhaps you share this perspective. Are you tired of punching the clock and would rather punch some dough?

As it turns out, budding home kitchen entrepreneurs come in many persuasions with a myriad motivations. Which one best defines you?

- Dream-catcher, eager to fulfill a lifelong dream of running a small food enterprise.
- Home baker, possibly with seasonal specialty items you want to share with your community.
- Stay-at-home mom wanting to earn extra income while keeping an eye on the kids.
- Someone with food sensitivities or allergies, who, after years of struggle, has found delicious recipes that work for you and might work for others, too.
- Dedicated locavore foodie, wanting to make a difference in the local food movement beyond your shopping habits.
- Retiree looking to stay relevant and active, plus make a little extra "fun money."

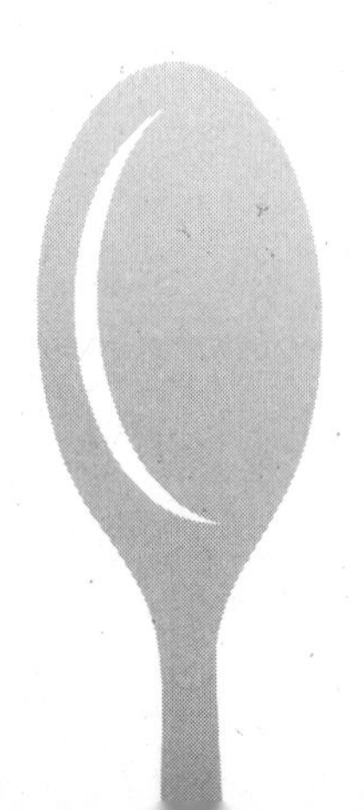

- Specialty cake and custom wedding cake maker looking for a chance to share your artistic talent and creative flair.
- Farmer looking to diversify your business by offering bread and other items at farmers' markets to boost your revenue.
- Economic survivalist who has found that Plan B, despite a college degree, is the new Plan A.
- Career changer from breadwinner to bread baker, looking to test your food-based dream before you quit your day job.
- Someone between jobs and searching for a quick way to earn some cash to pay the bills.

As we talked with cottage food business owners across the continent and interacted with many of them at the Home-based Food Entrepreneur Virtual National Conference, we discovered that launching a small food enterprise could be for anyone and everyone. While our non-scientific sample tended to skew female, there are plenty of men too, and food entrepreneurs are both young and old and come from various ethnic or socioeconomic backgrounds. They live in urban, suburban, and rural places. All share a passion for the culinary arts. Later in this book, we'll share more about who these aspiring and current cottage food operators, or CFOs, are thanks to the first-ever research assessment study on CFOs completed by Rachael Miller, a graduate student from the University of Wisconsin-Stout (a summary infographic can be found in Appendix A of this book).

"Lots of people are eyeing their kitchens right now as a way to earn a little extra cash in a bad economy."

— Emily Maltby, CNNMoney.com (July 2009)

Starting a food-based enterprise from your kitchen is an incredible opportunity, whether it resulted from politicians feeling the heat to do something as a result of the financial fallout from the Great Recession, was a way to deal with the realities of the pandemic, was spawned by the "buy local" movement, or came about because of pressure from the 99 percent who want to sell items directly to their neighbors and make a little money without wading through government regulations.

To help spur and support home-based food enterprises, many state governments decided to cut the excessive red tape and allow people to get to work and earn some money by becoming small business owners. In other words, they allowed Americans to be what Americans have always been: enterprising, community-focused, and hard-working. Forget the unemployment lines, food pantries, or minimum-wage McJobs. Make way for the muffin makers!

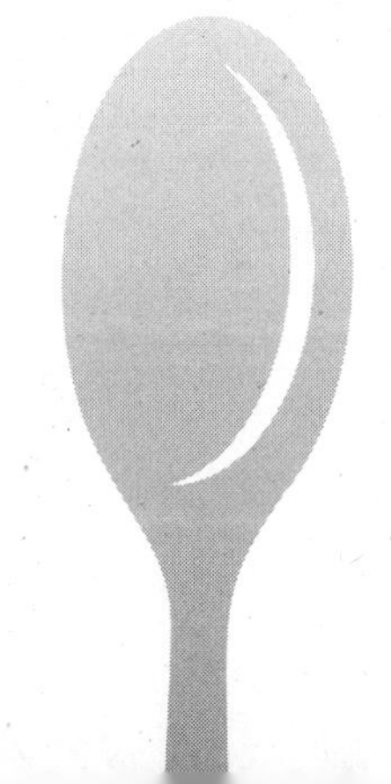

Perhaps encouraging cottage food businesses makes plain common sense. That's the way things were done in America for more than a century: neighbors selling to neighbors; fellow parishioners selling to fellow parishioners; local businesses selling to local residents. It's how business was done before the Age of Cheap Oil, industrialization, and globalization.

Buy Local and Sell Local

Our kitchen is the place we feed those who matter most to us: our family. We do so with love, care, and safety in mind. Would we really do anything differently when serving the public?

We can thank our current industrialized food system for the shift from homemade goodness to factory efficiency and the resulting disconnect from what we put into our mouths. Flash back to our pioneering *Little House on the Prairie* era when life centered on the hearth and home kitchens. You purchased those few staples you didn't raise on your homestead from the Oleson's Mercantile in town, a spot where you knew the shopkeepers, even their irritating daughter, Nellie.

But as our country increasingly modernized, embracing the lure of cheap factory-made products, food safety lost out. Horrid working conditions and unsafe food products rose to the public's priority list in the early twentieth century with the publication of Upton Sinclair's book *The Jungle*, a classic tale of the horrific conditions in the Chicago meat-packing industry. *The Jungle* influenced the laws that followed to regulate and clamp down on the food industry. While desperately needed at the time, these same laws have since been amended, expanded, and interpreted so broadly that public schools now ban homemade items for classroom birthday treats.

Today's cottage food movement cooperatively supports the burgeoning "buy local" movement across the country. The economic evidence of revitalized local community food systems is coming in. According to the Institute for Self-Reliance, in a comparison study of local and national chain retailers, the local stores return a total of 52 percent of their revenue to the local economy, compared to just 14 percent for the chain guys. Similarly, local independent restaurants recirculate an average of 79 percent of their revenue locally, compared to only 30 percent for chain eateries.

The same process can happen with cottage food businesses. Buy your ingredients from a locally owned, independent grocery store or food cooperative or farmer and sell your products to folks in your neighborhood, then return to the store and buy more flour, or canning jars, or strawberries. The money circulates within your community. You're not just a small home-based chutney-producing business, you're playing a role in changing our economic system, one cookie and neighbor connection at a time.

First-timer or Seasoned Pro?

We wrote *Homemade for Sale* as a comprehensive and accessible reference guide for home cooks unacquainted with operating a small business, as well as a more detailed book for business-savvy, but first-time, food entrepreneurs. Some of you reading this book may just need a little nudge to hang out your shingle. With you in mind, we've created the chapter Make It Legal: Establish Your Business in 7 Easy Steps.

For more seasoned entrepreneurs, we've offered several chapters on marketing, drawing from our experiences over the years in the public relations and advertising fields; we've worked at the full-service Leo Burnett Advertising Agency and know a bit about Tony the Tiger and Ronald McDonald. We write press releases for various clients as well as feature articles for national magazines, working both sides of the aisle. And if you want to improve your game using social media or a website, we'll dive into some nuances of hashtags and website SEO.

We also include plenty of guidance and resources that should help business owners eager to diversify or expand with new products they can sell to the public by leveraging cottage food laws. In our unique situation in Wisconsin, we had to organize and sue for the right to sell baked goods (more on that in chapter 21). We operate Inn Serendipity Fresh Baked Homemade Bakery and sell baked goods along with pickles and other high-acid canned items to guests staying at our Inn Serendipity Bed & Breakfast or at special events. In a business as small as ours, it could be the difference between operating

Cottage Food Pros and Cons

Pros	Cons
Little to no capital needed; you probably have everything you need in your kitchen already.	State regulations limit what products you can make, some more than others.
Fast start-up. Most states have a simple, low-cost registration process.	States may also have limitations on where and in what way you can sell.
May already have a recipe and be experienced in what you want to make.	With any food product, you're liable for what you make and need to insure yourself for the risk you take.
Sell directly to the customer and keep more profit.	Baking, canning, and other food preparation is hard work on your feet, especially if you have to make multiple fresh items at once.
	Bookkeeping is a must since you're required to keep track of sales, expenses, and inventory. A real chore, if you don't like crunching numbers.
	May stir up some negative vibes when viewed as competition by local businesses like an established commercial bakery.

at a profit or a loss. As we explore at length in our other book—*Rural Renaissance, ECOpreneuring, Farmstead Chef,* and *Soil Sisters*—we define success in ways far beyond financial wealth or prestigious corner offices or titles.

As a CFO, you're in charge and responsible for the outcome of your endeavor. This can be empowering and unnerving, satisfying and trying. It can also be enriching, in every sense of the word. When you operate your home-based food business, you can make some money, do what you want, and, maybe, even make a difference in your community.

It's Thyme. Why Now?

From "Buy Local" to "Small Business Saturdays," from slow food to fancy food, from farm-to-fork to handmade artisan breads, more people than ever are demanding real food made by real people—not by machines in factories, the same way they make cars and computers.

Let's be real. As more research findings surface on the improved health, nutrition, and taste of products made from real ingredients, the greater the demand for these products made with no preservatives, artificial flavors or colors, or mystery ingredients courtesy of the science lab. While laws labeling ingredients or products as containing genetically modified organisms (GMOs) have remained elusive, retailers are demanding transparency when federal and state governments do not. The growth of farmers' markets, specialty food products, and farm-to-table restaurants that source their foods directly from farmers, fisherman, or food artisans reflects this hunger for foods with ingredients we can pronounce, made by people who live at places we could visit, maybe even in our home town.

Added to this are the growing issues more Americans have with respect to what they eat. Allergies or sensitivities to peanuts, soybeans, gluten, and dairy products have exploded.

Cottage food enterprises address these growing trends, solving problems and meeting customer needs like few large corporations ever could. As a result, these micro enterprises often have a competitive advantage—beyond minimal regulations of the cottage food laws themselves. Their small size, direct connection and responsiveness to customer needs, and attentive detail to each and every product go way beyond large food companies.

The food industry is more crowded than ever with new players entering the field every day. In order to be successful, you must differentiate yourself by having a clear value proposition and a strong story that resonates with your consumers. As a small business your greatest asset is your ability to connect on a human level with your customers. That is something the larger brands simply can't do in an authentic manner and something that many food entrepreneurs overlook. Focus on building strong connections with your customers and engage them in conversation be it at the farmers' market, at the side of your food truck, or online via social media. Invite them to be part of your food business journey and they will reward you with their loyalty."

— 2014 *Plate of the Union Report*, Small Food Business (smallfoodbiz.com)

"Avoid food products containing ingredients that are (A) unfamiliar (B) unpronounceable (C) more than five in number or that include (D) high-fructose corn syrup."

—Michael Pollan, *In Defense of Food: An Eater's Manifesto* (2008)

While food products from most corporations are designed for shelf life, transportability, uniformity, and profitability, cottage foods, by their very nature, are small batch, fresh, and specialized. Fewer and fewer Americans are being fooled by mega-food producers' product labels that read fresh from the oven, all-natural, homemade goodness, artisanal. And more of us have discovered that Betty Crocker is a make-believe person created by the marketing department of General Mills.

Do you laugh when you hear Duncan Hines claim their cookie mixes are "Chewy, gooey, homemade good"? Or General Foods Corporation proclaiming "like grandma's, only more so"? While these mega-corporations feel the need to create an image of homespun goodness, your venture, by default, *is* authentic, transparent, and real. In our murky world where distrust runs rampant, the idea that someone can buy direct from someone they trust has a deep emotional appeal. It's much easier and simpler to trust the food you put in your body when you're on a first-name basis with the person who made it.

It's probably illegal, or practically impossible, to even visit most animal-processing facilities, commercial farming operations, or processing factories,

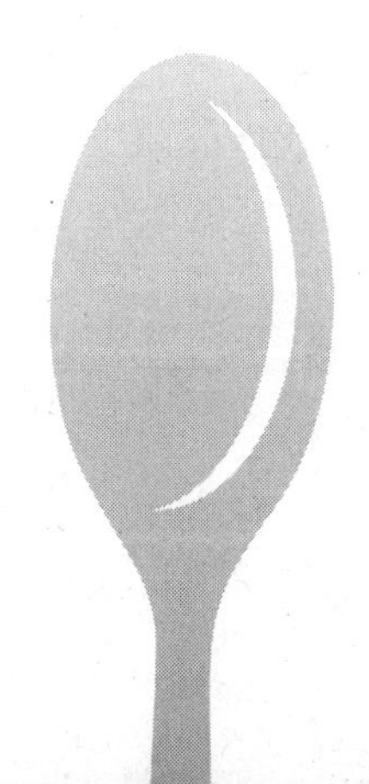

Contrast farm market stand with cottage food and corporate food factory. Above: *Slow Rise Organic Bakery, Gabriola Island, Canada.* CREDIT: MARY JANE JESSEN Below: *Rolls on a conveyor system.* CREDIT: ISTOCK: © WICKI58

where the vast majority of the food Americans eat is currently made. By selling to neighbors, co-workers, or community members, cottage food enterprises promise to usher in a new era of food-system accountability and transparency not seen since the days of *Little House on the Prairie*. If allowed by their state law, many cottage food operators welcome pickups at their house. There's a growing trend of pop up markets on home porches or driveways.

Key Elements of Cottage Food Laws

By their very nature, most cottage food businesses are:

- small-scale, grossing under $5,000 in revenue, at least starting out;
- independent and family-run, usually by only one person;
- home-based and use the equipment they already own in the kitchen.

So, with your only expenses being a license or two and perhaps a few safety checks, depending on your state, you may be able to get going with an investment of less than $200. Producers operating under cottage food legislation save costs and enjoy the ease and convenience of working from home rather than having to rent or build a commercial kitchen, as required by commercial food-processing regulations.

As well as some licensing steps, your state cottage food laws will specify what kind of sales, sales venues, and types of foods are permitted. Plus, your state will tell you exactly how much you can earn with your business. Nationally, this sales cap ranges from $5,000 on the extreme low end to the majority of states with unlimited caps where you could earn as much as you want from the comfort of your home. Increasingly, state laws are expanding to not only have no sales caps but also allow sales on a wholesale level to retailers or restaurants.

Organization of This Book

Homemade for Sale is broken into six sections. In the first section, Getting Started, we address in greater detail what cottage food laws allow, help you evaluate your goals, and offer tools to navigate your state's regulations and get you going through refining your ideas and recipes. Even with all the changes and growth of our movement, state regulations still vary tremendously in terms of what you can produce, where and how you can sell it, and how much you can earn. It's a true patchwork of changing rules and regulations, and this section will give you a basics understanding of what you can produce in your state.

The second section, What's Cooking: Product Development and Recipes, covers everything about developing your products and recipes, including off-the-shelf recipes you can adopt. We'll also take a deeper dive into the science basics behind non-hazardous and how to identify and sell safe products, as well as provide sample recipes, each tested in an independent lab to make sure they are non-hazardous.

The third section, Selling Your Story: Marketing, gets into the nitty-gritty of the all-important aspects of marketing and advertising, including branding and packaging, while setting accurate and profitable pricing. Good marketing will increase your likelihood of success, which is why this section of the book is the most detailed.

The fourth section, Organizing, Planning, and Managing the Business, digs into organizing your kitchen as well as managing your time and avoiding burnout, one of the key reasons a cottage food business will shut down, even if successful. The section also covers setting up your business, putting together a simple business plan, and accounting basics to keep your business in good fiscal shape.

The fifth section, Business Expansion, examines what to do if your amazing products appear to be the Powerball of the cottage food lottery, with sales growing to the point that they hit the gross sales cap for cottage food enterprises or are simply too high for your kitchen space to handle. You'll have to decide whether you want to keep it cottage-food-small or expand your enterprise. We'll explore scaling up your operations along a continuum, from a modest investment to a tens of thousands of dollars commitment.

Lastly, section six, Future of Cottage Food: Freedom!, covers the new and exciting frontier for home-based food entrepreneurs of food freedom, including what these laws are all about, dispatches from states that have implemented such legislation, and ideas for how you can advocate for a food freedom law in your state.

If you think you have the kind of products that can be sold nationally—and have the financing, research, and personal interest to take it to the next level—we'll briefly cover some potential next steps and point you toward resources that focus on these large-scale, full-time food enterprises. For the

Above: *Just because you're making money producing great products doesn't mean you can't have fun at it too when engaging your customers.* Credit: John D. Ivanko Photography

Below: *Cocoa bombs are big business for Jennifer Sinatra's Sinfully Sweets LLC, based in Dearborn, Michigan, where they're consistent sellers. Her attractively staged product photo, captured with an iPhone, is a social media scroll-stopper and brings in the customers.* Credit: Jennifer Sinatra, Sinatra's Sinfully Sweets LLC

majority of *Homemade for Sale* readers, however, keeping things small and home-based will be the recipe for success: a perfect blend of an independent entrepreneurial enterprise that shares a love for cooking with their local community.

Homemade for Sale also features seven inspiring story profiles of cottage food and food freedom start-ups and the individuals behind them. The people profiled address real-life challenges while sharing practical advice and opportunities about starting their business. These stories reveal specific financial, legal, marketing, and operational issues often absent in other start-up books. Either through the profiles or sidebars, every major direct sales channel and cottage food product category is represented in this edition, including decorative cookies, custom cakes, pickles, breads, preserves, dry mixes, candy, and cupcakes, as well as prepared meals sold under what is known as the Microenterprise Home Kitchen Operations law, or MHKO.

The cottage food movement represents more than an income source or a fun new project. You're helping to grow the local food movement in your community by providing "direct-to-the-food-artisan" connections. *Homemade for Sale* celebrates this and, as you read further, provides a pragmatic blueprint for success as you launch your dream food venture—right from your home kitchen!

Finally, a statement we made in the first edition of *Homemade for Sale* rings just as true today: "homemade" and "fresh from the oven" mean exactly what's written!

Getting Started

SECTION 1

1

Navigating Your State's Cottage Food Law

THIS CHAPTER WILL HELP you navigate your state's cottage food law. At the time of writing, every state has some form of cottage food law or judicial ruling that may allow for the sale of various food products made in a home kitchen. As noted in the introduction, while no Canadian province has a cottage food law, some provinces may provide specific exceptions, usually reserved for farmers, that allow for certain food product items made in a home kitchen to be sold at farmers' markets.

Addressed separately and much more detailed in section 6, the food freedom movement has emerged from the cottage food movement and may allow home cooks to make and sell homemade prepared meals and a wide selection of other food products, including some that require refrigeration or even be sold frozen.

To avoid possible confusion, when we talk about cottage food laws, we're focused on non-potentially hazardous, or non-hazardous, shelf-stable products, not prepared foods or meals that might require refrigeration.

Historic Roots, Back to the Homestead

While no one claims to have invented the term "cottage food," the phrase so perfectly and vividly captures the heart of this movement going back to the small and hand-crafted. When you think of the word "cottage," does a modest structure, typically one-story tall and designed with simplicity and modesty, come to mind? Maybe involving a few cute gnomes or hobbits? You making treats in your home kitchen then selling them to your neighbor epitomizes "cottage" and what built our nation. Local commerce, recirculating dollars amongst community members.

Back in those *Little House on the Prairie* days, we knew our shopkeeper, and business transacted abundantly between community members. We didn't need laws to regulate how such a sale took place because we knew each other and built our communities on trust.

Cottage food laws today revive this sense of trusted community connectedness in a way that no supermarket or big-box store ever could. These cottage food laws reveal a more authentic and tastier time filled with unique homemade items from small food artisans. These laws allow us to do much more than just launch individual businesses. They provide the catalyst for transporting our society back to an era when everyone shopped small with trusted neighbors. Despite what mega corporations might suggest, millions of Americans want to be on a first-name basis with their baker or food artisan. They don't want their food shipped in from 1,200 miles away and sold by scanning a UPC bar code.

Consider yourself a pioneer, leading this cottage food movement to new heights. Each of us through what we create in our businesses pave the way for others to follow. That collaborative spirit fuels the pages of this book, built on our own advocacy and educational leadership for over a decade. We've successfully sued the state of Wisconsin for the right for us to sell cookies. We've created a best-selling online Udemy course. And we sell Latvian sourdough rye bread and jars of dill pickles to our neighbors.

Having a Hobby Versus Operating a Business

A large point of this book is to celebrate operating a business, and not just having a hobby. If you're accepting payment for your product and trying to earn money and make a profit, you're a business according to the IRS. You need to, therefore, keep records, report this income, and, of course, pay some taxes on your profits. A hobby is something you do "for sport, recreation or pleasure," per the IRS.

One of the points we make often in this book is that because you operate as a business, you can also deduct expenses as a part of running your business and, at the end of the year, deduct losses if you have more expenses than revenues. You cannot deduct losses on your tax return for your hobby; this is the basic difference between a business and a hobby. Business losses allow you to offset other income, perhaps from the full-time job you still hold or your spouse's income if you file your tax return jointly. These losses potentially reduce your income taxes.

The IRS determines if your activity is a hobby or business, based on nine factors, including your personal motives, intent to make profits, and ability and success in making profit at least three of every five years. You, however, determine how much profit, or loss, you want to make in your business in

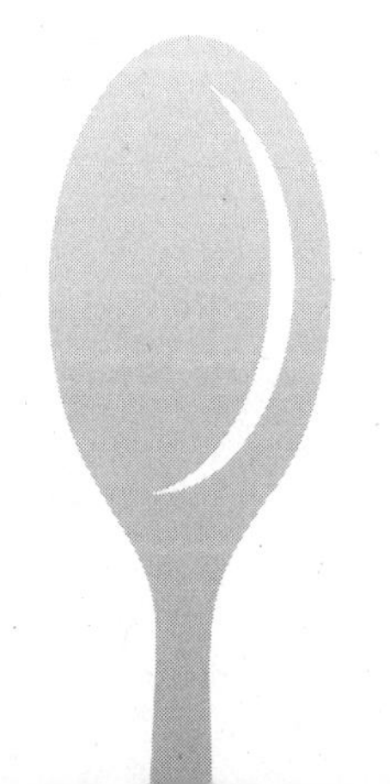

any given year—of course, based on meeting sales objectives. Lots more on business finances is covered in chapter 18.

Food Products Versus Food Service

Know the difference between food products and food service. It's an important distinction. We'll explain with one of our favorite ways to crunch: dill pickles. A sealed jar of pickles is a food product. You take it home, crack it open, and enjoy it alongside those hamburgers you're grilling up for family supper. In the context of cottage food products, the jar of pickles is exactly what is meant by a non-hazardous, shelf-stable item that does not require refrigeration. Typically regulated by your state's agriculture department, the jar of pickles you make must follow specific rules and regulations because this agency handles everything related to food products from supporting farmers to regulating exactly how the label must read.

What if we open up that jar of pickles and put one on a stick and sell it to you that way? Being from Wisconsin, how about we fry it first and then sell it? Either way, selling a pickle ready to eat on a stick now falls into the food service category from a regulatory perspective. Even though it's the same pickle that was in the jar ten seconds ago, when it's out on a stick ready to eat, that crunchy pickle suddenly falls under food service regulation, typically the domain of your state's health department since they regulate such areas that include restaurants, food trucks, and catering operations.

The exact same logic applies to baked goods. That chocolate layer cake, sold in its entirety and most likely displayed in a box, is a cottage food product. But when you cut it into individual pieces on-site and put it on plates with a fork, that's food service, with a whole slew of rules and regulations you must follow. Don't fret, since there are some generally acceptable work-arounds for baked goods. For example, individual cake pops or slicing and packing that pan of brownies into individual pieces while still in your kitchen can work. Unfortunately, there's no work-around for pickles.

With the growth of the food freedom movement, your state might offer options beyond non-hazardous food products. For clarity in this book, we'll focus first and foremost on the non-hazardous cottage food products since that's where the majority of opportunities exist. Cottage food products remain the most accessible on-ramp for food entrepreneurs to get started.

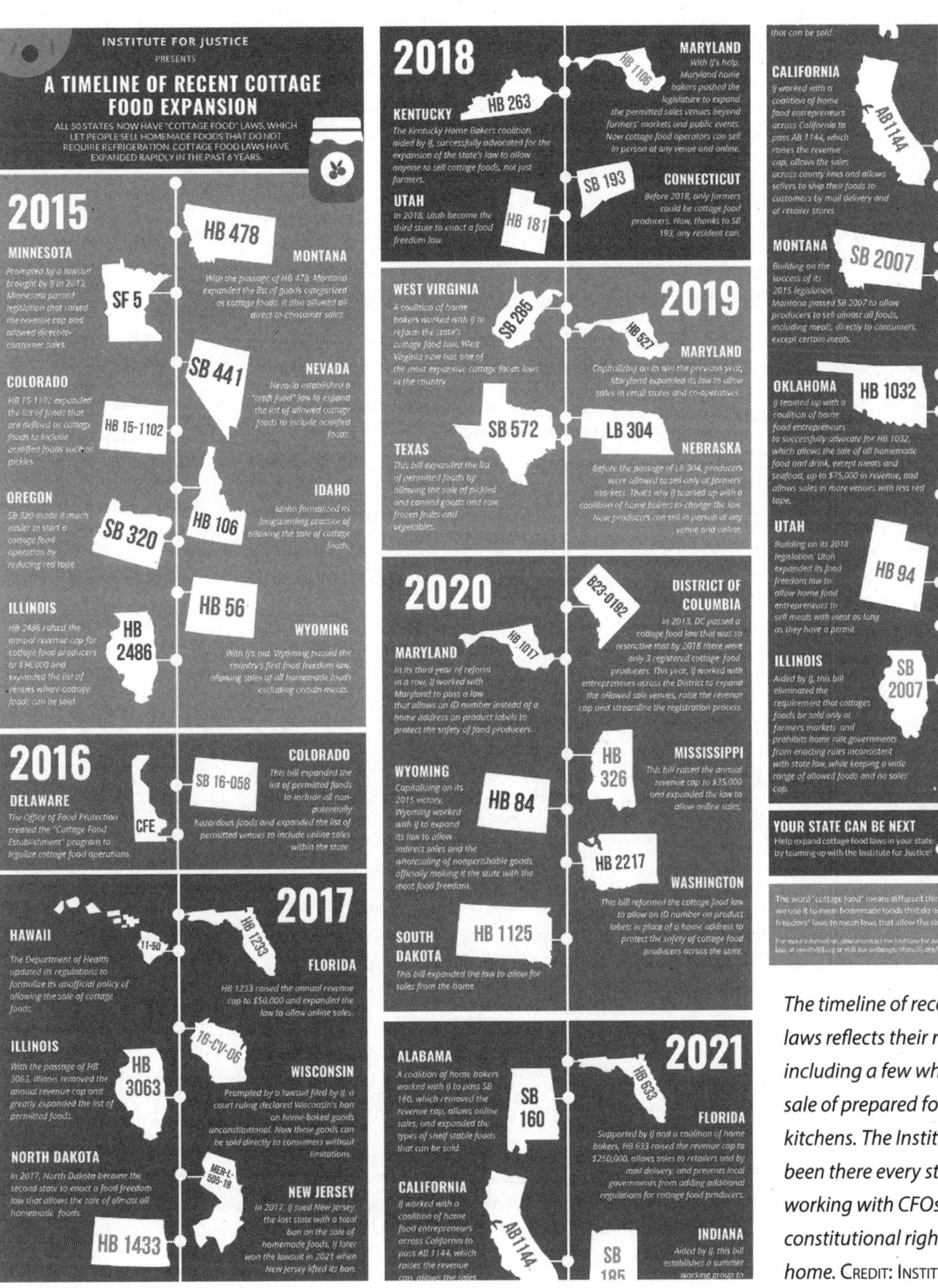

The timeline of recent cottage food laws reflects their rapid progression, including a few which also permit the sale of prepared food made in home kitchens. The Institute for Justice has been there every step of the way, working with CFOs eager to have the constitutional right to earn a living from home. Credit: Institute for Justice

Cottage Food Movement Is Growing

Tempted as we may have been when writing this book, we avoided having a chapter devoted to distilling and summarizing cottage food laws, state by state. Why? Because by the time you might have picked up this book, the law in your state could have been revised and expanded or broadened in completely new ways. As a result, step one in navigating cottage food law is to get your hands on the statute, what the law is referred to after it passes, for the state in which you reside. Most statutes have a number associated with them, but every state has a different system. State legislative websites usually have a "Search" bar where you can type in keywords to find a bill or statute. Some sites also have a "Find a Bill or Statute" function where you can type in the bill or statute number or name or search by keyword. Try searching under "cottage food" or, if nothing comes up, "home processing" or "home kitchen."

The Institute for Justice (ij.org), a nonprofit law firm that represents citizens like ourselves overburdened by governmental regulations, has been at the forefront of the growth of the cottage food movement, sometimes working with CFOs in their state, and their representatives, to draft the language that would go into a cottage food bill.

The Institute for Justice has also brought lawsuits on behalf of cottage food entrepreneurs with their attorneys representing CFOs when they were forced to sue their state over various aspects that were believed to be unconstitutional. To buttress their arguments in court, guide advocacy work, and help states better understand the cottage food movement, they've also conducted research. Check out *Flour Power: How Cottage Food Entrepreneurs Are Using Their Home Kitchen to Become Their Own Bosses*, a downloadable report of their 2017 survey of 775 cottage food producers in 22 states showing how restrictive laws can hinder entrepreneurship and how women continue to find cottage foods an appealing, easy business on-ramp, especially those in rural areas.

The progression of cottage food laws is covered in more detail in chapter 21. But to give you a sense of the rapid changes, the Institute for Justice's timeline reveals both the scope and breadth of the movement.

Tips for Understanding a Cottage Food Law

The following tips serve as a guide to understanding your state's cottage food law.

Review Your State's Cottage Food Law

Cottage food laws are administered by a state's department of agriculture or whatever department regulates "food production." This is usually not the same department that regulates and inspects facilities that prepare and serve food, like restaurants or catering operations. There's a big difference between "production" and "preparation"—so much so that each is handled by a completely different department with a completely different set of rules, regulations, and procedures.

As noted above, another key difference between the two involves "service." Once you start selling and serving a food item you made, the regulations and requirements immediately become more complex, often involving refrigeration, serving temperatures, food handling, licensing issues, and sanitation. Stick to just selling the whole chocolate cake. When you start selling individual slices along with a fork, you add another layer of regulations and cost. An easy work-around: offer cupcakes sold in single packages if you want to sell individual servings.

In Wisconsin, for example, the Department of Agriculture, Trade and Consumer Protection administers the cottage food law. However, the Wisconsin Department of Health Services administers, inspects, and licenses establishments that prepare and serve food to the public, like restaurants, caterers, and even our bed and breakfast. Can you see where things can get confusing?

Stick to Your State as Your Primary Source of Information

In journalism, articles can be sourced from primary or secondary sources. Primary sources are the people, companies, or organizations directly involved with the topic; secondary sources are people or organizations that may report about a subject. Primary sources of information are always preferred to secondary sources. That's one reason why Wikipedia can never be used as a primary source.

As cottage food laws expand across the country, websites are popping up to address the hunger for information about them, filling gaps where states often fall short: in providing readily accessible, easy-to-understand content. Such websites can also be a great way to connect with other food entrepreneurs in your state since many offer an online forum for discussions. At the forefront of mapping the movement is forrager.com.

While cottage food websites are a quick reference point with lots of useful information, avoid basing your information solely off them; they could

Direct-to-customer or Indirect (Wholesale)

While each state's cottage food laws vary on multiple levels, every law specifies to whom the product can be sold. This "to whom" then falls into two categories that probably sound familiar: direct and wholesale. Direct means directly to your customer. You, as a baker of brownies, sell some to me, the customer. I pay you directly and then, happily, am the one to eat them, give them as a gift, or do whatever else I choose to do with them, as long as I do not resell them.

Indirect sales, commonly known as wholesale, cover a wide range of other sales opportunities. If you live in a state that allows wholesale, you could potentially sell me those brownies and I could then resell them at a venue like my retail store or coffee shop. While you usually receive a lower price for wholesale transactions, the benefit is higher volume and, hopefully, more regular orders. If a retailer is reselling your item, they need to make some money, too, so you need to have a wholesale price that allows for this.

A growing number of states have passed laws that permit sales on a wholesale level; check to see if you're fortunate to have that opportunity in your state. Even if you can sell wholesale, you might find that giving up the profit margins required for selling through another retail shop might not be worth pursuing. As an added bonus, some states may permit other food categories like refrigerated baked goods and may not have a sales cap either. More on this in future chapters.

Bottom line to your bottom line if you're fortunate enough to live in one of these states that allows wholesale: you get to create close to a commercial kitchen arrangement without the cost and setup hassle such a facility often entails. In general, however, such states have more upfront requirements, including an on-site kitchen inspection, food-handling training certification, and other paperwork. Once you work through these, you can operate under a much wider range of product possibilities.

Consignment sales are those in which your products are placed at a retail outlet for sale, but the retailer does not place an upfront order for them. You only get paid if and when your products sell. If your items just take up space on a shelf and nothing sells at the retailer, the items are returned to you. No sales are ever made. In this way, retailers never have to commit funds to actually stocking their shelves with your product and may be willing to try them out.

For states with cottage food laws that prohibit wholesale, this seems to apply to consignment sales as well. For example, the law in Colorado explicitly states that a cottage food product cannot be sold from a retail food establishment like a grocery store or another outlet that also sells licensed and inspected foods for resale; on the CFO's product's label in Colorado, it even must include the line: "This product is not intended for resale." If you're not the one collecting the cash and making the sale at the consignment venue, then the sale is not direct. Covered more in the advocacy chapters, clarification of consignment sales, or the elimination of rules preventing it, might demand citizen engagement before you pursue such sales. Some states remain steadfastly opposed to wholesale or consignment sales.

Sometimes laws legalizing wholesale products produced in home kitchens come bearing names ☛

other than cottage food. Instead, they might have the word "home" in the title of the law. Make sure you know the right way to refer to this classification if you want to pursue it further or call the administering agency for clarification. In Iowa, for example, the license is for a Home Food Processing Establishment; in Maine, one of the first states to institute such a law allowing home food manufacturing in 1980, a CFO can now secure a Home Food License that came about as a result of the passage of the Food Sovereignty Law in 2017. While Virginia administers a cottage food law, it also has a separate Home Processor License that allows wholesale. California's law refers to cottage food but breaks it down into two classes of licensing: Class A-licensed operations can only sell direct to customers, but Class B-licensed operators have options to sell wholesale.

The consistent variable among states permitting wholesale remains the ability to use a home kitchen in a more commercial capacity. If wholesale interests you, ask about the possibilities, knowing those laws may be defined in ways other than as cottage food.

become outdated, contain factual errors, or suddenly disappear one day. In other words, these sites are secondary sources of information, perhaps more valuable to marketing than keeping tabs on what's happening in your state. Additionally, Facebook groups are usually overflowing with well-meaning advice and information; it's best to verify and confirm the information or direction before acting.

Your state's current cottage food law should be the only thing to direct the scope of your business. Treat it as your primary source. You are ultimately responsible for the actions of your business. The decisions you make must be based on the law as it stands. Avoid decisions based on what you hear or what someone else may be doing, particularly if it's in another state.

Throughout this book, we use illustrative examples based on laws that may change in the coming years. Change is constant, especially when it comes to legislatures creating, repealing, and amending laws. The great news is that cottage food laws are mostly bipartisan. Both Republicans and Democrats tend to agree on the importance of job creation, employment, and encouraging the growth of small business. Where they have a hard time working together and agreeing on is how.

Some states' cottage food laws are simple and short while others go on and on. These two extremes express two different approaches to writing laws. A shorter, more general law will enable the administering body (i.e.,

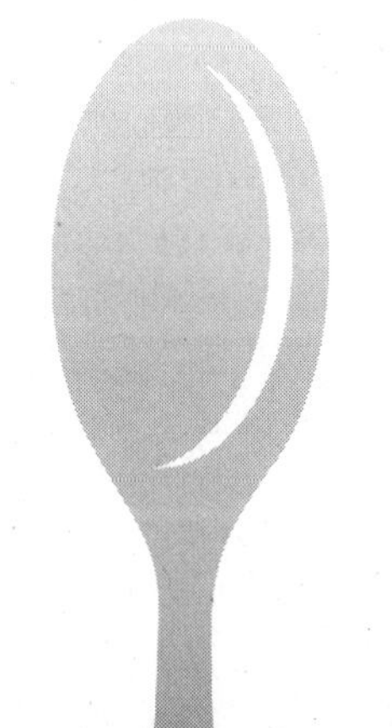

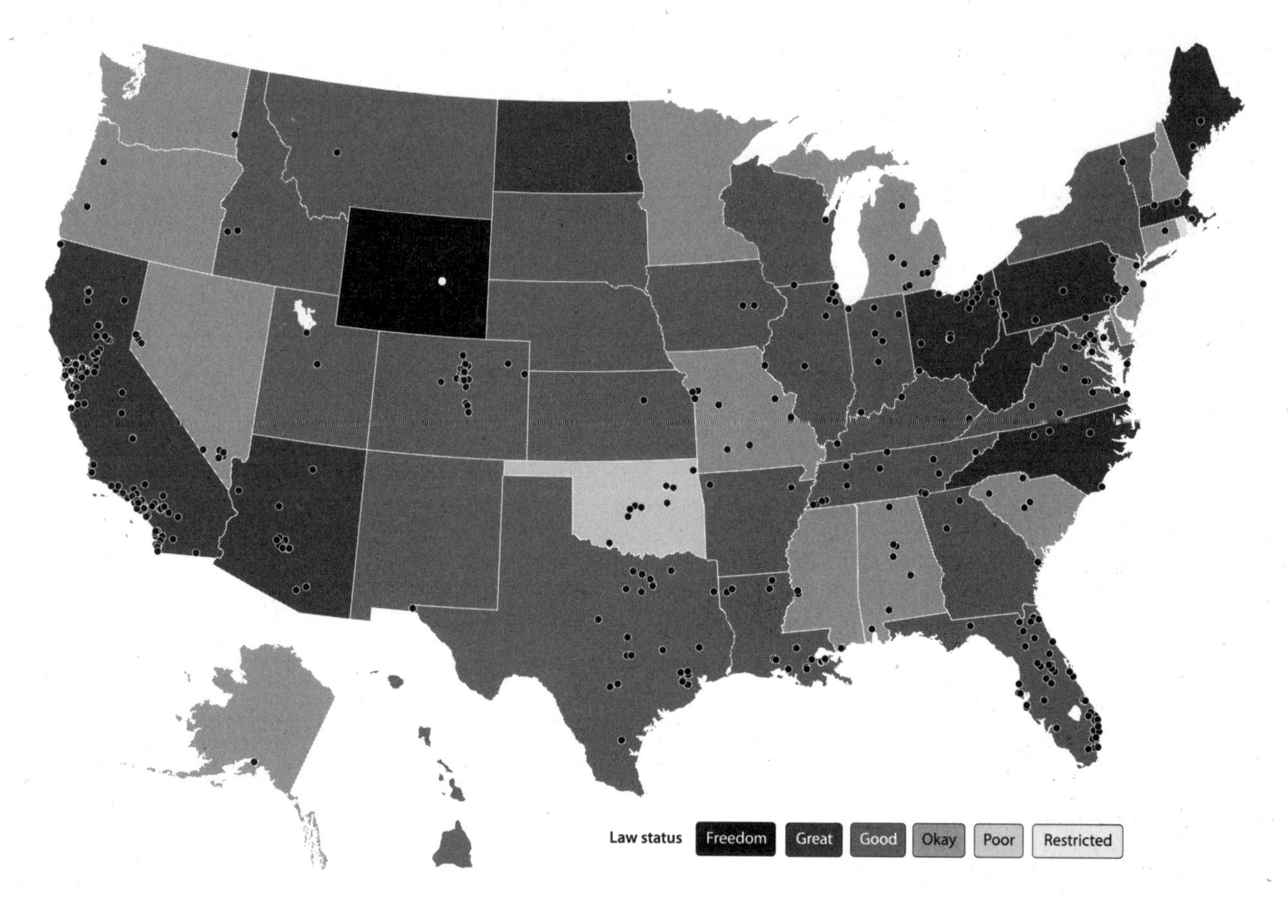

Forrager is an online cottage food community. It contains information about the cottage food laws, educational resources for starting a cottage food business, and The Forrager Podcast *that reveals strategies for marketing and selling food products successfully from home, online, at farmers' markets or special events, and in stores. At the bottom of each state cottage food law summary are links directly to the state-specific laws or statutes, for easy reference.* CREDIT: MAP COURTESY OF FORRAGER INC (FORRAGER.COM)

your state's department of agriculture) to address and answer questions and issues as they come up. A more detailed law aims to answer everything up front but leaves little wiggle room for questions or alternative interpretations. Keep this in mind when reviewing your state's law.

Tap State Resources to Understand the Law

You only have to deal with and understand your state's cottage food law. Some states have accessible, user-friendly, and easy-to-understand information on their cottage food law. Not all do. Depending on your state, you'll find yourself either muddling through some technical data and legal verbiage or proceeding easily with clearly defined guidelines and requirements. When in doubt, contact the department or agency directly to sort out issues and get advice on your specific product idea and your next steps.

Lobbying for an Expanded Cottage Food Law

The good news: With every state now having some form of cottage food law passed or some equivalent judicial ruling, you won't be needing to advocate for the passage of a cottage food law. But you may not be in love with your state's law. Maybe you find it limited—if, say, you want to mail your cookies directly to customers but your state's law requires in-person sales only. In this case, you will need to take democracy by the horns and advocate, lobby, and work to amend an existing cottage food law to include the expansions you would like. Depending on your state's legislative protocol, this expansion may require a whole new cottage food law. This may also apply if you're having a disagreement with your state regulator over a food product you believe is safe. In this case, you may need to take off your apron, put on your lobby hat; head over to chapter 21 for how to proceed.

States that truly embrace cottage food law opportunities couldn't make it easier, with many of them employing an easy-to-follow checklist approach to guide new food entrepreneurs. In the case of laws about pickles, preserves, and other canned products, university extension will often serve as a more objective educational arm and offer various online resources and in-person workshops and consultations. Don't, however, count on university extension agents giving you the definitive yes or no to your product; they're not lawyers or administrators of the law, nor may they have a talent for marketing.

In states with more clunky and hard-to-understand information, you'll need to educate yourself on the more technical terms used in cottage food legislation as it applies to your product.

If you feel like you're getting a runaround to your questions from the department handling the cottage food law—or no reply at all—go to the top! Contact your state elected representative and/or senator to see if they or their staffers can help. There's nothing more powerful to jump-start a less-than-responsive governmental office than a letter or inquiry from your representative on behalf of their constituency, you.

A word of caution, however, when dealing with legislators. You may need to bring your representative up to speed on the cottage food law. In your initial contact, it would be wise to reference the specific law and what you hope to accomplish in their district with your business. Making money and paying some taxes are two good selling points. Most politicians like to hear from their constituents, too. Don't forget to include your full address (not a PO box) when contacting your representatives.

Confusion or Denial of Cottage Food Laws

Even though you understand the specific cottage food law for your state, that doesn't mean that the agency, either the agriculture or health department, charged with establishing the regulations, rules, or enforcement of the law agrees with it, supports it, or even follows it. Some state regulatory agencies in charge of guiding the implementation of the cottage food law passed are enthusiastic supporters, doing everything they can to make it as straightforward and easy for cottage food operators to get up and running as possible.

However, agencies or local county regulatory bodies in other states may not be aware, ignore, or even deny an aspect of a cottage food law that was passed. They might even make up their own rule or requirements.

For example, an updated law in California, AB 1144, Cottage Food Amendments, went into effect on January 1, 2022. It "allows cottage food operators to ship anywhere within California, and to have higher annual gross income caps, $75,000 for Class A registration and $150,000 for Class B permit," summarizes David Crabill, founder of Forrager.com and one of the group of CFOs who worked with their legislators to get the amendment to the cottage food law passed. These amendments are in addition to the existing regulations that include securing a food-handlers training and certificate, Cottage Food Operation Permit and Sellers Permit.

"Local health departments cannot override this law or make up their own rules," continues Crabill, frustrated by a few counties in his state and their actions related to the amendments passed. "The shipping provision was written into the law in an unambiguous way and it applies to all cottage food operators in the state. Your health department cannot prevent you from using the new law! You can ship your products in-state without any permission from your health department regardless of what your application or cottage food operator permit says."

While addressed further in the food freedom section, suffice to say that you may need to understand your state's cottage food law, and you may need to educate and bring the local regulatory agency up to speed on exactly what you can do, operating completely, legally, within the law.

Madhavi Tandon, Maia Foods LLC, Aurora, Colorado

Adding a Dash of Spice to Life

Don't be fooled by the curvy road snaking through this quiet suburban neighborhood of Denver, Colorado, filled with family homes and tidy lawns. Madhavi Tandon lives in one of these homes and started Maia Foods LLC in October 2019, operated out of her home kitchen. And she's on a mission to transform taste buds with the flavors of India she grew up with.

Tandon's business, launched under her state's cottage food law, features garam masala spice mixes, various meal kits, Indian chai tea spice mix, traditional Indian biscotti that are made without eggs, and jars of ghee, a clarified butter that she produces in five flavors. Tandon sells her products at farmers' markets and takes special orders online through her website or via social media.

"When I saw jars of ghee for sale in my local grocery store in the fall of 2019, my first thoughts were: 'This is mainstream now. I have been making ghee in the US for over 30 years, I should make some and try and sell it,'" says Tandon, who is a part-time professor, teaching social justice and equity for minority student populations at the University of Colorado Denver. "The primary motivation at the beginning was not financial, but more about staking a claim to my food heritage and owning a product that has been in Indian kitchens for over a thousand years.

"My first step before starting a food product business was determining what I could actually sell under my state's cottage food law," outlines Tandon, eager to sell ghee, a clarified butter that's shelf-stable but unfortunately not on the approved non-hazardous cottage food list in Colorado Cottage Food Act. "I was the first home-based entrepreneur to propose ghee as a cottage food. So, there were many emails back and forth between myself and the Colorado Department of Public Health & Environment (CDPHE), the regulatory agency responsible for licensing cottage food operators in my state. I made the case that ghee has existed for thousands of years in ancient cultures of Asia and the Middle East where it is often made at home and used in daily cooking."

The process of making ghee involves simmering butter at a low heat until all milk solids become brown and stick to the bottom of the pan. The liquid will solidify as the ghee cools down, able to be scooped up with a

Name: Madhavi Tandon

Business: Maia Foods LLC (Aurora, CO)

Website: http://maiafoods.com

Products: spice mixes, meal kits, jars of ghee, biscotti

Sales Venues: direct orders, farmers' market

Gross sales: $5,000/year

Madhavi Tandon, owner of Maia Foods LLC, in her kitchen preparing an order of egg-free Indian biscuits made with ghee, whole wheat flour, and jaggery, a traditional unrefined cane sugar.
CREDIT: MAIA FOODS LLC

Ghee, a shelf-stable, clarified butter, made by Maia Foods LLC. Credit: Maia Foods LLC

CERTIFICATE OF COMPLETION

Madhavi Tandon

successfully completed

COLORADO COTTAGE FOOD SAFETY TRAINING

October 25, 2019

Instructor(s): Anne Zander, Mary Snow & Sheila Gains

COLORADO STATE UNIVERSITY EXTENSION

Instructor Signature

Valid Through: 10-25-2022

Food safety certificate for completing the online Colorado State University Extension course. The certificate is valid for 3 years.

Credit: Colorado State University Extension

spoon or knife. It's strained and stored in jars and remains shelf-stable for up to a year. Possessing a nutty, caramelized flavor, ghee is used as a substitute for oil or butter when cooking, as a spread, or as a base for marinades and salad dressings.

"It was mainly one person saying that it is not eligible under Colorado's cottage food law," continues Tandon, about the objection she first received from CDPHE. "Then another person with CDPHE said it was okay as long as I use commercially approved butter." Tandon was not the first person to ever to receive conflicting information from a regulatory agency involved with a state's cottage food law. Experiencing mixed messages may require due diligence or securing a second opinion regarding the safety of a particular food product. Once Tandon received approval for her ghee, she retained documentation should any questions arise in the future. No water activity level test was ever required by CDPHE. And with the approval of ghee in her possession, she never felt the need to engage her state representatives to help out on her behalf.

"Completing the Food Safety for Cottage Food Producers course from the Colorado State University Extension was step two," says Tandon, after she received the approval for ghee by CDPHE. "I have no professional training or certification in culinary sciences but do have over 30 years of experience cooking for my family." The Colorado Extension course, or an equivalent Colorado Food Handlers Card, was another one of the few requirements in her state to sell non-hazardous homemade products. The CSU Extension online course takes about four hours to complete and includes a test at the end. Like other CFOs in her state, she did not have to have her kitchen be inspected or licensed.

"I have been part of LLCs as an education consultant and knew it was an easy process in Colorado, so I started there," explains Tandon, on her decision to operate as a limited liability company (LLC) instead of simply as a sole proprietorship. LLCs provide liability projection. She also manages the risks associated with operating the food product business with a business insurance policy.

"I started experimenting with the meal kits right about the time my younger daughter was getting ready to leave Colorado for graduate school," smiles Tandon, looking to expand her product offerings beyond Maia Ghee. "I wanted to create quick and easy Indian meals for her that she could make in a crockpot or pressure cooker.

"As I did more and more farmers' markets and events, I saw other vendors selling soup kits or cookie kits, and this encouraged me to start testing the Indian meal kits," admits Tandon, reflecting a trait among many entrepreneurs: taking an idea from one product and turning it into something new for a different product.

"I continue to chat with customers and visitors about their favorite ingredients and flavors of Indian food," shares Tandon, reflecting her continued attentiveness to satisfying her customers' needs. Sometimes, the customers would tell her what they would buy, if she made it. "This gives me ideas for the ingredients and spices for the meal kits.

Maia Foods LLC meal kits.

CREDIT: MAIA FOODS LLC

"I buy almost all my ingredients from the local Indian, Asian, and Middle Eastern grocery stores and the restaurant warehouses," shares Tandon. "For the packaging, I have been ordering it online. The logo labels and banners are printed by a local printing company.

"Of course, there are now several brands of ready-made Indian food available at grocery and warehouse stores, and the market is growing," notes Tandon, not discouraged. "There are several brands as well as products in the snacks and condiments sections, too. This just makes me so happy because it tells me that customers are more knowledgeable about Indian food and are ready to try new tastes and textures." In many ways, those competitors have helped do some of the category marketing for her. They established that there is, in fact, a demand for Indian spice mixes where she lived.

"Another plus is the growing number of vegetarians and vegans in the US," adds Tandon. "Indian food has an ancient tradition of meeting the dietary needs of both groups, so it is very easy for someone like me to create meal kits for specific diets.

"My spice mixes I actually use daily in many of my family meals, so you could say testing and refining them has been ongoing for the last 30 years," laughs Tandon.

"The chai masala is rooted in a family recipe," adds Tandon, when explaining its origins. "My mother-in-law always kept a tiny steel tin with her homemade chai masala next to the jar of tea leaves. In summer, she would add a pinch to the pot of boiling water, and in winters she would add a bit more. I did not really need to experiment with it as it is a tried and tested product for me.

"The garam masala is another story," admits Tandon. "In India, every family has their own customized blend of garam masala based on personal tastes and the abundance of local spices. For example, I grew up in western India and my mother's masala has large amounts of dried coconut and cloves, but no fennel seeds. The garam masala that I make is a blend of flavors and spices that I have borrowed from my mother and mother-in-law, as well as all the other women who have passed on their food heritage to me.

"Keeping my eye on consistency and quality has helped with repeat orders," explains Tandon. "I stick with lentils and rice grown in India for the meal kits as changing the source does change the texture and taste. I tested lentils grown in Africa or Canada, for example, and there was a noticeable difference. According to my logic, agricultural products are a combination of the soil, water, air, and techniques, specific to a geography, just like wine. Basmati rice has the aroma and flavor because the paddy fields are fed by the rivers and monsoons of India; you cannot get that from, say, rice grown in Thailand or Japan." Unlike cottage food operations that mostly source local ingredients, Maia Foods does run a greater risk of possible supply chain interruptions for her India-sourced ingredients, a risk Tandon is willing to take to maintain her product's distinctive and authentic flavors, textures, and taste.

"Fortunately, Colorado is a very low-humidity state, and I do not have a problem with the moisture found in the air that might accidently get trapped inside my airtight packaging," acknowledges Tandon. Otherwise, she would have had to invest in a vacuum-packaging machine that would draw out all the air before sealing. "However, after grinding the masalas, I allow them to cool overnight before packaging them."

Tandon always envisioned her business based in her home kitchen. "Working at a commercial kitchen is expensive and involves more logistics," summarizes Tandon. "It's so very easy to use my home kitchen, and I can make the products all through the week, whenever I have the time. I work two to three half days per week on my cottage food products, balanced between by university teaching and training."

Maia Foods LLC spice mixes.
CREDIT: MAIA FOODS LLC

When it comes to marketing Maia Foods, Tandon relies on social media and her food and recipe website. "The holidays and holiday markets have been the most profitable, but I am more interested in cultivating a small set of loyal customers who become repeat buyers.

"The first product, ghee, allowed me to explore markets, see other products made by cottage food producers, chat with customers and business owners," Tandon explains, constantly welcoming customer feedback. "The next step was trying to build a profile of my ideal customer and then understanding what other products would be appealing to them. I learned that although many folks love Indian food and take-out, they tend to be intimidated by the number of spices and steps involved in Indian cooking. Therefore, Indian cuisine needed to be demystified and simplified for the mainstream customer.

"The website started as a way for me to share my home cooking recipes with my daughters as they left home for work and education," admits Tandon, recognizing that, in many ways, the business emerged from her passion and knowledge of Indian cuisine and her eagerness to share it with others. "Although my daughters are more adventurous in their food habits, they do seek the comfort of making simple Indian vegetarian meals, like dal and rice with a potato curry or dosas and chutneys. My website is a way for me to share vegetarian, Indian, and easy recipes that any novice home cook can pull off. I usually keep my daughters and their friends in mind when breaking the recipes down into easy step-by-step instructions.

"My other sales stream is through networking, which is a lot slower, where customers message me with their orders, and I will either deliver or mail their products," adds Tandon. "Through direct personal sales, I sell lower volumes but get the highest margin. My profits are slightly lower when I sell at farmers' markets because there is a booth fee to be paid upfront. Some farmers' markets also charge a commission in addition to the booth fee. I am constantly on the lookout for farmers' markets or events where they do not charge booth fees.

"I am also doing an Indian grocery store shopping video for a local magazine where I walk around the store and 'shop' for staple items like

Madhavi Tandon, owner of Maia Foods LLC, selling at an indoor market.
CREDIT: MAIA FOODS LLC

basmati rice, frozen rotis, paneer, and yogurt," says Tandon. "I know people want to try their hand at cooking Indian food but can be a little confused or intimidated by the large amounts of spices, lentils, and flours available in Indian grocery stores." The video is a natural carryover to help establish her brand and endear greater trust in her knowledge of Indian cuisine among the viewers, ultimately leading to product sales of Maia Foods.

"My customers tend to be balanced between women and men, well-traveled, health conscious, open to new adventures, love spices, like to cook, and are looking for convenient and easy meal ideas that reflect global tastes," observes Tandon, recognizing the importance of knowing the target market for her products if she was to be successful in meeting their needs.

"They tend to buy Maia products because they love Indian food but want to go beyond the usual tikka masala and aloo gobi they've been enjoying for years," adds Tandon. "More people are cooking at home and want to experiment with new cuisines and tastes. Maia meal kits provide all the ingredients and spices. They can make an Indian meal in an hour with the Jeera Rice and Dhaba Dal kits or throw the Bold Bombay Curry Soup ingredients in a slow cooker overnight to have a lentil and rice soup flavored with Indian spices ready the next morning." Each meal kit contains the ingredients, spices, and step-by-step instructions for cooking using an Instant Pot, slow cooker, or the stovetop.

Dhaba dal made with one of the meal kits from Maia Foods LLC.
CREDIT: MAIA FOODS LLC

"Indian cooking has always used pressure cookers for making dals," says Tandon. "Most kitchens in India have two or three different-sized pressure cookers. My daughters have switched to using Instant Pots instead of pressure cookers, so I adapted the recipes to Instant Pots as well as pressure cookers. Instant Pots are nothing but high-tech pressure cookers, so it was very easy to adapt my recipes.

"I'm hoping to offer small-group cooking classes," says Tandon, reflecting a trend among cottage food operators to share what they know through classes while also creating a new revenue stream for their business.

"I've always thought of Maia Foods LLC more as a side hustle," concludes Tandon. "I learn new skills, I get to feed people, and that brings me tremendous joy. Furthermore, food brings people together and allows us to bond and set aside our differences. Nobody is going to refuse a hot cup of masala chai, irrespective of their political, social, or ideological differences. So, let's drink chai and talk about what makes us humans and how we can make the world a better place."

Follow Your State's Registration and Review Process

What do you need to do specifically to get your business started? This can vary considerably from state to state. Some require annual registrations, licensing fees, and food safety training. Most require some form of business registration. We cover the seven easy steps to starting up your business in chapter 17.

Get It in Writing

Make hard copies of key pages off your state's website to document the cottage food law in case you're ever questioned. Just because your state has a law doesn't mean every state employee, farmers' market manager, or even your local bakery business understands the particulars. You may find you have to educate others—or defend yourself—about what it is that you're doing. Websites are inherently dynamic; they're always changing. Create a paper trail and cover yourself.

If you have specific questions on the law as it applies to your business, your best bet is to email the contact off your state's cottage food page and receive an answer in writing (again, keep a hard copy). This covers you if there are questions in the future, particularly if these relate to what you can and can't do under the legislation.

For example, if you're not sure that a particular product qualifies, send the recipe and receive and document a specific reply. Give this process time. The day before your market is not a good time to call. Even if you need to make a phone call to prompt a reply, get a confirmation via email as well. If you have a discussion with a state representative on the phone, one way to secure a reply is to send them an email outlining what you discussed and the direction you received; then ask him or her to just reply, confirming that you're on the same page.

"Think through your questions to make sure you're asking the right ones, and understand that answers will shift based on the details of what's being asked," advises Jane Jewett, Associate Director with the Minnesota Institute for Sustainable Agriculture and a dedicated cottage food educator and advocate. "Documenting answers received is always a good idea. Over time, you can build up a good knowledge base that covers lots of scenarios. It's important to understand that cottage food laws are complex and that changing a scenario even a little bit can change the answer about legality."

You'll sometimes hit walls when getting questions answered by your state agency associated with these laws. When it comes to navigating your

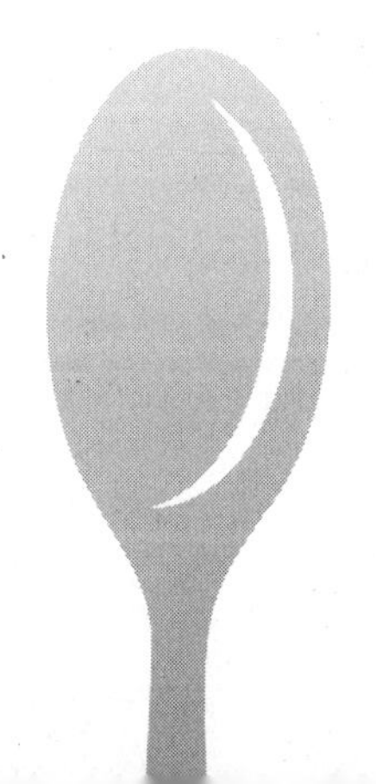

state's laws and regulations, you might be forced to advocate for answers. This may sound intimidating but think of it rather as democracy in action: By effectively voicing your questions and needs, you are directly improving entrepreneurship opportunities for all of us.

The great news is that cottage food laws have been successful, from both an economic and food safety perspective. You no longer need to "sell in" the concept of a home-based non-hazardous food product business—not the case when we penned the first edition of *Homemade for Sale* in 2015. Today, the discussions around cottage food laws are about refinements, clarifications, and their never-ending expansion.

There are times when you might feel that your state cottage food law is too restrictive and needs updating or improvement. If this is the case, put on your lobby hat and jump to section 6 to learn how you can lead the charge and make the change, or changes, you want.

Food Freedom: The Next Frontier

Get hungry for the next wave of home-based food entrepreneurship: food freedom laws. These state-specific laws expand the cottage food law concept to include other homemade food items, such as canned, pickled, and refrigerated goods, aside from those that contain meat, without any cap on sales or any licensing, permitting, or inspection requirements. At the time of printing, Wyoming leads this movement, followed by North Dakota, Oklahoma, Utah, Montana, and Iowa. Several states have potential legislation in the pipeline. Relatedly, California passed the first Microenterprise Home Kitchen Operations law, or MEHKO/MHKO, which enables counties to pass specific ordinances that let home cooks sell full homemade meals, basically just like take-out from a restaurant. Numerous states have or are considering similar MHKO laws as well.

Currently, the food freedom movement is where the cottage food laws were back in 2008 when they first started cropping up nationally. This is very new legislative territory and in need of education and advocacy, just like what was demanded of home-based food entrepreneurs during the early days of cottage food law developments. Food freedom and MHKO laws offer the potential to significantly boost your home kitchen entrepreneur opportunities far beyond specific food products.

Two things to keep in mind as you navigate your state's law: responsibility and perspective. Firstly, you're the one ultimately responsible for an

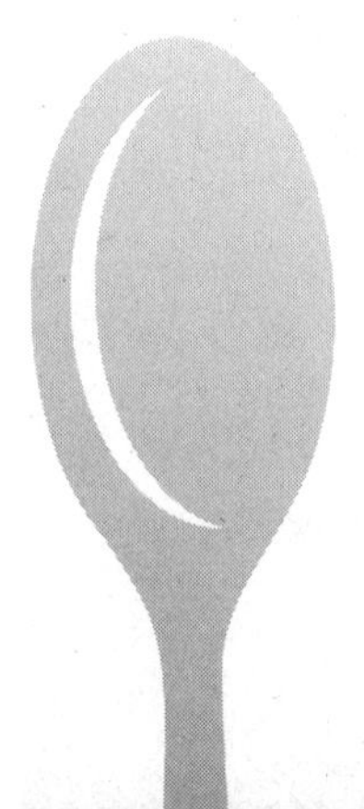

accurate interpretation of the law, to the best of your ability. We add "your ability" since you need to feel confident that you have fully researched the legislation and asked enough questions to know that you can sell focaccia or cake pops in your state. Don't expect everything to be crystal clear or black and white; you may find yourself with varying views from different sources in your state capitol. Do your due diligence and then proceed.

Secondly, carry a savvy businessperson's perspective. You're in charge of the cottage food law process. Sure, dealing with bureaucratic agencies and legislation can feel intimidating. But remind yourself that state agencies serve you, and if you have a less than ideal experience with those administering the cottage food law, make your voice heard. Your opinion and suggestions might improve the path for the next food entrepreneur and may even spark legislative change.

Navigating regulations and rules is part of any business, a part of the entrepreneurial life no matter what business you may be in, from cookies to construction. Ask questions and take charge of finding answers to what you need. We'll go into greater detail on non-hazardous products in the next chapter, which will give you more understanding and perspective in working within your state parameters.

Cake pops can be a delicious and unique way to celebrate a special event, or an easy and portable single-serving item for a bake sale. CREDIT: JOHN D. IVANKO

2

What's Cooking?

YOU MAY LOVE TO BAKE, can, or cook up a storm in the kitchen. That's a great foundation for a cottage food enterprise. But there are a few steps to go through transitioning from being a "home cook" or "hobbyist" to being a "food entrepreneur." This chapter examines some of your options and opportunities as a CFO, defined by the cottage food law where you live.

Cottage food laws vary a lot by state. The reason for this current patchwork of laws dates back to one of the underlying principles our country

Making Exemptions for Home-based "Food Establishments"

Most states' food safety laws are modeled after the federal Food and Drug Administration's (FDA) Model Food Code ("the Food Code"). The Food Code applies to any "food establishment," defined as "an operation that stores, prepares, packages, serves, vends ... or otherwise provides food for human consumption." Under the Food Code, if a food producer is legally a "food establishment," the operation is subject to the extensive requirements contained in the 767-page Model Code (or whatever portion of it has been adopted in that state) and other relevant state laws. The FDA advises against ever licensing or permitting any kitchen in a home as a food establishment, though it includes a limited exemption for producers that prepare certain foods in a private home and offer them at a bake sale for a religious or charitable organization.

As of 2021, all 50 states have innovated to expand the exception beyond that recommended by the FDA, allowing for sales of certain kinds of foods when made in a home kitchen. Many states either completely exempt home food production of certain foods from the food establishment definition, or replace the extensive "food establishment" regulations with more limited requirements that are better suited for home kitchens.

Harvard Law School Food Law and Policy Clinic (hls.harvard.edu/clinics/in-house-clinics/food-law-and-policy-clinic/), *Cottage Foods and Home Kitchens: 2021 State Policy Trends* (January, 2022).

was founded upon: states' rights. In the US, the Founding Fathers believed in giving independence and governing authority to the states on many issues.

The way that works today regarding food is the FDA publishes the Model Food Code, a model for the states to base their food regulation on—all 700-plus pages of it not including supplements. The Model Food Code provides a scientifically sound technical and legal basis for the food industry as a whole, and historically, states have generally abided by it as it relates to food establishments. But times are changing. As mentioned previously, both the Great Recession and the COVID-19 pandemic, among other considerations, have led states to abandon FDA food safety laws when it comes to foods produced in home kitchens. State exemptions made for foods sold at charitable bake sales have been extended to foods made in home kitchens. Because cottage food laws don't cross state lines, only concern yourself with what's required in your state. That's simple enough, right?

Fresh-baked pretzels can be a hit, especially if you make your own high-acid mustard to go with them.

CREDIT: JOHN D. IVANKO PHOTOGRAPHY

There are four key questions you need answered in your state's cottage food law before you get started:

- What products can you sell?
- Where can you sell your products?
- How are you allowed to sell your products?
- How much can you sell of your products?

Once you've answered these questions and understand how the cottage food law operates in your state, you'll then need to figure out whether what you love to make is worth selling. If people are clamoring for your pretzels, that's an excellent sign. In the end, your ability to sell products is based on creating items your customers want, need, and are willing to buy at a price that they, not you, determine. That's where marketing—covered in several chapters of this book—comes in.

Question 1: What Products Can You Sell?

There's a reason for you to first see what types of products you can produce under your state's cottage food law. It's the classic glass-half-full versus glass-half-empty scenario: focus on what you can legally make and don't waste time, energy, and money spinning your wheels on what you can't. Don't complain, just cook.

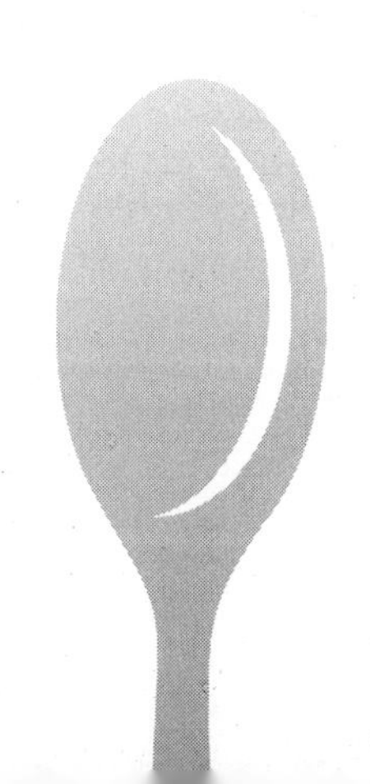

Your state's legislation will specifically outline those "non-hazardous," also called "potentially non-hazardous," food items you can produce under cottage food law. Some states also call these shelf-stable products "Time-or-temperature-controlled for safety (TCS)" foods. In the simplest terms, the conventions used to define such food are low-moisture and high-acid. Sometimes the legislation will itemize what you can or can't sell.

"While everyone from the media to Capitol Hill keeps spinning wheels trying to find the perfect panacea for job creation, especially in rural areas, they really need to look no further than our nation's kitchens. Our American history has roots in this idea of cottage businesses, from the butcher to the baker and other food artisans who create things at home that service their local community."

—Patty Cantrell, founder of Regional Food Solutions LLC

"Non-hazardous" is the keyword, which we'll use throughout this book. You don't see that term used in recipes, right? By scientific definition, it refers to an item, usually a baked good, that has a low moisture level, measured as a water activity value of 0.85 or less. Or it can be a high-acid food, measured by an equilibrium pH value of 4.6 or lower. Some state legislation includes this exact verbiage about moisture levels and pH values. Your state may also define other non-hazardous food items you're welcome to sell.

The two types of foods most widely approved under cottage food laws are low-moisture baked goods and high-acid canned foods like pickles or preserves, each explored next.

Baked Goods

Every state has cottage opportunities for selling baked goods. Baked goods are so prevalent in cottage food legislation because it's hard to mess up a loaf of bread or a chocolate chip cookie from a food safety perspective. Politicians, if nothing else, are mostly risk-adverse and conservative. Freshly baked non-hazardous baked goods are in a different food "safety zone" than something like canned green beans, a low-acid canned item you'll never see on an approved list.

A simple way to understand non-hazardous baked goods is by asking this question: Does your item require refrigeration? If, like a custard pie,

Pumpkin bread, baked with pumpkins grown on-site.
CREDIT: JOHN D. IVANKO

"I started my cookie business in 2008, from my home with $800. By my second year, I barely broke even. My business nearly quadrupled during my third year, bringing me from approximately 7 to about 28 orders per week. And last year, I averaged about 47 orders per week. Admittedly, I am *an optimist, but if you had told me ten years ago that I would be able to build a cookie business from my home, doing what I am absolutely passionate about and grossing six figures into my fifth year in business, I would have certainly told you, You are NUTS!"*

—Aymee VanDyke, owner of The Sugar Art Studio on Etsy

it does, then you cannot sell it in nearly all states with cottage food laws. However, here are some common examples of items you can bake and sell to the public:

- Bread loaves
- Muffins and scones
- Cakes
- Biscuits
- Cookies
- Crackers

Custom Cakes: Artistic, Time-consuming, Delicious, and Lucrative

One of the more popular and lucrative products made by CFOs are the artistic and delicious custom-designed cakes for weddings or special events like birthdays or anniversaries. Besides the skilled and labor-intensive nature of making these cakes, taking orders for them may require extra planning: a contract, invoicing, and even liability insurance might be necessary. Given the size and dollar amount of the order, getting everything in writing is a must, for both parties' sakes. Try to leave nothing to chance; some bakers even have swatches of color to serve as reference for their frostings to ensure they can deliver exactly what their clients or customers want. Accepting a nominal advance deposit would be expected if you are to hold a date; requiring full payment a month before the wedding date would also not be out of line. In addition to the wedding cake itself, another lucrative offshoot of cakes for special events are the dessert tables that can include a wide selection of cookies, cakes, and other treats. Just be careful not to cross the legal line of being a caterer instead of a cottage food entrepreneur.

Scones may add a unique item to your product mix.
CREDIT: JOHN D. IVANKO PHOTOGRAPHY

Understand what your state defines as a baked good as sometimes this also includes products that don't technically go in the oven but are perfectly non-hazardous such as rolled oats, nuts, and peanut butter to make an energy bar or trail mix. Depending on your state, these types of products may be covered separately in other categories (read on!), but they wouldn't be defined as a baked goods.

Check with your state's law for the definitive rule on what is allowed. You might live in the state with an oddball exemption, for whatever the reasons, to what can be baked in the rest of the states. Pennsylvania, for example, is the only state that allows dried meat jerkies so far. Iowa allows licensed home-based food operators to sell cheesecakes, cream pies, and even items made with either meat or poultry from a state-approved source.

"There is so much untapped business opportunity to showcase each state's baking heritage; in Wisconsin we have everything from Swiss bratzeli *cookies to Norwegian* lefse *to a multitude of other cultural specialties. In my work chronicling the state's culinary legacy, I've met many amazing home bakers who carry on Wisconsin food traditions. However, many of their baked goods can't be mass produced, and therefore you can't purchase them anywhere."*

—Terese Allen, Wisconsin's leading food authority and historian

Missing from the approved non-hazardous baked goods list are any items filled with something that needs refrigeration. Moist fillings increase the moisture level and thereby increase the potential for harmful bacteria to thrive. There are a lot of variations on what a "filled" baked good can mean. Again, some states give specific guidelines while others may require you to contact the agency for clarification.

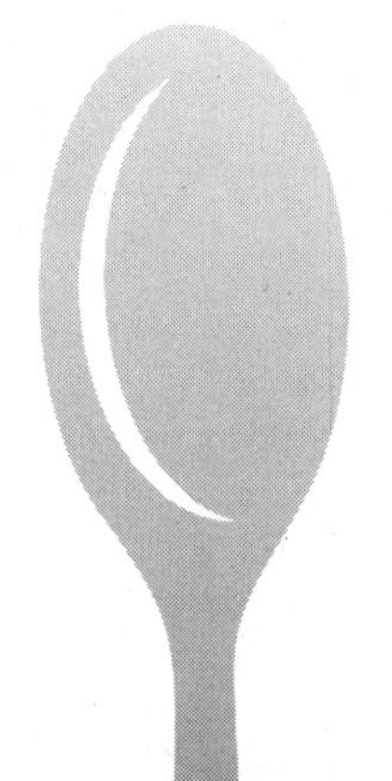

Low Moisture Means Baked Goods That Are Safe

Don't panic if you see a slew of technical detail and numbers in your state's law defining non-hazardous baked goods. You don't need to be a scientist; you do need to ensure the baked product for sale is safe by following your state's guidelines. These definitions generally follow the FDA's Food Code of a "water activity value of 0.85 or less."

These definitions describe baked goods with a low-water activity content, which inhibits mold growth and means they can be kept at room temperature. They're shelf-stable. If an item contains too much water, pathogens—the bad bacteria that cause disease—grow. In such cases, these items need to be refrigerated to prevent the growth of harmful bacteria. The lower the water activity level number, the more shelf-stable the item is because it is less prone to bacteria growth. That said, other factors can contribute to a recipe meeting the safe .85 or lower water activity level, including the sugar content: the higher the sugar, the better.

A state's law may list specifically what is allowed, such as breads and cookies, and what is not, like cream pies or churros that contain a moist filling. Anything made with meat is usually a no, unless you live in a state with some variation of a food freedom law.

What about frostings? A traditional buttercream frosting with lots of heavy cream will probably not qualify as non-hazardous by your state's definition, but there are various mock buttercreams alternatives that would. In chapter 5, we have several non-hazardous frosting recipes to consider along with other baked good recipes, each independently tested in a lab. Run the recipe and the test results by your state for approval before using them. Some scientists and state health officials, we've discovered, tend to disagree with one another.

"The Illinois law, called the Home-to-Market Act, is unique because instead of having a list of allowed products, the law contains a list of products that are not allowed, like meat or dairy items," explains Molly Pickering, Deputy Director of the Illinois Stewardship Alliance, regarding their updated law. "As long as you do not use ingredients that are on the list of prohibited products, you have a lot of flexibility to make whatever you want. It also carved out buttercream icing as an allowable dairy product."

"We had a lot of bakers and wedding cake makers tell us that they wanted to sell their cupcakes and cakes, but they couldn't do it because dairy products aren't allowed, except as an ingredient in a baked good," adds Pickering, regarding the buttercream icing exemption in Illinois. "We talked with food safety experts from the University of Illinois Extension and they felt that as long as raw eggs were not included in the buttercream, that it was a relatively safe and shelf-stable product. So we pushed for that. Most legislators liked the idea of more access to cupcakes, and it seemed incredibly logical to provide bakers with a legal pathway to sell these products."

As many of us witnessed first-hand during the COVID-19 pandemic, science may not always be definitive. When applied to cottage food laws, this may create time-consuming barriers for CFOs because they have to go multiple rounds with state health officials who may not have the science background to understand, per the FDA, that ☛

As long as no water or milk is added to the recipe, pecan pie is generally considered a non-hazardous food product because of its high sugar content. CREDIT: JOHN D. IVANKO PHOTOGRAPHY

butter or margarine on their own are safe products. Add in lots of sugar, which acts as a preservative, and most frostings are safe since they would meet the FDA requirement of 68% required to be a preservative. A typical American buttercream recipe lists 4 cups (1 pound of sugar) to the two sticks of butter, along with a little vanilla, and a little milk. By weight, this makes the recipe 64% sugar. Adding a little more sugar would take it above the 68% required to be a preservative. Straight from the source, the FDA writes, related to the water activity (aw) in foods: "If the water activity of food is controlled to 0.85 or less in the finished product, it is not subject to the regulations of 21 CFR Parts 108, 113, and 114."

Jars of Slow Jams, handcrafted and featuring Michigan produce and sugar. Based in Grosse Pointe, Michigan, the business was originally started by Shannon Byrne under cottage food legislation. Byrne's business did so well that the Detroit Food Academy, a nonprofit that works to inspire young Detroiters through culinary arts and food entrepreneurship, bought Slow Jams in late 2017. CREDIT: JOHN D. IVANKO PHOTOGRAPHY

High-Acid Canned Goods (Pickles, Preserves, and Salsa)

Second to baked goods, many cottage food laws permit high-acid canned items made in home kitchens. The "high-acid" refers to fruits and vegetables that are either naturally high in acid, such as tomatoes, or that become acidified through pickling or fermenting. To be considered high-acid, these products must have an equilibrium pH of 4.6 or less. If your memory of tenth-grade science is a bit hazy, this pH number measures acidity; the lower the number, the more acidic the food item.

Examples of high-acid canned products include:

- Jams and jellies
- Salsa
- Chutneys
- Pickled vegetables and fruits
- Sauerkraut (canned only)
- Applesauce

Cottage food laws only refer to canned items processed in university extension-approved methods such as a hot water bath. High-acid items that don't qualify in the legislation are refrigerator pickles or pickles made in a crock. Again, for the purposes of nearly all cottage food laws, if your product requires refrigeration, you can't sell it. Check with your state's law, because there increasingly seems to be a state or two that offers an exemption, for

Jam, jelly, and marmalade are high-acid canned products made by Renee Pottle, author of Profitable Preserves: How to Start an Artisan Jam and Jelly Business *(2020).* CREDIT: RENEE POTTLE

whatever their reasons, to some of the hard-and-fast rules. Illinois, for example, does allow certain fermented foods.

Unlike water activity level, pH can be measured at home if permitted by your state. You can use a pH meter, which needs to be properly calibrated on the day it is used. More common are paper pH test strips, also known as litmus paper; you simply dip these in a sample jar and the color will turn based on the acidity level and related pH number. Paper strips work best if a product has a pH of 4.0 or less; the strip's range should go up to a pH of 4.6. Depending on your state's rules, you may need to do a pH test on each batch or over a state-defined time frame. While expensive, a pH meter can provide a more exacting measurement of acidity.

Canning and creating high-acid products are very different processes than baking. Canning items, whether high-acid or not, is more science than culinary art. While you can alter, experiment with, and personalize your biscotti recipe until it is uniquely your own, this isn't the case with canning recipes. At best, you'll be able to adjust your spices and ratios of vegetables.

There are plenty of university extension-sanctioned recipes that have been thoroughly tested, from classic items like strawberry jam to more modern delicacies such as garden chutney and sweet pepper relish. Some states allow specific canning recipes from sources like the current edition of *The Ball Blue Book of Preserving*. But note that just because a recipe is in a canning cookbook doesn't mean it will qualify under the state law. Just follow the state-mandated recipes and protocol and you're good to go.

What if you want to use your great-grandma's special family recipe for blackberry preserves? Some states will allow you to alter and create your own recipes after you complete the Master's in Food Preservation course. This is similar in format to the Master Gardeners program, also through university extension. There seems to be a revival with this new home-canning movement. The Master's in Food Preservation is a one-day intensive class that goes into the nitty-gritty science of pH and food safety procedures. Once you complete it, you can serve as a community education resource for local folks with canning questions. Or a Master Canner in your community may be able to review and approve your recipe.

Canning Success with Renee Pottle

"There are all kinds of high-acid canned foods that we can choose to make and sell in our cottage home kitchens under your state's cottage food law, everything from jams and jellies, fruit, butters, shrubs, pickles, sauerkraut, flavored vinegars, chutneys sauces, even juice," says Renee Pottle, author of *Profitable Preserves: How to Start an Artisan Jam and Jelly Business.*

"So how do you know which product is the right one for you?" prompts Pottle. "Many of us have an idea with a recipe in mind, or maybe you grow an excess of apricots on your farm and you would like to make jam out of them. Perhaps you don't grow anything, but you have a famous peach chutney recipe that all your friends and family tell you that you should make and sell.

Renee Pottle preparing a new batch of her favorite Cranberry Christmas Jam, the recipe for which can be found on SeedtoPantry.com.
CREDIT: RENEE POTTLE

"First of all, whatever your canned product is, it should be something you love to make," advises Pottle, who's also a Master Food Preserver, getting started with canning as a child while hanging out in her Nana's kitchen. "You will be making this product over and over. So, if you're not crazy about the whole jelly-making process, don't choose a jelly business." This applies to any canned food product, not just jelly. The product has to be something you like to do.

"Do you have easy access to the ingredients needed to make your canned food product?" asks Pottle. "And are the ingredients affordable, if it turns out you buy them and not grow them yourself? Finally, when you add up the ingredient and packaging costs, plus factor in your labor, can you sell your products at a profit where you live?" Sourcing locally or regionally tends to be the best way to keep the costs down and secure the high-quality ingredients, harvested at their peak of ripeness and, therefore, flavor. Beyond affordable and accessible ingredients, she's quick to point out other potential bottlenecks, like the availability of canning jars, lids, or spices. Supply chain woes can crop up in unanticipated ways, so it's wise to have a backup plan so production delays can be avoided.

"Don't swim upstream," cautions Pottle. "Avoid choosing a product that you have to convince your customers to buy or that you have to overly explain. Most people understand jams and jellies and pickles and salsa. You might have to explain a regional fruit like marionberries, but people understand jam. However, they might walk right by your beautiful jars of mustard because they don't understand it as a pickled product.

"The biggest trade-off when working from our home kitchen is probably giving up a certain level of creativity," admits Pottle, "Low-acid foods, like pepper jellies, usually aren't allowed. Anything that includes alcohol, like wine jelly or ale jelly, probably isn't allowed either under a cottage food law. For example, your state might let you make peach jam, but they won't let you make persimmon jam. You might be able to make pickles from cucumbers, but not from carrots. The rules seem arbitrary, and to a certain degree they are.

"Some states will let you make jam at home," continues Pottle. "Some will let you make pickles at home. Some will let you make sauerkraut at home. Some will let you make two of those, but not the other. Some will let you make all three. So, before you get too excited about what you're going to produce, make sure that you've checked to make sure it's legal in your state. Either work with the cottage food law you have, or you'll need to become an advocate and get the law changed in your state.

"Because our products are in cans, the jars themselves sell your delicious home products at farm stands or pop-up food-related events," says Pottle, noting that the colorful canned item has plenty of eye appeal and doesn't need to be covered over by lots of labeling. "Be creative with labels, but there's no need to get carried away with it. Stick with easy labels. Same for standard jars rather than the more expensive imported ones unless you're sure you can get a lot more money for each jar sold. Otherwise, you'll be losing any profit you might have made.

"Starting a home-based business is always an exciting venture," shares Pottle. "I've started several over the past three or four decades and in various locations and various types. We're bubbling with optimism, but to keep that optimism, it's best to avoid costly mistakes. Don't get emotionally involved with either your product or your packaging. If something is too expensive, you have to be willing to give it up and move on to the next thing.

"Remember, you are making delicious canned food products you love," concludes Pottle. "You are sharing it with other people and they are paying you for it." That's the perfect recipe for business success.

Always check for jam set two ways: the spoon method and the temperature method, advises Renee Pottle, author of Profitable Preserves: How to Start an Artisan Jam and Jelly Business. CREDIT: RENEE POTTLE

Building Your High-acid Knowledge Base

While home canning goes back generations, don't forget it's a traditional art that has become safer over time thanks to our increasing scientific understanding of the process. Great-grandma's tomato sauce recipe based on yesterday's practices—which often did not include adequate water bath times or sanitation procedures—could potentially do more harm than good. Stick with current recipes from reliable and state-approved sources.

Another reason to steer clear of old recipes: some of the vegetables used today have changed in composition. Garden tomatoes, for example, have been bred to become less acidic to appease our taste preferences, a change that could significantly alter the results of the canning process and, therefore, the safety of grandma's original recipe.

Go through a reputable source for high-acid canned recipes, such as:

- *Ball Complete Book of Home Preserving*, edited by Judi Kingry and Lauren Devine (current edition)
- Cooperative Extension Offices in US: csrees.usda.gov/extension
- Home Food Preservation from Penn State University: foodsafety.psu.edu/preserve.html
- National Center for Home Food Preservation: nchfp.uga.edu
- The National Center for Home Food Preservation offers a free, self-paced online course, Preserving Food at Home: A Self-Study, for those who want to learn more about home canning.

Mixed Bag: Other Possible Cottage Food Products

Depending on your state, you may have an additional mixed bag of products you can sell that may include dried mixes, herbal blends, chocolates, butters, condiments, dried pasta, roasted products—even cotton candy! There's no rhyme or reason to the list, other than they all are non-hazardous. Some of the items could just be things some person in that state really wanted to make in their home kitchen to sell to the public. Don't be surprised if your state allows one product while a neighboring state does not.

Check your state laws to see if any of the following items are possible:

- Candy, such as brittle and toffee
- Chocolate-covered nonperishable foods, such as nuts and dried fruit

- Chocolate-covered pretzels, marshmallows, Rice Krispie treats, and graham crackers
- Cotton candy
- Dried fruit
- Dried pasta
- Dry baking mixes
- Fruit pies, fruit empanadas, and fruit tamales
- Granola, cereals, and trail mixes
- Herb blends and dried mole paste
- Honey and sweet sorghum syrup
- Nut mixes and nut butters
- Popcorn
- Vinegar and mustard
- Roasted coffee
- Dried tea and dried tea blends
- Waffle cones and pizelles

Rice Krispie "sandwiches" sold at the International Chocolate Festival at the Fairchild Tropical Botanic Garden in Coral Gables, Florida. CREDIT: JOHN D. IVANKO

Question 2: Where Can You Sell Your Products?

Each cottage food law will dictate where you can sell your product directly to the public. Only a few states still only allow you to sell at farmers' markets or special events like a holiday bazaar. Such limitations restrict your potential sales. Many states, however, offer a lot more flexibility in terms of the sales venues. The more options the better, in terms of reaching potential customers. The states with the greatest sales venue options often include direct delivery to a residence or an office, home pickup, pop-up markets in your community, and mail order shipped within your state.

Even if your state's law allows sales at a farmers' market, that doesn't mean this venue must allow you to sell there. Some farmers' markets have bylaws or rules that exclude cottage food enterprises. For example, the Dane County Farmers' Market held in Madison, Wisconsin—one of the largest in the nation—requires that canned and bakery products be made in a licensed commercial kitchen.

Handmade chocolates sold at the International Chocolate Festival at the Fairchild Tropical Botanic Garden in Coral Gables, Florida. CREDIT: JOHN D. IVANKO

Question 3: How Are You Allowed to Sell Your Products?

Regardless of the state, all cottage food laws permit direct sales to the public. Some of the more restrictive states, however, only allow sales that are direct-to-customer. Read: no indirect, or wholesale, sales to other businesses that resell your product. That said, in more than a dozen states, products can be sold through indirect or wholesale channels to restaurants, specialty food shops, the local food cooperative, or even Whole Foods Market. Check with your state to see what you can do.

Spritz cookies piled high on a holiday dessert table. Most CFOs can sell and deliver the cookies, but cottage food laws prevent you from arranging the cookies on a plate at a particular venue. The person who buys the cookies gets to do the arranging.
CREDIT: JOHN D. IVANKO PHOTOGRAPHY

If, or when, the time comes to scale up and turn your microenterprise into a macro-business and offer your products through a wider assortment of channels than are permitted by your cottage food law, you may have to rent a licensed food production facility, or renovate your own kitchen if allowed in your state. Expanding along a continuum, your business may either scale up modestly to serve a few small retailers or become an all-hands-on-deck, full-time endeavor with employees, production in a commercially licensed facility, huge financial demands, and plenty of governmental red tape to keep you busy seven days a week. At that point, it's no longer for a casual baker or pickle maker.

Generally, cottage food laws do not permit food service, and you are not a "caterer." You may deliver your products to a customer, but not display or serve them. You can produce certain foods in your home kitchen and have them consumed off premises—just don't slice, plate, or otherwise be involved in serving your product.

Covered in much more detail in the food freedom section of this second edition are the new food freedom and microenterprise home kitchen operation (MHKO) laws being passed in several states that are related, but separate from, existing cottage food laws. Under these laws and depending on the state, prepared meals can be served in a way that resembles a delivery of meals from a restaurant, except the items are made in a home kitchen.

With rare exceptions, your cottage food-approved products must, in fact, be made in your home kitchen. If you decide to scale up, you'll be renting a commercial kitchen somewhere or building one in your home. If in doubt, check the section of your state's law related to the "workplace."

Question 4: How Much Can You Sell of Your Products?

At the time of publication of this book, less than 20 states still have a gross sales cap on the products you're selling. This refers to the maximum gross sales your operations can reach per year and range from $5,000 to $250,000. (Not a typo; yes, a quarter million dollars, from your kitchen!) Net sales refer to sales after your expenses have been deducted. Remarkably, the majority of states allow unlimited sales and no gross sales caps, and other states are moving in this direction to allow for greater gross sales.

Decide What Products You Want to Sell and Which Are Worth Selling

Now that you have an idea of what you can legally sell in your state, what can you make that's worth selling?

Here's where the fun starts with testing out your food product ideas. If you already have a popular product, at least with the in-laws, friends, and co-workers, then jump to the next chapter and proceed. Otherwise, you'll need to sort out some details, including determining your products, checking your recipes, and figuring out your market niche. As we'll cover in the forthcoming marketing chapters, these considerations play an important role in the story about your product and business.

Product Selection

At this stage of your evaluation, what products did you have in mind? There are several approaches you might take to selecting your product.

- Ingredients: Are the ingredients or products going to be organic, whole grain, kosher, allergen-free, without preservatives or artificial ingredients, or gluten-free?
- Recipe focused: Are the recipes unique or rare family recipes that are popular with family and friends? Is the recipe an all-from-scratch item or do you take shortcuts with premade crusts or fillings? Is your focus on ethnic cuisine, cultural food items, or a seasonal specialty item?
- Sourcing of ingredients: Will your products come from your neighbor's fruit trees, your backyard, farmers' market, the supermarket, Costco? How local are your local ingredients? Depending on your products, some of the ingredients may come from a combination of these sources.

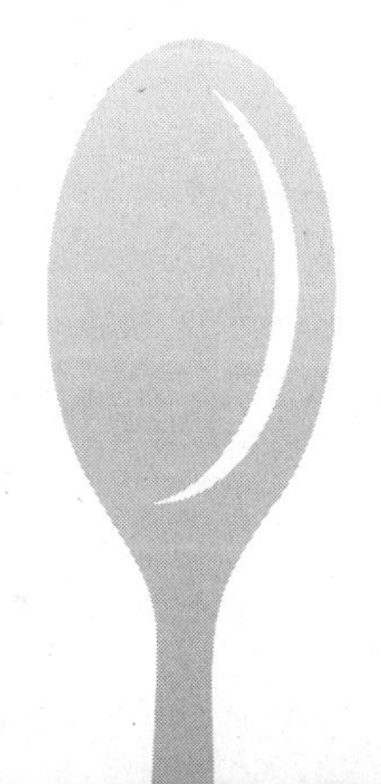

No Profits Allowed from Products Featuring Copyrighted or Trademarked Names, Logos, Designs, Emblems, or Characters

Avoid the temptation to create any products you sell that in any way infringe on the trademark or copyright of another company. The only way you can make a profit from a product you create using a name, logo, slogan, emblem, or character is if you get the expressed written permission from the company or person that owns it, or purchase a license for its commercial use (if allowed). Copyright protects the artistic or design elements (including cartoon characters like SpongeBob SquarePants) while trademarks protect the distinctive words, slogans, or phrases (like Nike or "JUST DO IT."). That means decorated cookies or cakes with Mickey Mouse, NFL logos or "Super Bowl," and the rings of the Olympics owned by the United States Olympic Committee are all off-limits. Even cookie-cutter shapes of famous characters like Batman are only for personal — noncommercial — use; they cannot be used for items you sell. How serious is this? The Michigan Cookiers Facebook group administrator has gone so far as to add a new rule to their group: "Posting trademark or copyright material/cookies is prohibited. That means no Disney, Star Wars, cartoon characters, TV shows, etc."

Avoid breaking the law like a commercial bakery did when selling decorated BB-8 cookies. BB-8 is a copyrighted character from the Star Wars movies. CREDIT: JOHN D. IVANKO PHOTOGRAPHY

The way the trademark and copyright laws are written, the owners of such protected intellectual properties are obligated to actually enforce their rights, otherwise they run the risk of losing those rights. In legal jargon, when someone illegally uses a copyrighted or trademarked element, the argument is that the loss of its distinctive quality causes "dilution." Interestingly, it could be argued that even if you feature a cake that you do not intend on selling on your website or Instagram page which features a company logo, but someone orders another of your cakes, you could be in violation of the law. The rationale: You used a famous logo or character, like Snoopy, to help generate a sale. ☛

Receiving a certified-mail "cease and desist" letter from legal department of the Walt Disney Company, or any other corporation, is guaranteed to ruin your day. The last thing most CFOs want is to be sued over a cookie because it features Mario, Luigi, or another famous video game character. It's best to avoid it. And if you see someone selling something with a logo on it, it doesn't mean it's legal; it just means that they haven't been caught — yet. Now, for our disclaimer: If you don't believe us, we encourage you to contact an attorney.

If your client or customer is set on having a certain copyright-protected character on their cake, let them buy the cake from you. Then mention to the customer that they can purchase a figurine of the character they want themselves, completely separate from your cake order, and place it on the cake after you deliver it. There's nothing preventing them from adding another decoration to a cake for their personal use. If it's a birthday cake, they'll probably add a bunch of candles anyway, so it's not that big of a stretch to add their own Jedi characters, Yoda, or Darth Vader.

Keep in mind that should you create a beautiful work of art of your own design in a cake, for example, and you take a picture of it and then post it on your website or Instagram, you are protected from someone else coming along and using it (without your expressed permission). So, such laws actually protect CFOs as well, assuming you have a unique enough design or concept and go through the efforts of registering it with the US Copyright Office. We did so for this book!

Market Niche

When you break down your ingredient list, what most of us are selling is nothing more than the following:

- Pickles: cucumbers, vinegar, salt, sugar, and spices
- Bread: flour, salt, yeast, and water
- Preserves: fruit, sugar, and water
- Cupcakes: sugar, butter, eggs, flour

In many cases, there may be similar products available where you live. What makes yours different—and better? In some cases, if your ingredients are from a neighbor's fruit trees, a cherished ethnic recipe passed down several generations, or a unique product you've developed and perfected yourself, these may be reason enough for a successful launch in your neighborhood. A market niche is a defined segment of a larger market you've identified as a potentially financially rewarding opportunity; more on this in chapter 6, when we dig in and define your product from a marketing perspective.

Follow the Trends

Your business might be small, but you can still take advantage of emerging food trends, creating products that target what shoppers currently seek. Some market niches to explore might be the following:

- Gluten-free: Only 1 in 133 Americans are diagnosed with celiac disease, unable to tolerate gluten in their diet, according to the National Foundation for Celiac Awareness. But gluten-free appears to be the hot health trend with more than 30 percent of Americas claiming to avoid gluten, reveals the consumer research firm NPD Group.
- Dairy-free: According to the Mayo Clinic, eight foods account for 90 percent of all food allergies, five of which are common in baked goods: peanuts, tree nuts, milk, eggs, and wheat (soy, fish, and shellfish also made the list).
- Organic: Total organic sales in the United States continue to rise, up more than 10 percent annually to more than $56 billion in 2020, according to the Organic Trade Association.
- Local: Research from Sullivan Higdon & Sink's FoodThink, "A Fresh Look at Organic and Local" 2012, finds that "70 percent of consumers would like to know more about where food comes from." They found that local was hot: "The vast majority of consumers (79%) would like to buy more local food, and almost 6 in 10 (59%) consumers say it's important when buying food that it be locally sourced, grown or made."
- Ethnic flavors: Does your own family heritage offer unique specialty items folks can't purchase elsewhere? Ethnic flavors continue to increase in popularity, particularly from Mexico and Latin American countries, according to the "Flavor Forecast" from McCormick & Co.
- Keto: A ketogenic diet is based on a strict low-carbohydrate, low-sugar, but high-fat intake. The metabolic state of ketosis is when your body burns fat, in the absence of carbohydrates or sugars. "Research showed that 8 out of 10 consumers intentionally avoid or reduce sugar in their diets and, of those, 70% find sugar reduction to be most important for baked goods," writes Melissa Kvidahl Reilly, in *Food & Beverage Insider* (September 23, 2021), based on 2021 data from ADM's OutsideVoice consumer insights platform.

Cupcakes come in many sizes. Will your cupcakes have lots of frosting or just a little? Shavings or sprinkles added too? Are they made with organic flour and chocolate? Who do you want to appeal to with your product?

CREDIT: JOHN D. IVANKO PHOTOGRAPHY

Recipe Testing

Getting the spices just right for your pumpkin cookies may involve plenty of trial and error, mixing and matching, and lots of tasting. Besides taste and flavor, you'll want consistency, since you'll get a bad reputation quickly if the delicious muffins you made one week are too sweet or flavorless the following week. McDonald's has built its quick-service restaurant empire around this idea of consistency—anywhere on planet Earth. It may not be the healthiest food in the world, but their Big Mac tastes the same in Monroe, Wisconsin, as it does in Hong Kong. Customers expect this.

When you make your product with your recipe, does it turn out the same every time, day in and day out? Or do humidity, temperature, or other factors create havoc with either your process or the ingredients?

Size is also an issue in consistency. Your cookies, cupcakes, or other baked items should be about the same size for the same price.

Product Testing

After nailing your recipes, it's time to test the product, since we're talking about something perishable. Your criteria might include taste, flavor, texture, shelf life (fresh, day-old, best eaten fresh, longer term), labor involved, waste, space needs, speed of preparation, and consistency.

It's important to have an honest and objective audience to help in your product testing. Is your pineapple salsa, pickled dilly beans, or magical muffins as good as everyone says? Many people, as well-meaning as they may seem, will tell you what they think you want to hear. As you develop your products or product lines, it's important to find honest and objective testers who can provide practical feedback. Don't forget to "hire" your son or granddaughter as marketing consultants; kids can offer incredibly honest and fresh perspectives on your products and how they taste.

Product testing at this phase is different than completing a market feasibility study, where you examine a host of other variables, many having to do as much with marketing considerations and customer needs as taste. More on this in chapter 14, after you've pulled together your ideas on marketing.

By now you hopefully feel ignited and inspired by the state of our cottage food movement and the opportunities the laws provide. But before we get into the kitchen, we're going to take a step back in the next chapter to more deeply understand the "why" behind what's motivating you to move forward on following your dream of starting a food business.

3

Ideas in the Oven: Identify Your Business Goals

BEFORE JUMPING INTO A BUSINESS, even a small home kitchen-based one, you'll want to sort out your personal goals for the enterprise and set forth some realistic expectations. Your enterprise will not suddenly make you rich, though a few of you reading this book might discover a path to personal wealth based on a combination of your culinary ideas, talents, and adept business decisions made along the way.

This chapter explores what it might mean to operate a business out of your home, helps you assess your current skill sets and talents, and completes a few quick checks to make sure you don't put the food cart before the horse.

My Kitchen, My Rules

For many food entrepreneurs, one of the best parts of running your business is calling the shots. Everything is on your terms, within the parameters set forth by your state's cottage food law, of course. The law defines what you sell, how you sell it, to whom, and when. You answer these questions yourself, perhaps with a little input from others you trust, respect, and admire.

Before starting, however, you'll want to have a clear idea as to what you want to achieve with your business. The following are some of the many reasons that CFOs open their operation.

Extra Cash for a Fancy Dinner with Your Spouse or to Pay off a Credit Card

Thanks to the cottage food laws created, in part, as a reaction to the recent trying economic times or the disruptions caused by the COVID-19 pandemic, turning a home kitchen into an income-generating profit center may allow you to splurge on a dinner out more often. Or it may be the difference between being able to pay the bills or not. Most enterprises will never be a

full-time endeavor; they can, however, add supplemental cash flow where it never existed before.

Enjoying and Fulfilling a Dream Passion

When money is not the object, many people would choose to do something radically different than what they do now. They have a dream of being a baker, making canned preserves from a favorite family recipe or just running their own business. We started our Inn Serendipity Bed & Breakfast based on our vision; now run a small bakery enterprise in our kitchen for the same reason.

Following your dreams and passion can be empowering, satisfying, enjoyable, and meaningful in ways that no paycheck—even a big paycheck—could ever be. In the world of human psychology, such self-driven motivation is referred to as intrinsic. The extrinsic motivation for most jobs is money, a health insurance plan, a corner office, or a gold watch; many of us have found that there never seem to be enough extrinsic rewards if you hate what you do or who you do it for.

"I didn't want the 9-to-5 rat race. I wanted to do something I'd enjoy."

—Angela Brooks-Van Niel, Redlands, California, home-based owner of Simply Fancy Cuisine

The Top 8 Traits of Successful Cottage Food Entrepreneurs

Simply put, since 2011, David Crabill has single-handedly put cottage foods on the map with his Forrager.com and *The Forrager Podcast*.

Based in California, Crabill is the technical wizard behind Forrager.com, the largest online community for the cottage food industry, providing the most comprehensive and up-to-date information about cottage food laws across the nation, as well as many other resources for starting a cottage food business. His dynamic and detailed map of the cottage food and food freedom movement in the US gets refreshed every time a law is expanded or a court case is decided. Forrager has helped tens of thousands of CFOs or home cooks better understand their state's cottage food law, connect with others in the community, and learn more about starting and growing a cottage food business. We've wondered, ourselves, if he ever sleeps, or if he's also built an AI-robot in his garage to help (he hasn't, yet).

As the host of *The Forrager Podcast*, Crabill interviews a wide range of entrepreneurs across America who legally sell their homemade food via their state's cottage food law. As one of the features on Forrager.com, each podcast episode reveals strategies for marketing and selling food products successfully from home, ☛

online, at farmers' markets or special events, and in stores.

Because of his knowledge and pulse on the movement, Crabill keynoted the Home-based Food Entrepreneur Virtual National Conference. In 2021, he also led the charge to expand the cottage food law in California, collaboratively working with legislators, other CFOs, and various nonprofit groups. He walks the talk, too, selling fudge during the holidays with his cottage food business, Crabill Candy.

"I've discovered eight of the most common traits that I see in successful cottage food entrepreneurs," shares Crabill, who has probably spent more than 1,000 hours so far researching, preparing for, or interviewing guests on *The Forrager Podcast*.

Crabill shares these eight traits of successful CFOs below.

Act and follow through

"The first trait I've noticed is that successful food entrepreneurs are consistent, and they show up," observes Crabill after talking with his many CFOs featured in *The Forrager Podcast*. "When they say they're going to do something, they do it. And they put in the work."

One of the many episodes on The Forrager Podcast, *hosted by David Crabill, founder of Forrager.com*
CREDIT: DAVID CRABILL/FORRAGER.COM

Doers, not talkers

"The guests on my show tend to be hustlers. They are action takers and they get things done. They do not often wallow in indecision, and they make the most of their time and produce a lot."

Serve others

"CFOs tend to love serving other people. They're very service-oriented and are always focused on providing the best service to other people as possible. They tend to be very humble people, which helps."

Have some food service experience

"A lot of food entrepreneurs on my show have had former experience in the food service industry, either working at restaurants or bakeries or some form of food service. I feel like the person who has food service experience just has a leg up over someone who's starting out brand new, and maybe hasn't seen how a food business would run." Sometimes that experience stretches back to working behind a counter in high school, taking orders. For others, it was before a sudden departure from a shuttered restaurant due to the COVID-19 pandemic.

Love being around people

"CFOs on my show tend to love people. They describe themselves as a 'people person.' They tend to be very social. Sometimes they're more extroverted, but not always. Generally speaking, they love going to events. They love going to farmers' markets. They love ☛

engaging with people and interacting with their customers. You can tell when a business owner really loves their customers, it just shows in everything that they do."

Know, and can share, their story

"Successful food entrepreneurs tend to be willing to open up and share themselves and their story with other people. And I think this makes them very relatable to other people. Even introverts are willing to open up in some aspect. Maybe it's not on social media, but at least telling their story on their website or engaging with customers at a farmers' market. These types of food entrepreneurs tend to do better with their businesses." They've mastered their "elevator pitch."

Have creativity

"CFOs are creative people. They tend to have art backgrounds or sometimes creative writing backgrounds, whatever it may be. They just tend to be more creative types. Obviously, this is correlated with the fact that a lot of the most successful cottage food businesses out there are customized businesses, custom cake businesses, custom decorated cookie businesses. Across the board, regardless of what kind of business people have, I've noticed that those who love to create, tend to do really well."

Partner with others

"Some of my most successful guests have partnered with someone else in their business. They're not solo entrepreneurs. Certainly, some of the CFOs were power couples or people that had some kind of business partnership. If you've gotten into business, you know there's a lot of moving pieces. There's the production side of things. There's the business side of things. And so being able to split up duties is essential to growing your business in a big way. I have had a ton of entrepreneurs on *The Forrager Podcast* that don't have a business partner and do very well with their business. But overall, I would say that those CFOs who have some form of help have a much easier time growing their business to the point where it can be the primary income for their family.

"Get to your first sale as quickly as possible," advises Crabill, for someone just starting out. It's based on the years of listening, of replying to questions, and responding to the never-ending stream of emails pouring in to Forrager. "Your recipes are already good enough to sell. Once you make that first sale, you can learn and evolve as you get feedback from your paying customers.

"This movement empowers individuals to use something they already have, a home kitchen, and something they already know, how to make amazing food, to create value in their local communities," concludes Crabill. "More and more states are learning that freeing up local food economies create many benefits, and come with very few risks. It provides opportunities to local artisan food producers by removing regulations which were designed for mass food production. People want to buy food from their neighbors, if only the government will let them!"

Profile

Tamsin Perfect, Tamsin's Cakes, Fort Worth, Texas

Name: Tamsin Perfect

Business: Tamsin's Cakes (Fort Worth, TX)

Website: https://tamsinscakes.com

Products: decorated custom cakes, cupcakes, paint your own cookies, cocoa bombs, South African baked items

Sales Venues: farmers' markets, direct orders from customers

Gross Revenues: $14,000/year

Baking the Perfect Cake Business

If there ever was a perfect cake, Tamsin Perfect, baker-owner of Tamsin's Cakes, bakes it. They're temping, delicious, creative, and diverse. Since 2004, Perfect has been customizing and decorating cakes for any occasion. Offering 15 cake flavors, nine fillings, and ten frosting options, she makes sure there's something for every birthday, wedding, anniversary, graduation, or bridal shower. Every cake is made from scratch with no artificial ingredients. She's also quick to jump on hot baking trends, like paint-your-own cookies and cocoa bombs, to boost profits when selling at markets.

Perfect is also a bit of a footloose baker, starting her business in South Africa, then again in Arizona, and finally settling down in Fort Worth, Texas. "I started my cake business in South Africa when my first daughter turned one and I realized that I wanted to make a cake for her," shares Perfect. It turns out she didn't just want to bake a cake, she wanted to bake a perfect one for her daughter. Plus, baking was her way to combat postnatal depression and express her creativity. "I attended a one-day class on working with fondant icing and made a '3 Little Bears' cake for my daughter. That was the start of the business after I sold a few cakes to my friends. News spread by word of mouth from there. South Africa didn't have a home cottage industry or any rules that I had to follow.

Tamsin Perfect standing behind her canopy booth at a community farmers' market. Credit: Tamsin's Cakes

"I had to do a lot of research into what I could and couldn't do here for my bakery," admits Perfect, after moving to the United States in 2013. A practicing registered nurse since 1998, she hoped that the baking business would complement her daytime job that she held while her two children were in school. "Every evening I come home and bake something. I start on Monday with my rusks that need time to dry. I typically make my cookie doughs early in the week so that they are ready to start baking on Wednesday and

Thursday evening. I spend most of Saturday working on the final packaging and making my cake pops."

Like many cottage food operations, Tamsin's Cakes has evolved into a family enterprise, with everyone pitching in as her kids got older. "I enlist the help of my teenagers with assembling boxes, labeling products and my bags. Besides assisting at the market, my husband does most of the supply shopping for me. My kids help with dishes and cleanup. I have a big white board in the kitchen with a list of upcoming orders and dates. I also start my week by listing all the items that I want to take to market. This helps me stay organized and gives me a visual of where I am and what I need to achieve. It also helps my family know what the week ahead looks like for preparing dinner and how much their assistance will be needed.

"After immigrating to the US, I started a home bakery in Show Low, Arizona, where I encountered the many rules associated with running a home cottage bakery. Then six years later, after moving to Texas, I decided to reopen and rebrand my business with a South African flower, the protea, in my logo as a reference to my heritage." It was in Texas that she formalized her business, completed the state requirements, created a website, and put an invoicing and ordering system into place using Google forms.

"I started making cakes and cupcakes," says Perfect, having quickly found both a passion and artistic talent for making unique customized cakes. "I had to change a lot of my recipes to the American palette as the flavors are different here. Americans typically prefer far sweeter flavors. Plus, there is a bigger range of culturally influenced cake flavors here." Today, she makes a diversity of baked goods, not just cakes, that appeal to those attending her local farmers' market.

"I also established a very regular client base for my South African treats," adds Perfect. "There are people who come to the market every week to purchase the same items. I have a few South African customers, but for the most part, it's Americans who have discovered our treats. I think the biggest selling point is that my baked goods don't use corn syrup and have a mouthful of flavor that lingers. It's not just pure sugar that you're tasting.

"Once I started looking into a farmers' market, I visited a lot of different markets around the Dallas Fort Worth area to see what was being offered by other bakers," explains Perfect, again echoing the important upfront research pursued by many cottage food operators. "I didn't want to be another cupcake or cookie baker. I knew that with my South African background I would be able to reach new customers."

Tamsin Perfect standing behind her canopy booth at a community farmers' market. CREDIT: TAMSIN'S CAKES

Tamsin Perfect's Chocolate Romany Cream cookies on a plate. CREDIT: TAMSIN'S CAKES

"The farmers' market gives me opportunity to be creative and try new recipes and ideas," beams Perfect, who takes great effort to transform her exhibit booth and table into an exciting and colorful mini-storefront. "I quickly realized that I needed to draw people to the table by having items that kids were interested in, like the cake pops with faces. Once the parents come closer, they start to show an interest in the different cookies. We have samples in little containers for our customers to taste, and this has definitely helped sell our products. I like to have some familiar items, along with the unfamiliar. The cocoa bombs are a fad that I'm more than willing to ride out. I saw how popular they were and decided to give them a try. I have learned a lot by making them and experimenting with new ways of doing things.

"With more than 80 regular vendors at the market every week, I have competition from other bakers," recognizes Perfect. "But this ensures that I constantly improve my presentation, packaging, products offered, and my interaction with the clients so that they return. After researching canopies, she made sure to secure a high-quality one with weights to hold the legs down and sides for sun and wind protection. Her table coverings stretch over the table legs so that the wind can't blow them away, along with her products.

"I avoid sitting down while at market," continues Perfect, who includes a gel mat behind her table to more comfortably stand on for up to four hours. "If I do need to sit during a lull in the crowds, I have a director chair that sits up higher. I encourage people passing by to try my samples, which generally leads to a sale. I also talk to people and smile at them, which draws them up to the table. My husband accompanies me at farmers' markets to pitch in with the setup, help with payments, cover that stand when I need a bathroom break, and restock items that are selling out quickly. It really helps to have someone not only to assist but also to encourage me when sales are slow or the weather is keeping people away from market.

"Doing the farmers' market has also taken me out of my comfort zone and forces me to interact with people," admits Perfect. "It helps me to get out of my head and meet new people. Selling at a farmers' market has been a great way to get my business name out into the community and for people to order cakes for their special occasions since they have an opportunity to taste some of what I make. My approach is that my cake needs to taste as good as it looks." Farmers' market sales represent about 80 percent of Tamsin's Cakes' revenues, with the balance resulting from custom order cakes for special events.

"I take orders for custom cakes and make them fresh for each order," says Perfect. "This way I can offer exactly what the client is looking for. I have made several wedding cakes, and make sure that I do not have a market going the same weekend, or that I don't take any other custom orders for the same day." She's quick to realize the time and effort that goes into producing her premium handmade baked goods. By curbing her orders, which she fills completely by herself, she avoids the stress of letting the business get out of hand or take over her life.

Tamsin Perfect displaying her three-tier pumpkin spice custom wedding cake, adorned with roses, carnations, and mums. CREDIT: TAMSIN'S CAKES

"After moving to Texas, I researched all the regulations for Texas home cottage bakery," explains Perfect. "There are, fortunately, only a few requirements, like having a food handler's certificate, correct labeling for packaging, and production of only shelf-stable products. There isn't a formal inspection conducted, but I do have to state on my labels that I operate out of a kitchen that is not inspected.

"I registered my business as a limited liability company, or LLC, rebranded with a new logo, changed the name of the business, and reorganized my house to accommodate the shelving and storage for bakery supplies separated from my household supplies," says Perfect, regarding the steps she took when opening up in Texas. "I registered the LLC in Texas so that I could keep my brand and make it easier for tax purposes, especially as I grow the business to a point when its more than a home-based cottage business." She also has the additional liability protection afforded by the LLC business structure, separating her personal assets from those of the company.

"Before rebranding, I held a think tank with a group of friends involved in different businesses and areas of expertise," continues Perfect. "We discussed ideas and created a new business model from that. My friends were compensated in cake! The new model was how to brand myself, how to create a social presence, what I needed to do to grow and build a customer base. This led to selling at farmers' markets, and it has grown from there.

"I had to purchase a lot of shelving and storage cupboards to accommodate the supplies," explains Perfect, recognizing the growing demands that

Tamsin Perfect's custard cookies arranged in coffee cup. CREDIT: TAMSIN'S CAKES

Tamsin Perfect's hand-decorated Sweet 16 custom marble cake. CREDIT: TAMSIN'S CAKES

her business placed on the use of her home kitchen. "I also started looking into bigger mixers, purchasing supplies in bulk. I might even look into moving to a new house with a better kitchen layout and storage space for the bakery.

"I market my business on Facebook, Instagram, and through my stand at the farmers' market. Every purchase at market is sent with the customer in a bag with my logo, website, and contact information sticker, along with a business card in each bag." She's already landed numerous orders for custom cakes through this effective packaging effort. Like many cottage food operators, she's surprised by how much time it takes to maintain Facebook and Instagram postings, along with updating her website. She also designs and prints her own labels. Realizing she was spending too much time to create her own stencils and cake toppers, she's outsourced them to artists on Etsy. "I know I can still offer a custom service by using my Cricut cutting machine, but I realized that I needed to save some time on the design portion."

Tamsin's Cakes' biggest sellers are paint-your-own-cookies, hot cocoa bombs, and custard cookies. But her most profitable items remain the paint-your-own-cookies and hot cocoa bombs that she only offers seasonally. "I didn't realize these cookie kits would be so popular. At market, one week I'll sell all 30 of one variety within a couple of hours. But the very next week, I'd sell hardly any of that same kit, so there's also a degree of unpredictability, which makes it hard.

"My first love and biggest passion is creating children's birthday cakes," confides Perfect, who tends to be very selective in taking wedding cake orders. "I'm just not into the bride drama." She's careful not to let potential stress associated with certain orders override the satisfaction and passion she has for baking. It's not just about the money.

"I plan to build my customer base to where I can have a bricks-and-mortar tearoom with a custom bakery," says Perfect, with a strong sense of confidence and the realization of the hard work that lies ahead. "We are giving the business three years to build a customer base. I feel my dream is bigger than I am right now." Perhaps that's okay, as long as she keeps making the perfect cakes, cookies, and other baked items.

Building community connections

A hundred years ago, people were interconnected and interwoven in their community in ways no Facebook group could ever be. Their survival, in some ways, depended on the support, kindness, and companionship of their neighbors. Citizens patronized their butcher, baker, and candlestick maker, who in turn supported their business. Money recirculated in the community. The made-in-China revolution sold by Walmart and made possible by relatively cheap fossil fuels was a century away.

Now "cheap" energy isn't cheap anymore and food costs are rising faster than our incomes. Plus, more of us are wondering just how what we eat is made and by whom, and questioning its safety. Some call this a food security issue. To reclaim our food supply, cottage food laws are expanding the reach to community-supported farms, food cooperatives, and farmers' markets, essaying a return—or at least a community option—to a time when we can buy from our neighbors again, legally.

Promoting Local Food

We now have a name for someone who loves growing, eating, and preserving food that's as close to home as possible: *locavore*. Thanks to Michael Pollan, author of *The Omnivore's Dilemma*. While he penned his tome from an ivory tower—in his case UC Berkeley, where fresh local food is available year-round—this idea of local food appeals to anyone aware that what we find in most grocery stores and supermarkets today has more frequent flier miles than Warren

Value-Added Products Are More Profitable

Take the vegetables and fruit you grow and create value-added products right in your home kitchen. One year, farmer John grew a huge 50-pound pumpkin that we could have sold for $15 as a Halloween decoration. Instead, Lisa made batches of her Estonian pickled pumpkin, a high-acid canned product, and we grossed over $150 with this one pumpkin!

We earn more by transforming pumpkin into value-added products through our state's cottage food law.

CREDIT: JOHN D. IVANKO PHOTOGRAPHY

Buffet. Thanks to the cottage food laws, as food entrepreneurs, we can close the local food loop with our value-added products, expanding the fresh selection of what's already available at more than 8,000 farmers' markets in the US.

Integrating Family

Akin to fathers fishing with their sons or mothers baking cookies with their daughters, going into business with a spouse, sibling, or other family member resonates in ways that no shopping excursion to the mall could ever do. Working with your family in a culinary operation provides a way to connect and build a relationship in an entirely new way. If you have older kids, what better way for them to learn about how to start a business and cook in the kitchen?

Needing a Project

Perhaps the kids have fledged the nest, off to college or life as a young adult. Or maybe you're among the roughly seventy-five million retirees in America, looking for something to do besides another round of golf or cruise. There's no shortage of research that shows that staying active and engaged is an essential part of staying healthy. But sometimes we just need a project. Starting a small business built around a passion for cooking and favorite recipes can be exactly what the doctor might prescribe (if they weren't so focused on prescription drugs, that is). For some, a cottage food business can act as a drug, providing a life focus and fostering interactions with other people and their community.

Recipe for Success

For many people, success has come to be defined by the size of their bank account, the square footage of their house, or the profitability of their business. Too often, the quality of your product, the satisfaction of your career, or your general level of happiness is trivialized or marginalized. It becomes an afterthought.

So when it comes to your cottage food business, how you define success will determine, to a large extent, whether you achieve it. Here are a few ways some food entrepreneurs have defined their success:

- Perfecting a great family recipe and sharing it with others
- Creating a unique product

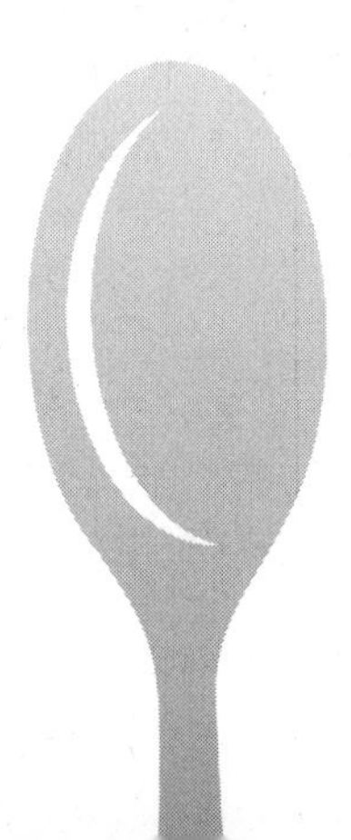

- Celebrating a passion for cooking
- Launching a small business and making a little profit, every year
- Enabling someone with a food allergy to enjoy something they couldn't before
- Being part of the celebratory process of a customer's special event, like a birthday party, wedding, or fiftieth anniversary

Intelligent Fast Failure: It's How We Learn What Works!

Civil and environmental professor and inventor Jack V. Matson, dedicates his life to practicing "intelligent fast failure," an expression he coined to capture the essence of innovation. It's captured in his irreverently titled book, *Innovate or Die: A Personal Perspective on the Art of Innovation* (1996).

In his book, Matson suggests that the goal with intelligent fast failure is to move as quickly as possible from new ideas to new knowledge by making small and manageable mistakes—intelligent failures. By moving quickly, we can determine what works and what doesn't, without draining the bank account or the energy devoted to developing the idea. When you come out with new products, some will catch on and some will fail. While you may love the taste of pickled radishes, there may not be enough other people that do too. Cottage food enterprises fit perfectly into this fast-failure mode. Everything you do is small batch and experimental. We take small steps as we grow, not giant leaps. Not sure which dry candy-combo harbors the most customer appeal? Make a tray of each and bring them all to market to see which sell best.

The key is to keep learning and try to avoid letting your intelligent fast failures negatively influence your emotions or self-esteem. And by all means, fail falling forward.

Author-baker Lisa is always on the lookout for new product ideas. This Christmas tree made with cookies and decorated with M&M bulbs and dollops of frosting for snow was beautiful. However, we could not find any customer willing to purchase it for the price we needed to charge to cover our ingredient costs and labor. All three that were made ended up being given away as holiday gifts — well appreciated, of course. You never know, until you try.

CREDIT: JOHN D. IVANKO PHOTOGRAPHY

When you define what you mean by success, you've put it in your terms. This perspective will lend itself well to putting your ideas down on paper in the form of a simple plan. It will also help silence snarky people who drift into your life or deflect the negativism, criticism, or cynicism you may encounter when you follow your dreams while others fail to realize theirs. Your vision, determination, and perseverance will transform your intent and actions into success, on your terms.

CFO Self-assessment

Do you have what it takes to be a CFO, a cottage food operator? More than an idea, recipe, or home kitchen filled with appliances, becoming a small food business owner will require a level of knowledge, skill, and talent, each addressed below.

Food Knowledge

What's your culinary know-how? Having a degree in food science, years working at a bakery, or a stint at a delicatessen would help you achieve the goals you've set for your business from the perspective of what you can accomplish in the kitchen. But don't underestimate the on-the-job experience of raising a family of four if you prepared most of the meals at home. Perhaps you're the legendary birthday cake maker of the family. Perhaps you already can enough food products to keep your family, friends, and a few neighbors stocked up each winter. Every item you make reflects your cumulative knowledge of cooking skills, techniques, recipes, and ingredient selection.

When determining what you want to make for sale, go with what you love and feel there's a market for. We'll cover the feasibility testing of your product in chapter 14. Do you love baking, making pickles, or mixing spices together? Is kneading dough a passion or something you procrastinate doing? Would a call for a large-batch production of 15 dozen muffins for a corporate retreat be stressful or a fun challenge?

Be realistic and honest in your self-assessment, but don't sell yourself short when it comes to your cumulative knowledge. Experience is the best teacher of all. When your recipes turn out the same every time you make them, that's a good sign.

If you like the idea of being a home baker but struggle because your recipes don't turn out as tasty or look as attractive as they appear to be on

the Food Network, recognize that you might want to learn some new skills (which can be fun, too) or cultivate your existing talents further. Practice really does make perfect. Many food entrepreneurs have spent months, if not an entire year, tweaking, modifying, and perfecting their customized decorated sugar cookies that they now sell for $2 to $8 each.

Expanding Your Knowledge Online

For more personal introduction to and exploration of cottage food and food freedom laws, and the opportunities they provide to launch a food business from your home kitchen, the following provide two online avenues where you can learn at your own pace.

Udemy Online Course: How to Set Up and Market a Food Product Business from Your Home Kitchen

The bestselling Udemy online course, How to Set Up and Market a Food Product Business from Your Home Kitchen, taught by Lisa Kivirist, offers a comprehensive overview of everything you might need to launch your business tomorrow. The course includes 5.5 hours of on-demand video instruction, more than 30 downloadable resources, and full lifetime access, so you can return as often as you want and take as much time as needed to complete the course.

"I found the course was extremely valuable, and it has put me on a whole new path I didn't even think was an option—just a few short months ago. Lisa's ☛

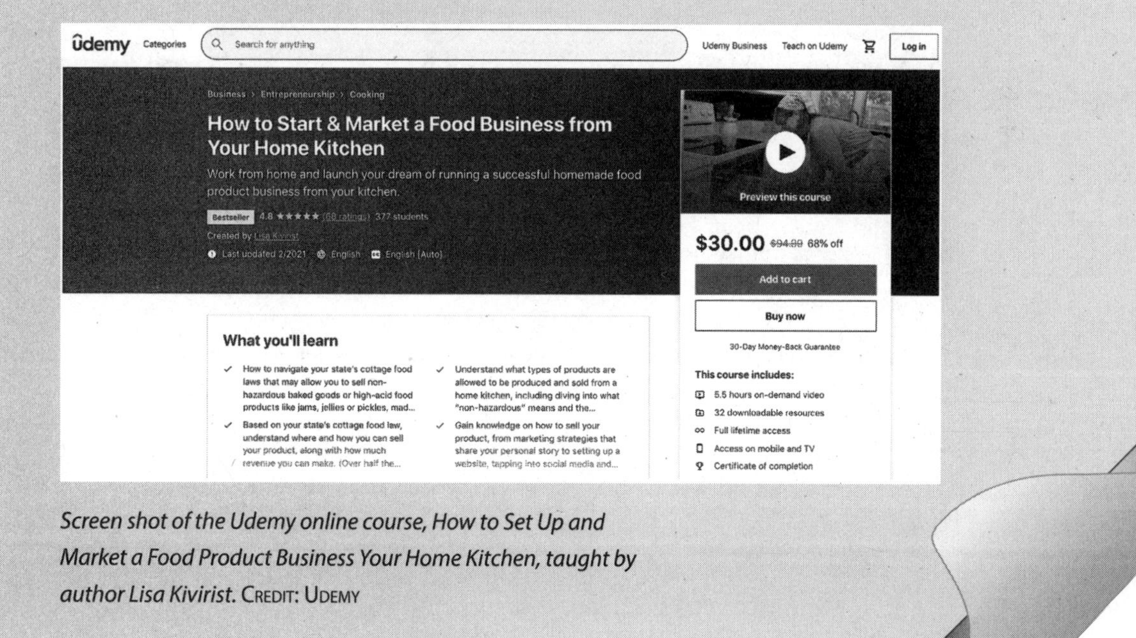

Screen shot of the Udemy online course, How to Set Up and Market a Food Product Business Your Home Kitchen, taught by author Lisa Kivirist. CREDIT: UDEMY

knowledge, expertise, and concise way of explaining the legality of the Cottage Food Law made this research less overwhelming."—Nicole B.

This course on starting a food product business from your home kitchen covers everything from licensing requirements for cottage food or food freedom laws to developing your product for market and managing your business to make sure it remains fun, lucrative, and successful.

YouTube overview video about the Udemy online course: https://youtu.be/1lwGVUVpbrM

"I feel far more equipped and confident to start my home baking business than ever before after taking this course. It was easy to follow and understand, and it provided a numerous amount of resources, guide, tips, and excellent examples. It made a molehill out of the mountain of moving from a hobby to becoming an entrepreneur." — Cecelia N.

Home-based Food Entrepreneur Virtual National Conference logo.
CREDIT: RENEWING THE COUNTRYSIDE

Like the content found in this book, Lisa Kivirist shares her direct experience as a home baker and canner, operating as a cottage food business. She also reveals what it's like serving as one of the three plaintiffs in a victorious lawsuit against the state of Wisconsin that lifted the ban on selling baked goods in her home state.

Home-based Food Entrepreneur Virtual National Conference

In 2021, the first-ever Home-based Food Entrepreneur Virtual National Conference was held online, bringing together cottage food business owners operating under their states' cottage food law along with educators and leaders in this movement with a goal to support these new entrepreneurs to launch and succeed. The conference showcased and celebrated the economic impact of this budding entrepreneurial movement and the local food economy.

All the speakers and live question and answer sessions were taped. You can listen to the lineup of speakers and question and answer sessions with questions submitted by more than 900 attendees from across the country at: renewingcountryside.gumroad.com/l/homebasedfoodentrepreneur

There are 9.5 hours of practical and timely content shared, including 4 keynote presentations, 12 workshops, and 16 question and answer sessions. Each session can be viewed via website access or a mobile app (free download) using the Gumroad platform. Once you pay for the online access, the conference can be streamed and viewed instantly. Viewing the sessions on the Gumroad platform would be similar to watching a webinar on YouTube, but with no ☛

Google advertisements. Depending on your Internet speed, there may be a brief pause when first watching the taped session to allow for video buffering.

The virtual gathering facilitated information sharing and discussion while:

- Examining the cottage food movement nationally and exploring what it might look like in the future
- Providing a platform for cottage food entrepreneurs to share best practices, challenges, and ideas
- Creating opportunity for networking and connections between states
- Spotlighting the up-and-coming food freedom movement
- Providing start-up information and resources for new entrepreneurs
- Addressing both the challenges and opportunities caused by the COVID-19 pandemic.

The conference offered practical, actionable ideas and information from leaders of the cottage food movement and from cottage food entrepreneurs who are running successful, and profitable, businesses from their home kitchens.

To set the stage, there are keynotes from the following acclaimed speakers:

- "A Cottage Food Recipe for Resilience" by Lisa Kivirist, co-author of *Homemade for Sale*
- "State of the States: Expanding Cottage Food Laws Across the Country" by Erica Smith Ewing, lead attorney with the Institute for Justice
- "Increase Your Sales Through the Power of Technology" by David Crabill, founder of Forrager.com and *The Forrager Podcast*
- "Food Freedom Frontier" by Alexia Kulwiec, executive director, Farm to Consumer Legal Defense Fund

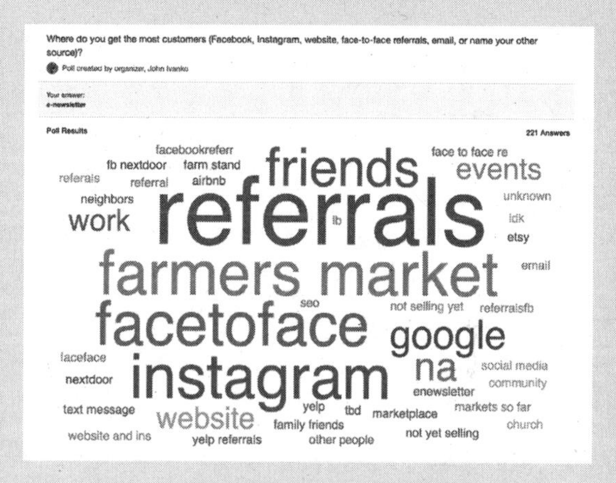

Word cluster replies from CFO conference attendees about where do CFOs locate their customers.

CREDIT: RENEWING THE COUNTRYSIDE

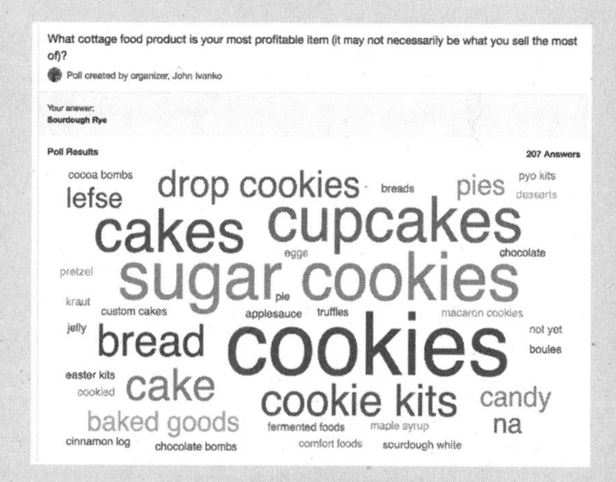

Word cluster replies from CFO conference attendees about what was their most profitable product.

CREDIT: RENEWING THE COUNTRYSIDE ☛

Various workshops offer practical and inspiring information related to marketing and social media, structuring your business (i.e., operating as a sole proprietorship or forming an LLC), insurance, operating as a business (not a hobby), developing hot new products like cocoa bombs, managing your time, pricing your items, and cultivating happy customers. A few of the story profiles featured in this book are also presenters at this conference, like Dave "Poppy" Sander's workshop that addresses whether building a commercial kitchen in your home might be a possibility down the line, with many step-by-step photos he took for his home-based commercial bakery.

The conference was hosted by Renewing the Countryside in partnership with a team of organizations and businesses dedicated to championing the cottage food and food freedom movements. Renewing the Countryside, a 501(c)3 nonprofit organization based in Minnesota, brought a strong track record of organizing such national conferences that support entrepreneurship.

Culinary Training

When starting in the burgeoning cottage food industry, you may be drawn by an interest in learning a new craft or doing something you've always wanted to do but just never had the chance to tackle. Until now.

If you need to pick up some skills or hone a few you already possess, a wide range of workshops offered by nonprofit or private for-profit organizations and university or community college-level courses could get you chopping, dicing, canning, and baking like a professional. YouTube, Vimeo, and TikTok videos offer hours of free instruction. From learning about artisan-style yeast-raised breads with recipes and techniques from around the world to cakes, cookies, and pies, these programs or online videos may open your eyes to what might be possible in your kitchen.

Some states, eager to help get people to work, have created programs or resources to support new home cooks and their businesses. That's helpful because these programs aren't cheap. Keep in mind, however, that you may be able to deduct these courses as a legitimate business expense; more on this in chapter 18.

The following shortlist of programs designed to help people jump-start their culinary careers may be worth a look. Be mindful, however, of your goals and aspirations, perhaps avoiding those programs or degrees that might push you in the direction of working at a restaurant, institutional kitchen, or similar operation. A good question to ask: How many of their students go off to start their home-based food enterprise? For the most practical experience, avoid classes or workshops heavy on food samples and light on educational content. You're not a recreational or hobby baker or cook. You're operating a business.

- Michaels, michaels.com
  This national arts and crafts chain store offers introductory to advanced decorating classes through the *Wilton Method of Cake Decorating,* covering cakes, cookies, cupcakes, and brownies. Workshops often cover topics like gum paste and fondant flowers.
- Williams-Sonoma, williams-sonoma.com
  They offer a variety of baking and other culinary classes, sometimes with a seasonal theme, such as Easter baking.
- The Culinary Institute of America (CIA), enthusiasts.ciachef.edu
  With campuses in New York, California, and Texas, the CIA offers culinary education programs in the form of Boot Camps designed around baking, pastry, specialty and hearth breads, and basic skills.

Beyond the accredited and non-accredited programs, workshops, and short courses, you may also pick up some quick experience in your area of interest by working at a bakery, restaurant, or catering business. If you love baking but want to see how another company does it, consider working part-time for a while at a bakery or one of those fancy cupcake-making places; you wouldn't be able to use their secret proprietary recipes, but you could walk away with practical knowledge about the industry you want to break into.

Another way to gain some experience might be as a volunteer at your church for events that involve food preparation; maybe you could handle the dessert or bread baking and test out your recipes. A nonprofit organization that regularly offers some food at their events could be another possibility. For example, our Monroe Arts Center in Wisconsin sets out various nibbles during their gallery openings; this could be a place for us to try out recipes and garner feedback without spending a cent of our money.

Exercising your "mind muscle," repeating over and over again the techniques needed for kneading dough or twisting croissants, translates to a more consistent, higher-quality product. The more practice you put in, the better the results. According to Malcolm Gladwell's book *Outliers: The Story of Success* (2008) and based on a study by Anders Ericsson, consider adopting the "10,000-hour rule," which states that it takes approximately this amount of focused practice time to perfect a skill. That's 20 years,

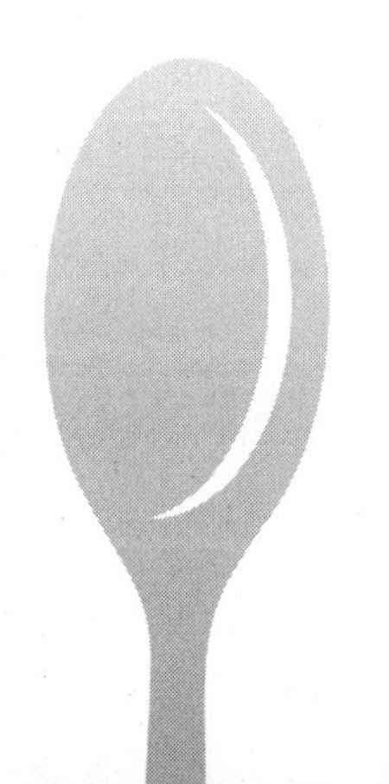

practicing an hour and a half a day. For many of you home cooks, you're already there!

Business Knowledge

What other talents or attributes do you possess that can help drive your enterprise? Can you write well? Are you a people person or someone with a knack for selling? Do you never grow tired of social media, always chattering on Facebook, posting photos on Instagram, or tweeting? Are you comfortable enough with software on your computer to make brochures, flyers, invoices, and receipts?

While you may bake a blue-ribbon-winning torte for the state fair, how much business aptitude do you have to help propel your business along? Even on a small scale, any skills with planning, marketing, and managing the financial aspects of your company can go a long way in helping to achieve your goals. The more you can do yourself, the less you will need to contract with a graphic designer for your labels, a freelance editor to help describe your product, a website designer, or a bookkeeper.

General Knowledge or Talents

How strong are your community networks? Would it be easy to share what you're doing, word-of-mouth, and then sit back and start filling orders, or are your community connections more limited to church, school, or place of employment? Are you an organized or tidy person? Both organizational skills and cleanliness are extremely valuable to any food enterprise. Can you manage multiple projects at the same time, or do you like to do things one at a time? While balancing your work and life, having the ability to multitask may make operating a home-based business less overwhelming.

Cottage Food Operator Assessment: A University of Wisconsin-Stout Research Study

In 2021, the first national Cottage Food Operator Assessment research study was completed to provide a snapshot of cottage food operators, those individuals operating a home-based food product business under their state's cottage food law. The results are summarized in the infographic created by Rachael Miller (see Appendix A), the principal investigator and graduate student attending the University of Wisconsin-Stout. They help us better understand how we fit into this growing movement, either as a CFO already

operating or as someone considering launching their dream food business from home. This first-ever peek into the home kitchens reveals some of the challenges, realities, and opportunities offered by cottage food laws.

Under contract with Renewing the Countryside, the online survey was made available to current and aspiring CFOs through cottage food-related nonprofit organizations, cottage food social media channels, and attendees of the 2021 Home-based Food Entrepreneur Virtual National Conference. Research study oversight was provided by Libby Smith, Program Director for the Master of Science in Applied Psychology at the University of Wisconsin-Stout.

A total of 902 individuals consented to take the survey, but not all of them answered every question. They were asked about their cottage food operation, commercial kitchen operations, business dreams, and demographics. Descriptive statistics were conducted on all variables to provide detailed information about this population sample. The demographic information includes all participants, while the non-demographic questions are split into two groups: aspiring CFOs and current CFOs.

The study reflects the geographic and age diversity of the movement. It came as no surprise to us that nearly a third of all CFOs were caring for kids at home while also operating their enterprise, perhaps reflecting the reality of the challenges of finding daycare for their children if they had full-time positions during the COVID-19 pandemic. Running a food business from home affords flexibility rarely found in corporate cubicles.

For aspiring CFOs, it was noteworthy that about a quarter wanted to sell food products other than cookies, breads, and cakes, perhaps eager to fill niches overlooked in their community or to avoid competing on price with an already crowded market for cupcakes. Reflecting the national interest in having a better work-life balance, less than half want to do it full-time and only a third wanted a storefront.

For currently operating CFOs, many found that what they sell the most of are not what generates the most profit. As echoed by many of the CFO story profiles in this book, the owners have carefully evaluated their menu offerings with a greater priority on pricing their products so that at the end of the day they actually earn a profit. That said, of those surveyed, most current CFOs generated less than $5,000 in gross revenues annually, suggesting that underpricing homemade products may be an issue for the cottage food industry.

We hope that CFOs take full advantage of the benefits of operating a business, as opposed to having a hobby, by deducting allowable expenses and, if operating at a loss, reflecting this operating loss on their tax return to reduce their taxable income. Deducting business miles for making deliveries with their personal vehicle and rent paid for a home office seem to be warranted, given the number of current CFOs who do both, according to the study. Chapter 18 covers how this can be done.

Now you've clarified your goals, completed a CFO self-assessment, learned more about other aspiring and existing CFOs through the University of Wisconsin-Stout research study, and gained a better understanding of what you might be in for. In the next section on product development, we'll demystify and clarify what non-hazardous foods are without requiring you to get science degree, then proceed in sharing some independently tested baking-related recipes you can possibly use, including those somewhat controversial frostings.

What's Cooking: Product Development and Recipes

SECTION 2

4

Understanding Non-hazardous Food Products

SOME STATE AGRICULTURE OR HEALTH DEPARTMENTS—or legislators—call certain food products "non-hazardous." To keep you on your toes, other states stick the term "not-potentially hazardous" or "non-potentially hazardous food (non-PHF)" on what is, simply, a non-hazardous food product. Not to be outdone, other legislators and food scientists like to use the acronym TCS, standing for "Time-or-temperature-controlled for safety." Leave it to the politicians and health experts to make a relatively simple thing complex. For the home-based cottage food business owner, however, the "non-hazardous food product" moniker—the term we use throughout this book—is a very important consideration when making your products for sale. There is a big difference between hazardous and non-hazardous, a hamburger casserole versus sugar cookies, respectively.

Adding to the mystery is the fact that recipes in cookbooks and online are never defined by this term. Recipes often include yield, ingredients, and directions but never a line about whether or not the recipe is hazardous to eat. Like most bakers, we'd rather talk about crumb, texture, or flavor.

As it turns out, you don't need to wear a lab coat and have majored in chemistry at college to be able to understand and then bake or can delicious non-hazardous food products. It comes down generally to either water content for baked goods or pH level for canned items sold in jars, which have core elements you can easily grasp.

This chapter takes you through the basics of non-hazardous food products, giving you a brief synopsis of what you need to know without digging into the complicated science behind the term. Neither of us have a science background, but picked up what we needed to know. Avoid skipping or hastily skimming this chapter. As food business owners, we need to understand our product from the legalities of selling to how it's produced. What we're aiming for here is providing enough fundamentals that you

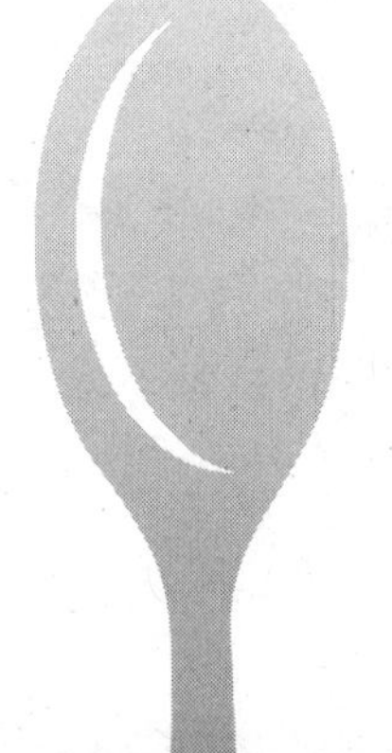

feel comfortable understanding basic concepts with no flashbacks to those potentially painful high school lab days.

Possessing a basic understanding of non-hazardous food products may also go a long way in diffusing possible objections a potential customer might have after finding out your product is made in a home kitchen not subject to licensing or inspection. Information can be an effective tool to close a sale or put a customer at ease and build trust.

This chapter focuses on non-hazardous food products, what is still the focus of cottage food laws for most of the country with lots of shelf-stable product opportunities such as cookies, breads, jams, and candies. With the growth of the food freedom movement, covered in chapter 23, some states have further expanded sales and product opportunities to include hazardous prepared foods just like those you might order take-out from a full-service restaurant. Live culture fermented foods, fully prepared meals, or food products that require refrigeration may be permitted if the business owner is properly licensed and other regulations followed. In this chapter, however, we'll focus only on the easy on-ramp for most CFOs: non-hazardous products.

Food Safety

Food safety is about ensuring that a product is safe to eat and will not cause any harm. The Food Code is the U.S. Food & Drug Administration's "best advice for a uniform system of provisions to address the safety and protection of food offered at retail and in food service." Even the FDA realizes this is a process that evolves and changes, hence the word "advice" versus etching requirements in stone. Revised every four years and comprising almost 1,000 pages with supplements, this document outlines detailed criteria and processes for our commercial food system so that when you buy that gallon of milk or package of bacon at the supermarket, it's as safe as possible.

Some of you, ourselves included, are shouting: "But wait, that system doesn't work! What about those regular product recalls and outbreaks?" Indeed, our food system is vulnerable to outbreaks such as listeria, a germ that causes serious infection when ingested, that you often hear about in spinach. The food system has grown so gargantuan, industrialized, and global that there is a wide and growing disconnect between the farmer raising the ingredients that ultimately end up on your kitchen table.

As cottage food producers, we're shifting the tides by providing authentic and transparent connections directly between producer and customer.

We're still an extremely small slice of the mammoth industrial food system, but we're pioneers in shaking that up and creating a direct connection between baker and buyer, canner and pickle lover.

Tap into Agency Resources

Before digging into the basics, recognize that you should already have an ally in navigating food safety and non-hazardous products through the department of health or agriculture or whomever is administering the regulations in your state. Unfortunately, agency attitudes do vary by state, both in helpfulness and expertise. Kudos to states where university extension has taken on cottage food producer education with various training and, importantly, an accessible point of contact where you can ask questions like "Is pecan pie okay to sell? What about my grandma's fabulous cheesecake recipe?" For the record, a traditional pecan pie is okay because the sugar content is so high, a topic we'll talk more about. No, on the cheesecake, since that item would not meet non-hazardous criteria related to ingredients, and it requires refrigeration (even on this, there are some states with exemptions).

While social media can be a useful source of information, don't rely on a random person telling you a product is safe to sell unless they have confirmation to back that up, either a lab report for an independently tested product or affirmation from their agency contact. You are ultimately responsible for your food products and their safety.

Non-hazardous Basics

Let's start with a rudimentary definition of this term: potentially non-hazardous. By scientific definition, it refers to an item that has a low moisture level, measured typically as a water activity (aw) value of 0.85 or less. Typical low-moisture level products include baked products such as bread and cookies—see below for a list of examples. Or if the item has a higher water activity level, it can still be non-hazardous if the item has a pH value of 4.6 or lower. The lower the pH value, the more acidic the food and therefore safer. Think of a jar of pickles that has lots of water but is still safe due to the high acid.

Some states may include an exact definition in the law or it may appear in the regulations. By "law" we mean the bill that your elected representatives officially pass and your governor then signs into law. "Regulations" refers to what happens after the law is passed related to specific rules and

details that come out of your health of agriculture department, the entity responsible for administering the law. Occasionally you might see different numbers or other forms of definition so, as always, be intimately familiar with your state's situation.

Common Non-hazardous Food Products

Cue the triumphant trumpets, proclaiming fantastic news when it comes to what you can legally produce out of your home kitchen! A wide range of food products qualify under this potentially non-hazardous definition. First, let's approach this as a glass-half-full scenario and celebrate what we can do, food businesses we can get up and running without the cost and encumberments of commercial kitchens and licensing. As mentioned earlier, that cheesecake recipe from grandma that your family loves won't be on this list, nor will custard-filled doughnuts and pastries, another item many CFOs ask about. Rather than focus on what you can't do, accentuate the positive and brainstorm as you scroll through this expansive and growing list below.

Many cottage food operators enjoy sharing knowledge with younger generations. Some businesses are even mother-daughter, marital or sibling-owned enterprises.
PHOTO: JOHN D. IVANKO PHOTOGRAPHY

Today you will increasingly see state legislations passing cottage food laws using the broader term "non-hazardous food products," referring to an extensive list of products like you see below. Early on in the cottage food days when this was so new, states tended to pass technically different laws for each category of product. You then end up with separate laws like a cookie bill covering baked goods and a pickle bill for high-acid canned items.

This process can get confusing and understandably cumbersome if you need a new law for every new product category. As a result, states moved toward a more general definition of non-hazardous products, enabling the regulatory agency to sort out specific product questions and issues. States like California have developed a streamlined online process for producers to ask if a certain product is legal to sell as non-hazardous. Once a decision is made, California then adds it to their product list if approved.

Non-hazardous baked products without cream, custard, or meat filling, including:

- Bar cookies
- Breads
- Brownies
- Biscuits
- Cakes
- Cake pops
- Cake balls
- Crackers
- Cupcakes
- Pastries
- Cookies
- Fruit pies
- Fruit tarts
- Pretzels
- Rolls
- Scones
- Tortillas

Candy, including:

- Brittle
- Caramels
- Chocolate-covered nuts and dried fruits
- Chocolates
- Cocoa bombs
- Cotton candy
- Fudge
- Hard candies
- Marshmallows
- Toffee

Dried items, including:

- Baking mixes
- Cereals
- Dried fruits
- Dried herbs and seasonings and mixtures
- Dried spice mixes
- Dried pasta
- Dry baking mixes
- Health bars
- Hot cocoa mixes
- Trail mixes
- Dried tea

High-acid canned items, including:

- Fruit butters
- Fruit jams
- Fruit jellies
- Fruit preserves
- Marmalades
- Pickles
- Salsas
- Shrubs

Other items:

- Waffle cones
- Pizzelle
- Granola
- Honey and sweet sorghum syrup
- Nuts and nut mixtures
- Popcorn and caramel corn
- Roasted coffee
- Vinegars
- Mustards
- Seasoning salts

Non-hazardous Testing Process

What should you do if you are not sure your recipe is non-hazardous? Best-case scenario remains to connect directly with agency resource staff who can answer that for you. Ideally such communication happens via email so you have a written confirmation that your recipe is safe to sell. Simply send in your recipe and receive an answer.

If your state unfortunately doesn't offer such streamlined support that can give you a concrete answer, the responsibility is on you to ensure what you are producing is safe. The main way to do that is to have your recipe tested in a certified laboratory to prove that it meets either the 0.85 water activity level or lower for baked goods or a pH value of 4.6 or less.

"Having a certified laboratory test is important because it ensures that the test is performed in a validated setting where all of the variables are recorded and consistent, from the temperature of the item to the humidity in the room at the time," explains Pratik Banerjee, associate professor of Food Safety in the College of Agricultural, Consumer and Environmental Sciences

What About Treats for Pets?

Can I sell pet treats, like dog biscuits made in a home kitchen? Given the number of enthusiastic pet owners out there, this could be quite a lucrative outlet. However, in most states, pet treats are not part of the cottage food law as they are not designed for human consumption and thereby need to be made in commercial facilities with appropriate licensing.

To add another layer of complexity, even if you want to sell just a few of those dog biscuits at the farmers' market, you may now fall under commercial feed regulations with the same requirements that apply to large-scale pet food manufacturers and industrial dairy operations. Check with your state, since some, like Illinois, allow specific categories of pet food to be sold that can be made in a home kitchen.

But in most places, pet food falls into its own special regulatory category and mostly under a law that's completely different than a cottage food law. Food for human versus animal consumption is treated differently from a regulatory perspective.

As a result, it's tough to be a mom-and-pop, small-scale pet food producer. It's not a question of food safety and protecting those cute pups. As a producer, you can readily make non-hazardous low-moisture pet treats in your home kitchen just as easily and safely as you can bake cookies for people. If the cottage food process is deemed safe for human consumption, wouldn't you think that it would also work for pets? If you hit this barrier on launching a home-based pet food enterprise, keep asking questions in your state and recognize that you might have to advocate for the right to feed Fido.

at the University of Illinois at Urbana-Champaign. "Additionally, you will receive a report from the lab with your test results that is the key document for proving your item is safe and non-hazardous."

Such certified testing labs generally are part of a larger food science operation that performs a variety of food testing and functions. Your state regulatory agency should be able to provide a list of labs in the state performing such services to get you started. The test is performed by you providing an actual sample of your product and not based on a written recipe. The lab does not need a large sample size; a small muffin-sized sample will be more than adequate.

Going back to the definitions we talked about in the beginning of this chapter, two primary tests validate that a product is non-hazardous:

Water Activity Test

Generally, to be non-hazardous, a product must have a water activity level of 0.85 or lower.

"Increased water activity increases the chance for food to get spoiled because of growth of the microorganisms inside," explains Banerjee. "Water activity is important because it determines whether microbes (including the ones that make us ill) can survive and grow. We do not want to make people sick."

Again, most baked goods like cookies or anything that is dry or crumbly will meet this water activity level. Water activity and food safety become an issue when you are looking at, for example, very moist products. Recipes that use ingredients that have a lot of water, such as the bananas in traditional banana bread, are often considered hazardous, and you would not be able to sell them because of that potential of microorganism growth. Items that use fresh produce like zucchini or squash can cause the same issue. However, sugar prevents microbial growth. For example, a bakery product high in sugar would be more likely to meet the water activity non-hazardous criteria.

The recipes in chapter 5 that might be suspect were tested in an independent certified lab to be non-hazardous. Some of these recipes include zucchini or pumpkin. We tested and employ a few sweet tricks to ensure food safety you'll read about.

pH Test

Some of you might now get that flashback of learning about pH in those high school lab days. The pH value stands for "potential of hydrogen,"

Sample Laboratory Water Activity Test

DEIBEL
LABORATORIES

103 S. 2nd Street Madison,WI 53704 ph: 608-241-1177 fax: 608-241-2252 www.DeibelLabs.com

Name:
Customer:
Address:

Order ID: MW-190806-083
Report ID: MW-190806-083.000001
Date Received: 8/6/2019 14:11:29
Reported: 8/7/2019 17:25:56
P.O. #: N/A
Page: 1 of 1

Report of Results

Deibel Lab #: MW-190806-083-001 Analysis Date 2019/08/06 Receiving Temperature: Ambient Sample Condition: Okay

Description: Muffin Pumpkin Chocolate Chip

Test:	Result:	Units:	Method:	Reference:	Comment:
Aw	0.8212@24.89°C	Aw	Dew Point - Chilled Mirror	AOAC 978.18	

Deibel Lab #: MW-190806-083-002 Analysis Date 2019/08/06 Receiving Temperature: Ambient Sample Condition: Okay

Login By: CG Entered By: PDH Approved By: SPENZA

The above test results only represents that portion of the product lot that has been sampled by the client and sent to Deibel Laboratories. This report conforms to 21 CFR Part 11 compliancy for electronic signatures. The final approval of this Formal Report is authorized by the individual labeled as 'Approved By'. Test results relate only to the analytical unit tested. This report cannot be reproduced except in full, and by the written consent of Deibel Labs. All information contained herein is Trade Secret and Confidential. See our updated terms and condition at www.deibellabs.com/termsandconditions

"Systems of Excellence"

This sample report from a certified lab (Deibel Labs) states the safe level of the water activity test at under 0.85. Other numbers found on the report refer to the exact process the lab used or other important variables, like the item temperature and equipment used. You only need concern yourself with water activity number, since that is what your regulatory agency needs to allow you to make the item.

Sample test report for water activity from Deibel Labs, an independent certified lab, for the Pumpkin Chocolate Chip Muffin recipe found on page 79. The recipe is non-hazardous, based on the test.
CREDIT: DEIBEL LABS

basically a scale to specify the acidity of a product. Solutions higher in acid, and therefore safer, have lower pH values and need to be 4.6 or lower to qualify as safe.

Let's go over that again because it can be confusing. For an item to be higher in acid and therefore safer, it needs to have a lower pH number. That's why "high acid canned goods" are typically considered non-hazardous cottage food products and they have a pH value of 4.6 or below.

"pH is your friend when it comes to food safety," affirms Dr. Banerjee. "While water encourages bad microbe growth, low pH is bad for microbe growth, so something high in acid, even if the water activity is higher, can still potentially be non-hazardous. You would think more water makes a

product more dangerous, but think about pickles. Pickles are a watery product but are safe because they are high in acid."

Bottom line, if for any reason you are unsure your recipe is non-hazardous, have it tested. They generally cost between $30 to $50 each. On a business note, the recipe test of your food product is a deductible business expense. The test both validates the safety of your product with that lab report if you are ever questioned and gives you peace of mind.

The science of cottage food represents an example of what we entrepreneurs encounter all the time: learning and researching as much as we need to know to make the best decisions, without digging too deep into the weeds and miss focusing on the more important business and marketing aspects covered in future chapters. Get comfortable with sometimes being uncomfortable with new terms or food science principles. So goes the life of running your own business.

5

Independently Tested Recipes for Non-hazardous Food Items

NOW LET'S MOVE ON from the science behind non-hazardous to recipes you could use possibly in your business. The tested recipes you'll find in this chapter are a part of the North Central SARE-supported baking cottage food project, with lots more recipes and information accessed on the website (cottagefoodhomebakery.com).

Meet the Woman-powered Recipe Team

Lisa and a team of her baker and farmer friends came together with a common goal of creating a collaborative, free, and growing tested recipe collection that tackles items that can often be suspect from the perspective of moisture levels, like baked goods made with zucchini as well as frostings. We experimented in our home kitchens to bring together this collection, drawing on inspiration from our own farmsteads and over-flowing gardens.

Like our cottage food community, we bring together a diversity of perspectives, sharing our strengths. Dela Ends from Scotch Hill Farm looked to the bountiful herbs and produce growing outside her kitchen window for inspiration. Danielle Matson added her pastry chef training expertise alongside Kalena Riemer, only 11 years old and dedicated to the craft with a dream of starting her own bakery one day. Linda Dee Derrickson, a spry seventy-something petite powerhouse, contributed a health mindset that enabled us to include recipes without a sugar overload, like her cracker recipe contributions. Ashley Wegmueller added creative ideas on display and packaging we'll cover in later chapters.

We invite you to pour yourself a cup of coffee or tea and join us in spirit at our Wisconsin farmstead kitchen tables as you read through our work, a cumulation of time in our kitchen working to ensure delicious taste followed by "pretesting" thanks to water activity testing equipment at our

A woman-powered team of baking and farming experts collaboratively came together to create a growing free collection of tested recipes. The original project team includes (left to right): Kalena Riemer, Dela Ends, Anastasia Wolf-Flash, Linda Dee Derrickson, Ashley Wegmueller, Danielle Matson, Lisa Kivirist, Jen Riemer.

CREDIT: JOHN D. IVANKO PHOTOGRAPHY

local community college. We then sent in the recipes for the final independent lab reports, shared on the website for the project.

Widely available high-acid canning recipes are based on free University Extension offices or in the *Ball Book of Canning and Preserving* or the National Center for Home Food Preservation. Testing of high-acid canning recipes is required only when you deviate from the recipes or want to produce an item where no recipe exists from Extension or acceptable book sources. Links to high-acid tested recipe resources can also be found on the *Homemade for Sale* website.

For baked goods, however, this is not the case, especially when involving certain moist ingredients, like pumpkin or zucchini. Therefore, most states require recipe testing, when in doubt. The recipes our group created are independently tested by Deibel Labs, an Accredited Laboratory under the American Association for Laboratory Accreditation, with three decades experience and facilities scattered throughout North America. We lucked out by having a Deibel Labs in Madison, Wisconsin, about an hour's drive away from our home so we could hand-deliver each set of our samples.

Best Practices and Kitchen Wisdom

For this project, our baking team focused on developing non-hazardous recipes that meet the 0.85 or lower water activity level and used seasonal and local produce. While these recipes were originally created with farmers in mind—often with a surplus of zucchini, pumpkins, or butternut squash—these recipes can just as easily be used if you have an overflowing home garden, regularly stock up at a local farmers' market, or found a fruit or vegetable on super sale.

Many cottage food bakers naturally follow the seasons and holidays with what they bake up and sell. These recipes offer yet another unique way to showcase the seasons by focusing on the ingredients themselves. They may also provide a way to connect with and partner with a grower at your local

farmers' market. As we discuss in the marketing chapter, you might find some farmers eager to collaborate and cross-promote, with you pointing customers to the farmer's stand for fresh produce and the farmer pointing their customers to your stand with freshly baked products. There are plenty of customers out there who don't want to grow fresh produce themselves or have the talent, time or interest to bake in the kitchen.

You'll also find two frosting recipes—again, independently tested by the licensed Deibel Labs. Frostings, especially potentially non-hazardous ones, seem to be the bane of the health and agriculture departments. The health department tends to like to play darts with our livelihood, our frostings. Try overcoming their inconsistency with education. For each of the recipes, the actual Deibel Labs test can be downloaded for proof from cottagefoodhomebakery.com, if needed. But just because we tested the recipes doesn't mean your state's health or agriculture department won't try to force you to complete another test. The first step may be to send them your recipe and the third-party Deibel Lab's test results to try to secure your approval the easy way.

Be sure to follow these recipes exactly as written, since free-ranging improvisation or adding different ingredients may impact the water activity number and result in the recipe no longer being non-hazardous. This is a super important point with these and any tested recipe you may use.

As we experimented with ingredients in these recipes that have a high-water content, we needed to develop and test creative ways to literally get the water out while still retaining the moist texture and great taste of the final product. This is why that typical zucchini bread recipe you probably have in your file would not be something you could sell since that loaf contains too much water to be non-hazardous. Too often, these sweet breads can be soft and gooey in the middle. While tasty, this situation becomes ripe for microbes to grow and taint the product. We totally agree with the health department or agriculture departments on this count, and selling such products should never happen. Ever. Safety first.

In these recipes involving such produce, the following unique techniques are used that make the end product non-hazardous:

- Draining the water from the ingredient (e.g., zucchini) prior to baking
- Shredding the produce versus chunks

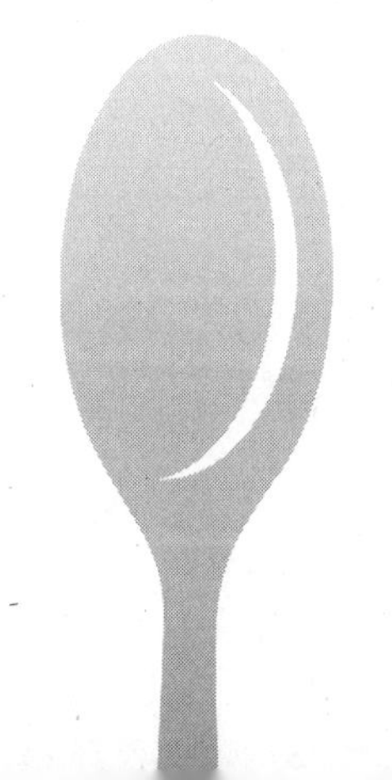

Nothing better than baking together! Our team of recipe testers sure had a lot of tasty fun cooking up this resource.
CREDIT: JOHN D. IVANKO PHOTOGRAPHY

- Adding elements like raisins and chocolate chips that can absorb moisture while baking
- Making smaller products, such as muffins versus loaves
- Using liners when baking

Recipe development like this takes time, including a fair number of failures that came in as "hazard-ous," but which we could still enjoy eating before tweaking it to work. That said, sometimes our experiments made something so dry or tasteless that they ended up as treats for our farmer team's array of happy goats and pigs. Once we found a recipe that worked, we did pretests at our local community college that had some of the water activity level equipment but was not a certified laboratory. After achieving a consistent test result as well as a consistently great-tasting product, we delivered a sample to the Deibel Labs for the official test, completed by people running around in lab coats in clean room environments.

Ingredients: Celebrate Local Foods and Grains

As the CEO of your cottage food operation, celebrate the fact that you call the shots and support other local businesses by using regional and locally produced ingredients in your products.

With a little research, you may be surprised by the variety of ingredients grown and produced nearby that can add both quality flavor and an interesting marketing twist to your goods. Being in Wisconsin, we only use organic butter and dairy produced there. Our state is also one of the country's largest producers of cranberries and maple syrup, other ingredients we like to showcase as well as our organic farm-raised produce and fruit.

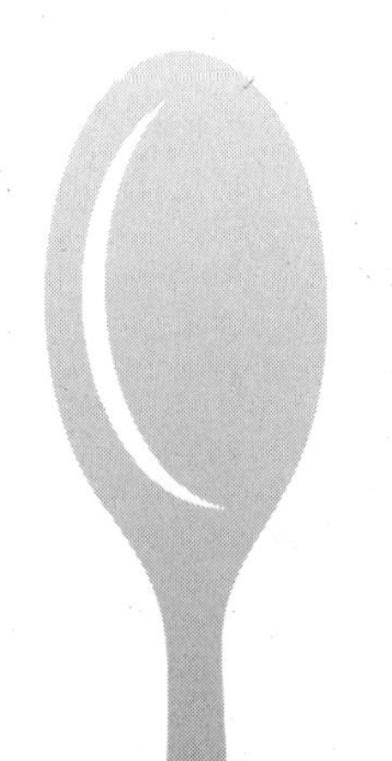

Regionally produced grains, from traditional wheat flour to specialty grains like rye, make up a hot new opportunity to showcase locally grown ingredients. Cultures throughout the world have been cultivating various grains that are well-suited to their climate for thousands of years. Today a growing renaissance across the United States is increasing the options and availability of grains for you as the baker and producer, thanks to the snowballing interest in supporting local farmers.

"By using regionally grown grains in your baked goods, you can amplify the impact of your cottage food business from selling a delicious product to adding a buffet of connected benefits, from strengthening your community's economy to helping the environment," explains Alyssa Hartman, executive director of the Artisan Grains Collaborative, a network of farmers, millers, maltsters, bakers, chefs, food manufacturers, brewers, distillers, researchers, and advocates working together to promote a regenerative grain shed in the Midwest. "Family farms in your geographic area directly profit from your purchase, instead of larger corporate entities. Those farms then purchase locally themselves, maybe even buying your products, and that economic vibrancy ripples and builds a healthy and connected community."

Additionally, regional agriculture supports a healthy ecosystem, one that does not need the heavy chemicals you typically find sprayed on most conventional crops today—you know, those flours sold by the case at supermarkets or big-box stores. The decreased shipping and transportation needed to get regional grains to you also results in less use of fossil fuels. These benefits quickly add up and are easy ways to making inroads to combat climate change if enough people switched to just a few localized grains.

"Another benefit of using local grains is outstanding flavor, crafting tasty and unique products far superior to mass-produced flours," adds Amy Halloran, local grain educator, advocate, and author of *The New Bread Basket*. "Not only do these grains improve your product taste, they gift you with a distinct and unique marketing element that quickly differentiates your product as unique and special."

Identify Your Options

Think of local grains as a palette of flavors, which will require you to step aside from using just that one-size-fits-all generic white flour. First, see what types of grains grow in your state or general region, which can vary depending on climate and geography. If you belong to a food cooperative, that's

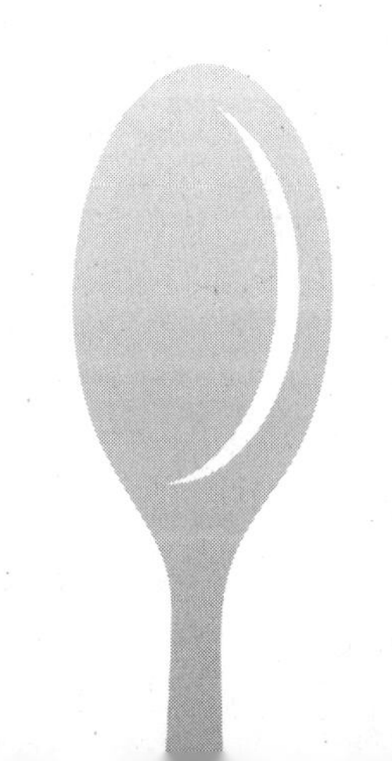

a fantastic place to start as they may have already done such research and offer local grain options. They may even get you discount pricing on 25- or 50-pound bags. Natural food stores or Whole Foods Market might be other options.

"This recent local grain renaissance is helping connect us cooks more closely with farmers and millers with perhaps the biggest benefit to cottage food bakers being the difference in flavor and nutrients the grains provide," shares Beth Dooley, author of *The Perennial Kitchen*. "Fresh isn't a term often associated with flour, but more and more bakers along with chefs are rising up in a battle against spongy bread and tasteless crackers. But unlike commercial bleached white flour, ground from grain treated with anti-molding agents and preservatives, artisan grain flours contain the nutrients of the whole grain." Because they are fresh, they are best stored in a cool, dry place, refrigerated or frozen.

Using locally grown grains and farm-fresh eggs add flavor to your products along with a unique marketing story to share.
CREDIT: JOHN D. IVANKO PHOTOGRAPHY

Depending on where you live, some local grains you may find that Dooley recommends exploring include barley flour for dense and rustic breads, cornmeal and corn flour, Kernza® flours, millet flour, oat flour, rye flour, and wheat flour. Also see if you have a locally grown oat option, an easy substitute for the commercial oats you're currently using in those cookies or streusel toppings.

Embrace Seasonality

"A plus of local grains is expanding your understanding of the concept of seasonality, the fact that because of factors like the soil type where the grains were grown, annual precipitation, or other weather patterns, certain grains may have different flavors from year-to-year, or, depending on the growing season, not be available at all," adds Hartman. Use this seasonal aspect to your marketing advantage by creating special limited-edition versions of your products, such as spring wheat sourdough loaves that will be different than what you bring to market in the fall.

Experiment with Small Steps

As a first step, experiment with some of your favorite recipes by adding just a proportion of a new grain to see how the flavor and texture evolves. For example, spelt flour is a local grain that we use for half of the unbleached white in some of our muffin recipes. It added a slight nutty flavor but didn't affect the already tender and fluffy texture of the muffin.

"Something to note is that flours from small mills are often whole grain, or lightly sifted, and the extra bran that comes along with them, or any whole grain flour, makes baked goods denser," advises Halloran. "Bran acts like little knives in yeasted or sourdoughs, cutting at the rising that happens. The extra bran will be less perceptible in cookies, just adding a superior texture."

Factor in Cost

Yes, local grains, as with many other locally produced goods, may cost more. Your own cookies, candies, or whatever you are making should then also be sold at a higher price than whatever commercially produced, shrink-wrapped product sits on your supermarket shelf. You should also consider marketing or display materials that explain your local sourcing to customers to help overcome price resistance. As owners of our own businesses leading the local food movement, we need to set the bar higher for valuing what's on our plate and paying fair and equitable pricing for the producers and farmers along that food chain.

Share the Tested Recipe Love

This recipe collection celebrates the collaborative spirit of our cottage food community of bakers, in that we intend for this to be an ongoing, free public resource for tested, safe recipes for us all to use. Our cooperative philosophy stems from the idea that we are stronger together and amplify our commitment to food safety by sharing such recipes. Each of them has a lab test result, downloadable from cottagefoodhomebakery.com under the recipes section. Bookmark the site, since new recipes will be added.

If you have a certified lab-tested recipe that meets the non-hazardous criteria, we'd love to add it to the database, with full credit to you, the chef, of course. Please contact us through the *Homemade for Sale* book website.

Pumpkin Scones

Scones need not be dry. These are moist and flavorful. Take this fall treat to market to showcase authentic pumpkin spice flavors and skip the chemical additives found in coffeehouse lattes.

Yield: 24 scones

These pumpkin scones are moist and flavorful.

Credit: John D. Ivanko Photography

Ingredients

½ cup butter (1 stick), softened
1 cup sugar
1 egg, beaten
¾ cup pumpkin puree (see Notes)
2 teaspoons baking powder
½ teaspoon baking soda
2 teaspoons cinnamon
½ teaspoon ground ginger
¼ teaspoon allspice
⅛ teaspoon ground cloves
½ teaspoon salt
2 cups flour
1 cup raisins
½ cup chopped pecans (optional)

Topping

¼ cup sugar
1 teaspoon cinnamon
⅛ teaspoon ginger

Directions

Preheat oven to 375°F.

Cream butter until fluffy. Add sugar slowly. Add egg and pumpkin and combine.

Mix in baking powder, baking soda, cinnamon, ginger, allspice, cloves, salt, and flour until just blended. Mix in raisins and pecans if using.

Drop tablespoons of dough onto lightly greased or silicon or parchment-lined baking sheets, two inches apart. Lightly flatten tops of scones with large spoon.

For topping: Stir together sugar, cinnamon, and ginger. Sprinkle mixture evenly on top of each scone.

Bake for approximately 10 to 12 minutes or until golden brown. Let cool 10 minutes on baking sheet and then remove to cooling rack.

Notes

Use fresh roasted pumpkin. Cut a pie pumpkin in half. Place cut side down on a foil-lined pan. Roast for 45 minutes at 375°F or until soft. Remove from oven and scrape out seeds. Return to oven for another 15 minutes to finish roasting. Allow to cool. Remove pumpkin flesh from skin. Puree. Fresh pumpkin puree can be refrigerated for 3 days or frozen for 6 months. Other winter squash can be also be used.

Pumpkin Chocolate Chip Muffins

Yield: 12 muffins

Ingredients

1¼ cups sugar
1½ cups flour
1½ teaspoons baking soda
½ teaspoon baking powder
¾ teaspoon cinnamon
½ teaspoon nutmeg
½ teaspoon ground cloves
¼ teaspoon ground ginger
¾ teaspoon salt
2 eggs
½ cup vegetable oil
¾ cup pumpkin puree (see Notes)
1 teaspoon apple cider vinegar

Fresh pumpkins used in delicious pumpkin chocolate chip muffins.
CREDIT : JOHN D. IVANKO PHOTOGRAPHY

Directions

Preheat oven to 375°F.

Whisk together sugar, flour, baking soda, baking powder, cinnamon, nutmeg, clove, ginger, and salt.

Combine eggs, oil, pumpkin, and apple cider vinegar.

Add dry ingredients to wet. Mix until just incorporated. Add chocolate chips.

Fill paper-lined muffin cups until ¾ full.

Bake at 375°F for 15 to 22 minutes. Check them at 15 minutes.

When done, muffins should spring back when pushed gently, and a toothpick should come out clean.

Remove from pan to cool.

Play around with the spices. More ginger will give a spicy muffin.

Notes

Use fresh roasted pumpkin. Cut a pie pumpkin in half. Place cut side down on a foil-lined pan. Roast for 45 minutes at 375 degrees or until soft. Remove from oven and scrape out seeds. Return to oven for another 15 minutes to finish roasting. Allow to cool. Remove pumpkin flesh from skin. Puree. Fresh pumpkin puree can be refrigerated for 3 days or frozen for 6 months. Other winter squash can be used.

Beet Chocolate Muffins

That's not a typo, but we understand if you never thought to add beets in your baked goods. A hidden gem, beets add color and flavor and a unique story twist to tell your customers. Maybe a great way to get kids to eat their vegetables! A dusting of powdered sugar on top or frosting would be a nice addition. This batter could also be used in other forms such as brownies.

Take the average chocolate muffin up a step with the seasonal, fresh local twist of beets.

CREDIT: JOHN D. IVANKO PHOTOGRAPHY

Yield: 12 muffins

Ingredients

2 cups sugar
2 cups flour
½ teaspoon salt
2 teaspoons baking powder
1 teaspoon baking soda
¾ cup cocoa powder
4 eggs
¼ cup butter, melted
½ cup vegetable oil
1¾ cups shredded beets
1 teaspoon vanilla
½ cup chocolate chips

Directions

Preheat oven to 350°F.

Combine the sugar, flour, salt, baking powder, cocoa in a mixing bowl.

Separately, lightly beat the eggs and add oil and butter. Mix into flour mixture just until blended.

Mix in beets and vanilla.

Fold in chocolate chips.

Fill paper-lined muffin cups until ¾ full.

Bake for approximately 20 minutes or until a toothpick inserted at the center comes out clean.

Zucchini Raisin Muffins

We're quite proud of this recipe as many farmers' markets don't allow anything made with zucchini because of the vegetable's high-water content. This one works! See the notes on squeezing out the water and be sure to use liners in the muffin cups.

Yield: 12 muffins

Ripe patty pan summer squash are perfect for these zucchini raisin muffins.
Credit: John D. Ivanko Photography

Ingredients

3 cups shredded zucchini, water removed (see Notes)
1⅔ cups sugar
⅔ cup oil
2 teaspoons vanilla
4 eggs
3 cups flour
2 teaspoons baking soda
½ teaspoon baking powder
1 teaspoon salt
1 teaspoon cinnamon
½ teaspoons ground cloves
¾ cup raisins

Directions

Preheat oven to 350°F.

Whisk together flour, baking soda, baking powder, salt, cinnamon, and cloves.

Combine zucchini, sugar, vanilla, eggs, and oil.

Add dry ingredients to wet. Mix until almost incorporated. Add raisins.

Fill paper-lined muffin cups until ¾ full.

Bake at 350°F for 17–20 minutes until a toothpick inserted at the center comes out clean.

Remove from pan to cool.

Notes

To remove water from zucchini, place shredded zucchini in a colander and sprinkle with salt. Let sit for about 30 minutes and squeeze water out by hand or by rolling and ringing in a lint-free dish towel. Doing a small amount at a time will yield a better result.

Pumpkin Whoopie Pies

Tap into the nostalgic cookies rage with this whoopie pie with a fall seasonal flavor twist.

Yield: 24 cookies

Ingredients

2 cups dark brown sugar
1 cup vegetable oil
1 cup pumpkin puree (see notes)
2 eggs
1 teaspoon salt
1 teaspoon baking powder
1 teaspoon baking soda
3 cups flour
1½ tablespoons ground cinnamon
2 teaspoons ground ginger
1 teaspoons ground cloves
1 teaspoon vanilla extract

Directions

Preheat oven to 350°F.

Mix brown sugar, oil, pumpkin, and egg and beat together well.

Add salt, baking powder, baking soda, cinnamon, ginger, cloves, flour, and vanilla. Mix well. Let batter sit 10 minutes.

Place heaping teaspoons of batter onto lightly greased or silicon or parchment-lined baking sheets.

Bake at 350°F for approximately 12 minutes or until firm to touch.

After removing from oven, let stand on baking sheets about 10 minutes and then move cookies to rack to cool completely.

To form Whoopie Pie: Use Cream Cheese Frosting or another non-hazardous frosting and glue two cookies together with approximately 1 tablespoon of frosting.

If you want your kids to enjoy pumpkin, try these whoopie pies.
CREDIT: JOHN D. IVANKO PHOTOGRAPHY

Notes

Use fresh roasted pumpkin. Cut a pie pumpkin in half. Place cut side down on a foil-lined pan. Roast for 45 minutes at 375°F. Remove from oven and scrape out seeds. Return to oven for another 15 minutes to finish roasting. Allow to cool. Remove pumpkin flesh from skin. Puree. Fresh pumpkin puree can be refrigerated for 3 days or frozen for 6 months. Other winter squash can be used.

Lavender Lemon Sunshine Shortbread Cookies

This recipe comes from Kriss Marion, one of the plaintiffs with Lisa in the successful lawsuit that made selling cookies finally legal in Wisconsin. This cookie was featured when the trio's story was showcased on *CBS Sunday Morning*. "This is a glorified herbal sugar cookie—snipped fresh rosemary or thyme will work instead of lavender—and lovely with a cup of English Breakfast tea," suggests Marion.

Yield: 24 to 36 cookies depending on size of cookie cutter

Delicious Lavender Lemon Sunshine Shortbread Cookie, baked by Kriss Marion of Circle M Farm.

CREDIT: KRISS MARION, CIRCLE M FARM

Ingredients

1 cup (2 sticks) butter, softened
½ cup granulated sugar
¼ cup confectioners sugar
½ teaspoon sea salt
2 lemons, zested (save to juice for icing)
1 tablespoon dried lavender (or 1 ½ tablespoons of a fresh herb)
2 large egg yolks (pastured or grass-fed will give you the great sunny color)
2 cups unbleached flour

Glaze

1½ cups confectioner's sugar
juice from the lemons (about ¼ cup)
dried lavender, more zest

Directions

Beat butter in a large mixing bowl until creamy.

Add the sugars, salt, zest, and lavender; beat until smooth.

Add egg yolks and beat until blended.

Add the flour all at once and mix until incorporated ONLY. Dough should look crumbly like wet sand.

Scrape into a ball and shape into a long roll (if cutting into thin wafers) or a flattened disk (if rolling out for cut-outs). Wrap in waxed paper and chill for an hour at least.

Preheat oven to 350°F.

Remove dough from fridge and soften slightly, then either slice into ¼-inch wafers, or roll flat for cut-outs. Place on a parchment-lined baking sheet 1 inch apart.

Slide sheet into a freezer for 10 minutes. Then bake in oven for 13–15 minutes until set but not browned. Watch carefully. Allow to cool slightly on sheet.

Mix ingredients for glaze, blend with a small whisk and let sit while you remove cookies to rack to cool completely. Mix glaze again to remove sugar lumps, drizzle over cookies, and tip cookies to cover completely. While glaze is wet, sprinkle with lavender flowers and zest another lemon over the top. When glaze sets up, flowers will stick.

Wisconsin Maple Dunkers

This recipe also comes from Kriss Marion of Circle M Farm, showcasing Wisconsin's maple syrup. She uses local eggs, too. Marion makes dozens upon dozens of these cookies for meetings or to share with journalists when they visit the farm.

Yield: 36 cookies

Ingredients

1 cup (2 sticks) butter, softened
1 cup sugar
½ cup maple syrup
1 teaspoon vanilla extract
1 large egg yolk
1 teaspoon salt
3 cups flour

Glaze

2 tablespoons maple syrup
powdered sugar

Directions

Cream together butter and sugar until light and fluffy, and beat in maple syrup, vanilla, and egg yolk until mixture is combined well.

Sift together salt and flour over mixture and fold in thoroughly.

Chill dough for about 15 minutes, then roll out on a floured surface and cut into shapes.

Bake at 350°F for about 10 minutes, but watch closely for browning on appendages, especially if you are working with a shape like Wisconsin! Allow to cool on racks.

For glaze, mix 2 tablespoons maple syrup with enough powdered sugar to make a nice thick glaze. Drizzle over cookies and allow to set before storing.

Wisconsin-shaped Maple Dunkers, baked by Kriss Marion, a signature cookie for sharing with guests staying in her rented vintage campers at Circle M Farm.
CREDIT: KRISS MARION, CIRCLE M FARM

Cheddar Herb Biscotti

Cheese can be tricky when used in baked goods. Dollops of cheese on top can make a product hazardous. Not these. This recipe uses shredded cheese baked into a dry biscotti so you are all good. Made with almond flour, these biscotti are even gluten-free!

Yield: 32–46 biscotti

Cheesy and crunchy, these savory Cheddar Herb Biscotti go great with soup.
CREDIT: JOHN D. IVANKO PHOTOGRAPHY

Ingredients

4 eggs
2 cups shredded Wisconsin cheddar cheese
2 tablespoons extra virgin olive oil
2 cups blanched almond flour
4 tablespoons fresh or 4 teaspoons dried savory herbs: thyme, dill, parsley, cilantro, rosemary, oregano
1 teaspoon baking powder
1 teaspoon xanthan gum
1 teaspoon salt
½ teaspoon pepper

Directions

Preheat oven to 350°F, line a baking sheet with parchment paper and set aside.

Place the eggs and cheese into a food processor and process until combined.

Add remaining ingredients to the food processor and pulse 3 or 4 times or until combined.

Shape the batter into two 8-inch logs (about 2 inches across) on the baking sheet.

Bake for 20 minutes or until firm to touch.

Cool for 20 minutes then cut into ½-inch slices.

Lay the slices flat, cut side down on the baking sheet and bake again until crisp, about 15 minutes.

Flip them over and bake an additional 10 minutes on the other side. Watch closely because these can burn quickly once they begin to brown.

Allow to cool completely before handling.

Notes

Let your customers know that if these need a re-crisp, wrap in aluminum foil and toast a few minutes before serving. Use any savory fresh herb that you have in your garden, or is seasonally available at the farmers' market.

These are quite crisp, so be sure to cut before the log cools completely, or they will crumble.

Sweet Potato Breakfast Cookies

Another unexpected vegetable in your cookie, the sweet potato! These cookies actually are an on-the-go breakfast, filled with oats and walnuts.

Yield: 2 dozen cookies

Ingredients

2 cups rolled oats
1 cup flour
1½ teaspoons cinnamon
1 teaspoon baking powder
½ teaspoon salt
¼ teaspoon ground ginger
1 cup mashed sweet potato
⅓ cup honey or maple syrup
⅓ cup melted coconut oil (or other vegetable oil)
1 teaspoon vanilla
¼ cup chopped walnuts
¼ cup chocolate chips

Whether for a healthier snack or as a quick breakfast, these Sweet Potato Breakfast Cookies help energize you for whatever is on the schedule.
Credit: John D. Ivanko Photography

Directions

Prepare sweet potatoes ahead of time: Bake at 350°F for an hour, then peel and mash and set aside for recipe.

Preheat oven to 350°F.

Combine oats, flour, cinnamon, baking powder, salt, and ginger.

Combine mashed sweet potato, honey, coconut oil, and vanilla.

Mix dry ingredients into wet until combined.

Fold in walnuts and chocolate chips.

Spoon onto a cookie sheet and bake for 20–25 minutes until browned.

Cider-Glazed Apple Cakes

While chunks of fruit in a baked good would typically make it hazardous, because these apples are shredded, this recipe works great. See chapter 7 for packaging ideas; these mini loaves individually as gifts could justify a higher price.

Yield: 12–24 mini bundts, depending on pan size

You'll love the apple flavor in these Cider-Glazed Apple Cakes.
CREDIT: JOHN D. IVANKO PHOTOGRAPHY

Ingredients

4 cups apple cider
3¾ cups flour
1½ teaspoons salt
1½ teaspoons baking powder
½ teaspoon baking soda
1 teaspoon ground cloves
1 cup vegetable oil
1½ cups brown sugar
3 eggs, room temperature
2 teaspoons vanilla
3 cups shredded tart apples, about ½ pound or three large apples. Drain extra liquid.
¾ cup powdered sugar

Directions

Place cider in a saucepan over medium-high heat and reduce to 1 cup. Set aside 2 tablespoons for glaze.
Combine flour, salt, baking powder, baking soda, and cloves.
Combine oil, brown sugar, eggs, vanilla, and remaining cider.
Add dry ingredients to wet until just incorporated.
Add shredded apple just to mix through.
Portion into greased mini loaf pans, filling ¾ full.
Bake at 375°F oven for 15–24 minutes.
When done, loaves should spring back when pushed gently, and a toothpick should come out clean.
Remove from pan to cool.
Combine the 2 tablespoons cider reduction and powdered sugar for the glaze.

Basic Crackers

Think of crackers as the hidden gem of cottage food products. Everyone eats them but few make them. Most bakers don't make crackers, but once you do, you'll discover they are so much tastier than the commercial ones. These crackers can stand alone, but suggest to your customers all the things they can be paired with from other local food businesses: cheese, relishes, ferments, pates, dips, summer sausage, wine, cider, micro beers. Try using fun-shaped cookie cutters such as animals. See the flavor variations at the end to make this recipe your own.

Spelt flour adds a healthy, local grain twist to these crackers.
CREDIT: JOHN D. IVANKO PHOTOGRAPHY

Yield: 3–4 dozen crackers

Ingredients

2¼ cups spelt flour
¾ teaspoon baking soda
¾ teaspoon salt
1½ teaspoons cream of tartar
¼ cup melted lard (cooled)
½ cup water
Coarse salt for sprinkling on top. Himalayan pink adds gourmet touch.

Directions

Preheat oven to 350°F.

Line baking sheet with parchment paper or silicon sheets.

Combine first 4 ingredients in bowl, mix well. Add lard and work in until mixture is like coarse meal.

Add water and stir until dough forms ball (add more flour or water as needed).

Dough can also be made in a food processor by lightly pulsing.

Turn onto lightly floured surface and roll out very thin, as thin as possible, to keep them crispy.

Cut shapes with a cookie cutter or 1- to 2-inch strips with a pizza cutter or pastry wheel. Then cut the other direction into squares, rectangles, or triangles. For fun, cut on diagonal for diamond shapes.

Bake 15–20 minutes until crispy. Cool on wire rack.

Crackers

Variations on the basic cracker recipe:

- **Pumpkin Patch Crackers**

  After rolling out basic dough, brush with tamari and sprinkle with shelled pumpkin seeds.

- **Rosemary's Baby Crackers**
  (good teething crackers or on a cheese platter)

  Chop and add to basic dough 3 to 4 tablespoons fresh rosemary leaves.

- **Dilly Girl Garlic Crackers**

  Finely chop/mince and add to basic dough 3 garlic cloves and 3 to 4 tablespoons fresh dill weed.

- **Going to Seed Crackers**

  Whisk together and spread on crackers before putting in oven 1 egg, 2 teaspoons sugar, 1 teaspoon apple cider vinegar. Sprinkle with hulled sunflower seeds or sesame seeds.

American Buttercream Frosting

This frosting tastes closest to what you'd expect from in a classic buttercream, sweet and similar to those supermarket sheet cakes but much better without the additives and chemicals. Works great for a quick frosting on cupcakes. To create such a stable buttercream, lard adds a smoothness and savory flavor offsetting the sweetness.

Yield: 5 cups, enough for 8- or 9-inch cake, two-tiered, or 24–30 cupcakes

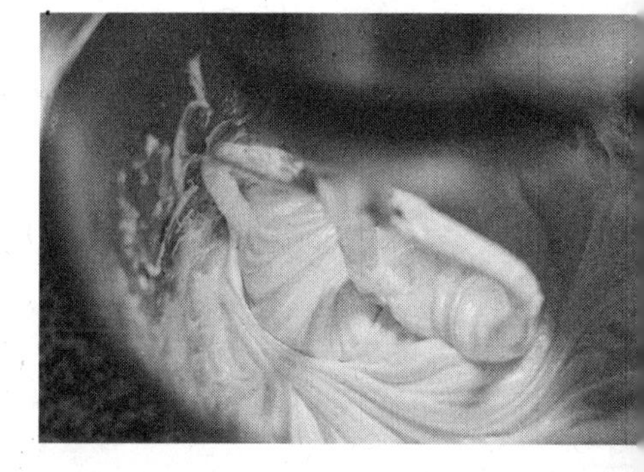

Frosting being churned in author Lisa Kivirist's stand mixer.

Credit: John D. Ivanko Photography

Ingredients:

¾ cups unsalted butter (1½ sticks), room temperature
¼ cup lard, room temperature
3½ cups powdered sugar
½ teaspoon salt
2 teaspoons vanilla or other extract
1 tablespoon hot, near boiling, water

Directions

In stand mixer bowl, combine butter and lard on medium speed until smooth.

Add powdered sugar and salt. Mix on low for 1 minute or until powdered sugar is incorporated. Increase to high speed and cream for 5 minutes, until light and fluffy.

Add vanilla and hot water. Mix for an additional 1 minute on high.

Flavor variations:

- Chocolate: melt 2 ounces chocolate, let cool, add after butter and sugar is creamed. Add no water.
- Jam of any kind: add ¼ cup

Cream Cheese Frosting

This frosting is super versatile and adds the tang of cream cheese to offset the sweetness. Swap out vanilla extract for other extracts or add lemon or orange zest.

Yield: 5 cups, enough for 8- or 9-inch cake or 24–30 cupcakes

Ingredients

8 ounces cream cheese, room temperature
½ cup (1 stick) unsalted butter, room temperature
4 cups powdered sugar, sifted
1 tablespoon vanilla extract

Directions

Cream together cream cheese and butter until light and fluffy, 4 minutes.
Add powdered sugar on low for 1 minute.
Increase speed to high and cream for 5 minutes, until light and fluffy.
Add vanilla on low.

Sugar is a key ingredient that helps make frosting non-hazardous. Frosting adds value to a regular muffin.
CREDIT: JOHN D. IVANKO PHOTOGRAPHY

In the next section and chapters on marketing, we'll turn your "half-baked" ideas and recipes into products ready for market.

SECTION 3

Selling Your Story: Marketing

6

Product Development: Design, Name, and Logo

A WIDE RANGE of different elements go into defining a great product, including the uniqueness of your recipe, the quality of the ingredients, the packaging, perhaps the specific process of its small-batch production, and even the messaging you've created around your product.

As we touched on earlier, marketing is a term that covers a variety of considerations associated with selling your homemade item. Most business schools cover the 4 Ps of marketing: **Product, Price, Place** (how you distribute your item), and **Promotion**, both in the form of paid advertising and free public relations.

We explore three additional Ps in our *ECOpreneuring* book, in part because marketing has become so pervasive and integrated into day-to-day routines, often in subtle or clever ways. It permeates our life through product placement in movies, naming rights for stadiums or campus buildings, Facebook updates, or reviews on Yelp. These three extra Ps of marketing—**People, Partnerships,** and **Purpose**—reflect our values and belief systems and connect us to our community.

Because marketing plays such a pivotal role in the success of any product, we've broken the 7 Ps of marketing down into several chapters. Realize, however, that the most effective marketing efforts are those that combine all elements into one cohesive and clear plan that can be effectively implemented.

Niche, Target, and Positioning

Before getting into the product aspect of marketing, we'll touch on three very important concepts first: finding your niche, defining your target market, and positioning your product.

Finding a Niche with Potential

Nearly all food businesses, large and small, assess potential markets, carving out a niche that seems most likely to earn enough money by selling a

product to make it worth pursuing. If you don't make some profit, at least three out of five years, you're not in business, according to the IRS; you're just a hobby. We'll cover this more in chapter 18.

A niche is a segment of a broader market where you believe your product can do well. Because of its unique characteristics, better quality, or because it faces little competition, you may find greater flexibility in how you market and sell it. If you define your niche too narrowly, or if there aren't enough customers who want what you make at the price you're asking, then this niche doesn't have the market potential to make your business viable. Don't throw in the towel, just re-evaluate your goals and examine ways to expand your market without being everything to everyone.

Defining Your Target Market

While a niche is often product-focused, your target market is the audience or potential customers you want to reach, serve, and satisfy with your products. The 7 Ps of marketing are guided or defined by who you select as your target. In other words, the customers most likely to purchase your products in a large enough quantity at the price you've determined will allow your business to prosper.

There are a number of ways you can define your target market:

- By demographics: age, gender, geography, and income level, among many other variables
  Example: ages 30–40, female, living in Smalltown, New York, earning $50,000 to $100,000/year
- By psychographics: attitudes, beliefs, and value systems
  Example: a Cultural Creative locavore who loves artisanal food products, especially when organic and made without preservatives. Different from Traditionals and Moderns, Cultural Creatives are more attuned to environmental and social issues.

You'll need to define and understand your customers in both demographic and psychographic ways. Think about it this way: demographics helps you understand who your customers are while psychographics help determine why your customers buy what they do. Keep in mind that the needs of your customers may not even be real; they could just be perceived. In other words, your customers may not even know they need your

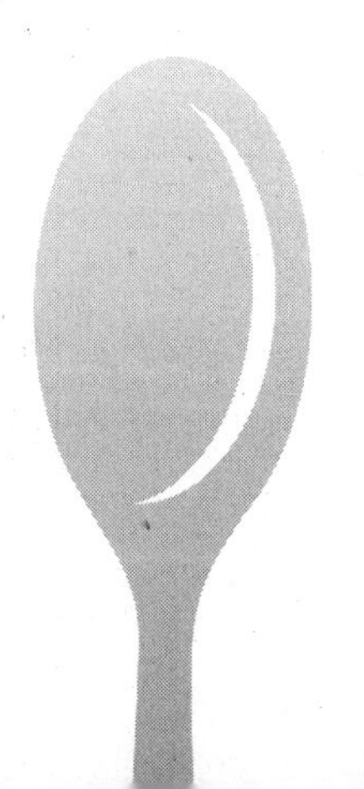

product, even if they do. Think: impulse purchases. From this information, you can then develop your marketing strategy and from that, a marketing plan that addresses those 7 Ps.

Due to your familiarity with and assessment of the marketplace, you may already have a solid grasp of who would buy your products. You'll probably start by selling to neighbors, family, or friends already clamoring for your products. Maybe they attend the same church, work in the same office or school, serve in the same civic organizations, or attend the same youth soccer games. This works great until you find yourself wanting to sell more products and ramp up your operations to reach customers beyond your immediate network. At that point, you'll need to flush out the target market more thoroughly if your marketing efforts are to be effective.

Positioning Your Product

In marketing jargon, the expression of differentiation is called positioning: the combination of marketing elements that go into defining your product and why it's different than the competition. Some marketers may also call this idea your unique selling proposition, or USP. Drawing on your strengths, the USP showcases the unique benefit or benefits associated with your product and brand that helps set what you offer apart from the competition. Your positioning and USP are what results in customers choosing your products. Ultimately, you're selling a promise and the customer needs to trust that you'll deliver.

Defining exactly how your product might appeal to your customers' needs or desires and the benefits it provides can be tricky. While you may believe you have the most unique and tasty fruit-flavored graham crackers ever, in the end, your potential customers need to share this perception and feel that it meets their needs as a healthy snack (assuming that's one of the benefits of your product). Product development research and a market feasibility study, covered in chapter 14, guide this process.

Positioning can consider all 7 Ps of marketing, plus how your product might be used or the solution to a problem it addresses. Often, positioning can involve a combination of several variables. For example, your sugar-free sweet rolls could be a solution as a breakfast item for customers seeking ways to cut back on their sugar. Or that same sugar-free roll could be a delicious and healthier way to savor a snack, perhaps with a cup of coffee or tea.

Keep in mind that there's a big difference between being product-focused and market-focused, especially if your aim might be to scale up your operations. The market—your customers—are the ones telling you what they want, what benefits they perceive, what problem is being solved, or what needs are being met with your product. Are gluten-free breads absent in your community? Is a well-attended local arts show missing a food vendor, with hungry art shoppers with no place to go for a snack?

With positioning, you're conveying what your product is, how it's different from the competition, and why a customer should buy it. One path to success may be to come up with a signature product, something unique. Perhaps it's your uncommonly good approach to a common recipe. Bonus points for being clever, creative, or distinctive in describing it. Even when you have no competition for your product, its taste will ultimately determine whether customers come back for more.

What you're actually selling could be much more than just the taste, flavor, texture, size, or appearance of your food product. If you package

Ideas Everywhere

When exploring how to label, package, price, and sell your products, there's nothing wrong with seeing how other food entrepreneurs do it. Wander the aisles of a Whole Foods Market or a specialty gift store that sells food products. The following are a few more places to check out.

- Specialty Food Association's Fancy Food Shows, held on both coasts every year, and their informative website (specialtyfood.com)
- igourmet.com — if you're looking for how other food artisans create gift baskets and design their labels, check out this online gourmet food and gift retailer
- stonewallkitchen.com — another source of ideas and to see how a Maine company thrives in the specialty food business
- Natural Products Expo, East and West, focus on natural, organic and healthy-lifestyle products (expowest.com and expoeast.com)
- Good Food Awards (goodfoodawards.org), organized by Seedling Projects, is the first national awards platform to recognize American craft food producers who excel in superior taste and sustainability. The awards for outstanding American food producers and the farmers who provide their ingredients are given out at a ceremony and marketplace at the Ferry Building in San Francisco. The 11 categories are beer, charcuterie, cheese, chocolate, coffee, confections, pickles, preserve, spirits, oil, and honey.

Every Christmas holiday season, Chris Sachs takes orders for his Grandma Staada's Christmas Stollen, made in his home kitchen.

CREDIT: JANELLE MASSEY

or distribute it as a gift for tourists or the holiday season, your approach will be far different than if it was a product offered at a farmers' market. Depending on your item, you may even offer some form of service, like a guarantee of satisfaction.

For example, a Swiss-style cookie sold in a Swiss community with lots of tourist traffic might be positioned as an edible gift or a souvenir. The name, packaging, price, and label should aid in this by eliciting a clear and prompt "I should try this now!" thought in a potential customer's mind while they're browsing the arts and crafts fair where you've set up a small stand.

Price can appeal to a customer on a limited budget or deter an upscale clientele who might happily pay a premium for an item with high-quality ingredients or fresh from the oven. For many impulse purchases, convenience, comfort, or hunger may drive the exchange; customers may pay a premium for any one of these qualities. How your product is different can take interesting forms; perhaps you deliver by bicycle. For example, Domino's Pizza, the national pizza chain, is famously known for being in the delivery business, not the pizza business. That's how they do pizza different.

Depending on your marketing strategy, you may be able to create an entire experience around the enjoyment of your product and the love that went into making it. Starbucks sells an experience, not just coffee. Who knew so many Americans would pay a lot of money to order a double tall skim vanilla latte and hang out in a coffee house instead of a bar. Starbucks identified a perceived need among people and delivers a "coffee experience" in a way that differentiates them from the hundreds of thousands of coffeehouses and cafes that already exist.

A supermarket now contains, on average, more than 42,000 products, according to the Food Marketing Institute. Our modern-day marketplace is about choices, providing something for everyone, with companies vying for market niches and every dollar of the consuming public's disposable income. With 70 percent of the US economy based on "consumer spending," your product is directly linked to this broader economy. Making a great-tasting product is only the start.

There's no "right" way to position your product; the choices are infinite. But if you're stuck with a bunch of unsold items at the end of the day, you'll need to re-evaluate both your product and your marketing efforts.

Elizabeth Berman, Small Oven Pastries, Shelburne, Vermont

Baking up a Macaron Empire in a Small Oven

Name: Elizabeth Berman

Business: Small Oven Pastries (Shelburne, VT)

Website: www.smallovenpastries.com

Products: French macarons, tartlets, and other small pastries

Sales Venues: online sales, pop-up markets, and farmers' markets

Gross Revenues: $35,000+/year

"After being in higher education for some 15 years, I burned out," says Elizabeth Berman, owner of Small Oven Pastries, chief confectioner, and flavor master. "While I was trying to figure out my next move professionally, I doubled down on baking. I immersed myself in learning the science and art of baking. I started unloading my treats on friends, neighbors, my husband's colleagues—and everyone was loving what I was creating!" exclaims Berman, on her career pivot, launching her business in 2020.

"I loved the challenge of perfecting the world's most difficult cookie," Berman adds. "I went all in on starting a business with no experience with entrepreneurship, no professional baking degree, a move from Boston back to Vermont." Now, by nearly every measure—including enticing first-time customers, attracting plenty of repeat customers, and a degree of profitability on the inaugural first year—her Small Oven Pastries is well on its way to establishing a French macaron empire in Vermont.

"With my multidisciplinary experience in academic libraries, I was adept at researching cottage food laws and business planning, possessed a degree of marketing and social media know-how, could build websites, and was familiar with good customer service," recognizes Berman, who shares business and life experiences common among many new cottage food entrepreneurs. "Those skills gave me an extraordinary head start, especially with respect to the website and social media, because it allowed me to put myself out there professionally from the very beginning and focus on making the best macarons in the state of Vermont."

Berman, and her business, demonstrates the KISS principle: Keep It Simple Stupid. For her online sales, she primarily focuses on macarons and takes them in multiple directions in terms of color, fillings, and flavors. "Find your niche and own it," Berman advises. "Don't try to be all the things to all the people because that will lead to burn out. Your customers will find you when they know exactly what you provide."

Elizabeth Berman, owner of Small Oven Pastries, in her home kitchen.
PHOTO CREDIT: ISORA LITHGOW

While French macarons are small, they offer big flavors. The Small Oven Pastries website offers a gallery showcasing a dizzying array of flavors arranged by season, holiday, or theme. There are boozy macarons, like mint julep that has a mint almond shell with Woodford Reserve bourbon and fresh mint Swiss meringue buttercream, and summer macarons, like peaches and cream, made with white chocolate ganache and vanilla peach compote. A selection of approximately two dozen flavors are available at any given time in the online shop, based on "seasonality, access to ingredients, and chef's temperament." Berman's top sellers include raspberry, salted caramel, and birthday cake.

"I also experiment with other small pastries, including tartlets, financiers, meringues, and madeleines, which have performed very well at farmers' markets and pop-ups, but less consistently in the online store," continues Berman. "It's an area I'm continuing to explore and experiment with.

"I started with the French macaron, a notoriously difficult pastry to perfect, as the foundation for what I sell because of its popularity," explains Berman. "The name of my business, Small Oven, is a play on the English translation of the French term *petit four,* which gives a nod to the variety of bite-sized confections I specialize in and keeps me focused on the vision of my business: small treats, big flavor.

"Know your numbers," says Berman, when it comes to arriving at the right price for your products. "Know what your recipe costs, the amount of labor you put in, the per item cost of each thing you sell, what your margin is, and your profit and loss. Knowing your numbers can make the difference between being a successful business or an unprofitable hobby.

"When I was dividing my time more equally between macarons and tartlets, this hindered my bottom line because they were two very different processes, with different mindsets to create—and different cost of goods sold," discovered Berman. "I actually generated less profit overall when labor was accounted for." Understanding the labor and pricing differences has ultimately shifted her approach to production and the products she offers on a regular basis. With this knowledge, she's able to think more strategically about how to introduce new products into the market.

"On the business side, I intentionally wanted to make sure I was making the best possible macaron

Naughty and Nice Macaron Collection 2021: Spiked Eggnog, Candy Cane, Blue Christmas, Grinch, O Christmas Tree, and Hot Cocoa.

Photo credit: Elizabeth Berman

and to provide a unique product in a crowded home-bakery and commercial bakery landscape," explains Berman. "I'm a sole proprietor, so I worried about spreading myself too thin and being proficient at many things but expert at none.

"No local food system is a closed system, and I do need to rely on products grown elsewhere to create my treats," acknowledges Berman. "Vermont is lucky in that we have not only a strong small farm system but also some larger players in the food industry game including King Arthur Flour and Cabot Creamery. While I cannot source sugar, chocolate, or almond flour locally, I do work directly with local vendors for my dairy, eggs, flour, fruits, honey, and other flavors that I use to infuse my macarons, as well as fair-trade or B-Corp certified local importers of coffee or spices. When items aren't locally available, I work with artisans, small farms, and other B-Corp certified suppliers to get my ingredients. For example, I work directly with Alldrin Almonds for my almond flour.

"My lens on participating in the local food system is not just about promoting 'local ingredients' but about making lasting connections with farmers and producers and investing in and bolstering the local economy," continues Berman. "This includes working with local businesses for my labels and stickers and marketing materials and packaging."

For macarons, it's all about colors and flavors—and being responsive to customers' needs. "I know that bright colors attract kids, so I make sure there are always brightly colored kid-friendly flavors in my display when doing in-person markets," observes Berman. "I also know some of my more adult flavors of macarons don't sell as well at farmers' markets, but they sell well in prepackaged collections via the online store. I'm still learning and always alert and receptive to what my customers are looking for.

"I tried using only natural colors via different nuts, spices, and freeze-dried fruit and vegetable powders," says Berman. "But those naturally colored macarons did not have wide consumer appeal. Customers want a beautiful, Instagram-worthy jewel

Sour patch kid macarons. PHOTO CREDIT: ELIZABETH BERMAN

box of macarons! So, I found a company that sells hyper-pigmented powdered food coloring where a little goes a long way and still use natural colorings when I can.

"My business is run 100 percent by me," smiles Berman. "I do all the baking, packaging, marketing, website creation, photography, and cleaning." She's assisted by her daughter Natalie, laughingly described as queen boss of quality control and delivery co-pilot. As many cottage food operators know, kids make great taste-testers and can be great helpers. "My husband does a bunch of grunt work behind the scenes, helps with deliveries and word-of-mouth marketing. Having them work alongside me has made the business more fun, which helps mitigate burnout. It's family time!

"I wanted to protect my family's finances and keep them separate from my business's finances," says Berman, regarding her decision to form an LLC. "It's a simple and straightforward structure that's easy to maintain. I also wanted to make sure I was doing everything legally and aboveboard, so having the structure in place from the get-go was essential to me." Berman also has a business product liability insurance, in part recognizing that most farmers' markets and pop-up venues required a Certificate of Insurance, or COI, in order to participate. Vermont's home bakery license requires an annual in-person kitchen inspection.

"I started intentionally as an online store, direct-to-consumer," explains Berman, who realized early on that one of the most important skills she brought to the business was having experience in website design and development. She also understands the importance of an attractive and easy-to-navigate website.

"When you want to find out more about something, you Google it, so you need to have something to Google. In today's world, I believe that it's essential to have a web presence, both a website and social media. The website is marketing, demonstrates professionalism, and provides a very user-friendly and accessible way for customers to order and communicate with you." She also created a free Google business profile.

"There are lots of software options to create websites these days without any need to learn coding," Berman encourages. "Just plug and play. I used Wix to design and build the framework for my website as well as provide the e-commerce platform so I can sell online." While she pays for a Wix business account that includes an e-commerce platform, there are free accounts with the only cost being a registered domain name.

"I put the most time and energy into my Instagram account," Berman shares. "Then I cross-post to Facebook to target my ideal demographic target market: female, ages 24 to 50, educated, and who might be called 'foodies.' I capitalize on the visual appeal of food photography, so-called food porn."

She also maintains a newsletter list to communicate directly with her customers which drives the sales because these are a self-identified group of customers who are most interested in buying her products. "I paid for Google Ads and Instagram Ads early on, which generated some business, but the return on investment wasn't great, so I've ceased putting money into those activities. I wasn't able to engage directly with people who saw the Google Ads, another negative. This is a huge part of why I prefer building a community of followers on social media."

Berman does experiment with new online marketing avenues, like PastriesPERKS. "I started seeing all these rewards programs on many of the online stores I shopped at, so I looked into the software Smile.io," says Berman. "There's a free version, so I tried it out and established PastriesPERKS on my website to see whether it was a motivation for customers and help drive sales. So far it hasn't been widely adopted, but my core customers have definitely taken advantage of earning points and redeeming them for macaron purchases. It doesn't generate additional sales, but it creates loyal customers."

Farmers' markets, like Shelburne Farmers' Market, and pop-up markets provide face-to-face sales opportunities for Small Oven Pastries. "I loved the direct human connections I was able to make with customers, to be able to talk about my product, and answer questions," observes Berman. "It energized me, and I look forward to more in-person events.

"I've found that a beautiful display of 12 flavors of macarons sells themselves better than pictures on a webpage," Berman adds. "Plus, there's the potential for future collaboration with like-minded vendors that grows both our customer bases." Her long-term goal is a sales mix of 50–50 in terms of online sales and in-person events. Since

Natalie Berman, daughter of Small Oven Pastries' owner Elizabeth Berman, selling macarons at pop-up event in Burlington, Vermont. PHOTO CREDIT: ELIZABETH BERMAN

the cottage food law in Vermont sees no difference between selling retail to consumers vs wholesale, Berman also wholesales to Lu*Lu, a local storefront bakery and ice cream parlor.

"If I didn't have the farmers' market, my business would not have been profitable during the summer months," Berman admits, on the importance of cash flow and recognizing seasonal ups and downs of her business. "But on the flip side, I sell a product that is meringue-based, which means it's susceptible to humidity and heat. It's sort of insane to be selling it outdoors during summer heat waves." She's astutely mindful of the realities of weather and her focus on maintaining the quality and consistency of her macarons, regardless of seasonal variability.

So far, Berman's biggest order was for 60 dozen custom macarons for a wedding, delivered on the same weekend that she sold about 45 dozen at a local farmers' market. That's 1,260 macarons, worth $2,520 at retail. "That was stressful," Berman confides.

"But stress is inevitable as part of the job," continues Berman. "Macarons are finicky pastries with a good number of fails. I limit myself to stop working for the day when my daughter gets home from school. It's a physically demanding job, so I build in breaks throughout my day to relax by taking a walk, reading a book, or painting. It's important to take your mind off the business side of things for a while. In order to survive as a baker, womanpreneur, and solopreneur, actively practicing self-care in whatever form it takes is the only way to be successful.

"Figure out what you enjoy doing and build a business plan around you focusing your energies on that thing then work with others to fill in the gaps," Berman suggests, to keep it in control. "For example, my primary focus is production of baked goods and recipe development, then social media marketing, then order fulfillment, then finances. I am at the point where I am working with a bookkeeper to help with my finances. I enlist my husband to do deliveries so I can keep baking. I am looking for a local photographer to take a gallery of easy-to-use product photos. I know the things I eventually need to let go of. So, I am planning accordingly. This also is a form of self-care to stave off burnout. You may be a sole proprietor but you are not alone on this journey."

Product Design and Attributes

While largely guided by your state's cottage food law, there's plenty of breathing room for what you create in your kitchen to sell to the public. The combination of your ingredients and the packaging, presentation, and pricing—plus the story you build around your product —gives it identity or personality. How you define the attributes and aspects of your product help differentiate it from others in the marketplace.

There are, however, certain industry conventions that you'll need to follow, since that's also what your customers are expecting. Size and quantity are two important considerations. If your muffins are double the size of others at a community event, are you sure you can charge double the price, or do you even need to? Alternatively, people are used to getting discounts when they buy extra. Consider having a sliding scale for items sold by the half and full dozen.

If you're like us, you may already have a few well-tested recipes for products. We just need a marketing plan for sharing the products with those who might want to buy them. Our distinguishing attributes are organic ingredients, many from our farm, which is completely powered by the sun. Following our concern for the environment, our packaging is made from recycled content and is compostable.

Tools for Product Creation

There are lots of tools used by inventors, entrepreneurs, and people working in creative fields, most of which work perfectly for developing new food products. Here are a few you might want to try if you don't have Auntie Emma's secret recipe.

Brainstorming

Among the more common ways of coming up with creative ideas and solutions to problems, brainstorming encourages a free-flowing and spontaneous list of ideas with few limiting constraints. After assembling the list, whittle it down to a shortlist of the most promising ideas.

Free Association

Sigmund Freud made it famous, making the unconscious conscious. But free association can work for more than patients with psychological problems. Let your mind go when dreaming up new concoctions in the kitchen. Have a family member make a random list of various words or a targeted list of culinary words and see what pops into your head.

There's no limit to your creativity. Take it from Jacqueline Weber, owner of Junie Pie's Baking Company in Madison Heights, Michigan. "I'm obsessed with desserts that are disguised as savory foods," laughs Weber, who created an amazingly convincing dessert charcuterie board. "Everything is edible except for the board and serving tray!" Perfect for the Superbowl, or any party.
CREDIT: JACQUELINE WEBER/JUNIE PIE'S BAKING COMPANY

Opposite Attractions

Sometimes it works for marriages, so why not see if some opposite attractions work for your culinary creations? When it comes to flavors, explore pairing sour and sweet, like mangoes and salsa or balsamic vinegar and raspberries. Salty and sweet are a well-known match made in heaven. Keep a notepad next to your bed in case an idea suddenly appears; the moments just before and immediately after you sleep can be very creative times for some people.

Discordant Events

Disagreement and conflict can breed new ideas, even if they're odd, like the invisible dog or a pet rock. Why did it take so long to put wheels on luggage so we wouldn't have to drag our suitcases through the airport? One of the tastiest ideas in recent times is turning a flower bouquet into a cookie bouquet. When can something that clashes become something brilliantly creative?

Drawing a Map for Success

What would it look like if you made a picture of your dream business? Sometimes pictures are worth a thousand words. Some of us think visually. Try sketching a map or visual representation of your route to success, tracing the ingredients from the garden or a local supplier to your end product. Or use one of the many online apps or a free website, like FreeMind, to guide your efforts.

Naming Your Products and Business

For the chocolate lover, but not overly sweet. This Chocolate Pastry Tart, made by the author Lisa Kivirist for her Inn Serendipity Fresh Baked Homemade Bakery, has a decadent chocolate filling and topped with chocolate frosting, plus sprinkles. Handmade with organic sugar, organic butter, and Equal Exchange Fair-trade-certified organic cocoa. Just don't call them Pop-Tarts®. Her ingredients don't include TBHQ or high-fructose corn syrup. CREDIT: JOHN D. IVANKO PHOTOGRAPHY

There is no right name for your product. But there are names that tend to elicit a smile, convey a mood or feeling, or are just plain fun. While the name you give it should be true to the product and reflect the ingredients or contents, there's plenty of evidence that a catchy name grabs the attention of a potential customer passing by. In that fraction of a second, you'll either have a sale, or not.

Take chocolate biscotti. Perhaps it's crunchy, made with fair-trade-certified cacao powder and almonds and can be enjoyed as a snack with coffee or tea. Why not call it Double-Down Chocolate Almond Crunch? Adding a little alliteration, plus including another defining ingredient (almonds), may trigger a pang of hunger—and spur an impulse purchase.

Avoid obsessing over naming your product, but have fun with it. Keep your market, positioning, and other marketing considerations in mind, since your name should echo the others aspects of your marketing. If you are planning a product line, consider a name that can be easily carried across the entire line in some way.

Before settling on a name, try running it by the Internet to make sure you're not violating any existing trademarks. "Cease and desist" notes from an attorney representing a company with a product by the same name as yours can sour an otherwise exciting product launch. Here's one of the items that came up on our search for our hypothetical Double-Down Chocolate Almond Crunch: Creamy Almond Crunch SQUARES™, trademarked by Ghirardelli, a multinational. Given this, we'd feel okay to proceed with our product name since it's different from the one owned by Ghirardelli. If we wanted to take this product national and scale up, we'd complete a trademark search with the US Patent and Trademark Office (see Company Name sidebar) to be 100 percent certain, while protecting our name from infringement by another company.

A Company Name

Besides coming up with memorable, descriptive, relevant, or provocative names for your products, you'll also need to decide on the legal name for your company itself. Many CFOs have a fictional business name used with the public that's distinctive, easy to say and spell, memorable, and that captures the essence of your goods or evokes feelings you want associated with your business. This fictional name is referred to as a DBA, "doing business as." There's nothing wrong with using your own name in it, or a variation, like Bonnie's Baked Goods (with alliteration) or Aunt Emma's Pride. You may have a more personalized name for your business, too, if you operate as an LLC or corporation (covered in chapter 17), plus a DBA. Your business name is part of your marketing, so take the time to choose it carefully.

Before you proceed, run the name by friends and family for feedback. Check to see if the domain name is still available in case you want to create a website. If you think there's a possibility you might scale up later on, check to see if you can trademark the name with the US Patent and Trademark Office (USPTO). The website domain name can be checked for free on whois.net; to complete a free USPTO search using the "trademark electronic search system," type your name into their search engine on uspto.gov. Even if you do not want to trademark your name, you will still need to register it in your state through your secretary of state or other licensing department; your state will have some form of free search feature to see if the name you want can be used there.

Another popular way to present information about your products, company, and brand is through a Quick Response, or QR, code, a matrix barcode that can be readily scanned by mobile devices. The free code can be affixed to your product labels or used in other ways to promote your business and can foster greater customer engagement through a mobile device. The effectiveness of its use will largely depend upon your potential customers being familiar with and desire in using them. QR codes, however, cannot be used exclusively or as a substitution for the state-required language on your label.

Given the proliferation of social media and the heavy dependence upon it by many CFOs, cleverly deciding upon a name can be echoed in your social media handle, your website URL (universal resource locator), your packaging, then turned into your business card. We'll cover more on the social media and advertising in chapter 12.

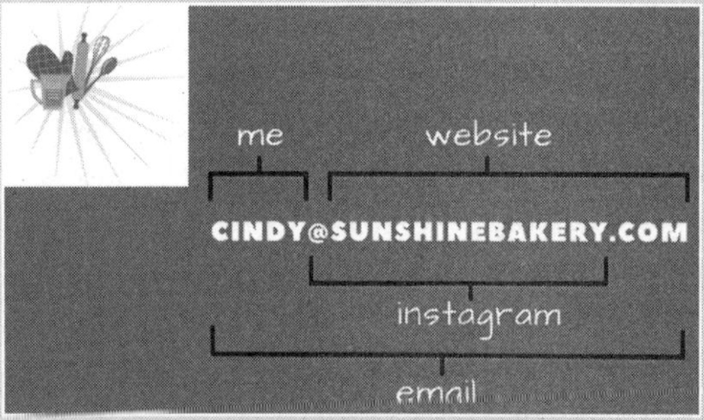

Bonus points for CFOs who are clever and creative with a business card that incorporates their name, website, email, and Instagram handle (the unique link to your profile).

CREDIT: JOHN D. IVANKO

Logo: Picturing Your Product, Company, or Brand

Whether it's a symbol, a graphic, a word, or a creative combination of two or three of these, a logo helps define your company and its products and makes your products more memorable to your customers. A logo can be as simple as Nike's swoosh or as intricate as Harvard University's shield with its Latin motto, *Veritas*. While you don't need one to operate a business successfully, a logo can help, especially as you expand. A well-designed logo lends credibility and an aura of professionalism, and may help reinforce your price strategy if it's on the higher side compared to your competition.

When designing your logo, consider how and where you might be using it. Will you be paying to reproduce it in four colors on a label, or photocopying it in black and white at the top of your solicitation letterhead? Maybe you'll be doing both color and black and white. Detailed logos can rarely be reduced to small sizes on product labels and still be legible.

For basic low-cost logo options, review various online logo makers such as LogoGenie (logogenie.com) or Graphic Springs (graphicsprings.com). These websites walk you through the logo design process for free online. If you like what you created, you can download the final art for less than $10.

Putting a face to her food products, Delights by Dawn logo featuring Dawn Belisle. See the story profile on page 238.

CREDIT: DELIGHTS BY DAWN

Slogan

- "The Freshest in the Business"
- "Bottling up Nature"
- "Quality. Taste. Baked right, every time."

Similar to a logo, but written as text, a slogan, or tag line, captures in a phrase what your business is about in a memorable, catchy, and creative way, with the intent of helping close a sale. If you distilled your product to its essence, what words would you use to describe it?

Also like a logo, a slogan, while not required, can help position your products in the minds of your customers and reinforce the personality of the brand you're creating. If you say "fair and balanced" enough, people believe it (even if it isn't necessarily true). Can you complete these sentences?

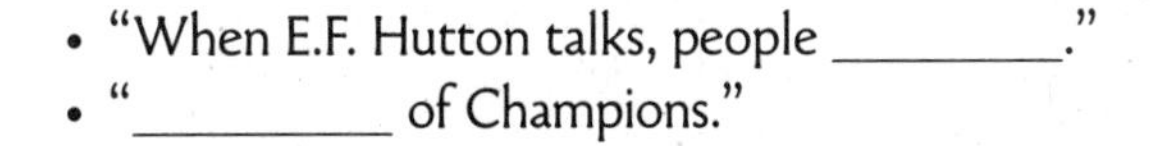

- "When E.F. Hutton talks, people ________."
- "_________ of Champions."

If you can't fill in the blanks of both slogans, it means either you weren't alive when they were used or you weren't in the target market for these products.

When working at a large ad agency in Chicago years ago, we became familiar with the expression "selling the sizzle, not the steak." In some cases, the actual product attributes themselves were tangential to the messaging and claims made about the product. We were creating a personality or image around an item, a national brand, and having that personality carry over to the product itself, so people would be persuaded to buy it next time they needed a box of cereal. What does a cartoon character have to do with a nourishing way to start your day with a cereal breakfast? The answer is, it doesn't really matter, so long as the customer feels the emotions and connects them with a certain product so that as a result they select one brand over another. Finish the sentence: "They're _______!"

Slogans can be used on your letterhead, website, beneath your company name, or tied to your logo in some way. They should be catchy and easy to remember. Home baker, Yuliya Childers, a speaker at the Home-based Food Entrepreneur Virtual National Conference, has "Flour + Water + Salt + Love" as her tag line for Wild Yeast Kitchen. Unlike your business name and logo, however, slogans can, and often do, change over the years. In 1979, Toyota proclaimed: "Oh, what a feeling!" Now, it's "Moving forward." So if you discover a more compelling slogan, perhaps something a customer says or if your product line expands, change it.

Just because your business is small, it doesn't mean it has to look or appear that way. With some thoughtful effort, your company and its brand can be just as memorable and valuable with the right combination of name, product design, and business logo.

7

Better Labels and Packaging That Increase Sales

CONGRATULATIONS! Now you have this fantastic-tasting, unique product and are ready to start selling. Onward to figuring out how to successfully get your items into the hands of what will eventually be loyal returning customers. There is a creative marketing art to this next step of labeling and packaging that can both increase your sales and provide an opportunity to express yourself.

Think of cottage food packaging as if you were wrapping a gift, something that will safely get your product to its destination and delight the taste buds of the recipient. As we'll explore in the next couple of chapters, sprinkling in a dash of strategic thought on how your final product looks from the eyes of your customer can go a long way in making a sale. Many of us buy with our eyes, so what you're selling has to look great, not just taste great.

Identify Packaging Goals

From bags to cellophane wrap to boxes, you will find a wealth of options for packaging your products. Before ordering anything, check with your state regarding any packaging requirements. Typically, states tend to focus on the label not packaging. A state could, for example, require an item to be fully wrapped if you are selling at a farmers' market.

We'll go over some specifics on actual design in chapter 8, but the following goals should be met by your packaging.

Protection

Before we talk about the fun side of cute and engaging packaging, don't forget an important element of packaging is that your item gets your cake pops, brownies, cookies, or cupcakes to their end

Commercial bakeries love to add the word "homemade" on their products, but with ingredients like aluminum phosphate and diglycerides, they are anything but! Celebrate the authenticity of your products as being truly homemade through your choice of label and packaging. Credit: Lisa Kivirist

destination safely while preserving the integrity of the product. This can range from your customer taking hamburger buns home from the farmers' market to a larger custom cookie order that must stay perfectly intact, not broken, chipped, crumbled, or crushed.

Think about the type of product and how to best get it to its destination. For crispy goods like pizzelle cookies, the packaging should both protect these brittle items and keep them crispy. Others, like moist muffins, can stain a package if it isn't the right material. Be sure to do some test runs with your packaging before showtime to make sure it's working as you want.

Communication

What packaging will best showcase the yummy side of your product, highlighting the quality ingredients and time you put into producing this unique item? For decorated sugar cookies, a clear cellophane wrap will feature your designs. If you have multiple identical items, such as a dozen muffins or a bag of crackers, your customer would just need to see a sample.

Professionalism

Try to not use anything currently in your kitchen as packaging. Yes, it's time to upgrade from what you use for your kids' lunch box. You are running a cottage food operation, not just selling at a school bake sale. We'll talk more on economical packaging ideas in the next chapter and ways to increase your professionalism. Operating from your home kitchen doesn't mean your products are in any way inferior to what might be made or sold by a bricks-and-mortar bakery or found in an upscale gift shop. If anything, yours are better. And packaging matters.

Labeling

Great news. The cottage food law for your state should dictate what must be on the label. If you're not selling wholesale, you won't need those UPC symbols or the product nutritional information panel you see on packaged goods. While not required by many states' cottage food laws, a weight measurement can be added; note, however, that weight is always net, referring only to the contents and not the packaging.

One role of the label is to specifically capture and reflect your state's requirements for your product. Their goal is to protect the customer by ensuring transparency between you and them. While states may be very

specific in terms of the mandatory verbiage on labels, they generally do not detail anything related to aesthetics and creative aspects, fonts, colors, graphics, or other brand-related design elements. That's where you can add your creative touch.

In general, most states require label language such as the following examples.

- A statement like: "This product was made in a private home not subject to state licensing or inspection." Or "Manufactured in a home kitchen." The exact wording is usually specified by your state.
- A list of ingredients in order of greatest to least use by weight, including any allergens. The eight most common allergens are milk, eggs, fish, crustacean shellfish, tree nuts, wheat, peanuts, or soybeans.
- The date the item was made.
- Your name/business name and contact information, which may include your home address.

Only food companies with "annual gross sales made or business done in sales to consumers that is not more than $500,000 or have annual gross sales made or business done in sales of food to consumers of not more than $50,000 are exempt" from nutritional labeling requirements, according to the FDA; for lots more detail, see their website, fda.gov.

UPC Codes for Wholesale Customers

A universal product code, or UPC, is a series of bars and 12-digit numbers, Global Trade Item Number, unique to each packaged item you may sell, issued by the GS1 US Partner Connections Program (gs1us.org). Though they are not required by law, UPCs are usually a necessity if you offer your products wholesale to retailers and distributors, as they allow these customers to store, stock, and track sales of your items. These codes can also be secured and printed by companies like ABB Labels (abblabels.com) or Simply Barcodes (upccode.net). Each UPC code includes both a manufacturer identification number and a unique item code. Note that UPCs are different from Stock Keeping Units or SKUs, covered in section 5.

While often not explicitly required by many state cottage food laws, it's advisable to take extra precautions by labeling your product and identifying any allergens, such as milk, eggs, tree nuts, soy, peanuts, and wheat. For example, if they have allergens in their kitchen, many CFOs elect to add a sentence like "Made in a facility that processes peanuts, soy, and wheat." For most operators working from a home kitchen, this would be the case.

Be careful about any health claims you make on your label or in any marketing materials. If you say that your product reduces the risk of a disease or medical condition, this claim must be approved by the United States FDA, a process both highly involved and complicated. If you claim that an ingredient improves a function, such as "calcium builds strong bones," you will need to compile legitimate research from reputable and neutral sources. If you make a nutrient content claim—such as your muffins are high in fiber, low in fat, or low-glycemic—the package must have a full nutritional label that could be more complicated and costly than you may want.

Beyond including state cottage food requirements, the label design is usually up to you. Thanks to color printers and various self-adhesive label options for home printing, if you have some computer mastery, take great photographs, or have talent as an illustrator, you can pull off a homespun label in very small quantities to stick to your jars, boxes, containers, or tins, whatever their size.

If you have enough volume, however, there are many options for printing professional-looking labels on par with anything you'd find at a supermarket or specialty food store. Thanks to breakthroughs in digital printing, Lightning Labels (lightninglabels.com), Wizard Labels (wizardlabels.com), PrintRunner (printrunner.com), and YourLabelsNow (yourlabelsnow.com) quickly produce smaller print runs at reasonable prices.

Safely Packaging a Powerful Punch Line

With your name, label, and logo in hand, the next step is packaging your item in a way that ensures its quality, safety, and compelling presentation. One thing is certain—as much as possible, your packaging should allow the customer to see your product. People eat with their eyes first.

By their very nature, many specialty food products and cottage food items are impulse purchases. You could be selling muffins at a community event where hungry kids tug at a mother's sleeve or setting out stacks of your granola bars at a Little League game. Besides being able to see what

your product looks like, having a professional and engaging package and label can be the difference between landing or missing a sale.

Whether or not your state law specifically requires product packaging, safely wrap your item for three compelling reasons:

- sturdy packaging prevents food contamination
- it ensures a more protected transport of your product to prevent breakage or damage
- unique packaging can be a marketing advantage

The first and most important issue is food safety. Wrapping your product makes sure it will not be exposed to the elements, either as you transport it to your sales venue or customer or when your customer brings it home or delivers it to its destination.

Your style or design of packaging depends on what you're selling, but it's especially relevant to baked goods, candy, and anything what won't already be in a jar, like jam. For your first sale when you're testing things out, sure use plastic bags or things you have at home already. But as soon as you sell more product, amp up your professionalism and check out a bakery packaging supply outlet to order bulk bags or various-sized cardboard pastry boxes.

Thoughtful, colorful packaging draws customers in and can showcase your product. For baked and other goods, the range of packaging options can be overwhelming. There are clear plastic sleeves, paper bags, display boxes, decorative tins, and for the eco-minded, corn- or soy-based biodegradable alternatives. Each has a cost that needs to be considered when fixing the price for your product, a subject covered in the next chapter.

If you're selling baked goods directly, perhaps by delivering them to an office, large boxes might be a good choice. You might even explore reusable plastic delivery boxes, with a deposit that comes in the form of a discount off a future order. If you're selling a fancy edible cookie bouquet for the holidays or anniversaries, then a food-grade basket and plastic wrap might make the most sense.

Some packaging costs more. You'll have to decide if it's worth it to elicit an impulse buy or increase sales. You can buy cupcake boxes that hold two cupcakes in an insert and come with a carrying handle and a window, a plastic section on one side so you can see what's inside. These can cost up

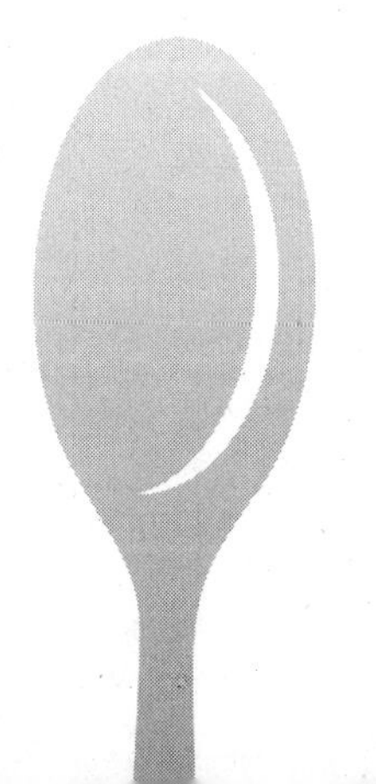

to one dollar each but may make your customer feel like they have received a beautifully wrapped present. If you're selling at a market or event and someone is carrying around that cute box, they may serve as a free walking advertisement for your product. Adding a piece of colorful tissue paper in a bakery box may add a frilly gift appeal.

"The whole presentation, the pink box, the ribbons, the way it was put together was really, really cool. Everyone loved it."

—Harmonie Kuhl, Corona, California, a customer raving about Cookies Your Way

Because standard boxes for baked goods come blank, don't forget to add a sticker label or stamp that displays your business name and contact info prominently, so customers can reorder or have a quick reference for referrals, in addition to meeting any state label requirements.

For canned items, glass jars work perfectly; they are, by default of health and safety issues addressed by hot water bath processing, the only way such goods can be sold. But you can still add a little frugal extra to dress these jars up and boost your item's perceived value. We'll cover dressing up your jars in detail in chapter 9.

Four Basics of Product Labeling

Moving beyond what is required for your label based on your state's cottage food law, think of your label as the welcome mat for your product: the primary means to quickly communicate what your product is, its ingredients, and your brand. It should entice customers to pick it up and engage more and beg to be purchased. We so often eat with our eyes, so make the label and packaging pop.

The following elements are part of an effective cottage food product label.

Include Easy Contact Information

In addition to being a welcome mat, your label also serves as your business card and an easy tool to keep repeat customers while generating new ones. For whatever means you want to be contacted for future orders—be it Facebook or Instagram, your website, email or a phone number—include that information clearly on your label.

Including this contact information on your label is especially important should your product be given as a gift. While most cottage food products are indeed consumed by the purchaser, some may also be given as a thank-you gift for a teacher or a housewarming gift for a new neighbor. Embrace this opportunity for new customers by making it easy for them to contact you after they've enjoyed your product.

Showcase Small Batches

Celebrate the simple but important fact that you are not producing high volumes of those decorated sugar cookies or jars of strawberry jam. One easy way is by individually numbering each label by hand. First, count how many of a certain item you will be selling, such as five loaves of sourdough bread. Hand-write on the label, identifying each individual loaf of bread as "1 of 5," "2 of 5," etc. This—the same strategy you would find in an art gallery where a limited-edition fine art print is numbered and signed by the artist—creates a specialness about that loaf and an urgency to purchase at a premium price.

This idea works best if you are selling at a market or public event where your primary sales are coming from impulse buyers when they read the label and realize that sourdough loaf is one of a batch of six and there's only two left, they may be motivated to buy it quickly before they're gone.

We number the jars in each small batch of our bread and butter pickles to communicate the special limited offering.

CREDIT: JOHN D. IVANKO PHOTOGRAPHY

Sprinkle in Both Personal and Consistent Branding

Your label can be an easy means to tell your personal story as well as the brand and values of your business. Your brand is what sets your product apart and is the big reason you choose the labels and packaging you do.

This approach to branding was taken with our Pucker Up Pickles. We're a small family-run business, and when our son, Liam, was growing up, he would always be with us at markets, engaging customers and helping at the booth. Our Pucker Up Pickles label featured Liam making a cute face expressing the tart flavor of this product. Attendees would often pick up the jar and easily engage in conversation with Liam, asking if that's him on the label. And not surprisingly, these conversations often led to a sale as people love that direct connection, along with supporting a family business.

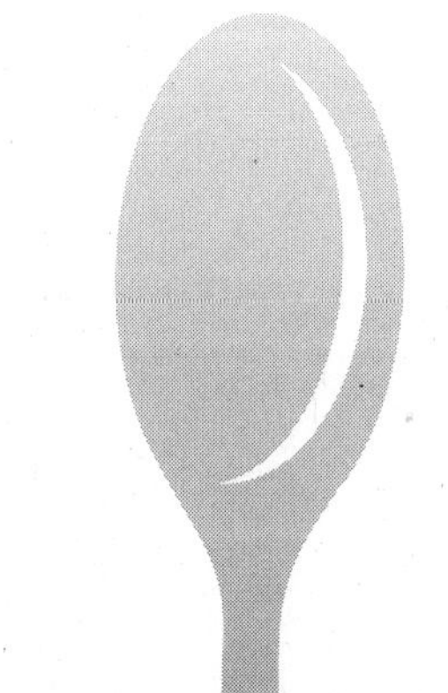

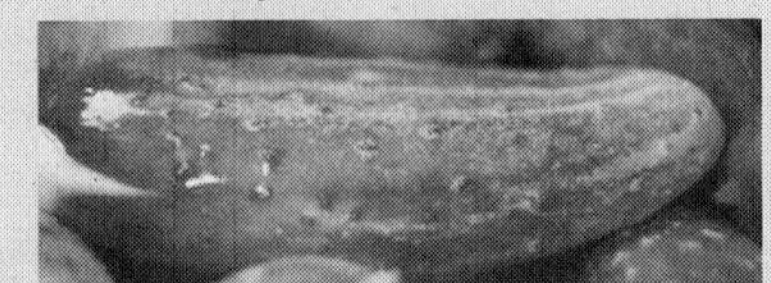

Our Pucker Up label for our pickles showcase the fun family-run aspect of our farm business, Inn Serendipity.
CREDIT: JOHN D. IVANKO PHOTOGRAPHY

Your label can also showcase the unique and quality ingredients you devote to your product. While your state's labeling requirements will include an ingredient list, remember to highlight those that make your item extra special. Do you use organic squash you grew on your farm? Or if you buy ingredients from specific local farms, give them a shout-out.

Tie in your logo color scheme on your label. Steer away from boring black and white, unless that is part of your slick ultra-modern brand. When first starting out, we didn't have a color printer and only printed a few labels. We'd quickly add a pop of color with some hand drawings, using markers or rubber stamps, that showcased the handmade, small-batch artisan feel.

Place Label to Showcase the Product, Not Cover It Up

Unless your state's requirements indicate differently, you can choose where to place the actual label. Think about what is the most effective placement strategy, based on your product.

Sometimes the product itself is so attractive you don't want to cover it up with a label, such as decorated sugar cookies or the bright red of strawberry jam. For example, one clever way to cover the labeling requirements is to use the top and bottom of the jars for the product name, ingredient

list, and other necessary verbiage. In this way, your customers can see your wonderfully preserved relish or pickles.

To make the task of packaging more practical, the next chapter will illustrate numerous ways to enhance yours with step-by-step ideas, some crafted from supplies you might already have in your kitchen cupboard.

Bottom of the jar label, with required information presented per the cottage food law in your state, like the date, name of person doing the production, and the "private home" disclaimer line.
CREDIT: JOHN D. IVANKO

Top of the jar labels from Equinox Community Farm, with key information presented, including company and product name. CREDIT: JOHN D. IVANKO

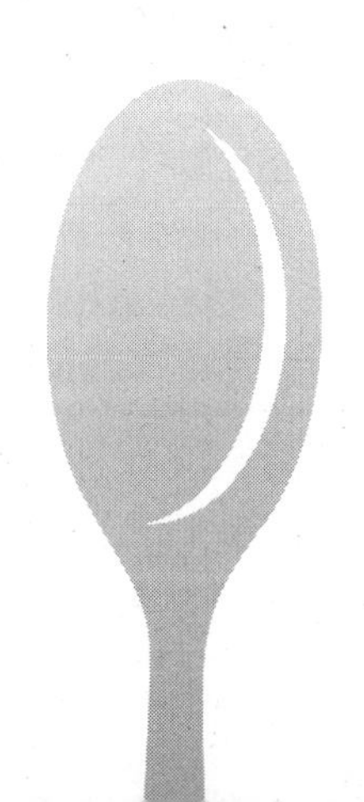

8

Packaging Ideas to Increase Sales

YOU MIGHT ONLY be bringing a few dozen muffins to the farmers' market, but that doesn't mean they can't look like they came off the shelves of a fancy bakery store. Those chocolate truffles may have been made in your modest apartment kitchen, but you know their hand-crafted taste rivals any gourmet specialty retailer. In these cases, making the successful connection between that potential customer strolling by and you landing the sale is often the packaging.

DIY cookie decorating kits provide the ultimate in convenience to a busy mom and a fun activity for the family during the holidays. Jessica Rae McPherson, owner of Baked with Love Cookie Shop, sold so many over the Christmas holiday that she's planning to do them for other holidays as well. CREDIT: JESSICA RAE MCPHERSON/BAKED WITH LOVE COOKIE SHOP

In this chapter, we'll detail specific cost-effective ideas for packaging products such as bakery treats, candies, dry mixes, and other non-hazardous items. In the following chapter, we'll focus on jarred products and cover ideas on how to pretty up those jars of everything from blueberry jam to bread and butter pickles. Considering most baked goods sales at a market are impulse buys, how they are packaged can go a long way in nailing the sale.

Fortunately, there are many cost-effective, creative packaging options through which you can showcase your brand and personality. Packaging is your chance to tell the story of your product. The effort you take to design, package, and display your goods correlates with customer expectations and should reflect the care, love, and pride that went into making them. Your choice of packaging and display echoes your brand and its uniqueness.

Three Purchase Scenarios: Impulse, Gifts, Snacks

Let's cover how packaging affects three different purchase scenarios.

Impulse Buys

Especially when creating the packaging for your market display, focus on a professional, detailed-oriented, and personalized look. These three aspects working together will showcase your products so that any passerby can tell that they were made with care and dedication. Having a professional appearance in packaging at a market stand tells everyone that you take your products seriously and they can expect the very best. Details like adding a pop of color with a ribbon or a handwritten element showcase why your product is different than what you'll find on a supermarket shelf.

A fun example of that is how we sell Lisa's Latvian sourdough rye bread through our Inn Serendipity Fresh Baked Homemade Bakery. Rye bread baking is rooted in Lisa's heritage. In Latvia and Estonia, where her parents immigrated from, rye bread is a culinary tradition reaching back thousands of years. This version of Latvian sourdough rye—*saldskaaba maize* in Latvian—offers a dense, hearty sweet and sour flavor, perfect with a slab of butter, cheese, or sausage. In the homeland, the rye is often paired with herring.

A simple red-and-white ribbon wrap adds a Latvian flag vibe to Lisa's traditional saldskaaba maize, *Latvian sourdough rye bread. It just so happens, red and white are also the colors of the University of Wisconsin Badgers.*

Credit: John D. Ivanko Photography

With Lisa a first-generation Baltic-American baker, that loaf comes with a story of history and cultural perseverance, along with a quality product. The loaf itself weighs one and a half pounds. We package the bread, about an eight-by-four-inch loaf, in gallon-sized clear cellophane bags wrapped in a wide red ribbon with a white strip through the middle, an accurate representation of the Latvian flag!

A fun plot twist is the fact that we live in Wisconsin with a big fandom for the University of Wisconsin Badgers whose colors also happen to be have red and white. Our community is naturally drawn to those colors, which especially inspires engagement at markets. It gives Lisa a story to share about how those colors actually don't represent the University of Wisconsin but her culture and culinary history. The simple packaging engages and generates sales. People buy from people they connect with, and this gives Lisa a story to share of her homeland. Add in the fact that these loaves take 48 hours with fermentation time, and we typically sell out of these premium priced loaves at markets.

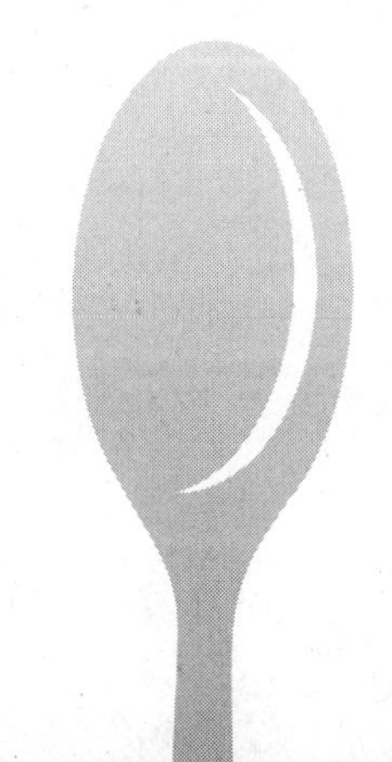

Packaging several mini items together makes a lovely gift parcel. CREDIT: JOBEA MURRAY, JOBEA BAKES

Gifts for Others

Cottage food products are often given as gifts, particularly those that are gift-ready with attractive packaging. Would you rather have another bauble for your bookshelf or a cocoa bomb? We rest our case. Strategic, special, and cost-effective touches elevate those muffins to a housewarming party gift. Nothing says "I care" more than a delicious, thoughtful edible gift.

Snacks

Attractive individual packaging in cellophane bags is perfect for hungry shoppers looking for a snack. While as a cottage food vendor you are not licensed to do food service, you can package small amounts or single serving-sized items that probably won't make it home from the market. Examples include cake pops, biscotti, or small packs of caramel corn.

Display Your Values

How can you use your packaging to truly express your values as a business and person? For us, running an organic farm powered by renewable energy, sustainability, and stewarding the Earth reflect our core values, both in our business and personally. We're increasingly finding we're not alone. Having eco-friendly packaging is vital. It is one way to do your part to reduce or eliminate landfill waste while also creating marketing appeal with shoppers wanting to support businesses with a conservation commitment. A growing number of suppliers offer reasonable quantities of products made with recycled-content materials, items that are able to be easily recycled or even made from compostable materials.

Adding personal details like these to your products doesn't have to be time-consuming or complex; a little goes a long

Home baker Sol Cruz's indoor market display perfectly captures her brand and company name, Home Sweet Bakery, based in Lake Worth, Florida. On her Facebook page, she asks "How can I make your life sweeter?" She takes preorders online and sells at pop-ups around town. CREDIT: SOL I. CRUZ/HOME SWEET BAKERY

way. If you use twist ties, tie a ribbon around the top for added color and style.

Add a simple band of paper or ribbon around basic items, like a loaf of French bread, for an extra eye-catching look. CREDIT: JOHN D. IVANKO PHOTOGRAPHY

Encyclopedia of Packaging Options

The good news is that there is an increasing wealth of packaging options and materials. The Launch a Farmstead Bakery: Recipes and Resources, found on this book's website, has a downloadable spreadsheet with various packaging suppliers that cater to smaller-scale orders and are made of recycled content or are compostable.

Cellophane

Think of cellophane as the professional version of grocery store plastic wrap that can instantly amp your professionalism yet keep that homespun appeal. Cellophane is a plant-based material. The "cello" in cellophane stands for cellulose, the structural component of plants. Cellulose film can be made from a variety of natural sources, including wood, cotton, hemp, and corn.

Make sure you are using a food-grade version of cellophane. There's the food-grade cellophane used in the packaging we'll talk about in the following examples but also a non-food-grade version instead for gift wrapping and crafts.

Cellophane bags come in every imaginable size and are inexpensive, adding just a few cents to your product cost even if you order in small quantities. For example, small cellophane bags can be used to package individual cookies that warrant a higher price and potential gift sale than if you sold them in a dozen batch.

Another reason to use food-grade bags is the ability to seal them with a heat sealer. This saves you time, particularly on large custom orders. Most cellophane bags work with a heat sealer, but be sure to check with the manufacturer. A heat sealer that saves you money and adds to your profit margin is also a full business deductible expense. See chapter 18 for more on managing expenses.

Cellophane bags easily add a professional look to your products. CREDIT: JOHN D. IVANKO PHOTOGRAPHY

Inexpensive parchment preserves your product and communicates homemade. CREDIT: JOHN D. IVANKO PHOTOGRAPHY

The flat bottom of gusset-style bags allows you to pack more product. CREDIT: JOHN D. IVANKO PHOTOGRAPHY

Parchment

Parchment paper is cellulose, eco-friendly, plant-based paper that has been treated to make it nonstick and moisture resistant. Parchment can be readily used for an extra layer of protection, especially if you are worried that an item might bleed into and stain say a cardboard box. Lisa lines cardboard bakery boxes with parchment when she packs the butter-heavy Alexander Cake to avoid that unappealing look.

Parchment is available in various precut sizes for easy wrapping of larger bread loaves. A simple parchment paper wrap, fabric wrap, and twine tie make an ordinary bread loaf very eye-appealing.

Parchment also comes in sandwich bag size that works well for cookies and small nibbles, especially products that probably will be eaten immediately after purchased. A little ribbon and a bright label dress up a simple bag to make it look like a package worthy of gift-giving.

Gusset Bags

Gusset is an industry term for a bag with a panel that folds, especially used to make a bag bigger. Gusset bags have a flat bottom so they can readily stand up on their own and expand to include more items. Coffee bags come with a clear window that nicely displays your product and are typically lined to keep freshness.

These bags are also good for packaging the following products:

- Granola
- Crackers
- Croutons
- Roasted coffee
- Various mixes

Bakery Boxes

Bakery boxes remain the ultimate in professional packaging. While they do add cost, their sales appeal may be well worth the price.

A great example of bakery boxes taking an item from average to special and gift worthy is this bundt cake in a small box (below). That item is basically the same amount of batter as one muffin, but between the appealing bundt shape and cute box, your profit margins increase. These bakery boxes pictured are made out of natural kraft paper, unbleached and compostable.

There are times when a premium bakery box is warranted. This harvest-themed bakery box (below right) includes a unique cutout of autumn shapes, laid up against a cellophane window so the box is fully sealed. It's a unique box, again worthy of gift-giving, that may warrant the $1.50 price. Lisa uses these types of bakery boxes with cutouts for her

Bakery boxes transform those muffins into a treat worthy of gift-giving for special occasions.
Credit: John D. Ivanko Photography

The right box can catapult a simple item into a premium-priced gift.
Credit: John D. Ivanko Photography

Unique boxes increase the price you can charge for your premium products. Credit: John D. Ivanko Photography

Communicate fresh from the kitchen with a coffee filter wrap.
CREDIT: JOHN D. IVANKO PHOTOGRAPHY

Alexander Cake special orders. With the higher ingredients' costs for raspberry and currant jelly, along with the time-consuming nature of the recipe, she charges a higher price of $25 for a dozen small bars. As a premium product, the box investment is worth it.

Coffee Filters

Sometimes with a dose of creativity, some inexpensive kitchen items you probably already have can add professional packaging polish, such as basket-shaped coffee filters. These mini bread loaves are wrapped in coffee filters tied together with a bow, adding a homespun, unexpected touch.

Keep an Inventory

Avoid stress by keeping an inventory of your packaging on hand. With constant pressures on our global supply channels, you never know when a certain item will be out of stock. Nothing is more stressful than having a large order and you don't have enough of the right packaging. Having extra inventory on hand can help alleviate that.

You may already have an amazing tasting product, from classic chocolate chip cookies to unique ethnic specialties that no one could find anywhere else, like Lisa's Baltic treats. Think of packaging as a means to truly make what you created shine and look and taste the very best. Like the right frame around a painting, the right packaging simply enhances the beauty and quality that is already there.

In the next chapter, we'll take a closer look at ideas for your jams, salsas, and pickles—those high-acid canned items—as jars come with their set of variables to create a visually appealing product.

9

Amp Up Your Jams and Other Jarred Products

Now let's turn to a distinctly different aspect of packaging, jarred products. For those selling high-acid items like salsas, dill pickles, or rhubarb jam, the product must be processed in a canning jar per tested recipes to keep it safe. Or you might see dry mixes in a canning jar, such as attractively layered ingredients for making cookies. Occasionally you'll see canning jars used for premium packaging for a special event where your clients may want to pay more for the impressive factor of a jar, such as favors at a trendy farmstead wedding event.

This chapter delves into details on simple, yet effective, ways to create a unique jar that will catch a customer's eye and result in a purchase. By adding your personal, creative touch to the already artisanal nature of a cottage food product, you catapult it way above the product in the jar. It's a gift, a visual treat leading to a tasty experience, whether the customer ends up eating it themselves or sharing it as a gift.

We use hand-written signage with chalk on a mini-blackboard to communicate the homemade, farm-fresh appeal of our pickles. Credit: John D. Ivanko Photography

One bonus of selling canned items: shelf life. Whatever goes unsold can be brought to the next market. That's not the case with baked goods. If the packs of muffins don't sell out, that package and corresponding cost is lost. For baked goods at markets or pop-up events, you'll need a plan for what to do with any unsold items, covered in chapter 12, like flash sales, sample donations to prospective customers, or freezing them to enjoy during your next family holiday celebration.

Generating Attractive Labels

Consider the canning jar not just as a container for your product but as an opportunity to communicate your authentic brand, your identity. For farms, this means you are selling a piece, a taste, of your farm experience—packaged in a jar. It's an opportunity to connect with your customers emotionally, to share values that lead to loyalty that then adds up to a profitable business for you.

There's nothing ho-hum about your products. So, avoid boring and nondescript white labels with black type slapped on jars with packing tape. Give your product the professional look it deserves. With today's improved printers, along with more options for preformatted labels, you can readily create a professional-looking label right at home.

If you're just printing a small amount, companies like Avery Custom Labels offers a wide variety of shapes and sizes specifically designed for small-batch processing. They also offer free online template software for creating your label. For our high-acid canned items, we use Avery Print-to-the-Edge Glossy Oval Labels True Print 22820, the larger 2-inch by 3⅓-inch size fits nicely on both half-pint and pint jars. We add the required state verbiage "around" the perimeter of the label, which you can readily do with the Avery template. This approach meets our state's label requirement.

There's a balance between your products looking too slick and professional and overly informal and homespun. The fact that your product is crafted by hand in small batches compared to a mass-produced item from big food conglomerates is something to showcase in your product.

"Think carefully about what message, what story, you want to communicate about your farm or home business and how that can play out in the packaging of your product," offers Brett Olson, Creative Director at Renewing the Countryside, a Minnesota-based nonprofit that supports farmers in a variety of training and programs. Are you more minimalist and modern, or playful and informal? "From the font you choose for your labels to the colors of additional elements like ribbon or fabric, these choices communicate to potential customers what you are about."

However you may use them, canning jars add a premium price to your product. If you sell at a regular market with loyal customers who love your

strawberry jam, you can add an incentive to return their jars for you to reuse. Perhaps you can offer a discount on your customer's next purchase or an added freebie of a different item as a sample, like a cookie.

Adding Effective Visual Appeal to Jars

Simple, effective add-ons can literally "add on" to your sales by attracting customers to your visually appealing jars. Depending on the look you are aiming for and the market venue you will be selling at, consider the following creative ideas.

Jar Toppers

A fabric circle adhered to the top of your jar adds color and creates a homespun yet premium look. When deciding what fabrics to use, consider these two design ideas.

- Select similar color families and patterns. It's appealing to the eye to have patterns from one color family or theme. This creates a more professional look. Don't hesitate to use different patterns for each of your products to make them easy to differentiate, especially when setting up your display and packing up at the end of the event.
- Choose seasonal-themed patterns for winter market sales. At the end of this chapter, we'll cover the creation of gift baskets, a way to add value and increase that premium price even more.

Don't be afraid to mix it up with the cloth pattern toppers. Different designs can add a whimsical touch to your display at market. You could even make different types of pickles correspond with different patterns, to make it easier at the market to sort out the bread and butter sweet pickles from the sour dills.

CREDIT: JOHN D. IVANKO PHOTOGRAPHY

Adding a topper with a holly or snowflake pattern increases the incentive for someone to buy these as gifts or stocking stuffers.

CREDIT: JOHN D. IVANKO PHOTOGRAPHY

Follow these easy steps to add fabric toppers to your jars.

Step 1: Create a template pattern, either an 8-inch circle for pint jars or 6-inch circle for half- or quarter-pint jars.

You can either cut out a heavy-duty cardboard circle as a template or use a plate or container lid of the appropriate size. CREDIT: JOHN D. IVANKO PHOTOGRAPHY

Step 2: Use this template to draw a circle with a marker on the back-side of your fabric. Cut out the circle.

Pinking shears, with a serrated blade, add an interesting zigzag edge and help prevent fraying. CREDIT: JOHN D. IVANKO PHOTOGRAPHY

Step 3: Use a hot glue gun to add a dot of glue to the middle of each jar lid.

Place the center of the fabric circle on the glue dot. This helps keep the fabric on the lid and makes it easier to attach the tie (Step 4). CREDIT: JOHN D. IVANKO PHOTOGRAPHY

Step 4: This last step is easier as a two-person job: One holds the glued fabric tightly down and around the edge of the jar while the other person ties a ribbon around the tight fabric.

Teamwork allows the second person to tie a tight knot. CREDIT: JOHN D. IVANKO PHOTOGRAPHY

For a more rustic look, use twine instead of ribbon. CREDIT: JOHN D. IVANKO PHOTOGRAPHY

Cut-out Paper Toppers

A cut-out paper circle on the top of a jar adds color and creates a clean modern look. Using various colors of the same pattern can be eye-catching, as seen with the chevron pattern, as pictured.

Step 1: Using a clean jar lid, trace the exact size circle on to your paper.

Cut out the paper circle.
Credit: John D. Ivanko Photography

Step 2: Place circle on top of the lid and screw on the band.

No glue is needed to attach paper topper.
Credit: John D. Ivanko Photography

Step 3: Experiment with similar patterns in different colors.

Complimentary colors can spice up the display. CREDIT: JOHN D. IVANKO PHOTOGRAPHY

Baking Cups

Standard-sized paper baking cups work well as toppers for jars with regular sized lids (not wide-mouth). With the increasing variety of colorful cups on the market thanks to the cupcake craze, lots of options are available at craft stores with larger cake decorating departments.

Paper toppers can be changed and replaced, so you can readily modify your jars to tie into a Christmas market or other holidays, like red for Valentine's Day or orange for Halloween. CREDIT: JOHN D. IVANKO PHOTOGRAPHY

Burlap readily adds a popular shabby chic aesthetic to your product. CREDIT: JOHN D. IVANKO PHOTOGRAPHY

Washi tape, a high-quality masking tape made of rice paper, is very attractive, yet the low-tack adhesive makes it extremely versatile and easy to use and stick. CREDIT: JOHN D. IVANKO PHOTOGRAPHY

Here are two other simple ideas to add a hand-crafted, creative touch to your product.

- Wide ribbon wrap: Add a wide ribbon around the jar's center; affix with a hot glue gun. Place label on top of the jar.
- Washi tape: In the hip and unexpected element category, wrap washi tape around your jar for an easy pop of color.

Combining Items to Create Attractive Holiday Gift Baskets

Holiday markets offer the potential for higher pricing and increased sales volume for canned items. Everyone is in a festive shopping mood, and shoppers might likely be willing to pay more for special pickles for their mother-in-law at Christmas than for an average family supper. Grouping a few items together in a basket adds value.

Keep an eye out at Goodwill or garage sales throughout the year for inexpensive baskets. CREDIT: JOHN D. IVANKO PHOTOGRAPHY

The following two simple design ideas can increase holiday sales:

- Incorporate natural elements, such as pinecones or dried greenery, to add seasonal charm to baskets.
- Change jar toppers to holiday-themed patterns and ribbons.

Wired garland ribbon adds whimsical sparkle. Credit: John D. Ivanko Photography

Label and Package Efficiently

Keep sales and profit your number one goal as you plan how to manage your time in creating your jar packaging. Your time management plays a big role here in your bottom line, so keep the following in mind:

Use Your Off-season, Slower Time

A big bonus when selling canned products is you can readily do both your processing and packaging ahead of time, on your own schedule. This avoids the "night before market stress" that cottage food producers go through by default of having to make fresh items close to the event, often at night or early in the morning.

If canned items include your home-grown ingredients, summer undoubtedly racks up as your busiest time for dealing with bushels of fresh seasonal abundance. Focus your energy on just processing and canning these goods. Keep records of your batch processing per your state's requirements, but deal with other issues in the off-season.

Use the dormant winter months to create your labeling and adding other design elements. But what if your blueberry jam brings in such high demand that you need to sell it as soon as you make it? You can still tap into the winter months to do some prep work such as cutting fabric toppers and measuring ribbon ties to save time during the busy summer season.

Create Systems

Having your supplies in one place ensures an efficient production process. Keep items specific to labeling and packaging in one place, such as the cardboard templates for fabric toppers.

Cut out and create multiple elements at a time. It's much easier and more efficient to cut the paper circles out at once and then place them on jars in one batch.

Enlist Help—and Make It Fun!

Sticking on labels and cutting out patterns is an easy way to involve children and other family members. This process helps kids to start understanding the entrepreneurial process and seeing how a product goes from "field to market."

The look of your product—its name, label, logo, packaging, and display—is just the start. In the following marketing chapters, we'll explore some of the other aspects of building a brand and growing a customer base eager to purchase your products and support you and your business.

10

Getting the Price Right

BY NOW, you realize that there's a lot more to a food product than the product itself. Sure, it has to taste great, but plenty of other factors determine whether customers will try your product and keep coming back for more. The right price can be a big part of the equation. It can be the difference, too, between actually making money and just having a hobby.

Business Expenses

Before getting into the nitty-gritty of pricing your product, you'll need to get some sense of what it may take to get your business off the ground from a financial perspective. Below is a breakdown of the three general types of business expenses we'll cover in greater detail in section 4: Organizing, Planning, and Managing the Business.

- Start-up expenses: including local and/or state licenses, registration fees, a possible fee for a required food handling course, educational materials, like this book or Lisa's Udemy online cottage food course, and new kitchen utensils or storage containers needed for the business
- Fixed expenses: while very limited, these could include the hosting cost for your website and domain name registration
- Variable expenses: including ingredients, packaging, gas for delivery, or rental fees for a booth or exhibitor table

Unlike a food company that produces their items in a commercial kitchen, licensed home kitchen, or rented space in a licensed facility, you don't have this expensive start-up or fixed overhead expense due to your state's cottage food law. You're working from home. However, because of your setup, you cannot deduct your utility costs (electricity or natural gas) or the use of home kitchen as business expenses since they are shared by others in your household.

Self-worth: Valuing Your Time and Skills

It's perhaps one of the more vexing issues of our day: How much are your time and skills worth? While the never-ending debate rages on about the minimum wage and exorbitant CEO salaries, when it comes to considering your labor involved in your business, can you get away with charging enough for your goods to pay yourself, too? Price your products too high, and you may only sell a few; price them too low, and you may not earn enough to pay for the ingredients or cover your labor. Economists call this "elasticity of demand": the relationship between price and quantity demanded by customers. Your market feasibility study, covered in chapter 14, will help you determine your product's fair market value. Ultimately, the customers decide. Many CFOs drop products from their menu that just aren't profitable enough to sell.

You may feel your hard work and skills are worth $50 an hour when decorating a four-tier wedding cake that takes about 12 hours to make and deliver. But what if where you live the going rate for a comparable wedding cake is only $350? This is far below your labor costs and other variable costs, including the high-quality ingredients you decided to use. If they're just starting out, some CFOs may proceed anyway, looking to grow customers by referrals, increase sales volume, and then, down the line, when they have a great reputation, raise prices to better reflect the costs and skilled labor involved.

Ultimately, your hourly rate is largely based on your culinary skills and ability to entice and attract customers who are happy to pay the rate you feel compensates you for what's involved, including order correspondence, invoicing, bookkeeping, cleaning, and making the item itself. In other words, if you make a great product, you just need to attract those customers that respect your work and who will happily pay for it. Anyone who owns an Apple product knows there are "cheaper" alternatives. Promotion to those who might purchase your product is as important as the product itself. This is why we've devoted so much space to promotion and marketing in this book. Cultivating a customer following who desire to purchase your product at a rate that covers your time and skills is essential of you don't want to work for free.

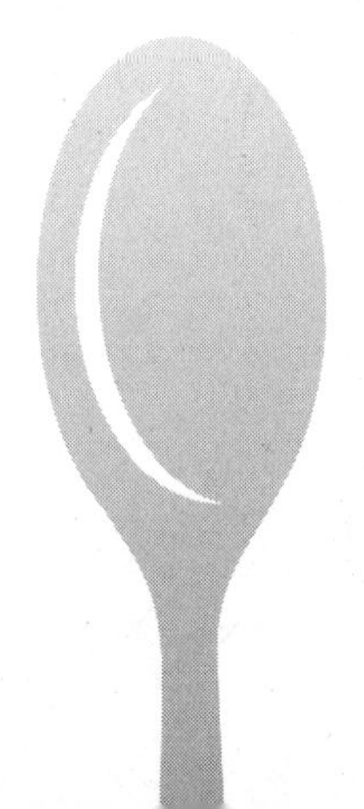

As explored previously, some of us define success beyond the merely financial. Maybe it's about time for delicious, local, and organic sourdough breads to be available where you live, but due to the realities of the economy, your customers are only willing to pay $4.50 per loaf. In cases like this, the joy of running your own business, making social connections, and a host of other considerations can compensate you in ways cold hard cash may never. Plus, when the economy picks up and ingredients get more expensive, you can raise your prices with it; economists call this relationship inflation.

Pricing Your Product

Now that you are aware of some of your business expenses and the tricky part of determining the value of your labor, you can consider how to price your product. Unfortunately, there's no steadfast rule, guideline, or principle for this.

The following are some of the ways to determine retail prices for food items sold directly to the public.

Parity Pricing

By far the easiest way to price your product is to just sell it for a little more or a little less than a similar product already sold in your community. If the going rate for a dozen muffins from an area bakery is $17, then your price could be about the same if you adopt this approach. Once your customers taste the difference, most will choose your better-tasting muffins.

This approach may hit a snag if you decide that your competition is the bakery department of a local supermarket, selling that same dozen muffins on special for $12 per dozen. It's unlikely they use the same quality ingredients and probably don't make them from scratch like you do. At this point, your product positioning, packaging, and other marketing come into play, to differentiate your product and justify the higher price you'll need to charge.

WHY DO COOKIES COST SO MUCH?

what goes into 1 dozen simple custom cookies

1/2 hour Customer Interaction	$7.50
1/2 hour research/design	$7.50
Cost of goods	$15.00
Packaging	$2.00
1/2 hour dough making	$7.50
1/2 hour cut/bake	$7.50
1/4 hour icing/mixing colors	$3.75
2 hours decorate	$30.00
1/2 hour photos/edits	$7.50
1/2 hour clean up	$7.50
What we should charge:	$95.75
What we actually charge:	$55.00

*based on $15 hour wage

Because our time is worth being paid correctly

@TheSpeakeasyBakingCo

Why do cookies cost so much? Because there's a lot that goes into making them. "I keep a hand written time log of everything I do," says BrieAnna Arteaga-Marcel, owner of The Speakeasy Baking Co., based in Oakley, California. "This helps me to average out my time spent on each step. This is the best way to price out your cookies based on your speed and skill level."
CREDIT: BRIEANNA ARTEAGA-MARCEL/THE SPEAKEASY BAKING CO.

Cost-input Calculation

A far more accurate way to price your item would be to add together your ingredient costs then multiply that by three to six times to cover your labor, packaging, overhead like electric or gas use, and delivery. The higher multiplier would account for the quality of your ingredients and other personal variables, such as more difficult recipes to prepare or the venue fees. To simplify this calculation, some CFOs just use the most expensive ingredients as a benchmark and go from there to calculate a fair retail price.

There are growing number of online and mobile apps that can help in capturing your ingredient costs, packaging, labor, and variable costs and even add in your desired profit margin for particular items. Some cost calculators may be simpler, but free, while others are more sophisticated and have a fee. A few of the more commonly used ones, which tend to be designed for home bakers and cake decorators, include CakeCost (cakecost.net), CookKeepBook (cookkeepbook.com), and ReciPal (recipal.com).

Many CFOs also create their own cost calculator using a spreadsheet program like Microsoft Excel. They use these calculators to make sure they're covering all their costs as well as their labor and talent. As mentioned previously, however, you still need to attract customers willing to pay the price you charge for a particular product. Many CFOs choose to not sell certain products because there is just not a market for them where they live.

Market Value

While related to parity pricing, market-value pricing carefully considers where you're selling your product. As we'll see in the next chapter, the distribution of your items may dictate what you're able to charge for them. Selling muffins at a weekly farmers' market where other vendors are competing with baked goods and edibles may be very different from selling them at a holiday bazaar where you have the only baked goods display and everyone is in a festive shopping mood; the holiday bazaar should naturally lend itself to higher prices.

The more high-end or upscale the event or place, the more you can charge, because in most cases, your customers will not be as price sensitive as people browsing the aisles for a deal or special. Don't underestimate the pricing power of attractive packaging. Dressing up your box with some ribbons and colorful fabric can reinforce your premium price.

Like buying stock in a company or investing in real estate, the price is determined by what someone is willing to pay. Your customer is always

queen or king. If your product is priced too high, what you sell doesn't match your target market's aspirations, or your packaging doesn't reflect your positioning well enough, you may find yourself returning home with what you made. Decisions about ingredients, packaging, and labeling play a direct role in determining the profitability of your product.

Never fear. Your market research and feasibility study will help you to better determine realistic pricing for your items. Don't feel you should, or even have to, compete on price. In most cases, your products will be far superior to most of the competition already in the market where you live because yours are homemade, fresh, or custom ordered. Whatever you do, don't pay people to buy your product because you are selling it for less than it is worth.

On the flip side, your products may be the only premium-priced items in the market, allowing you to command the top dollar from those customers eager to get their hands on something available nowhere else. Interestingly, there are people who, for various reasons, will only buy the most expensive item on a restaurant menu or at the jewelry store or winery. Justified or not, they equate quality with price. In marketing jargon, it's called a premium pricing strategy, also called "skimming," as in taking the cream off the top of a bottle of milk. If you can back up such an approach with your great-tasting product, why not? It's worked well for Apple, Tiffany, and Tesla for their respective products.

Lauren Cortesi, Bella's Desserts, Glenmoore, Pennsylvania

Name: Lauren Cortesi

Business: Bella's Desserts (Glenmoore, PA)

Website: https://bellasdesserts.com

Products: specialty cakes, cupcakes, and other desserts for weddings, birthdays, and other special events

Sales Venues: custom ordered by phone or email, then delivered or picked up by the customer

Gross Revenues: $20,000/year

Marketing Might After Two Decades of Selling Homemade Custom Wedding Cakes, Custom Cookies, and Specialty Cakes

With a wide grin of accomplishment, Lauren Cortesi is quick to say that it's been a long and wonderful journey. She's the sole owner of Bella's Desserts, operated out of her home kitchen in a quiet small town about an hour outside Philadelphia. As an award-winning cake designer, Cortesi could be among one of the longest-operating cottage food operators in the country, before "cottage food laws" and "cottage food operator" were even a thing. To this day, Pennsylvania does not have a specific cottage food statute. Rather, they have a law for a limited food establishment.

"I got started in 2002 because I was going stir crazy after making the decision to quit my career and be a stay-at-home mom," admits Cortesi, who named her business after her daughter, Bella. "Catering from home is illegal unless you have a separate kitchen, so I settled on baking because that is legal here." Since 1994, the state of Pennsylvania has allowed home-based food product entrepreneurs who produce certain non-hazardous products to operate as a "home food processor," later renamed "limited food establishment," licensed by the Pennsylvania Department of Agriculture.

Lauren Cortesi putting the final touches on her cake, made in her home kitchen.
CREDIT: LAUREN CORTESI

"My daughter was born allergic to dairy and eggs as well as other foods, and I realized on her first birthday, there was nowhere to buy a birthday cake," explains Cortesi. "This was the spark for my business.

"I had originally had two menus," continues Cortesi. I had an allergen-free menu focused on kids that was called 'Bee's Delights.' My regular menu was 'Everything Desserts' which included cakes, cupcakes, pies, tarts, cookies, brownies. All of this was easy because it was 'to order' only, so I didn't need to keep inventory on hand.

"I discontinued my Bee's Delights menu as a result of a scare related to a parent at my daughter's preschool ordering an allergen-free cake for her son. Unbeknownst to me, it was served three days after it was purchased.

She had left the cake out in the open, and by the time she served it, something must have happened because her son had an allergic reaction to it. The reason why I know it wasn't an issue directly related to my cake was because she had also ordered cupcakes that I had made the same. Still, it was enough to scare me, so I decided to no longer offer an allergen-free menu for kids.

"I realized that couples, adults, and kids struggle with getting beautiful delicious desserts, so this was an important part of my business and inspired my business slogan: 'No one should go without a beautiful delicious cake on their special day.' Of course, today, most bakeries offer allergen-free cakes. But they don't all taste great. Mine do, which is why people keep coming back for those items. Everyone is so thankful that I offer them.

"I added wedding cakes over a decade ago, and that is my biggest profit center, then and now," adds Cortesi, astute to adapting and adjusting her business based on her customer needs and profit objectives. "I changed my business model in 2015 because I wanted to make more money, as my daughter just started high school, so the cost of college was just four short years away. I stopped selling less profitable cookies, brownies, tarts, and pies. Today, I mostly sell specialty cakes and, pre-pandemic, did about a dozen wedding cakes per year." Over the years, Cortesi has also perfected her craft by training at Le Cordon Blue Paris and receiving instruction by world-renowned cake designers that include Colette Peters, Liz Marek, and Bronwyn Weber.

From start to finish, this Modern Geometric Cake took approximately two hours to make. Photo credit: Right Start Photography

"When I broke into the wedding market, I purchased insurance which is only $200 a year," says Cortesi, who has worked hard to be as professional as possible with her business. "You have to have product liability insurance because it makes you look like a real business. Plus, many venues require it."

Another way to manage risk for Bella's Desserts and head off potential customer headaches is by having customers sign a contract for every order. "Contracts are more important than anything else these days," Cortesi says, now requiring a two-page contract for weddings that covers all the issues she's experienced over the years, from bounced checks to wobbly tables. "I also have a one-page terms of agreement contract that lays out how to place

Lauren Cortesi's ornate sugar flowers adorn her Pantone's 2019 color-of-the-year inspired, Living Coral wedding cake. Credit: Lauren Cortesi

an order for me, deliveries, pickups, and refunds. I can't emphasize how enough important contracts are. Not only for you, but for your customers. It clarifies your rules about refunds and takes the guesswork out of it for you."

Sample Terms of Agreement for Orders

Credit: Bella's Desserts

Company Logo
Address
Telephone number
Website
Email

TERMS, PAYMENT, CANCELLATION, AND REFUND POLICY

This Contract represents the entire understanding and agreement between the parties with respect to the subject matter hereof, and supersedes all other negotiations, understandings, and representations (if any) made by and between such parties.

Payment:
Payments may be made via Square or Venmo.

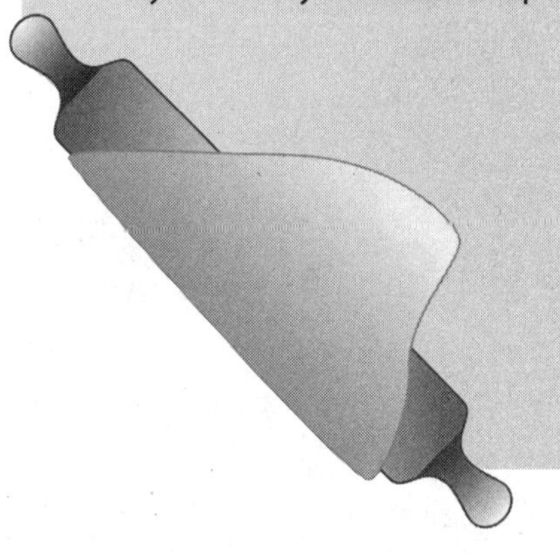

Retainers:
We require a 50% retainer to reserve your wedding date. Without the retainer, we cannot hold your date and priority will be given to the paying customer. We ask that you be absolutely certain that you would like to work with us, as all retainers are nonrefundable. The remainder of the balance is due 4 weeks prior to delivery and is nonrefundable. No desserts will be delivered if payment is not received. All returned charges will be assessed a fee of $50, and will not be delivered until paid in full by cash or bank check only at least 2 weeks prior to your event.

Alteration to orders:
Any alterations to the original order must be confirmed in writing and may be subject to an additional charge. Late changes to orders are sometimes possible and every effort will be made to accommodate these, however this cannot be guaranteed.

Cancellation of orders:
In the event of cancellation, work already completed is chargeable, and retainers are non-refundable. If an order has been paid in full, only 50% will be refunded if cancelled one month prior. If an event is cancelled within one month of the event, all money paid will be non-refundable. ☛

Transportation:
If you or your representative elect to pick up and set up the cake, you assume all liability and responsibility for the condition of the cake once it leaves Bella's Desserts possession.

Serving sizes:
A cutting chart will be provided to you or your venue, with the proper way to cut the cake to guarantee you get the numbers of servings you paid for. We guarantee that what we deliver is the number of servings you paid for. We cannot be held responsible if the person cutting the cake did not follow measurements and instructions.

Allergens:
Our products may contain or come into contact with: milk, wheat, nuts, soy, and other allergens. You agree to notify your guests of this risk and hold us harmless for allergic reactions. Please let us know if there are any allergies, so that we can take precautions, although this still does not guarantee an allergy free product since Bella's Desserts is not an allergen-free environment.

If you aren't satisfied:
We take pride in our desserts and cakes. If you are dissatisfied with your order and/or purchase, immediately notify us (within 24 hours of pickup) of your concern and return your dessert/cake to us. We will give you credit for use toward a future purchase. All refunds will be provided as an in-store credit of Bella's Desserts within five (5) business days upon receipt of the returned item. We do not provide cash refunds.

Printed name: ______________________________

Client Signature: ___________________________

Date:______________________________

"For larger orders, I require final payment due two weeks prior to the event," Cortesi mentions, when it comes to the money side of things. "This way everything's paid for, and my customers know they're going to get their cake, and I know that I'm getting paid for it. This took years to learn.

"My decorated cookies start at $4, but average $6 per cookie," Cortesi says, ever mindful to make sure that she is actually making some profit on every item, given the work involved. "This reflects the type of cookies I do, from start to finish: from making the dough to rolling it out, to cutting, baking, frosting, decorating, and finally drying time. Technically, it takes two days. Since the majority of that production time is for the icing to dry, I can make about 50 cookies over two days, depending on the level of decoration. I do a lot of watercolor, and I do a lot of drawing, opposed to piping, because I'm better at it.

Lauren Cortesi has found a strong market for creating baked items for the dessert table at weddings and other special events. Photo credit: Lauren Cortesi

Lauren Cortesi has a consistent following for her beautiful drip cakes. Credit: Lauren Cortesi

"My very first order was from a mom in my mom's group," smiles Cortesi, on her humble start like so many cottage food operators. "What I offered then spread by word of mouth. After several months, I decided to build a free website, which really didn't do much. But because my baking business was a way to keep busy, I wasn't concerned about marketing at the beginning."

Things changed when her daughter started going to school full-time in 2006, and she had more time to bake. Lauren discovered that a free website or pages on social media only go so far. "Anyone that is serious about their business needs to build a real website," she encourages. "Don't rely on Facebook and Instagram. Social media have algorithms that bury pages that don't have a lot of traffic, so I find I don't get as many hits from them."

Today, Cortesi finds that about 75 percent of her business comes from Google. "If you are serious about growing your business, you need a website, not just a Facebook page. It shows that you're a real business, and it gets listed on Google and all the other search engines. Because I paid to have my website optimized, it shows up on the first page when people searched. Yes, it can be a bit overwhelming, but I taught myself to code. Then, as I got busier, I bartered with friends and hired professionals to get my website where it needed it to be."

Cortesi doesn't turn down free marketing opportunities when they arise. "I offer all my couples a free anniversary cake in exchange for a professional photo and a review on Google or Wedding Wire," she says. "If you like to write, contact blog sites and ask to be a guest blogger. I've had people come to me because they found my website online and asked for an interview. I also have guest bloggers on my website. Anywhere you can add value results in more traffic to your website and, possibly, turn into orders.

"The old 'times three' method is a myth when it comes to pricing your products. You are paying people to come get your items if that's the way you're charging," Cortesi explains, having discovered, early on, that on more than one occasion she was selling products for less than what it took to make them. "Pricing correctly takes a lot of work, but to be successful as a cottage food operator you have to put the work in behind the scenes. Before I price ingredients, I figure out the following: my salary, how many hours it takes to make the product, overhead—which includes electricity, water, heat, air conditioning, trash, phone, Internet, rent, gas—and I add all that to the cost of ingredients. You need to figure out how much you want to pay yourself. I pay myself $25 an hour. The overhead costs are easy to figure out, it just takes some time. Mine is $3.83 a day, but that changes annually.

"I use software to help figure out my ingredient pricing," shares Cortesi. "It helps break down ingredients and measurements and everything else you put in your recipe. It includes your boxes, your labor, and everything else. It's a great piece of software. Here's the important point: If you feel that people don't want to pay that much for a pie, for instance, once you figure out how much it costs to make like I did, take it off your menu. If you feel in your area that no one will pay what you need to charge, this isn't the right menu item for you. After I learned how to price, I pared down my menu dramatically. I took off all the pies. I became profitable.

"If you look at BellasDesserts.com, my website is geared toward large events, featuring tiered cakes, specialty cakes, mini desserts cupcakes, and decorated cookies," adds Cortesi. "My website also features other goodies for dessert tables, which are becoming a bigger part of my business. So, I would take a look at your menu once you learn how to price and figure out what you need to take off.

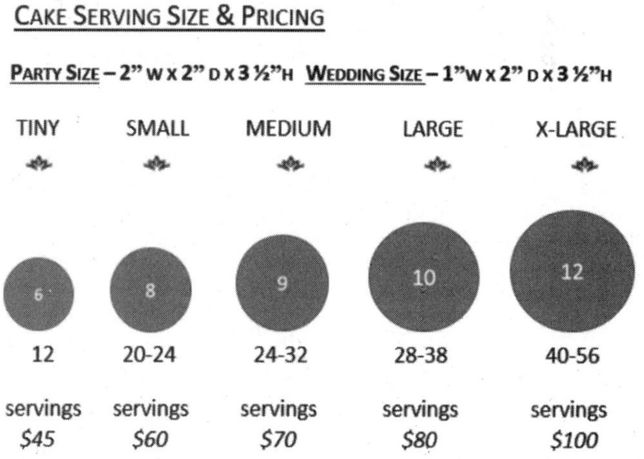

Cake Serving Size & Pricing

Party Size – 2" w x 2" d x 3 ½"h Wedding Size – 1"w x 2" d x 3 ½"h

TINY	SMALL	MEDIUM	LARGE	X-LARGE
6	8	9	10	12
12 servings	20-24 servings	24-32 servings	28-38 servings	40-56 servings
$45	*$60*	*$70*	*$80*	*$100*

Cake serving size and price chart from Bella's Desserts, clearly displayed on Bella's Desserts website. Credit: Bella's Desserts

"My ideal customer today is someone who wants a delicious, beautiful dessert, regardless of the price," admits Cortesi. "I've been in business for decades, so I'm okay to be focusing on the high-end clientele. My first 12 years was spent charging too little and offering too many items and being unsatisfied. It makes me feel good that I'm getting paid for my work, and that people are just as appreciative as they've always been. My favorite is to get an engaged couple, do the shower, the wedding, the baby shower, and then their children's birthdays. It's so satisfying that they want your cakes to be a part of their lives. And don't forget to give your customers a reason to order from you and solicit testimonials from them, adding these reviews on your website.

"Customer service is so important for cottage food bakers," concludes Cortesi, who admits she can be impatient at times or have an off day, just like anyone. "It's super hard to grit my teeth and be nice all the time, especially with unreasonable customers. You can choose to not do business with that person, but you never want them to decide not to do business with you due to your attitude."

Father's Day breakfast of pancakes and eggs (It's cake!). The maple bacon cake with maple buttercream was inspired by Liz Marek of the Sugar Geek Show.
PHOTO CREDIT: LAUREN CORTESI

Variable Savings

While we touched on the value of your labor and some of your fixed start-up costs, where you can cut corners without impacting the quality of your product may be with the packaging and the ingredients themselves.

Slashing Ingredient Costs

There's nothing like sourcing some of your ingredients from your own gardens or growing fields. From pumpkin for muffins, raspberries for preserves, and cucumbers for pickles, using your own ingredients (if your state's law allows it) can cut your variable costs considerably.

If that's not feasible, bulk up. Don't overlook ways to buy bulk ingredients at prices just over wholesale through a food cooperative or buying club. Food cooperatives are member-owned grocery stores that specialize in more health-conscious food options. Membership fees are nominal and give you access to discounted pricing and better sourcing options with a focus on local and sustainable agricultural products and specialty foods. Food co-ops often have bulk aisles; they can special-order a 50-pound bag of flour or sugar for you, often at an additional discount.

If you don't have a food cooperative where you live, check and see if there might be a buying club that offers similar options. A buying club allows a group of people to collectively place an order with a distributor. Because of the volume, the distributor can offer wholesale pricing. Other options include United Natural Foods (unfi.com), food wholesalers, or food distributors that specifically serve food businesses in your community. We regularly use Frontier Coop (frontiercoop.com) for our natural spices and organic dried herbs and Equal Exchange (equalexchange.coop) for our organic baking cocoa.

Don't rule out supermarkets. Some chains, like Whole Foods Market, offer a bulk aisle and may be able to order a full bulk bag for you. Warehouse clubs may also be an option for large case-size packs of key ingredients; increasingly some warehouse clubs, such as Costco, sell large bulk bags and even organic items.

Another way to cut down on your ingredient costs is by purchasing "seconds" or overstocks directly from area farmers. You don't need perfect tomatoes to make salsa; a box with a few blemishes you can cut around will work fine. This works great if you're into producing preserves, marmalades, salsas, or pickles. Some of these farms might end up partnering with you by

Take it from Shelby Emrich, a mother of four, who started Mollylocks and the Three Bears: Customer engagement is easy with an editable "cookie care card" from Etsy. She added some tasty thank-you cookies that cleverly mirrored her business logo.
CREDIT: SHELBY EMRICH/MOLLYLOCKS AND THE THREE BEARS BAKERY

Besides sharing key marketing information about the business, the two-sided cookie care card helps reinforce messages about maintaining quality of the product and food safety. CREDIT: SHELBY EMRICH/MOLLYLOCKS AND THE THREE BEARS BAKERY

selling your value-added products to their customers (if allowed by your cottage food law).

Penny-pinching on Packaging and Kitchen Supplies

The cost for various packing materials can add up, reducing your profit per item. So why not try to locate some of the materials you might need that may cost you little to nothing? The following short list offers several ways to locate packaging, kitchen supplies, and other items at prices much less than full retail.

Etsy: Etsy.com

This e-commerce website features handmade craft items and supplies. It can also be a place for packaging design ideas or, if your cottage food law allows it, online mail-order sales. Some CFOs have used Esty crafters to supply them with labels or other related products, since they'd rather be baking.

General Merchandise Retailers

One reason to join state or topical Facebook groups is to network with other collaborative CFOs, be they cookie bakers, cocoa bombers, or canners. Retailers, like Target, sometimes have items perfectly suited for selling boxes of decorated Christmas cookies. Fellow CFOs readily share where these can be found and if they go on sale.

Thrift Stores and Auctions

Don't underestimate your local thrift store for attractive baskets, containers, boxes, ribbons, or other packaging materials for pennies on the dollar.

Your pricing may also need to account for any promotional costs and food samples given away at events. But as we cover in the next chapter, most cottage food enterprises will launch without the need to spend much on promotion.

11

Moving Your Product to Market

GROWING YOUR CUSTOMER BASE is essential for growing sales. While people may love your product, they can only eat so much of it. If you want to maintain or increase your sales, you'll need to attract new customers through referrals, seek out new sales venues, or explore other marketing approaches related to this P of marketing: the Place where you're selling your items. We'll also be addressing the closely related aspect of the ways you can sell, like pickups, deliveries, or by mail. Both the where and how you can sell are covered in this chapter.

Just as it defines your product, the cottage food law in your state will specify the venue or venues where you can sell your products. The law will also address the more nuanced aspect of how you can sell the product. The where could be a farmers' market. The how could be direct sales at your market booth or a customer picking up an order already placed and prepaid for through your online storefront. Some states readily allow online sales while other states only allow informational websites, but no e-commerce transactions. After selling at a market, for example, would your state allow you to do a "flash sale" of any unsold products through your Facebook page, with customers picking them up at your home that evening? Some states remain sticklers for direct orders made in person, face-to-face.

There is a difference between advertising your business online and accepting money online. Every state now allows advertising online, usually by having a website or Facebook business page. At the time of this book printing, only 38 states (and Washington, DC) allow online sales and the ability to accept money online for your product. While that number is much higher than before the pandemic, there's a way to go until this barrier has been eliminated for every state. The pandemic revealed just how crucial online sales are to small business survival. Monitor what your state allows since it's likely to change.

The greater the flexibility in sales channels permitted by your state, the better the opportunities for distribution, allowing you to reach a wider market and generate more sales. If you're forced into only a few sales venues or channels, then you'll have to see how many different outlets you can sell at to achieve your sales goals.

For many CFOs, distributing your product is the easiest part of your business; if your family members can't wait to place advance orders, your office co-workers just need an order form or your church has already welcomed you to set up a display in the lobby of the community room after Sunday service to distribute advance orders. Many CFOs prefer direct sales since they like the certainty of the advance order, especially if it comes with a prepayment or deposit. In many cases, promotional costs are negligible.

Selling to family, friends, or office workers may be awkward at first, or make you uncomfortable. It's not unlike teens reaching out to neighbors during school or organizational fundraising campaigns. How did this disconnect happen? Somewhere along the line, as our local economy evolved into a global marketplace, we lost the personal connection between products and the people who make them. Today, most foods are made by anonymous people (or machines in factories) located thousands of miles away. As a result, selling to friends can feel awkward.

But why wouldn't your best friend buy your granola bars instead of some national brand—especially if yours are priced fairly and taste great? Chances are your muffins, cookies, or pickles are far superior to those shelf-stable national brands because you don't pack them full of preservatives, chemicals, fillers, or other mystery ingredients. Your heart went in to making them.

If you find yourself suddenly grappling with the fact that you're charging for what you once gave away free, think about coming up with new products your friends have never tried. Or emphasize how your friends are linked to the marketing story: they're helping support your dream, your business, and a shared local economy. In the end, people are more likely to buy things from people they trust, admire, respect, and care about. Of course, you can always donate some of your products to a fundraiser or silent auction when your friends give you a call.

Sales Venues: Where and How to Sell

At the time of printing, over 20 states permit selling wholesale, a process by which another retailer sells your product to a customer for you. In this case, your products could be found throughout your city or even the state. The remaining states require you to sell directly to the customer. The variety of ways to sell your products are covered below. Naturally, the where and how you can sell are often interrelated.

Most states provide multiple venues where you can sell your goods to the public and many allow mail order within your state, a huge change from a decade ago, in part, from the realities of the COVID-19 pandemic. Because of how the cottage food laws are written, and with rare exception, no sales of your products can be made in a state other than the one you reside in. Be aware, however, that rules governing this may change. After all, a cookie is a cookie, no matter what state the baker is in. Kudos to the Commonwealth of Pennsylvania for leading the way by being the first state to allow out-of-state mail orders for products made under their limited food establishment license.

"Not allowing sales across state lines is ridiculous and also unconstitutional," admonishes Erica Smith Ewing with the Institute for Justice. "The reason so many states don't allow sales across state lines is because they mistakenly think federal law prevents it. But we have talked to the FDA and USDA multiple times about this, and they have confirmed to us in writing that it is perfectly okay as long as you are not shipping meat products and certain dairy products like raw butter across state lines." It could be just a matter of time before individual state laws concede, realizing too, that enforcement is practically impossible. Seriously, how could a state agency track a box of inbound cookies from another state?

Sampling out HeathGlen's Farm & Kitchen products at a community event.
CREDIT: COURTESY OF HEATHGLEN'S FARM & KITCHEN

Farmers' Markets and Community Events

One of the more popular ways to distribute your products directly to your customers is by going to where your customers are. Holiday festivals, shopping bazaars, arts and craft fairs, farmers' markets, community markets, walk-a-thons, and community-wide tourism-related events may welcome cottage food vendors. While there is usually a fee associated with a booth space at these events, it may be worthwhile if the event draws a large crowd and has strong marketing support—the organizers may even promote your enterprise as a vendor on their website, in printed materials, via social media, or all of the above.

One of the easiest ways to pick up new customers is one bite at a time through samples, assuming the community event organizers or venues allow it. Because your products are non-hazardous, you'll have an advantage over other commercial vendors who may have products requiring refrigeration. That doesn't guarantee, however, that a health inspector passing through the event will like how you're putting out the samples on toothpicks or spoons. The event may also have a policy restricting what you can sample and how—or require, if you give sample items, additional liability insurance beyond which you feel you want to commit. Individual packaging may be required in some states.

Even if an event draws in a crowd, there's no guarantee you'll blow out of your products. There is an uncertainty that comes with selling at an event: inclement weather reducing attendance; guessing how much of which product you should bring; a competing vendor with a cheaper product in a booth across from yours. One barometer you can use to gage the potential market for your products is the number of vendors already selling

How to Move Extra Products: Flash Sales and Marketing Samples

When selling at farmers' markets or other events, of course you'll want to have your table looking full and enticing. But rarely will you sell every item. And if the weather happens to put a damper on the turnout one day, you might return with more items than you and your family could possibly enjoy. For canned goods, it's not a problem. But for baked goods, it can be. Having a plan in place for the leftover baked products helps avoid any waste; these extra products could be possibly used to attract new customers.

If you have an online following in social media, have a "flash sale" to move your remaining freshly baked items. Some CFOs have found Facebook Marketplace another avenue to quickly announce items for sale, distinct from their main business page (more on this in chapter 12). The one-off flash sale also helps avoid customers associating discounts or cheap prices with your products, unless that's one of your main benefits of your brand. Your extra products could also be dropped off at area businesses or organizations with the idea that they might place an order down the line. Food pantries, hospitals, schools, police departments, and fire stations might also be options to share your treats. Just because they didn't all sell at a market doesn't make them any less delicious or appreciated.

Holiday Bazaar or Farmers' Market Packing List

If you think a packing list for attending and selling an event is overkill, don't. The difference between a fun, organized, successful, and profitable event and one that's not can be as simple as a forgotten money belt (or change drawer), an attractive tablecloth, or a chair to sit on when there's a lull in the crowds.

- [] Table
- [] Chair
- [] Tablecloth
- [] Pop-up market tent with pegs and/or leg weights if applicable to the venue
- [] Display gear: cake stands, baskets, risers, etc.
- [] A company banner or similar sign to promote your name and brand identification and loyalty among customers
- [] Pricing cards for each item; people want to see what something costs (without having to ask you)
- [] Money belt or change drawer, with plenty of small change and the ability to break large bills without a crisis
- [] Credit card processing forms and device, if you accept them
- [] Attractive table signage with your business name and other particulars
- [] Business cards or order forms for your products
- [] Masking or duct tape
- [] Permanent marker
- [] Bags for customers

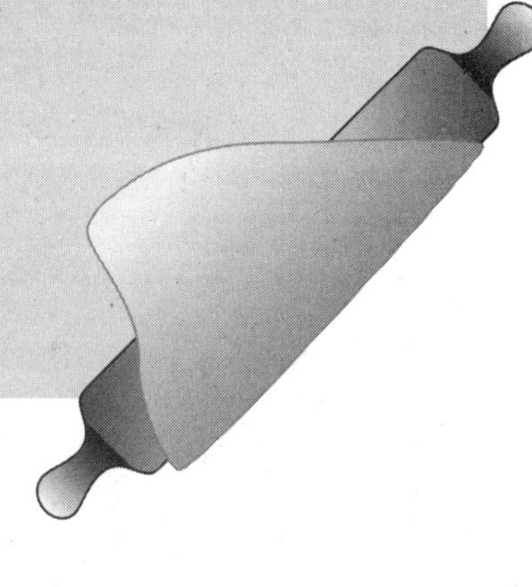

there and the number of years they have been doing so. Another consideration is the appropriateness of your product to the event itself. For example, pickles and chutneys may be a hit at a farmers' market while dried soup mixes or decorated cookies may draw greater interest at a gift-focused holiday bazaar.

Sponsoring a community bake-off, can-off, or cook-off may be a quick way to reach potential customers, sample out some of your products to participants or spectators, and establish credibility, brand or company awareness, and interest in your products. You may even be able to be one of the judges on the panel. This may require a financial investment or, if you approach it right, an in-kind (i.e., non-cash) donation of products that will be given away to winning participants or volunteers helping out.

Selling at Market: Tips to Return Home "Sold Out"

Hard to believe, but in the early days of cottage food, some states limited you to only selling at farmers' markets and some even limited CFOs to only farmers. Fortunately, those days are gone, and today markets serve as a great opportunity for product sales for everyone. Some ideas to boost your market or event bottom line include the following:

The display of HeathGlen's Farm & Kitchen products features signage that conveys how their products can be paired with cheese, meat, and wine.
CREDIT: COURTESY OF HEATHGLEN'S FARM & KITCHEN

- Cross-promote
  What do you sell that pairs perfectly with something else at the market? Do you make relish and someone else sells sausages? Do you sell pound cake and another farmer sells fresh strawberries or blueberries that would make the perfect complement? Connect with these vendors and explore your cross-selling opportunities.
- Cater to kids
  You always see kids at markets. Often, they look a little bit bored while their parents or caregivers negotiate more time to linger and shop. Provide a solution: small treats for the kids, something to occupy them and satisfy their hunger. Selling something easy to hold and eat in a kid-appealing shape could score some points, like a cake pop or cakesicle.
- Offer multiples
  Everyone loves a special deal. Look at how some of the farmers promote their produce. Borrow a couple of tactics like "buy one, get one free" or volume discount pricing: "3 for $10."
- Seek shade
  If possible, visit the market beforehand and see how the sun hits it. Try to confirm a booth space in as much shade as possible to help preserve your products, especially if you have baked goods or candies.
- "Gift exchange" (technically, avoid calling it "barter")
  At the end of the market, especially if you have extra fresh fare like loaves of bread, gift exchange with other vendors for some take-home treats. Common after the market has closed, these gift

exchange scenes provide an extra bonus: building community and cultivating relationships. According to several tax accountants we've consulted, it's best to call these "gift exchanges." What you call it apparently matters to the IRS, since they want to try to collect tax on it. A gift is freely given.

Direct Customer Deliveries

After selling at farmers' markets and community events, direct customer deliveries appear to be the most common way CFOs get their products to their customers. This may result from their desire to provide the best possible customer service, saving their customers a trip to their home. Many coordinate deliveries around other daily errands, making them as efficient as possible. In cases where the customers are away, a safe, secure, and sheltered place is arranged where the products can be left, often on a porch or in a breezeway.

If you're set on delivery, ask yourself: Are you in the delivery business or the bakery business? Since gasoline or diesel fuel isn't getting any cheaper, evaluate just how far you need to go to deliver your product to your customers. Besides fuel costs and possible tolls or parking meters, consider how much time you want to be stuck in traffic or running around the city dropping off orders. Thanks to third-party delivery services like DoorDash, more people than ever before are becoming accustomed to paying for deliveries. Use this to your advantage and potentially charge for deliveries.

Evaluate your set of wheels. Do you have the right kind of vehicle to transport a large and fragile wedding cake? If you're using your vehicle more, it's reasonable to anticipate that there will be additional repair and maintenance costs. If your markets are nearby and your orders are small, see if delivery may be made by bicycle or on foot. Depending on your state, you may not be able to use third-party delivery services, like DoorDash or Postmates, owned by Uber. While the pandemic led to a massive uptick in the use of these delivery services, many cottage food laws are written in such a way to ensure that direct-to-customer connections are preserved and prevent CFOs from using them.

One of the more lucrative outlets for your products might be weddings or special community or corporate events. Due to the high value of

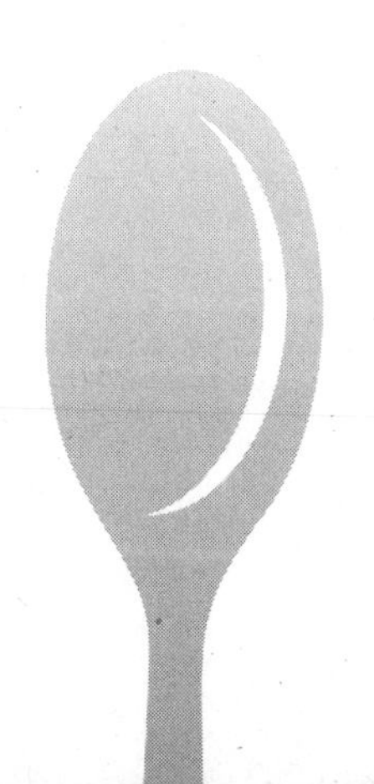

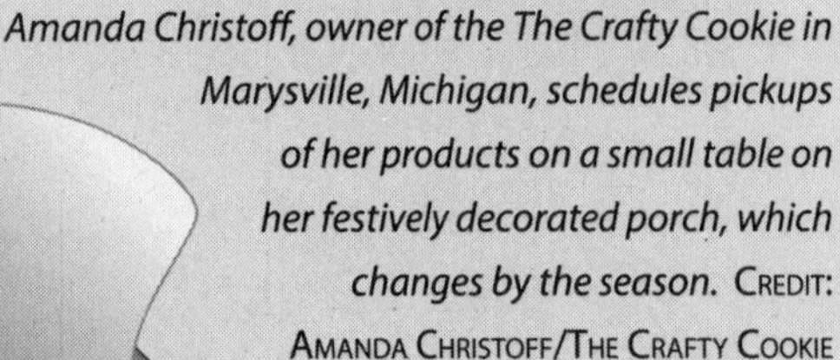

Amanda Christoff, owner of the The Crafty Cookie in Marysville, Michigan, schedules pickups of her products on a small table on her festively decorated porch, which changes by the season. CREDIT: AMANDA CHRISTOFF/THE CRAFTY COOKIE

custom-decorated cakes or large quantity of items that might be ordered, they're often delivered.

Home Pickup

Certain states allow cottage food products to be picked up at your home. Such pickups could involve interaction with the customers, where they ring the doorbell and you hand-deliver and thank them for their order. Other CFOs have creatively designed a porch pickup area and allowed the customers to come and go on their own, completely contactless. A few even schedule their pickups. These days, given the increased variability and unpredictability of weather, you'll need to make sure your products are safe from the elements. Unfortunately, depending on where you live, you may also need to have a way to secure your products so they don't disappear off your porch, taken by someone other than your customers. The more well-known you become, the more likely your business might be targeted for theft.

To encourage pickups, a discount off a future order could be extended to those customers who do so, since having them pick up their order saves you both time and money for fuel. You'll need to evaluate, however, if you want to offer this option. People get busy, miss appointments, or come at the wrong time. You'll also need to check with your city and zoning department

Risk Realities of a Business Operated from Home

While many cottage food operators use their home as a pickup point, especially when selling to neighbors and community members you know, the reality is we live in a society with increasing risk of random violence or malfeasance.

When we first wrote *Homemade for Sale* in 2015, we could whole-heartedly say there had been no reported incidents of issues with cottage food pickups or deliveries at private homes. But, in 2019, came the first case of sexual assault of a cottage food producer in Iowa during a pickup in her home. As the CFO industry grows, we're tragically not immune to such issues since we're operating within the broader society. By the very nature of business, a transaction is based on trust. This should go both ways.

Perhaps applying the same degree of caution that you might with staying at an Airbnb or getting into a car operated under Lyft or Uber, consider ways to make your business operations and transactions more secure, safe, and trackable for both you and your customers. Restricting time and location of pickups or drop-offs or adding a front door security camera might be ways to build trust while discouraging or preventing malevolent bad actors. A visible camera on a porch may also provide a natural deterrent for possible theft. Clear order processes and contracts can also add clarity and trackability. Be mindful of your order process as well, since using PayPal, for example, may allow a customer to cancel a payment after picking up their items. It's happened to a few trusting CFOs.

Don't rule out that some of those missing boxes of your products could have happened completely by accident. Often, the customer placing the order may not be the person picking it up. A remote-working mom might place the order, but the husband picks it up on the way home from the office. To address this, many CFOs schedule pickups. Others have opted to hand the orders directly to their customers. The latter two alternatives also avoid a possible roaming dog, cat, or squirrel prying open a box of "treats" left unattended on a porch.

If you're wary about including your home address on the label and it is your state's requirement, contact your health or ag department that manages your state's regulations to check on alternatives like a PO box or website. Again, the state's goal in asking for an address is to be able to quickly trace any foodborne illness outbreak back to the producer. Given the need for safety, some states are allowing CFOs to list a website, email, or other means of contact versus a home address.

to see if any current restrictions apply to you, like parking restrictions or limits on traffic.

One of the emerging trends for both home pickup orders and deliveries are subscription services created by CFOs for regular deliveries of their products on a weekly or monthly basis. This service would provide a package of various products, at a specified time, often paid for in advance and usually with a changing menu over the course of the period covered. Subscription sales not only maintain consistency in customers and demand, they do wonders for smoothing out cash flow from one month to the next, covered more in a later chapter.

"I sold out in 17 minutes," says Leigh Hittner Liesemer, owner of Sweet Delilah's Cookies, based in Aldie, Virginia. Her pop-up on the front porch of her home featured two tables of decorated cookies for Valentine's Day. Another table had an engagement contest where customers could guess how many chocolate kisses were in the jar for a chance to win 50 percent off an order of a dozen custom cookies.

"I had a line of people off my porch and down the walk to my driveway, and boom, no more cookies!" Her plan for leftover cookies to pass out as teacher gifts, donate to the firehouse, or give to friends was saved for another day.

CREDIT: LEIGH HITTNER LIESEMER/SWEET DELILAH'S COOKIES

Pop-up Markets

If you're not into deadlines or demanding custom orders, some CFOs have found pop-up markets an effective way to sell to neighbors and others in their community. Suddenly your porch or driveway could be a temporary sales venue, assuming you get the word out to your customers so they can stop by to shop. Pop-up markets happen on your schedule, and you control what you sell and how much you produce.

Pop-up markets can also happen in partnership with a local store, where you basically set up a booth and sell your wares. This works especially well when you offer a complementary item that the retail store doesn't sell, like a pop-up for candy in a flower store before Valentine's Day.

Typically, pop-up markets have more to do with local zoning regulations than your state's cottage food law in terms of legality and additional rules that must be followed. For example, ask your local zoning department if you can have a table right outside the retailer you are partnering with and if the table needs to be a certain size to keep the sidewalk open.

CFOs work out a variety of arrangements with the host retailer so it's equitable for everyone. Maybe you pay the retailer a percentage of your sales, or better yet, they see it as an opportunity to bring through their door new customers that are looking for you. Pop-up markets can also take place, with permission, in parking lots outside retail establishments, at a church function if granted permission, or in conjunction with an event, such as a table at a community summer concert night in the park.

Pop-ups you run right from your home can make the time and effort it takes to go to a market disappear. You can set your own schedule and don't need to schlep everything at the crack of dawn to a market. Most CFOs allowed to do pop-ups at their home tend to create an attractive tented space on their lawn or a part of their driveway instead of the "garage sale" approach, sticking a table in the garage next to the lawn mower and garden tools.

In an interesting twist, some CFOs have started to transform vintage trailers into cute mini-storefronts when permitted by state laws. Viewed differently than fully licensed food trucks where food items are prepared, the trailers have been accepted by some state regulatory agencies as simply "fancy" display stands. One of the key variables to secure trailer approval, in these cases, seems to be that no preparation or cooking is involved. Food trucks, however, are typically viewed as "itinerant restaurants" and must be licensed and inspected as such, in much the same way as a restaurant or catering operation might be.

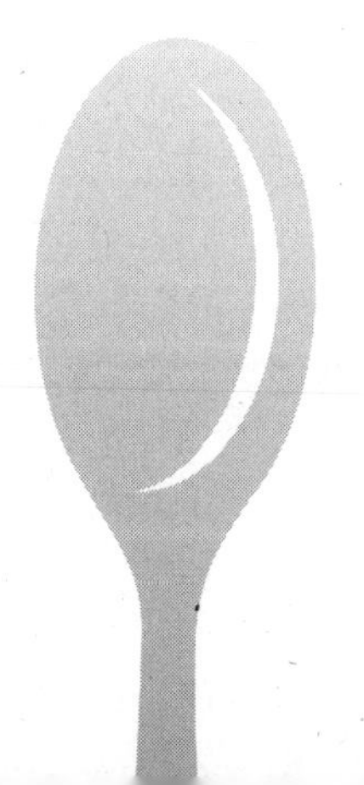

Wholesale (Indirect)

More than a dozen states allow various forms of wholesale or indirect sales, which encapsulates both the where and how questions. Permission to sell wholesale allows you to sell to a venue like a retailer, gift shop, or restaurant that then resells your product. For these transactions to take place, you will often need to go through a more involved home kitchen inspection and licensing process, plus meet a host of other requirements specified by the retailers or distributors themselves, like having UPC codes for your products so they can scan and stock them. Depending on your wholesale client, you may need to guarantee production and regular delivery of a certain quantity of product that, of course, meets impeccable quality and consistency standards. More on this in chapters 19 and 20.

Mail Order

Most states, over 30 at the time of printing, allow mail order within their own state. However, a few states with broader "home processor licenses" allow products to be sold wholesale as well as mail order.

Stay on Target for a Bull's-eye

While the enthusiasm might be there to pursue more than one of the sales venues detailed above, we caution against it, at least when just starting up. It's best to begin by targeting the venue with the highest probability of strong sales and repeat customers, to establish your business within your financial and time limitations. You can always expand later, once you have a track record and firm footing.

Thematic Table Displays to Boost Sales

If you are a food entrepreneur selling at farmers' markets, craft fairs, and other events, think of your display as an important part of your food business success. First and foremost, your display communicates your products. You want your loyal customers and even more importantly, potential new buyers, to be able to see them, and view them in a way that reflects the time and effort and love that went into making them.

Secondly, your display should encourage repeat customers, especially if you're at a regular event like a weekly farmers' market where vendor locations might change. You want a distinct look that reflects your brand and personality so that previous customers can easily spot you and come back and buy again.

Next, you want your display to be eye-catching and distinct. This is especially important at something like a holiday event with people wandering around, usually having a fun time, and probably not having a shopping list for exactly the unique items you offer. You want your display to lure them over to start talking, ask questions, and look at what you have, inspiring impulse purchases.

And lastly, your whole display should be easily transportable to go from event to event and preserve your product from the elements, especially if you're outside for a farmers' market.

Elevating Your Displays

Everyone starts with a basic flat table at a market. But you can stand out in the crowd by easily adding height to your table display. As potential customers wander the market, eyes are naturally drawn to what stands out on your table. Having some of your products at a higher level does just that.

Keep it simple with a basic board placed on top of upside-down terra cotta pots. Who doesn't have extra pots or boards sitting in the garage? They easily come apart and store for setup and transport. The rustic feel of the items adds to us authentically communicating our fresh-from-the-farm message.

Place your premium products on a riser to catch the eye of someone wandering the market.
CREDIT: JOHN D. IVANKO PHOTOGRAPHY

Author Lisa Kivirist selling at an indoor Winter Market in Madison, Wisconsin. CREDIT: JOHN D. IVANKO PHOTOGRAPHY

A farmstead display theme showcases homespun and fresh ingredients. CREDIT: JOHN D. IVANKO PHOTOGRAPHY

Here are four different display themes to play around with, based on you, your vision for your business, your brand, and your products.

Farmstead

A farmstead display theme readily works for our cottage food products because people associate homemade as from the farm, whether or not you literally live on one.

A gingham tablecloth pattern always communicates homespun and fresh, just like a summer picnic at your grandma's. Rustic and hand-drawn, chalkboard signage communicates homemade. A metal three-tiered stand adds height to your table and adds space to display more product than just on a regular banquet table. This added staging can attract your customer's eye at different levels, wherever they may be looking.

Wooden crates placed on their side are handy for packing and transporting your product and stack up easy for transport. Colorful mixing bowls communicate kitchen and add a pop of color to your table.

The galvanized metal feed buckets and chicken feeders came directly from the farm supply store. Even if you're not in a rural area, you might want to make a road trip to a farm supply store for items like this handy three-compartment chicken feeder, a perfect display piece as it is divided into sections, made out of lightweight metal, is inexpensive compared to home décor, is easy to transport, and communicates a message—fun, rustic farmstead.

A bohemian-themed display communicates your inner artist with pops of color. CREDIT: JOHN D. IVANKO PHOTOGRAPHY

Bohemian

Bohemian styling celebrates your artsy, funky side with splashes of vivid color. A bright paisley tablecloth communicates whimsy and fun.

We traded the chalkboard signs for creatively repurposed place card holders, shaped like little birds. Place card holders you would traditionally use for a dinner party table also work well for product signage on your table and can easily be changed for different events. They bring height to your display, making your price and product description easy to spot.

Metal baskets flipped upside down add a height element along with that important storage element for conveniently transporting your products.

Upside-down glass vases with a plate on top add a classy pedestal-like display element to showcase specific premium-priced products you want to be most noticed because you're selling them at a higher price.

A black tablecloth and metal accessories adds a contemporary look to your table. Credit: John D. Ivanko Photography

Modern

A minimalist clean look creates a modern-themed display, trading color for a sleek black tablecloth topped with a sequenced runner adding a pop of sparkle. Imagine you were setting the table for an elegant gourmet dinner party.

A blend of metal and ceramic communicates modern. Shiny metal adds a high-end contemporary feel, but it can be an inexpensive item. Upside-down plates on bowls again provide height to your table.

Cheerful

A cheerful-themed display would be something to use at the first farmers' market of the spring season, communicating needed fun and whimsicality that customers crave after a long winter.

A warm-cream tablecloth with a bird pattern hails the newness and freshness of spring. You see a lot of bird themes on this table, such as the return of the place card holders for signage. The wooden crates are back for that garden-fresh theme.

Cheerful-themed displays capture a light-hearted fun look. Credit: John D. Ivanko Photography

Whatever theme you create, do a full setup of your display prior to that important first event. Set up your table and display gear, even if it's right in the middle of your living room, to make sure everything works exactly how you envisioned it and you're not forgetting anything. It's a simple rehearsal, addressing details beforehand, like ironing a tablecloth, that will make your life so much easier when you set up on the event day.

There are many ways to approach each and every topic covered in this book. You'll need to evaluate which make the most sense to you, your situation, budget, goals, and, of course, your state's cottage food law.

When you are testing your display, take a few photos to share as teasers on social media for what you're bringing to the market and to help folks identify you when they attend.

CREDIT: JOHN D. IVANKO PHOTOGRAPHY

12

Promotion: Persuading Customers with Advertising and Public Relations

If the target audience for your products happens to be your neighbors, family, or co-workers eagerly awaiting your kitchen creations, then produce, package, and deliver your product and let the money roll in as you keep them stocked and happy.

For most food entrepreneurs, however, you'll need to let potential customers know your company exists to serve their needs with products you've tested and know they'll love. You'll need to reach out to connect with these potential customers, whether they're in your office, school, church, or neighborhood.

You need not empty the bank to promote your product, however. Depending on your skill set, comfort with a computer, time, and budget, there are many free or nearly free promotional opportunities covered in this chapter. Despite the saying "you have to spend money to make money," we've found that the less you have to spend in promotion, the more you earn selling your products. The trick is to find the most cost-effective way to reach your target market.

Capturing Great Photography

Great photography helps sell more of whatever you make. The Internet and social media have made visuals essential to effective marketing. With powerful digital cameras—including most current models of mobile phones—plus an array of free apps to enhance photos, capturing stunning photography or videos has never been easier. For quick photo enhancements on the phone, it's just a matter of easily passing it through an app before posting to your website or social media.

While DSLR (digital single lens reflex) or mirrorless cameras offer amazing results with lots of artistic freedom, mobile phones from companies like Apple or Samsung, with their automatic settings, provide stunning results

French macaron baker Jill Drobiak knows how to capture the perfect photo of her mouth-watering creations. Shooting through glass, creatively arranging her macs and some of their toppings, she takes a visually stunning layered photo. It's a social media scroll-stopper.

"I take my photos on my iPhone 11 Pro, edited in the Lightroom app," explains Drobiak. "The glass pane is set on top of two pint glasses over a white foam board I purchased at Michaels. It's simple, but creates a neat effect." She was careful to remove any shadow or reflection of herself or her camera.

Entice your customers scrolling through social media with a stunning photograph.
CREDIT: JILL DROBIAK/SWEET LIFE CONFECTIONS

Using a glass table, Jill Drobiak created a visually engaging image of her macarons.
CREDIT: JILL DROBIAK/SWEET LIFE CONFECTIONS

and will meet most CFO needs. Thanks to the magic of computational photography, these mobile devices automatically add saturation and vibrance, contrast, warming tones, and a host of other enhancements to the image.

As a result, capturing consistently amazing photos at home has become more about learning a few tricks of the trade, like creating the composition and bouncing indirect daylight on your products, perhaps arranged on a table beside a bay window. For product shots, staging photos is essential, thus the fascination within Facebook groups around beads, vintage kitchen items, and other props that can be used to enhance the image and better showcase your product. It's about making your images pop. A boring plate of chocolate cookies can be transformed by adding a vintage sifter, rolling pin, wooden cutting board, and a few chocolate chips sprinkled around the cookies. Practice makes perfect.

The good news is that most CFOs already own the essential tool for great photography: the mobile phone. Just don't forget to take a few photos, both horizontal and vertical, of you in the kitchen, at the market booth, interacting with happy customers, or even making your products in your nice clean kitchen. These can be used for advertising and public relations, covered next.

For a mini home studio to capture your product shots, experiment with white foamboard set up on a chair facing a window for indirect light. Credit: John D. Ivanko Photography

Promotion

Promotion is what most of us think about as marketing, the applied art form of persuasive communication by graphics, words, and such to help sell goods. Creative, innovative thinking thrives through your approach to promotion, communicating information—telling the story about your business—that leads to customers wanting to buy your products. Effective promotion helps them realize they have a need that will be satisfied by purchasing your product.

Marketers often refer to brand as the embodiment of your product in the form of your name, logo, and other design aspects. The goal, of course, is to devise communications that help your customers understand and remember what your business is about and why they'll love your products. While multinational corporations spend millions on developing their brand, you can do it with almost no money at all by harnessing the power of the Internet and a home computer, plus your own creativity.

Included in promotion is both advertising and public relations (PR). Advertising is purchased while PR, whether solicited or

Remember to take photos showcasing you in your kitchen, in action making your treats and beside your finished products. These are great shots to have on file for whenever a reporter calls for a story but can't send their own photographer. Credit: John D. Ivanko Photography

unsolicited, is free. The smaller the business, the less you'll need to focus on paying for traditional advertising in media like magazines or newspapers and the more you might want to focus on PR efforts, since they involve investing time, not money. PR is covered in more detail later in this chapter.

Promotion decisions include developing a sense of what your company offers with words, graphics, and other communicative elements. These often include your logo, product slogan, and unifying colors, styles, themes, and images expressing what you do, for whom, and why it matters. They position your product in the marketplace.

Advertising

In the traditional sense, advertising is paid forms of communication via outlets such as newspapers, magazines, TV, and radio. Depending on what products you're selling and your existing networks of friends, community connections, and comfort with a computer and the Internet, most of your promotional efforts can be accomplished by spending little to nothing on traditional paid advertising. Save your money and focus on Internet communications and PR instead.

However, don't rule out the possibility of exchanging your products for a display advertisement in a newspaper. Publications, particularly regional or nonprofit newsletters, may be open to creating a giveaway of your product (perhaps as an incentive for renewals) in exchange for a "free" publication advertisement, which will garner you conventional advertising exposure through an unconventional means. So if you get a local newspaper sales call, float the idea by them as a marketing promotion.

Business Cards, Posters, and Flyers

For most CFOs, if you're planning to spend anything on advertising, it will be on a business card or printed flyer to pass around to your neighbors or co-workers, a poster to be displayed at the local library and other public places, and maybe a few nicely crafted letters to area businesses or organizations announcing your new venture, with a product order form attached (and, if appropriate, some samples in a box). As mentioned previously, clever CFOs often use any unsold products from a farmers' or pop-up market as marketing samples for future customers.

How you advertise will be predicated on what you're selling and how, based on your state laws. On this book's website, we share a few examples

as a guide. Don't leave out contact information, any order specifics (like minimum orders), and whether or not free delivery is included.

Direct Marketing

In the same way many CFOs sell their products directly to their customers, direct marketing connects your messages directly to those you wish to reach. While social media can be viewed as direct marketing, many other channels are used to elicit direct responses from potential customers. Some of the most widely used include promotional letters, newsletters, and postcards sent via mail, email, or text messaging.

Postal Mail

Most of us are familiar with getting catalogs and credit card offers in the mail. While they're becoming less common thanks to the exploding use of electronic communication, sending a polished snail mail letter, perhaps with a few product samples, to potential customers can be effective, particularly if you are trying to land a large account like a weekly bakery order for an office. But you must reach the right decision-maker, or your solicitation letter may end up with the junk mail. You may need to make a few cold calls to receptionists or secretaries before you send your samples and introductory letter.

Email List Campaigns

Like catalogs in the mail, spam in our email inbox has become an accepted, albeit unwanted, aspect of using this form of direct communication via the Internet. With the widespread availability of free email, more people than ever have adopted this means of receiving and sending messages.

Besides crafting simple emails that announce a new product or event you will be selling at, you can also design more sophisticated emails using graphically rich templates from many email systems, perhaps ones you already use.

You may, however, encounter a limit as to how many emails you can send out at one time—in part, an (unsuccessful) effort by technology companies to curb spam. So if you have a large enough database of names, you may find yourself needing to use various free or low-cost email management systems, plus a host of other marketing features. Among some of the most widely used service providers are Sendinblue (sendinblue.com), MailChimp (mailchimp.com), Constant Contact (constantcontact.com), and Emma

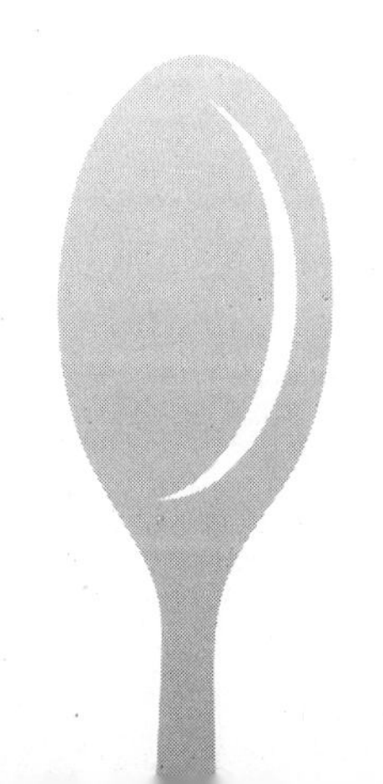

(myemma.com). Each email service provider may offer various analytics and other customizable options and design templates or features. Even if your state forbids sales via the Internet, you can still have a website to share general product and company information and take an order over the telephone.

A word of caution, however. Keep what you email out relevant, helpful, and informative, otherwise you run the risk of turning off the very customers you want to excite and engage. If you send too many messages, too often, some recipients may see the constant contact as a constant annoyance.

Websites

One of the easiest ways to raise awareness and establish a degree of professionalism around your product and company is to create a website. This digital presence allows you to share information about your business. For whatever reasons, a few states' cottage food laws prohibit any Internet-based advertising or communication; double-check to make sure this restriction doesn't apply to you. Even if your state forbids Internet sales, you can still have a website to share general product and company information and take an order over the telephone.

The website would, of course, include your company name, products, contact information, order forms (if allowed in your state), and the backstory to your business. Consider adding a schedule of your markets, events, and other sales venues so people know when and where to find you—just make sure to keep it up to date. While there are lots of opinions about what makes a great website, ease of navigation remains important. Most websites have either a navigation bar across the top or along one side containing words or a graphic that connects you to key components, or pages, on the site.

Be sure to include a slice of your personal story. This helps differentiate your products from the mass-produced ones on the supermarket shelves. A simple "About" page could include a photo of you in the kitchen preparing your products, plus a lively question-and answer format that helps support and promote your story. Replies to the following questions may be a great place to start:

- How did you get started making your product?
- What makes your product unique?
- Why did you start (your business name)?
- When you're not in the kitchen, what are you doing?

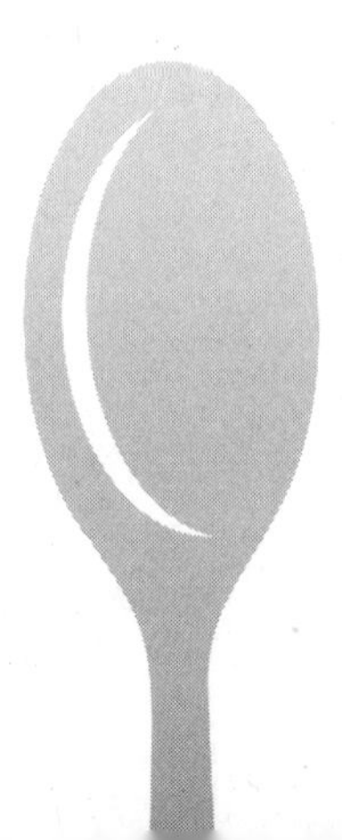

Another important feature may be a "Frequently Asked Questions," or FAQ, page. This can deflect time-consuming telephone or email questions and clarify your policies and procedures. An FAQ page is a great place to try to establish boundaries for your business, like confirming hours to avoid late night calls or last-minute orders. This is also another place to reiterate your written policy for late pickups or no-shows. Many CFOs keep adding to the FAQ page as new customer questions arise, such as the following:

- How can I get your product?
- Do you have a minimum order?
- Can you deliver?
- What kind of payment do you accept?
- How quick is your turnaround on an order?
- When are you available to discuss an order?
- What happens to my order and payment if I have to cancel last minute or miss my pickup?

The graphics, style, and feel of your website should echo your products in terms of the design, color schemes, and other creative elements. For example, if you decide to use a red gingham pattern for your products, this could also be cleverly worked into the design of the website. Featuring customer endorsements, testimonials, or media coverage you may have received will help reinforce the quality of your products and the reputation of your company.

Search engine optimization, or SEO, refers to ways you can improve both the traffic to your website and the number of on-target potential customers who might visit your website from search engines like Google. Like anything else related to marketing your business, it's a good idea to have an SEO strategy before jumping in and producing your website. SEO is important because that's how potential customers actually find you when searching the Internet.

Depending on your time and interest, there are numerous tools and resources to better understand your customers visiting your website, traffic patterns, and so forth. For example, if you plan on using Facebook ads, Facebook's pixel can be installed for free on your website; it's a snippet of code that allows you to measure, optimize, and build audiences for your ad campaigns. If you're someone who likes to know details on what works for one person but not another and testing ideas, you could examine conversion rate optimization, or CRO, testing what works best on your website to

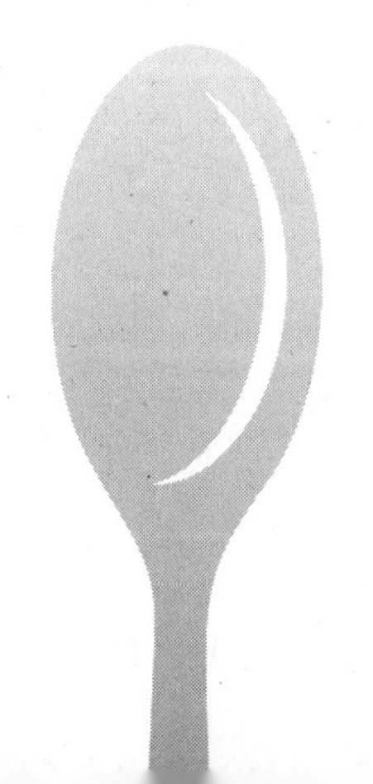

generate leads and sales. SEO helps drive traffic to your website; CRO helps convert those visitors by enticing them to act in some way, like signing up for a newsletter or buying your products.

There are two ways to approach a website for your business, one involves money and another that is free. Gone are the days when you needed big bucks for a website. Since many cottage food businesses may be just getting off the ground, starting with a free website might be the simplest and wisest choice.

Free Websites

The following companies offer the ability to customize easy-to-use templates for your business; there are many other options as well. If you have some computer experience, the intuitive nature of their websites makes them easy to navigate, and instructional videos will guide you through the design, so there's no programming or coding involved. These websites do have some space and creative limitations and may come with small ads that also appear on your website. But for most first-timers, you'll be amazed by the results. Just register for the template you like the best and start

Use Google My Business, It's Free

One of the first things we did for our Inn Serendipity B&B was get a free Business Profile on Google My Business, sometimes called GMB. Helping customers more easily find your business and the products it offers is a breeze via Google, once you set up an account. Now more than ever before, your location is being recorded by your browser, cell phone, and so forth (unless you've disabled this feature). When you make a search, Google might reveal how others may search for you at the bottom of the first search results page, like the following examples:

- baked goods near me
- best pastries near me
- fresh bread bakery
- birthday cake bakeries near me

If you have a GMB, you are making it easier to be found by your neighbors. Besides putting you on the map, GMB allows you to personalize your profile, which you control, with photos, special offers, and key contact information, including website address/URL—which is important for SEO. It allows you to highlight the fact that you're a woman-owned business or, perhaps, a US veteran, whatever applies to you and your story. ☛

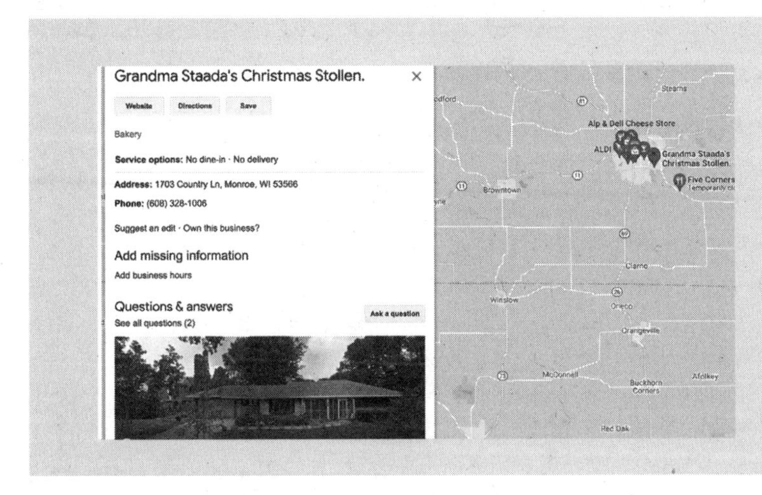

Grandma Staada's Christmas Stollen, made by home baker Chris Sachs, pops up with the supermarket bakeries in the small town of Monroe, Wisconsin, even though his bakery is only operated during December. SEO success!
CREDIT: GOOGLE SCREEN CAPTURE.

uploading text and photos. There's plenty of free storage space. Test out the site before you go live, even completing a test order.

wordpress.com

It's so easy an 11-year-old can do it. Really. This is the leading blogging interface that can be adapted easily as a business website. For the record, "blog" stands for a "web log." If you love writing about your products, ingredients, or journey as a food entrepreneur, this option will be particularly attractive.

wix.com

Containing numerous templates, many product-oriented, this popular cloud-based website builder focuses on easy drag-and-drop design elements. Its simplicity will appeal to less tech-savvy people and get you quickly set up on the Internet. You can design websites that are both mobile and computer-screen optimized. Newsletter sign-up, social media integration, and SEO options make this a robust option. More features are added regularly. We intentionally created the website for both this book and our Inn Serendipity Homemade Bakery.

Inn Serendipity Fresh Baked HOMEMADE BAKERY website created for free with Wix.
CREDIT: INN SERENDIPITY FRESH BAKED HOMEMADE BAKERY

squareup.com

Another solid visuals-driven interface, especially after Square (used for e-commerce and payment processing) acquired Weebly, a cloud-based website builder. Use this referral link—squareup.com/i/HOMEMADE22—and you'll receive free processing on up to $1,000 in sales for the first 180 days. It can include an e-commerce platform.

Low-cost Websites

More experienced entrepreneurs who want greater control over their name, products, design elements, and capabilities can purchase their domain name (the name you select to represent your company) and then host their own website. Both the domain name and hosting fees cost less than $100 per year from companies like BlueHost or GoDaddy. Most free websites also allow paid upgrades that include a registered domain name.

Hosting and designing your own website may require greater computer knowledge than you have the time or interest for. If so, you could hire a designer, depending on your budget, design goals, and intended purpose of the website within your business. Some CFOs find a family member, friend, or neighbor happy to help design a professional-looking website, perhaps in exchange for a regular supply of cookies or jams.

At the time of printing, Shopify (shopify.com) and Squarespace (squarespace.com) were among the popular e-commerce-focused platforms used by some CFOs to accept orders, process online and in-person payments, and display menu offerings. Monthly fees are based on the features you select. Like the free website builders, tools for SEO allow you to add meta descriptions, product details and tags.

Social Media

Everything you do is about sharing your story. Don't overlook ways to let your customers do this for you as well. To build awareness around your product, you'll need to get people to try it, love it, and share what they like about it with the rest of the world. With the explosive growth of the Internet—plus access to it through computers, mobile phones, and tablets—social media have become an increasingly important part of an advertising campaign. And it need not cost you a penny to get started.

Your most effective advertising are the satisfied customers themselves. Word of mouth has always trumped a four-color display ad in a magazine. People are much more likely to trust their friends than a company trying to sell them something (even if what you're selling is really great).

Thanks to the proliferation of social media, many options are available for sharing your story with the world, in characters, updates, photos, and

video. The multiplier effect cannot be overstated. But it does require a different modus operandi, where talking becomes typing and a printed poster becomes a "folder" of incredible photos of your products, your home kitchen, and your customers savoring a bite of your creations. Because there aren't enough hours in the day to do them all, carefully select the social media your customers use most.

Regardless of the social media you prefer, there are two elements which should be considered for each post you make: hashtags and tags.

Have fun coming up with creative ways to engage your customers on social media.
PHOTO: JOHN D. IVANKO PHOTOGRAPHY

Hashtags and Tags

The "hashtag" in a social media post refers to a metadata hash symbol, #, followed by a keyword or phrase related to a topic, that enables others to discover it when searching for that topic. For example, using #cookies, #MonroeWisconsin, and #valentinesday for a Valentine's Day cookie pop-up market in the local community of Monroe, Wisconsin, would help people discover what you are selling at a specific time and location.

For Facebook and Instagram, using the @ sign allows you to tag specific people, companies, or organizations related to your post, assuming they have a social media page. For example, if you're selling at a specific farmers' market for Valentine's Day, then you could use a tag for the specific market, @ElkGroveFarmersMarket (Elk Grove Farmers Market in Elk Grove Village, Illinois). In this way, you let the farmers' market receive a notice that you tagged them and hyperlinks to the tagged profile. This is what's commonly referred to as being "mentioned" in a post. If you're active on Facebook, and may have liked the tagged organization's page, it's possible the Facebook algorithm may display that post to other Facebook friends. Yep, that's free advertising. In general, the more likes, shares, or replies you get or make—your engagement—the more Facebook might expand the reach of your post.

The more your customers rave about your products to others on the Internet, the better. People who love your product can, in spirit, be your "in-house" advertising agency. They can tell their friends, share links to your products on Facebook, "like" on Instagram, or tweet about their favorites, too.

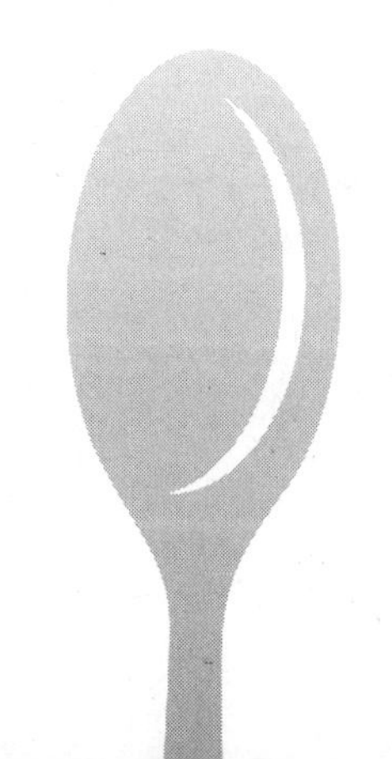

Catapult Your Business Forward with Some Miraculous Digital Marketing

The dynamo and dynamic marketing twins, Heather and Corrie Miracle, co-owners of Sugar Cookie Marketing, pack a punch when it comes to marketing insights and ideas, especially in the digital realm. Raised on smartphone feeds and cookies, the Miracle twins stake the value and timeliness of their guidance — often presented with a touch of humor and irreverence — on delivering results for cottage food operators across the country since 2020. While focused on cookies, their suggestions easily translate to marketing other cottage food products.

Based in Virginia, Corrie and Heather manage a vibrant free Sugar Cookie Marketing Facebook group where members join to learn how to take better cookie photos, sell more effectively, and price high enough to pay yourself. They were both speakers at the Home-based Food Entrepreneur Virtual National Conference and the masterminds behind the Cookie College, a membership-based online subscription that allows you to access courses that help get your bakery business seen when it comes to online marketing. Sugar Cookie Marketing focuses on making dough, as in "money," not how to make or decorate cookies, there are plenty of other online outlets and YouTube videos for that.

Heather and Corrie Miracle discussing which cookies they're going to start baking in their home kitchen.
CREDIT: SUGAR COOKIE MARKETING

Corrie and Heather also love baking and decorating sugar cookies. Eating them, too. And they sell their cookies under Virginia's cottage food law. "We can't ship, but we haven't found that to hold us back when it comes to making sales," admits Corrie. "The best part is that there are tons of people in the area that we can benefit from when it comes to online marketing right here where we live!

"Photography in this day and age is so important," explains Corrie, endlessly eager to share her knowledge on digital marketing. "What better way to get in front of your potential audience than with an awesome photo to stop that endless scroll on social media. Most people buy with their eyes. So, for the best shots, find some indirect natural light. This type lighting is what makes your photography go from blah to awe.

"Whether you take your baked goods down to a sliding glass door in the basement or use a bay window in the living room, indirect natural light is the best prop available for your photography," continues Corrie. She's quick to point out that all you'll need is the cell phone you already own due to the quality of their cameras. Corrie suggests downloading the free limited-feature version of the Adobe Lightroom ☛

app for your phone to do a little post-processing, lightening up and enhancing photos to really make them stand out in social media feeds.

"Macarons are beauties," Corrie explains, holding them up as an example. "But where the value is at is truly in the fillings, so showcase them. I love when macaron people take a bite or break one open so you can see exactly what you are buying. Boy does it create some delicious 'FOMO,' fear of missing out. So, I usually leave one or two macarons without their top shells so I can photograph those gorgeous vanilla beans or showcase a specific filling that will get people to reach into their wallets. For my pumpkin cheesecake macs, I went for an autumn feel, so we brought in woods and warmed up our shadows. They scream, 'put me on the couch and wrap me in a burrito blanket,' doesn't it? Half our sale is done before we even start typing. I use aeCore Backers for my photography backdrops, and here's why: They are food-safe, rigid, stain-resistant, scratch-resistant, and waterproof."

"I know I'm not hitting any headlines, but you need to be on Facebook and Instagram," jokingly chimes in Heather. "Creating a great Facebook post is more than just a couple of words and a prayer. A converting Facebook Post consists of a scroll-stopping creative, either a photo or video, an attention-grabbing headline, and a strong call to action. These factors combined will capture your viewers' attention, inform your audience, and guide them to the next steps of the sale. Think of your photo as what catches the eyes and your headline or first line of your copy to be what captures their interest. The rest of your copy is building value and your final send-off is a call to action telling them what to do next."

"Food porn" shot of Corrie Miracle's macarons.
Credit: Sugar Cookie Marketing

"A call to action is a command," further clarifies Corrie. There's little doubt that the two are, in fact, twin sisters. "We often tell our kids, 'Wash your hands' before they eat. That is a call to action. We are telling our audience what to do next. 'Click on the link to order' or 'Message me to book.' These are examples of strong calls to action that can help guide your audience to the next steps in the sale. You may think of call to actions as being pushy, but they aren't. We, as consumers, want to know what to do next. Don't leave ☛

your audience guessing. Help them by giving them the directions they need to buy what you are selling."

Tags are another important element of a social media post. "Good tags are ones that can benefit you and the person you are tagging," says Heather. "Tagging random accounts that have nothing to do with the content you are posting is both annoying for them and wasting their time. It can cause the opposite effect to what you are going for where they either remove the tag or block you from doing it again.

"Getting blocked or banned by Facebook can cause your business to go to a full stop, and we don't have time for that in today's online buying world," cautions Heather, related to other issues that might come up on social media. "To avoid getting banned or blocked, familiarize yourself with Facebook's terms of service and their Community Guidelines. Make sure that what you are selling and who you are selling to is in line with its guidelines. It's great to take a few seconds to go back and read the guidelines rather than posting and learning the hard way."

"With social media, be consistent," advises Corrie. "There's nothing that will cause zero sales more than not posting for the whole year or posting once and hoping that someone buys from you. With consistent regular posts, your audience will turn into a hot market for your items, ready to buy. You need to be consistent in your message, your branding, and your posts. Use Facebook's scheduling software to make it easy. You could schedule right from the platform. Plus, you can know when your audience is going be most active, and you can make sure a post goes up at the best time, increasing the likelihood of it being seen and lead to an order."

"Don't just set the scheduling software and forget it, though," adds Heather. "You need to be there engaging your clients, interacting with your potential customers so that there's a conversation going on. People buy from those they like know and trust. So, let them get to know you and let them like you."

"As for which is better, Facebook or Instagram, the answer really comes down to who your target audience is," says Corrie. "Are they an older generation with college-age students? Odds are you will find them on Facebook getting their daily dose of news and family updates. Are they a younger crowd, perhaps recently graduated college and into the first years of starting a family? You better believe they are on Instagram hashtagging away! Take the time to really know your audience. It will help you decide which platform is the best time spent for you and your business."

"The reality is that if you want to reach people from the comfort of their own phones, you need to make the time," says Heather, on the reality of posting and engaging customers through social media. "You don't need to be a social media influencer to be effective, but a few minutes on a Monday spent scheduling out your posts on scheduling software can help keep you and your product top of mind and keep those sales coming in."

"You don't have to believe in the platform to use it, but you do need to be where your target audience is to reach them," adds Heather. "Do you need to post a million times a week? Absolutely not. But three times a week can definitely grow your business and help people discover you."

"Be creative with your content!" exclaims Corrie. "Show them behind the scenes, and let them get to know you. You don't have to be selling in every ☛

single post. People buy from those they like, know, and trust so let them get to do just that with your posts. You'll find that you'll start enjoying the platform, even more, when you can form relationships instead of just sales."

"If you've got the swing of things on social, then consider making a transition from just a Facebook page and an Instagram profile into Facebook ads manager," says Heather. "It's not just boosting a post. Facebook ads manager is taking the training wheels off on ads and allowing you to create an advertisement that is served to your target audience. If the boosted post is a shotgun, think of Facebook ads as a sniper rifle; you find that target audience, that person who is likely to pay you, and you serve them an ad at the time that they're probably going to reach into their wallet. Facebook ads manager has quite a learning curve, and it is a quick way to lose a lot of money, so proceed carefully."

"Another easy tip is to start learning Google forms," says Corrie. "Google forms makes it easy for your client and your end user. And it also saves you a bunch of time and energy. Time is profit. So, the less you can spend on actually trying to chase down customers and information, and the more you can spend on marketing and advertising, is more money in your pocket in the future." Like creating a Facebook page for your business, Google forms are free.

"If you have no website, you're losing sales. Plain and simple," says Heather. "A website is the single biggest thing that you can do to move your business forward. At the end of the day, we don't own our Facebook pages, our Instagram accounts, or our TikToks, but we do own our websites." She's quick, however, to convey that it's not just about throwing up a bunch of product photos and descriptions on a website.

"Search engine optimization, or SEO, is critical in online selling," adds Heather. "SEO is a great way to get your website in front of your target audience. By optimizing your website for searches, you are placing yourself right in front of those who need you most."

"SEO is the process of building your website to rank better in search engines like Google," chimes in Corrie. "You know when you search 'Best pizza places' and a list of websites pop up? They are ranked in Google because people find their websites helpful to their search for the best pizza. Imagine if everyone who searched for what you sell actually found you first. That's a lot of new customers and a lot of potential sales. SEO is powerful, and when it's done right, it's life-changing when it comes to online marketing and sales." They regularly follow a general Local SEO strategy outline, to make sure they're covering all the bases.

"All SEO falls under either 'on-page' tasks or 'off-page' tasks, meaning that you're performing SEO either inside of a website, 'on-page,' or external to the website like building backlinks and social signals, 'off-page,'" explains Heather. "With local, we have a bit more strategy because we have the ability to rank in maps and quite a bit less competition since we're only competing with our locality or service area. To attempt to rank first for the keyword 'cookies for sale' would be a national keyword and requires a much different strategy than 'cookies for sale near me' which would be associated with a local search intent."

For the off-page SEO, Heather and Corrie emphasize the importance of securing and optimizing the Google Business Platform, or Google My Business. ☛

Local search engine optimization (SEO) strategy overview from Sugar Cookie Marketing.
CREDIT: SUGAR COOKIE MARKETING

You need to get a sense of what keywords people would use to find you when searching. It's also very important to establish backlinks from Facebook, since this impacts SEO results; the more relevant backlinks from your Facebook page and other customers' Facebook pages who love your products, the better.

If you're going all in on SEO, you could pay to play hardball. "'Gray hat' is skirting the blurry line between what is ethical SEO, called 'white hat,' and what is considered manipulation of SEO, referred to as 'black hat,'" further explains Heather. "The gray hat SEO uses techniques of both to create a strategy that lies somewhere in between. While Google would like us to earn backlinks by creating quality content and hoping it's discovered, we can purchase backlinks instead. Because those links weren't earned but rather purchased, it's considered not a white hat to purchase links." Buying backlinks is accomplished through various link builders found online.

For the on-page SEO strategy, the Miracle twins advise thinking through what you want to do before jumping in. Building out a wire framework for your website is like understanding the skeleton of our body and how everything is connected. The wire framework is the structure of the website, not the aesthetic design. Numerous online guides detail some of the particular tricks of the trade related to developing content for your SEO-optimized website — or you can hire an SEO copywriter. Word choice, the size of images so they can quickly load, providing alternative text for each photo, strong keyword-oriented sub-headers, and a number of other considerations come into play for achieving the results, for example, someone searching for "gluten-free children's birthday cake, your city, your state."

"Google provides two main reporting dashboards to understand more of how Google views your site in search," says Heather. "The most common is Google Analytics, but Google Search Console is a huge tool many overlook because it's overshadowed by the more notarized Google Analytics. Formerly called Webmaster Tools, Search Console can be enabled through domain verification or cross-authorization from an active Google Analytics accounts. Google Analytics is user-oriented, providing data related to those who visit and interact with your website. Google Search ☛

Console, on the other hand, is search-engine focused, providing tools and insights that can help site owners improve visibility and presence in the search engine result pages."

"Silos are a metaphor for content that supports strategic content," describes Corrie. "The silo strategy uses all portions of the website — the home page, blog, pages, categories — to create a content structure around a keyword or phrase. A silo page can be any page on a website that's been included in a silo content strategy. Siloing content also benefits the website in that crawlers, those computer programs that search documents on the Internet, can better understand your content, how it's structured, and how to rank it. It's also beneficial to end users who typically click for information, then click within that info for additional information on the topic being researched."

"You need to ask for product reviews in our line of work," encourages Corrie, since reviews lend credibility, can be featured on your website or echoed in a social media post. "After you complete an order, follow up with the customer with a Facebook private message or email: 'I hope you enjoyed that order. If there are any issues, let me know. If your order met your expectations, I would love it if you can support my small business by leaving a review.' Then give them the website address that goes straight to the recommendation area on your Facebook page. The less work you have to make them do, the better."

"We don't have to reinvent the wheel when it comes to marketing, you just take what's working and then put your spin on it," sums up Heather. "Do some market research, by setting up a Google alert, on alerts.google.com. You put in keywords, your company name, your name, or even a big local competitor. Then you'll get notified every time somebody on the Internet types in those words. It's a great way to see what your competition's doing. And frankly, it's a great way to see what the Internet thinks about you."

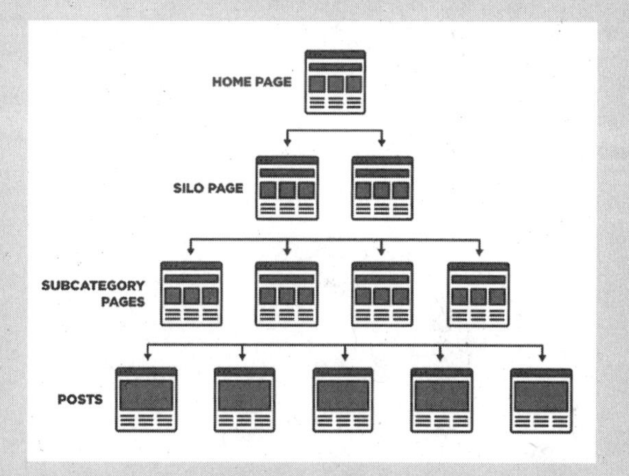

Diagram of a silo from Sugar Cookie Marketing.
CREDIT: SUGAR COOKIE MARKETING

Facebook: facebook.com

Currently, the dominant social media networking service where you can keep connected to your customers and share regular social updates, such as a new product or an upcoming event where you'll be selling. As part of their marketing strategy, some companies are now choosing to make their business Facebook page their de facto "website."

When you start your Facebook page for your venture, be sure to select and create a "business" profile, not a "personal" page. This keeps your business professional and opens up opportunities you won't have on your personal page, including the ability to schedule posts in advance, assign other people as administrators (to help you), access analytic tools, and implement targeted advertising campaigns, if you choose to do so later. Many CFOs have also tapped into Facebook Marketplace for local outreach and connections for sales, especially flash sales. Note, however, that Facebook Marketplace tends to attract more bargain shoppers.

Reeling in Customers with Social Media

Malina Lee's best-selling Letter/Number Cake, promoted, when allowed, on various social media groups she joins.
Credit: Malina Lee/Sweet Grace SA

"I posted my best selling and most profitable item, my Letter/Number Cake, in every single Facebook group I was allowed to," says Malina Lee, owner of Sweet Grace (SweetGraceSA.com), based in San Antonio, Texas. The cake is topped with macarons, roses, and pretzels. "Wherever I post it, I get sales. Moms love it for their daughters, friends love it for their friends. Everyone loves it, and it's easy to sell. Plus the profit margin on it is absolutely wonderful. It's made of cake, and the cake board is 13 inches by 9 inches. Each digit is made of two layers from a half sheet of cake. I charge $100, plus $2.50 per macaron. These take me about two hours to make from start to finish, not including baking and cooling time.

"If you are allowed to market in the mom groups in your area, do it!" exclaims Lee. Her business is a full-time job. "I had a total of about 750 likes off the postings in the mom groups in my area this month and around 70 comments and more than 50 order inquiries. Ten of my January orders, worth about $1,000, came from the wonderful mom groups where I had to pay nothing to post. I marketed myself as someone who had availability to 'make all of your kiddos' birthday dreams come true.'" Lee's sales for the month of January totaled $2,550, which included $300 in customer tips and $750 in TikTok payouts. She uses JotForm to take and process orders; her website is powered by Shopify.

As it turns out, Lee is so effective at using Instagram and TikTok, she's become a bona fide social media influencer and creates reels, those short video clips, posted on social media. Her hard work engaging customers translates to an additional income stream for her business. "You have to be eligible, and then there needs to be a bonus 'opportunity,'" Lee explains, about her TikTok videos. "It just popped up for me when I started posting my reels consistently on TikTok. You get paid for how many views you get."

CREDIT: MALINA LEE/SWEET GRACE SA

Instagram: instagram.com

Instagram provides a platform to share the story of your business via photos, enabling you to develop an authentic personal narrative with potential customers and create engagement with you, your company, and your brand. When your product wins a state fair or is enjoyed by your state governor, share that candid photo here with the appropriate hashtags.

Twitter: twitter.com

If you like texting, then this online microblogging website is perfect for sharing what's happening with your business in 140 characters or less. This is a mainstay for news media outlets.

TikTok: tiktok.com

Share short video clips captured with a mobile phone, whether more polished or spontaneously funny or creative. It's not just for the kids anymore.

Pinterest: pinterest.com

Think cork bulletin board with photos, embedded on an Internet page. This pinboard-style website can spread images of your food products through the Internet if your photos are beautiful enough.

YouTube: youtube.com

Owned by Google, this free movie-sharing website is particularly useful if you have the talent and interest in creating videos around your products and their use in the kitchen, perhaps as cooking demos.

LinkedIn: linkedin.com

This professional business network can connect you to people once impossible to reach, if you can get into their inner business circle. It's all about degrees—or links—of separation. Try it out and see if you're only six degrees of separation away from everyone you might want to meet. It could be used to connect with partners at a law office or bank branch managers in town who might just need a nudge before ordering some cookies for a "customer appreciation day."

Just because you have 742 Facebook "friends" doesn't mean these friends see every "status update" you post. Make no mistake, not only are Facebook and other social media sites mining personal information about you and your online life, they're making money off you, too. In fact, if you have your "cookies" disabled on your browser, you cannot even sign in to use the site; cookies track everything you do. Facebook and many other social media companies have proprietary and secret algorithms they use to control how many people see your updates.

If you want to boost your reach and increase your audience on social media, you have to pay for it. This is called "pay-per-click." You can focus on people who like your page and their friends, or broaden your reach to people you target. Right on their main business page, the social media site will show you how you can increase your reach and how much it will cost you; heck, they even create a sample advertisement out of the content you just provided.

All you have to do is enter your credit card and set your parameters, including your budget, target market, and duration of the campaign. Then with a click of a button, your ad will reach a segment of the population so specific that it's a bit creepy, at least to us. The good news, however, is you can effectively target a market at a potentially very low cost; your update will show up in their "news feed."

Listing on Free Directories

While most cottage food businesses can't sell by mail or cross state lines, getting listed on one or more of the many free national Internet directories

can help locals find you. This will also be another means for media to access your information. And links from other websites to your website boosts your company website's SEO.

Forrager: forrager.com

It's billed as the "cottage food community," a space where home cooks, bakers, and decorators can learn and share with each other. Solely focused on the cottage food industry, Forrager has grown from an information portal into an online community, where people can ask and answer questions, connect with each other, and add their cottage food operation to the directory.

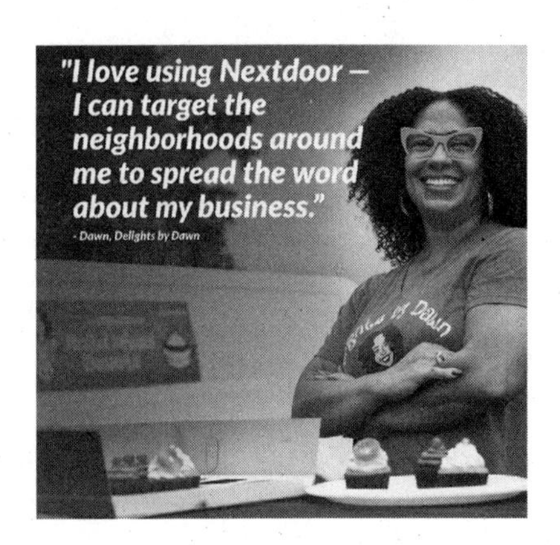

Dawn Belisle featured in a Nextdoor advertisement. *See the story profile on page 238.* CREDIT: DELIGHTS BY DAWN

Nextdoor: nextdoor.com

Billed as a hyperlocal social networking service for neighborhoods, this app and web-based network can connect you to potential customers in your community.

Etsy: etsy.com

This e-commerce website, developed to sell handmade items, has a growing listing of baked goods. Just make sure your state law doesn't prevent you from taking online orders.

Specialized Online Marketing and Sales Platforms

Another way to garner sales and streamline your entire marketing, ordering, sales, and bookkeeping processes may be through marketing and sales platforms especially designed for cottage food operations or home-based prepared food enterprises that might be operating under food freedom laws or licensed as a microenterprise home kitchen operation. They could be an alternative to having your own website, depending on your overall goals and priorities with your business. Some CFOs find Facebook or Instagram meet their needs in terms of drumming up sales.

At the time of printing, several marketing and sales platforms are available, with various features, cost-structures, and capabilities. Each provides a way for food entrepreneurs to market their homemade food online and a way for potential customers to search for, order, and pay for the homemade products or prepared foods that interests them. Castiron (castiron.me), My Custom Bakes by Borderland, and Tastebuddy focus on food product businesses, including CFOs. FoodNome (foodnome.com), Shef (shef.com), and

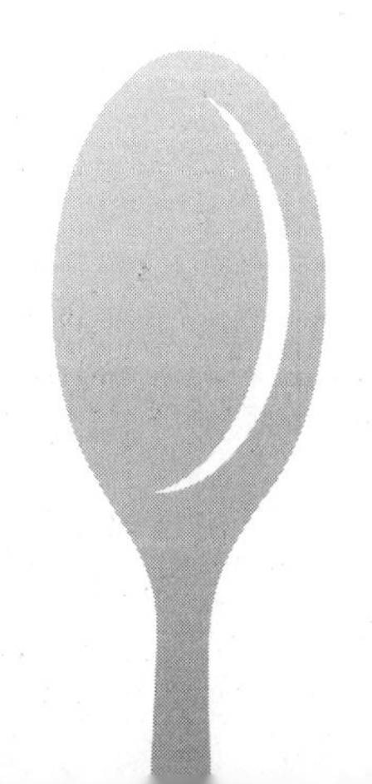

YouFeed (youfeedapp.com) focus on home-based prepared food businesses established under food freedom or operating as a microenterprise home kitchen operation.

Some platforms are both website and app-based, while others can only be used through a mobile app. Given the growth of the cottage food and food freedom movement, and the fact that many state laws currently prohibit the use of third-party delivery services like Grubhub, DoorDash, and UberEats, there will likely be a proliferation of such services in the coming years. Research or try out, if possible for free, various options to see which best serve your needs.

5 "Cast Iron" Strategies for Using an Online Marketing and Sales Platform

When it comes down to it, most cottage food operators or home-based food entrepreneurs prefer to focus on what they love, making delicious food products or, in the case of those home chefs with food freedom laws in their state, prepared meals.

Designing websites, sending out newsletters, and keeping track of customers or sales are what we must do if we're operating as a business. But most of us prefer to minimize the amount of time doing tasks outside the kitchen. The growth of specialized online marketing platforms makes it easier than ever before to take orders, initiate marketing communications with customers, and keep track of sales.

"Castiron is a mission-driven e-commerce company that elevates how independent kitchen-based creators sell to their customers and provides them with resources and community to support their whole business," explains Mark Josephson, CEO and Founder of Castiron. "The world's best bakers, juicers, canners, jammers, caterers, meal-preppers, private chefs, and other culinary artisans use Castiron as a central hub to sell their products online, connect with customers, grow their businesses, and save time and money so they can focus on making what they love."

As one of the sponsors of the Home-based Food Entrepreneur Virtual National Conference, Castiron was eager to learn about CFO needs as they developed an online platform to best serve them. Here's what they recommend when it comes to considering whether an online marketing platform is right for you.

When searching for an online sales and marketing platform, Emily Brungard, Marketing Manager at Castiron recommends that you look for the following key components.

Ease of Use

No one should have to be a coder or website designer to have an effective storefront to sell your cookies, cakes, or jars of jelly. Look for a platform that is easy to use without sacrificing the features you need for your business.

One-Stop Shop

You don't want your new technology to make things harder for you, do you? Ideally, your website introduces your customers to you and your business, while also showing them what you have to sell, accepting orders and payments, and even helping to secure repeat purchases through marketing. At the end of the day, the platform should be complete and flexible.

Help Line with a Real Human

Tired of chatbots or electronic FAQs that never answer your questions or solve your issue? Make sure your platform of choice offers quality human customer service. Look for fast response times — minutes or hours instead of days or weeks.

Built-in Marketing Optimization

Just like you shouldn't need to code your website from scratch, you also shouldn't have to become an SEO expert or an email marketing pro to market your business. Look for tools that automatically optimize your website so that it's search-engine friendly, or so that you can easily keep customers updated on your newest products and coupons.

Domain Expertise

Look for a sales platform that specializes in what you are selling. Some tools can be a mile wide and an inch deep, meaning they're catering to everyone instead of just businesses like yours. The best platform for your business will offer features that are unique to the needs of a cottage food operator — things like hiding your home address until pickup time for privacy, product templates to help you get selling faster, or automatic allergen and dietary information on product listings.

While we have a Wix website for our home bakery business and use Square to process credit card orders online and for in-person events, we decided to harness the power of an online marketing and sales platform as well. If you already have nice photos of your products, a logo, a headshot, and text that describes your products and your business, you could be operational with an online storefront in a matter of an hour since their easy-to-follow, step-by-step guide takes the CFO through the entire process. It took us 45 minutes on Castiron. The built-in payment processing is accomplished through Stripe, with us directly connecting it to our business checking account.

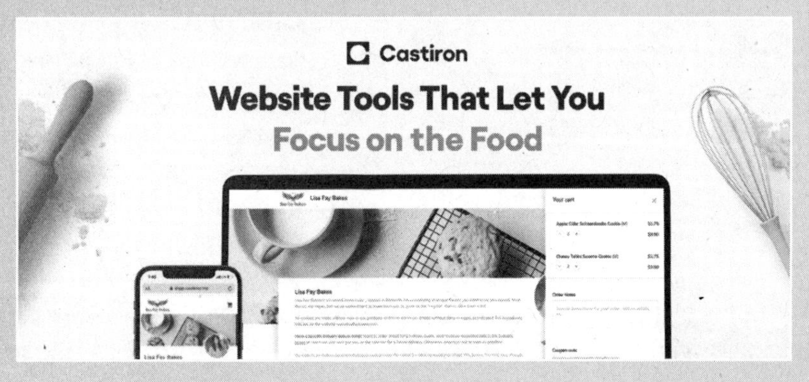

CREDIT: CASTIRON

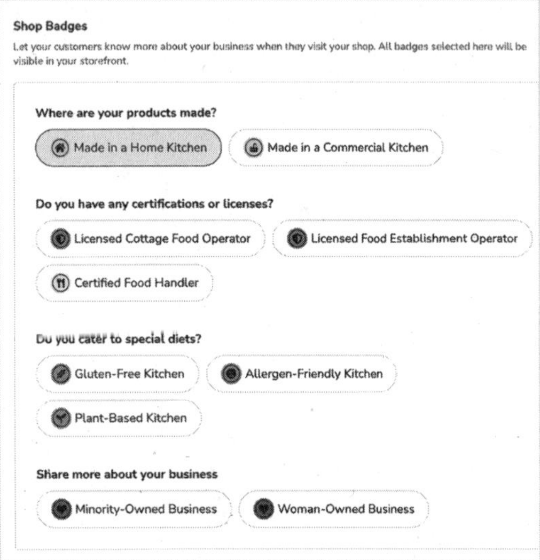

Shop Badges
Let your customers know more about your business when they visit your shop. All badges selected here will be visible in your storefront.

Where are your products made?
Made in a Home Kitchen · Made in a Commercial Kitchen

Do you have any certifications or licenses?
Licensed Cottage Food Operator · Licensed Food Establishment Operator · Certified Food Handler

Do you cater to special diets?
Gluten-Free Kitchen · Allergen-Friendly Kitchen · Plant-Based Kitchen

Share more about your business
Minority-Owned Business · Woman-Owned Business

Castiron's easy-to-use setup process allows CFOs to showcase noteworthy attributes of their business with Shop Badges. CREDIT: CASTIRON

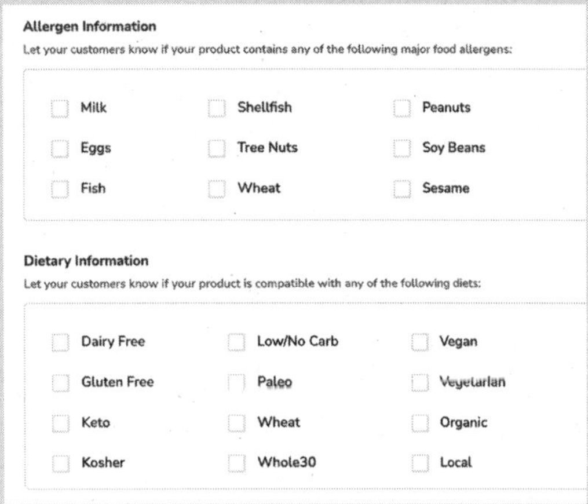

Allergen Information
Let your customers know if your product contains any of the following major food allergens:

Milk	Shellfish	Peanuts
Eggs	Tree Nuts	Soy Beans
Fish	Wheat	Sesame

Dietary Information
Let your customers know if your product is compatible with any of the following diets:

Dairy Free	Low/No Carb	Vegan
Gluten Free	Paleo	Vegetarian
Keto	Wheat	Organic
Kosher	Whole30	Local

Castiron's easy-to-use setup process allows CFOs to highlight key product dietary attributes as well as potential allergens. CREDIT: CASTIRON

Unlike the limitations in Wix, Castiron offers the ability to highlight key aspects of our business, like where the products are made, any certifications received, or whether the business is woman-owned. They call them Shop Badges.

"Shopify is built for everyone — not just the cottage food operator," observes Josephson, about another popular website platform. "When you use a one-size fits-all product, you're bound to run into some limitations. With Castiron, you're getting a product that was built as a result of thousands of conversations with cottage food business owners. Shopify can be overwhelming, especially for someone who doesn't want to spend a lot of time coding or designing their website. With Castiron, you're getting an intuitively designed, easy-to-use website that you can go live within minutes, no coding or design chops required."

The platform offers unlimited product listings, custom orders, invoices, and transactions. Just about any credit card can be securely accepted, as well as Apple Pay and Google Pay. They offer an automated customer list, and you can receive order notifications and status updates. It's nice, if there's ever a problem, to be able to quickly connect with a human being should an issue arise — something that's never an option with Facebook.

"At Castiron, we believe in total transparency about the fees we collect on orders," says Brungard. "On your Order Detail pages, you'll be able to see exactly which fees were collected, who keeps them, and how much each fee was.

"We only make money when you do," adds Brungard. "We make money through a transaction fee, paid by your customer at checkout. Castiron collects a service fee on all orders. Additionally, sales tax and ☛

payment processing fees are applied to your customer's total and paid at checkout." There is no listing or monthly fee. Their payouts are weekly. Sales reports can be generated easily, and Castiron issues a 1099-K at the end of the year.

Castiron also offers a free membership to the artisan community in the platform called The Kitchen where food artisans can ask questions, interact with other food artisans, and share real-world experiences, like how to ship cookies without damaging them.

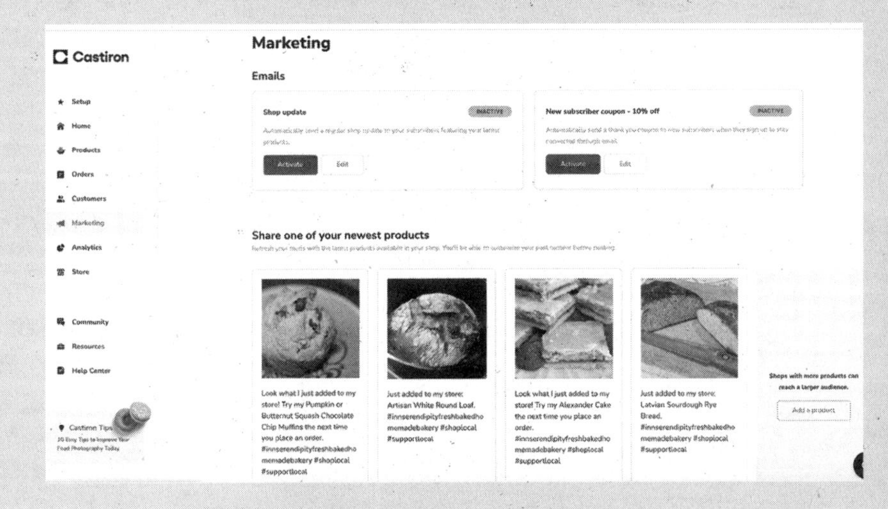

Castiron features click-to-use marketing options to reach out to customers with an update, share new products on social media, and make a coupon offer.
CREDIT: CASTIRON

Having some form of online marketing is essential for any CFO. But there's no hard-and-fast rule for what you should do. Some CFOs focus exclusively, and profitably, on farmers' markets. Others use two or more digital channels and realize that Meta owns both Facebook and Instagram. A poll created by keynote speaker David Crabill at the Home-based Food Entrepreneur Virtual National Conference revealed a diversity of answers to this question: Where do most new customers first discover your business online?

Facebook	49%
Instagram	21%
Website, via search engine query	14%
Google maps (Google My Business)	2%
Other	10%

With more online marketing platforms being created and our evolving use of digital technology, these results are surely to change.

Product Demonstrations and Sampling

Sampling out your product, whether on the table at a farmers' market or in a sampler box you give a prospective company that hosts regular morning roll days or birthday gatherings for employees, is an effective way to get potential customers to try it without any financial commitment on their part. If your items taste as good as your market feasibility studies suggest, then you're just an order form away from landing a new customer.

Every happy customer can lead to two or more down the line. Most catering and cake decorating companies, for example, thrive off referrals. It may take months, or even years, to build this buzz, but once it happens, the work you'll have to do marketing your business will be greatly reduced, depending on your sales goals. Thank those loyal and supportive customers,

Samples Anyone? A Word of Caution

HeathGlen's Farm & Kitchen products with single-use sampling spoons.
CREDIT: COURTESY OF HEATHGLEN'S FARM & KITCHEN

If your sales venue offers the possibility of sampling your product, that's one of the best ways to clinch a sale. But thanks to numerous regulations and requirements, you may find this more problematic and a hassle than it's worth.

At many farmers' markets around the country, trolling health inspectors have effectively put the kibosh on product samples because of fears of food spoilage, customers contaminating the samples, or on other grounds. You'll need to check the specific rules for each venue, such as wearing food service-grade disposable gloves to serve samples. Check with other vendors, too, since they can tip you off if the market or craft fair, for whatever reasons, is on the watch list for the health department.

perhaps with special gifts during the holidays or discounts with every referral they send your way.

Public Relations

PR represents your reputation and brand image. It's what both you and the public say about your business or product. Securing solicited or unsolicited media coverage can be far more cost-effective than any paid display advertisement or classified ad.

By sharing your product story effectively and strategically with various media outlets through a PR campaign, you will:

- Increase visibility of your products and business
- Add credibility to your operations
- Enhance your image
- Sell more products without having to spend a cent
- Create more interest in a "buy local" movement and economy

Hosting Private Product Parties

Another option may be to host a private "product party" along the lines of a Pampered Chef or Tupperware gathering. Invite your friends, neighbors, and other community members in your target market to a private party to taste your products and learn more about how you make them. If you make it an invitation-only event, you may sidestep legal regulations; the health department, for instance, should only concern themselves with public events where food is sold or served. *Private* is the keyword.

This unique format could welcome people into your home kitchen to see where and how you make your products. Besides giving samples, you might offer suggestions on hosting a brunch based around your products or pairing them with others. You could do a blind tasting to get people talking about how your product is better. Such parties can be ripe for testimonials, provide new product ideas, and create a buzz in social media. Everyone likes being invited to a party, especially if the food is homemade and delicious — and free.

You may want to generate press clippings, gather endorsements, collect testimonials, or grow your customer base. If you cast the net wide enough to include invitations to some local newspaper reporters, it's possible they will create a news story about you and your new products (covered in the PR section of this chapter). To make your private product party more newsworthy, tie it to national event, like Bake Cookies Day in December (if you're a baker) or Canvolution, organized by Canning Across America (if you're a canner or have your own line of pickles).

Ways to Generate Media Coverage

Everyone's business and food products could make a great topic for an article. But what's your hook and news angle to get free media coverage? The following ten steps will help increase the likelihood of receiving the media exposure you deserve.

Step 1: Identify your media goals

In addition to increasing awareness of your products and business, what specifically do you want to accomplish with your media efforts? You may want to generate press clippings, gather endorsements, collect testimonials, or grow your customer base. For example, do you want to introduce a new product or invite your community to a product demo party event?

Step 2: Create your compelling story

Identify your strengths, unique characteristics, and what makes your products and background special. Keep your story simple and describe it as if you're talking with a friend.

Step 3: Develop a media list

Compile a list of media contacts, including the names of writers, journalists, or producers who regularly cover related topics. Start a file of articles published or aired by those journalists, since this might be a way to make an initial contact. If you have the time and inclination, build relationships

Win Some Awards

You know you have a great-tasting product, and your current customers do, too. But to reach new customers and grow your business and reputation, there's nothing like winning an award for your pickle relish or artisanal sourdough bread. Whether it's a People's Choice award, a state fair ribbon, or a prestigious Good Food Award (goodfoodawards.org) from Seedling Projects, such an accolade can boost your reputation and solidify your position as a leader with a third-party endorsement. It will also allow you to add "award-winning" to your marketing materials and may even include attractive medals you can use in your market displays. Depending on the nature of the award and the fame associated with it, you may also draw media attention and new customers eager to try out the next great food product.

with journalists before you pitch your first story idea. Thanks to LinkedIn, Twitter, and Facebook, this is easier than ever before. When contacting someone, it often helps to tell them how much you enjoyed a story they wrote or produced.

Step 4: Write a press release

Follow the standard press release format. See the sample press kit on this book's website (homemadeforsale.com) for a downloadable template.

Step 5: Capture visuals, both photographs and video

A picture is worth a thousand words, it's often said. Don't miss an opportunity to share your story visually. High-quality digital single-lens reflex (DSLR) and GoPro video cameras make taking great shots a breeze. With the quality of cameras in mobile devices these days, video or images from your phone may also suffice. Make sure you capture images at a high resolution so they can be used in print or even on TV. With photos or video, you can turn a small mention into a larger feature or product profile. Shrinking budgets at various media with limited photography capability may allow you to showcase your story more effectively. Visual content is in demand more than ever, by magazines, newspapers, and even the Associated Press. Plus, *you* can capture the images you want, presenting your products in the best light.

Step 6: Time your press release

Most magazines work ahead from three to six months (or more) when covering a story. Newspapers work a week ahead. Don't forget about local radio, since people interact with the media in many ways; those who watch lots of TV may not regularly listen to the radio. Internet media, like food bloggers, are always eager to cover stories and enjoy passing out free samples to their readers; plus, their blogs can sometimes go viral, which means what they write gets picked up, over and over again, by other bloggers.

Step 7: Submit your release

Email your release to a specific person or media contact, then follow up with a telephone call or email about one or two weeks later to make sure they received it. Ask the assignment editor, producer, or journalist if the story has been assigned or if it's still being reviewed. While targeting major outlets, focus on the media you believe you have the best chance of reaching; perhaps they cover topics related to your products or regularly include human interest features.

Step 8: Accept and manage the interview (and photography session)

The interview or meeting can be the most enjoyable part of working with the media. Relax and just be you. Your enthusiasm will carry the interview, but make sure you share your story about your products. Avoid going off the record about anything and minimize detailed or complex issues. A little warm hospitality goes a long way with journalists; send them home with some of your product.

Step 9: Offer thanks for the media coverage

After an article or story has run or aired, send a thank-you note and keep in touch as future story ideas arise.

Step 10: Keep track of it all

Keep a list with links to media articles about your products and your business. An easy way to do this is to set up a free Google Alert via Google with your name and the name of your products and business. Google will send you a link via email every time they track something with your name in it. Once you've received a glowing review or business profile, don't let it stop there. Share the media article or coverage on your website or social media, making sure to tag the writer or media source using the @ or # sign, depending on the platform, so it shows up on their social media page.

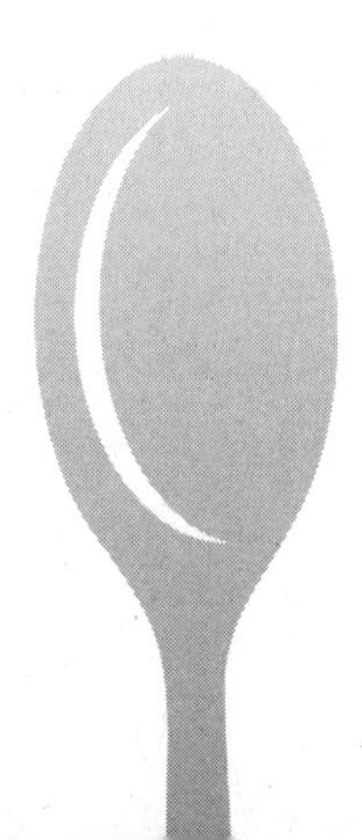

13

People, Partnerships, and Purpose

THANKS TO a fragmented marketplace and the advent of powerful new technologies, marketing is playing an increasingly important role in the success of a product. Besides the traditional 4 Ps of marketing covered previously, we added three Ps to address the growing importance of People, Partnerships, and Purpose in the success of your efforts.

People

One way or another, your food product will satisfy some need of your customers in a delicious way. The need could be for a convenient and tasty snack at an event or an attractive Valentine's Day tin of heart-shaped, hand-dipped chocolate pralines. People are people, but how you determine whether they're customers or consumers can improve your bottom line. Are they enjoying your product themselves or sharing it with someone they love? Are they interested in the taste alone or the experience they have enjoying it?

Customers Versus Consumers

When defining your target market, you may notice that sometimes the person buying your product is different from the person eating it. In marketing circles, we talk about decision-makers as well as decision-influencers. Take kids and their parents, for example. Who has more pull when it comes to that jar of jelly on the shelf or type of cookie in the cookie jar?

A mother may be the decision-maker with the bucks to buy a loaf of your healthy whole-grain bread to make sandwiches for her family that week. She might also be the parent who breaks down at an art and crafts fair and picks up your decorated cookies after being nagged by her hungry kids. It may be the husband, however, who seeks out an anniversary treat he and his wife can share together. Or a customer may, on impulse, pick

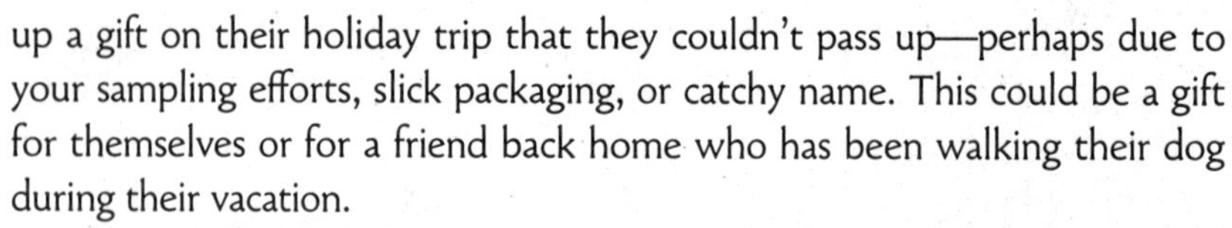

up a gift on their holiday trip that they couldn't pass up—perhaps due to your sampling efforts, slick packaging, or catchy name. This could be a gift for themselves or for a friend back home who has been walking their dog during their vacation.

> *"Your creations are experienced on a visceral level; your passion comes across in every bite. More than musicians, more than writers, you live the virtues of authenticity, passion, community, and connection. Every food crafter has by necessity created a tight-knit community around them. Your work is a true and authentic expression of tradition. And like any good artist, you walk this path not for the promise of a pot of gold at the end but from a drive to express what is deep inside you."*
>
> — Sarah Weiner, Founder of the Good Food Awards (goodfoodawards.org), addressing the 2014 Winners

When thinking about who might buy your product, decide whether you are going to target the customers with the cash or the consumers who actually end up savoring it. Your marketing can be designed to reach one or both of these audiences, albeit with different messages and goals in mind. Back to that jelly example: the kids need to know that your brand of jelly tastes great on a PB and J, but Mom or Dad (whoever gets the groceries in the house) needs to know that yours is made with local organic fruit and has no artificial colors or flavors.

As we cover in the Business Expansion section of this book, when you're selling wholesale, this customer-consumer dichotomy becomes even more complex. In some cases, you may be two or three layers removed from the end consumers of your products. You may be selling first to a food broker, distributor, and/or retailer before your product is purchased at retail. Each of these layers has industry standards—and pricing demands—which must be met.

Products or Experiences?

You determine the experience your customers may have with your product. Interactions with customers move beyond transactional relationships, seeking to establish unique, emotional, and uncommon experiences for individual customers. Your product has the potential to develop so much more than merely an exchange of money for a cupcake. The marketing research firm Strategic Horizons, founded by Joseph Pine and Jim Gilmore, examine this idea in their book *The Experience Economy: Work Is Theatre and Every Business Is a Stage*: "Experiences are as distinct from services as services are from goods."

With cottage food products, this thinking involves creating an experience around the enjoyment of your product and not simply focusing on its attributes, such as taste, flavor, or size. Adding an experiential dimension of your product is another way to differentiate it in the marketplace and connect you on a relational level with those who enjoy eating what you love making.

Next time you visit a farmers' market, notice the relationships between farmers and their customers who will eat the food they grow. Your booth selling pickles, preserves, or freshly baked products extends this local

economy and naturally thrives there. Many who frequent farmers' markets are there for the friendship, the ecological connections to the land, and a sense of hope and optimism for the future—far more than for the potatoes, pea pods, or your homemade salsa. What you're selling is adding to this richness of community.

As well as being a neighbor, a colleague at the office, or a familiar face at your local YMCA, you're many people's personal connection to the local economy. You complete the growing interest in buying local by selling local. The trust and respect you earn from the relationships with your customers differentiate your products from the made-from-mixes, mass-produced, or factory-generated products made somewhere far, far away.

"The New Artisan Economy has become hotter than hot in our cities. This trend is especially visible in the form of new small-scale companies focusing on local craftsmanship. Consumers are more and more demanding for local products that are produced in a sustainable way, with care for the environment. Keywords in the New Artisan Economy are local, authentic, and sustainable. One thing the companies of the New Artisan Economy have in common are the strong stories that come with their products."

— Ted Pouls, PopUpCity.net

Taking Care of Customers

Taking care of your customers is part of the experience you create around your product. Maintaining a high level of customer service is the best thing you have going for your business, leading to word-of-mouth endorsements and referrals. Regardless of the product you sell, building relationships with your customers demands a few key ingredients:

- Selling a great-tasting product at a fair price
- Promotional efforts that are honest, authentic, and never misleading
- Professional and courteous service, with on-time deliveries

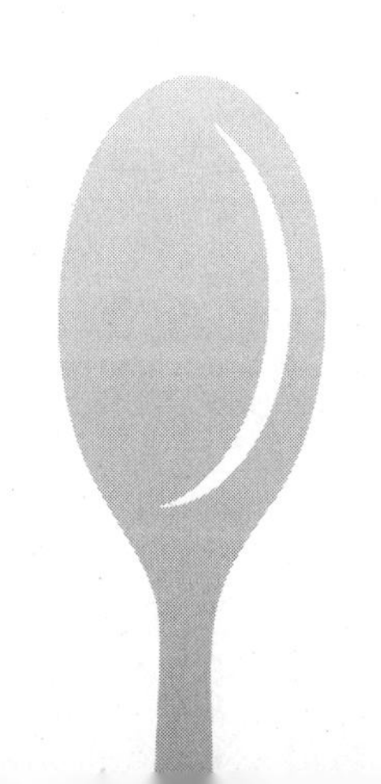

- Accurate invoicing and billing
- Extending some form of thanks for every referral, tweet, or "Like" on Facebook
- Taking any criticism or feedback constructively, never personally

The more you can deliver every order with a smile, the better. Never lose sight of that connection: you're the face of the food.

The 80–20 Rule

From the first telephone call to the delivery of a product, how you interact and form relationships with your customers solidify your position in the market. Many companies or organizations we've consulted for or interviewed use the 80–20 rule to help prioritize their marketing efforts and focus on building long-term relationships and loyalty among a select group of customers.

Practical experience has led many business owners to observe that about 80 percent of their sales come from only 20 percent of their customers. Covet the 20 percent and do everything possible to keep them happy, since they're the ones that are repeat customers or big on referrals. If you host special tasting events, make sure they're on your VIP list. If you carefully manage your customer database and can keep track of birthdays and anniversaries, send a congratulatory note or small food gift.

In part due to your relationships with your customers, you can help them help you. As discussed previously, customer referrals remain the most powerful form of unpaid advertising or public relations. The words of a satisfied customer craft a long-lasting message about you and the reputation of your company and its products. Don't hesitate to ask enthusiastic customers for an endorsement to quote on your website.

Never underestimate a personal touch in communicating with your customers. A handwritten thank-you note to a customer who referred a friend adds a lasting impact for the price of a stamp. In our world of rapid technology and emails possibly lost in a flurry of spam, a personal touch can go a long way.

Collaborators and Vendors

When we talk about People in promotion, we're not just talking about reaching customers. There may be aspects of your business where you need

Maintaining a Customer Database

Every business must both attract and retain customers. Once you have customers, maintaining records about them can help you sustain and grow your enterprise. From tracking their orders and preferences to capturing useful information like birth dates and anniversaries for relationship-building marketing efforts, your customer database serves as the fuel to propel your business. Without customers, you won't be in business for long.

Keeping written records of important customer details in a notebook or on index cards has increasingly given way to various computer or electronic-based programs or systems. Among the simplest is a spreadsheet, like Microsoft's Excel program, where you can list contact information, orders, anniversary dates, customer referrals, frequency of orders, and product preferences, among other details.

While it used to be very expensive to take it up a notch with a custom-designed client database that could link to direct marketing efforts as well as invoicing and bookkeeping functions, now numerous low-cost email services are available that may work well for your marketing and as a customer database. Among these are Sendinblue, Emma, Constant Contact, and MailChimp.

Because we already use many of the Google tools, we opted to keep our company database online, in the cloud, with Google Contacts. This robust database can easily be exported for use in newsletters and for other purposes while being synchronized with our electronic devices, including our mobile phone. Most online credit card processors like Square, plug-and-play website builders like Wix, and online marketing platforms like Castiron also provide customer database features. You'll need to decide what works best for you and your situation.

In today's world of identity theft and privacy concerns, be attuned to your customers' requests and make sure the data you collect is secure. Keeping credit cards numbers or check information on file electronically seems to be a disaster waiting to happen. And avoid selling your customer information to any third party, since you run the risk of violating your customers' trust in you and your business.

assistance, like graphic design, website development, public relations, or computer technology. While you could hire people or companies to help you take on various projects, some of these individuals may want to collaborate with you in exchange for the products you create. Addressed in greater length in *ECOpreneuring*, this is called a "gift exchange," one of the oldest forms of commercial relationships.

The companies or individuals that supply your ingredients are also a part of this People equation in marketing. They could likewise share the stage as you craft a story around your products. These vendors, be they farmers or specialty food providers, may also be your biggest cheerleaders as your business dashes from the gate. It's a symbiotic commercial relationship, so they want you to succeed as much as you do and can help share your story, your product, and your aspirations. They may also send customers your way. If you are sourcing some of your ingredients from other interesting food artisans, showcase and share their stories on your website.

Partnerships, Networking, and Cause-Related Marketing

Partnerships can be magnified by cottage food entrepreneurs. While steering away from traditional paid advertising outlets, you may discover strategic partnerships that open new doors to connect with your target audience. When dollars do exchange, like when your business makes a donation or takes out a membership with a nonprofit organization, the money goes directly to furthering your shared mission. Explore ways you can thrive on connections with like-minded organizations. For example, can your bakery products be an add-on to a share for a farm that follows a community supported agriculture (CSA) model?

Or can you join an existing statewide industry association and dovetail your marketing to coincide with their efforts to support artisanal food enterprises? In Wisconsin, we have Something Special from Wisconsin, managed through the Wisconsin Department of Agriculture, Trade and Consumer Protection, a state-sponsored marketing program for any business, no matter how small, with at least 50 percent of the product attributable to Wisconsin ingredients, production, or processing. The Certified South Carolina (certifiedscgrown.com) program is a cooperative effort among producers, processors, wholesalers, retailers, and the South Carolina Department of Agriculture (SCDA) to brand and promote South Carolina products. There's also the Vermont Specialty Food Association (vermontspecialtyfoods.org), among the nation's oldest specialty food association. See if your state has a similar program.

By joining with nonprofit organizations or various causes to help advertise a product, your small enterprise participates in what is commonly called "cause-related marketing." This benefits both the charity or nonprofit organization and your business. You cultivate relationships that echo your values, reinforce your business' commitment to the issues you care about, and connect with people who share your interests, passions, and sense of purpose.

Rather than making donations, with cause-related marketing you create meaningful relationships that help serve the partner organization. This mutually beneficial relationship is particularly salient to a cottage food business since it offers the ability to co-mingle with much larger organizations that might be trying to improve their brand image and become more supportive of the local community and its businesses. More and more schools, hospitals, and larger corporations are exploring ways to keep their money local. Your cottage food enterprise is a solution to their problem.

Whatever your focus, there's a nonprofit group out there with like-minded members. These groups often seek speakers for various events, especially local service organizations like the Kiwanis, Rotary Club, and the Optimists. Why not let it be you? As a part of your presentation about your new business, make sure you have plenty of samples—and business cards and order forms, too. Like the saying goes: It's not what you know but who you know that matters sometimes when landing a sale.

Once you're up and running, contributing donations to various nonprofit silent auctions can expand your reach to people who might appreciate your generosity to a like-minded cause. People like to buy from people they know, like, and respect. Seek out an auction where you can showcase what you make, perhaps in an attractive gift basket. Avoid offering a gift certificate instead of your actual product, since this takes away the eye-candy appeal. If you become over-burdened by donation requests, consider opportunities where you have a visible presence; perhaps you could set up a small sample display during the final night of the auction.

Purpose and Passion

All CFOs work their passion, at least to some extent. You can do what multinational corporations never can to the same degree: communicate honestly, openly, and authentically. Everything is personal when you're just starting out. There's no need for customer numbers or mother's maiden name. You'll be on a first-name basis with your customers. Many are also your friends, neighbors, or community members. Instead of a fictional farm representing your strawberry jam, consider putting a picture of the real place on the label. Avoid hiding or downplaying that your products are truly homemade. If you have spectacular photos on your website, an engaging social media presence, and present yourself professionally—which you should, of course—conveying up front that you work from home will avoid

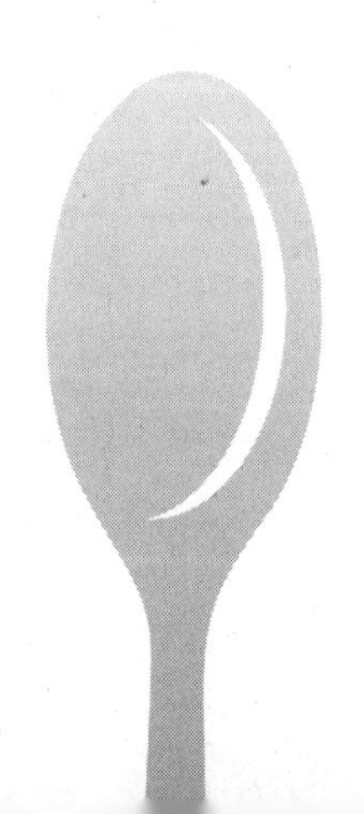

the possibility of a confused customer looking for a bakery at your address when they pick up an order. It's entirely possible that how you present your business and your products may outshine commercial bakers in your neighborhood; you may seem bigger than you actually are.

Purpose-based marketing provides the ultimate in competitive advantage for a small business; the bigger the operation, the less likely it can maintain its values throughout the organization. This is such a challenge for large corporations that whole books are devoted to just this issue. Your sense of purpose and passion can be reflected in everything you do. This compelling message, a part of your inspiring story, puts a face to the food item that your customers then savor, one bite at a time.

By associating your business and product with organizations you support, like the Women's Club, a local entrepreneur group, or a chapter of the Sierra Club, you can garner support, build awareness, and advocate for issues near and dear to you.

Tips on Nurturing Your Purpose and Passion

By addressing the following issues, you can nurture your purpose and passion.

Know Your Elevator Pitch

An elevator pitch is a brief speech that succinctly describes your cottage food enterprise, something you might say to a stranger chatting with you in an elevator. The most successful CFOs are those who conceived an idea and could express their passion for their product in a way that others could readily understand and support. The elevator pitch is both the "what" you do and the "why."

Maintain Your Passion

Keeping up your own energy and enthusiasm for your livelihood is important. There will be people who don't care for your product, think you have better things to do with your life, or flat out don't care that you're happy selling your product and running your own business. Some of the least supportive people might be closest to you, including parents or siblings. Therefore, maintain a network of like-minded people, organizations, or businesses to support and encourage you to stay the course and keep at it, even if you accidentally burn a tray of cookies. It happens to all of us.

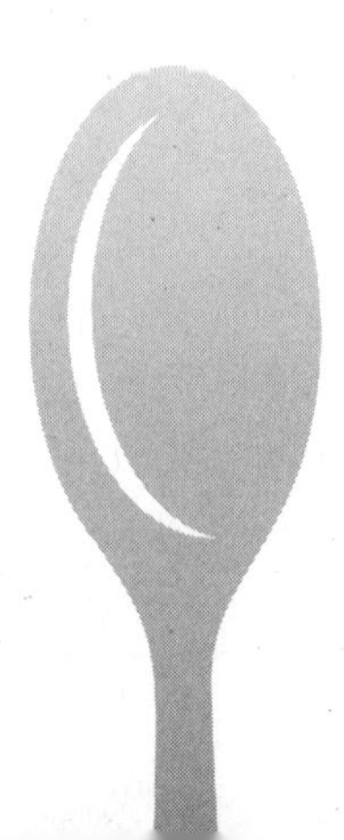

Find places where you can meet and interact with similarly spirited souls. Such contagious enthusiasm, blended with new insights, often prove to be inspiring.

Manage Competition

Unfortunately, you may sense resistance and even be on the receiving end of negative jabs from competing local business owners, especially if they're established enterprises operating in state-licensed commercial kitchens. These businesses may perceive you as competition, which you may or may not be. They may not welcome the fact that you just launched your business from your kitchen with little or no out-of-pocket start-up costs.

Your best play is to keep your head high, remain focused on your customers, and ignore the flack. If your product is better than theirs, so be it. In a free market where customers choose the best products at the best prices, that's how it works. In general, competition is a positive force that benefits your community, especially if you account for other aspects of how your business operates, like how it impacts the environment or how it builds a stronger local economy. Who knows—you might even improve your competitors' game too.

Question Each Other

Like a ping-pong ball, challenging questions should banter back and forth between you and your customers. Ultimately, your business is about serving their needs. Positive in nature, such exchanges stem from the idea that passion should never stagnate. Be open to suggestions, feedback, and criticism. That doesn't mean you have to rework your recipes, but one novel idea from a customer could lead to a whole new product line that outsells all the others.

Find Mentors and Sensei

In ancient Japanese culture, *sensei* guided the training of ninja and other warriors who practiced the martial arts. In the *Star Wars* world, Jedi Knights are responsible for the training of their Padawan learners. Whenever we step outside our comfort zone and leave behind the safety of routine or seeming normalcy of a job with clearly defined responsibilities, we face the unknown. Seek out a mentor or two who possess the sage knowledge and a willingness to serve as a guide, a sounding board, or a lifeline as you develop

and grow your cottage food enterprise. These mentors can keep you on track, pick you up when you're down, and point you in opportunistic directions you never dreamed of.

It's time to put the 7 Ps of marketing together as we dive into testing your products in the marketplace in the next chapter. In reality, many CFOs start out with one or two sales to eagerly waiting customers (sometimes they're cheerleading friends or family members) or as a one-time trial at a farmers' market, before jumping in with both feet. The more agile and flexible the CFO is to their plan, also covered in the next chapter, the more likely they'll exceed their customers' expectations and end up with a thriving home-based enterprise.

Fellow bakers in your community can make great mentors.
JOHN D. IVANKO PHOTOGRAPHY

14

Proving the Market and Getting a Plan

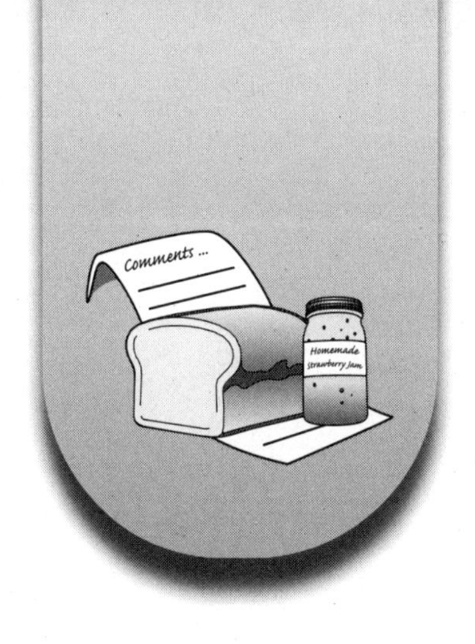

NOW THAT YOU HAVE a handle on your state's cottage food law, set your personal goals for your business, sorted out some possible recipes that might work, and embraced the 7 Ps of marketing, it's time to test the market, size up your competition, and commit your plan to paper. These final steps are covered in this chapter.

Market Feasibility: Testing the Market

While you may have a great-tasting product, you still have to test it in the marketplace. It's one thing if everyone you know loves your muffins—especially, if they're free. It's something completely different to see if customers will buy them at $2 a pop. The same holds true for your organic pickles, which you calculated should retail for about $12 a jar.

This process of testing the market for your products, often called a feasibility study, may take the following steps.

(1) Testing

This may involve evaluating taste, pricing, portion size, packaging, labeling, and even the sales venue itself. Many CFOs share samples of their products with friends, neighbors, or family to taste test. At the early stages of the business, some CFOs have a pre-launch event or soft launch at a farmers' market to assess viability. Some even try different farmers' markets or pop-up markets to determine which get the most traffic or customer interest. Weeks can be spent refining and testing recipes before some CFOs feel they have the best quality, most consistent product that they're proud to sell. Expenses associated with testing are often considered start-up business expenses and can be deducted, covered in more detail in chapter 18. One approach a few CFOs have taken: throw a party and showcase your products.

(2) Feedback

Provide comment cards, send short online product surveys, or have a system in place to collect customers' comments about your product. While some feedback may echo what they think you want to hear (not what you really want), other times it could highlight an issue, sometimes in a brutally honest way.

Besides reaching out directly for feedback, you can also explore incidental sources of information about your most promising markets. How are other food enterprises selling their products? Having some competition is a great thing, since that means there's a market for what you want to sell. Evaluate each of the 7 Ps of marketing, covered in earlier chapters, in relation to your competitors to determine how your products are different—and better.

(3) Refinement

Take what you've learned, by way of direct customer feedback or observing decisions made by your customers or the marketplace, and refine, modify or adjust your product and marketing accordingly. For example, did your blueberry muffins sell out in the first hour, but you returned home with your wild cherry version? Did a volume discount pricing strategy for your gift jellies allow you to profit more by selling a greater volume than if you sold them individually at full price? Did a flavor sampler set sell better than a four-pack of the same flavor? A slow and steady approach to growth helps minimize costly mistakes or shortcomings should you have gone all-in on a pop-up sale without doing the important upfront work first.

Keep refining your product, pricing, or sales venue options until you've reached a level of confidence that you have the best version before a full-on launch. You need to have a product that enough customers want and will pay a fair price for to leave you with enough profit at the end of the day to make it worth undertaking.

(4) Product Launch

Finally, synthesize your testing, feedback, and refinement into your final product and implement your launch campaign.

Keep in mind, however, that change is constant. Customers can be fickle, follow fads, or have tastes that change. One year, gluten-free is the rage; three years later, it's sugar-free or low-sugar. In most cases, even though your feasibility study may reveal solid products to sell, it's always possible that market conditions will change, a new competitor will show up across

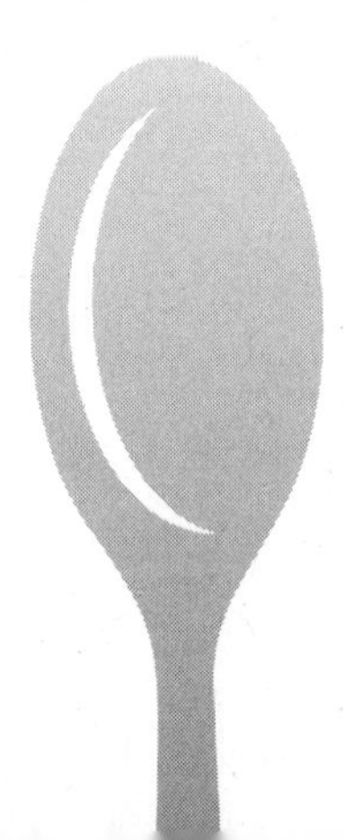

from your booth, or some of your key customers will move away. The longest-running, and usually most satisfied, CFOs are the ones that evolve their business, try new products, and eliminate menu items that are not profitable enough. These CFOs listen closely to what their customers tell them they want to buy, and at what price.

Garnering Feedback

As a small CFO, you don't need to spin wheels and spend lots of money to figure out the value and sales viability of your product. Depending on your products, options to connect with your customers and garner actionable information may include:

- Follow-up emails requesting customer comments or feedback
- Testing out products at mini-markets. By selling at small sales venues, you can adjust various marketing approaches, including price, to determine the potential for your product.
- Snail mail a letter with a small survey to return in a self-addressed stamped envelope.
- Try out the widely used SurveyMonkey (surveymonkey.com), a free online system that allows you to invite customers to complete a survey about your products; SurveyMonkey provides various analytic tools to ferret out key insights.
- Large marketing companies often use focus groups, inviting potential customers to taste samples and offer their opinions. You could do something similar, perhaps in a less formal way at your home or a community room at your local library, if they permit it.

Regardless of how you collect feedback, make sure you incentivize your customers' participation. As thanks, perhaps offer a giveaway draw of your products. In your early market feasibility study, you may want to avoid social media until you're satisfied with your products and feel comfortable that the public feedback you receive will generally be favorable. Ideally, minimize the possibility of customers venting negatively about your product, especially if you're still refining your recipe or the marketing. If you've ever read restaurant reviews on Yelp or Trip Advisor, you'll recognize the power of one that's well written but scathing.

While what you make is ultimately for the customer's pleasure, not everyone will agree with your choice of frosting color, design, or crumb of your bread. Dry and moist cake is a subjective opinion. Take cookies, for example, some are chewy and some are crunchy.

While respecting and valuing your customers is essential to being in business — they are paying you after all — not everyone will be 100 percent happy with every product, every time. Have a plan for the rare occurrence of a rejected order or dissatisfied customer. What will you say? How will they be refunded? What do they need to do in order to get a refund? Client or customer bashing is never advised in any situation. Negative trolling, bullying, or a bad review might happen. Part ways and chalk it up to a learning experience. Move on. Avoid letting a complaint, or a reduced rating score on a review page, bring you down.

The food industry, particularly specialty food products, can be cyclical and very sensitive to economic booms and busts. By their nature, many of these food items are perceived as impulse purchases. A breakfast of chocolate croissants is not the same thing as a hearty spaghetti dinner in the eyes of many, even if both cost about the same.

Be realistic, adaptable with your products and marketing, and you'll do just fine. And keep listening to the needs of your customers. They might even point you in the direction of the next great thing.

Competitive Analysis

Early on in your product development, you'll need to undertake some form of competitive analysis, carefully examining the potential markets for your products. This will give you a sense of what other companies are selling and how their products are the same as or similar to what you want to offer. Observe pricing, product features, and other marketing aspects.

Competitive analysis can be informal, via the Internet, or merely anecdotal, perhaps as you browse the aisles of a local farmers' market or arts and craft show, jotting down notes on the selection, pricing, and quality of baked goods. An easy way to record your findings is by creating a chart or matrix that lists other companies and their products, along with any distinguishing characteristics or special features.

Many enterprises come about because a particular food product is completely missing where they're located. Perhaps there are no organic pickles, gluten-free baked goods, or decorative cakes made in a nut-free kitchen. In these cases, you'll have the opportunity to "own the market" and be the only one offering such an item. But be warned: this doesn't guarantee success or mean you can charge anything you want. You'll still need enough customers in your community to buy your products at prices that make your enterprise worth undertaking.

Taking a macro view of your business can also help avoid falling down a trapdoor and keep you realistic about what you want to, and can, accomplish. For guidance, a SWOT analysis can be used to examine the strengths, weaknesses, opportunities, and threats to your business. This analysis assists you with strategic planning and management. The resulting situational awareness can help keep your customers, competition, and costs more top of mind. Some CFOs complete a SWOT analysis every time they launch a new product line or explore a new marketing channel. If you complete it honestly, you may discover that going to a farmers' market with lots of low-cost competition for breads or jars of jam may not be the best, or most profitable, use of your two hours standing behind a booth in hot, humid weather. If it's not fun, or profitable, what's the point? Is this the best use of your time, energy and passion for your food product?

The more ambitious your plans and sales goals, the more astute you'll need to be with respect to the details, competition, and marketing considerations. Understanding your competition is essential to breaking into the market with your products. The more crowded a market, the more you'll need to find your niche and clearly identify your target audience, both covered previously in chapter 6.

S STRENGTHS	W WEAKNESSES	O OPPORTUNITIES	T THREATS
• Aspects that make you stand out, like culinary experience or unique recipes • Well stocked kitchen • Neighbors who already love your products	• Limitations, like time or space • Things that others do better than you • Unfocused & trying to do too much at once	• Growing market for your products • Unique products • Fill a gap & meet unfilled needs, like gluten-free baked goods • Attract free press coverage	• Changing tastes & preferences of customers • Difficult operating environment, i.e. supplies being hard to purchase • Competition & price war

An example of a SWOT analysis for a cottage food business. CREDIT: JOHN D. IVANKO

Planning for Profits

Finally, the time has come to put it all together. If you've followed along in the previous chapters, making notes, testing recipes, coming up with product names, talking with potential customers, and making labels, it's time to summarize everything in a plan and then put that plan into action.

The Back-of-the-napkin Plan

If you fail to plan, you plan to fail. Some of the most innovative ideas or tastiest recipes never make it to our mouths because the people with them couldn't get their ideas down on the drawing table or, worse yet, jumped into a business before thinking it all the way through. Please don't let this happen to you.

Given that most cottage food businesses will have modest or humble beginnings, we're recommending that you forget about writing a full-blown business plan with a vision statement, company description, product details, strategy...ad nauseum. At this point, you don't need to impress a bank to get a loan to start your business. It's too early to tell if your cookies are going to be a $10,000 or a $100,000 hit.

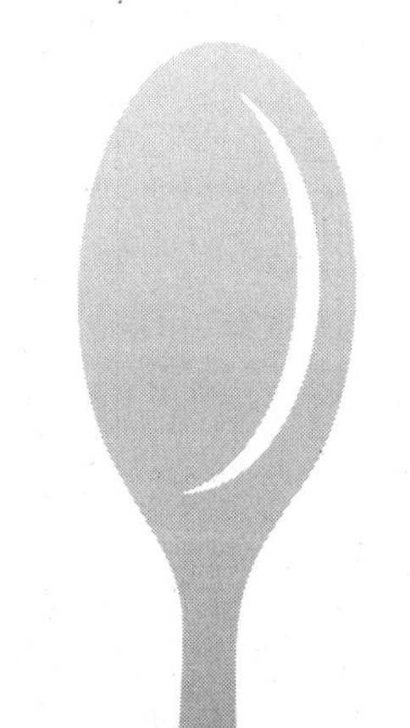

That said, if you love writing or like to meticulously detail every step, decision, and ingredient, by all means do so, but know that such a labor-intensive undertaking is unlikely to make your business more profitable when you're just starting out. It's the process of writing the business plan that's most valuable. It forces you to evaluate every aspect of your enterprise and get these details down on paper.

If, in the future you need and want to expand, you'll have plenty of time, enthusiasm, and determination then to pull together a business plan that would impress an MBA professor, lure money from the deep pockets of bankers, and convince the rest of your family you're serious about turning your cottage food business into a big business, covered later in this book. There are plenty of free online resources that guide you through writing a

Inn Serendipity Fresh Baked Homemade Bakery

Products: Latvian sourdough bread, biscotti, Alexander cake, artisan bread, granola, organic muffins, decorated "plug-in to solar power" sugar cookies

Author-baker Lisa uses a cast-iron pot for baking her Artisan Bread.

CREDIT: JOHN D. IVANKO PHOTOGRAPHY

Sales Objective: $2,000

Target Markets:

- Primary: Inn Serendipity Bed & Breakfast guests; direct on-farm sales or local deliveries
- Secondary: Attendees at various community events; direct-to-customer sales at a booth

Niche: Baked products made with organic and locally sourced ingredients, containing no artificial flavors, colors, or preservatives

Positioning Statement: Inn Serendipity Fresh Baked offers discriminating foodies great-tasting, truly homemade, organic, and locally baked goods that contain no artificial flavors, colors, or preservatives. These premium-priced products are unlike any available in the Monroe, Wisconsin, area.

Sales Venues: On-site, plus some high-traffic community events like the Midwest Renewable Energy Association Energy Fair or Monroe Cheese Days ☛

business plan, from a vision statement to pro forma income statement and balance sheet. In case you're curious, here are a few that you can customize for your needs: enloop.com, sba.gov (follow the link to writing a business plan).

Besides providing resources for small businesses, the Association for America's Small Business Development Centers (asbdc-us.org) offers an assistance network in the United States and its territories. Its mission is to help new entrepreneurs realize their dreams of business ownership. Small business owners and aspiring entrepreneurs can go to one of approximately 1,000 local SBDCs for free face-to-face business consulting and at-cost training on writing business plans, marketing, or regulatory compliance.

But for now, let's go with what we call the "back-of-a-napkin plan" that, if nothing else, makes sure you don't forget the great ideas you've come up

Start-up expenses: $0, the state license ($65) and registered office registration ($25) are already covered as a part of Inn Serendipity B&B.

Fixed expenses: $0, liability insurance is covered by existing homeowner policy from Cincinnati Insurance Company as a part of the B&B; the B&B is listed as "incidental to the home" and comes with an annual premium of $69. Additionally, $1 million umbrella liability insurance policy is also taken, costing $165 per year. DSL Internet service ($34/month), domain name ($10/year), and website hosting ($120/year) are already covered as a part of the business.

Authors selling at an exhibit booth at the Midwest Renewable Energy Association's Energy Fair, the longest running event in the country, in Custer, Wisconsin.
CREDIT: JOHN D. IVANKO PHOTOGRAPHY

with to get your product to market. Plus, it might keep you on track. As an example, the adjacent sidebar provides a sample napkin-sized plan for our Inn Serendipity Fresh Baked business; a general template is on this book's website.

When searching for resources to help you launch your business, you'll sometimes notice a bias against being your own boss or becoming an entrepreneur. Our mantra: give your business idea a shot, get a plan together, and go for it. So, take any negative vibes you might encounter in stride and recognize the source. It could be coming from an ivory tower.

Here's how one less-than-positive startup guide written by Kenneth W. Wood from the Mississippi State University Extension Service puts it:

> "Do I want a hobby, or do I want to make money?" It is very difficult to introduce a new product into the market place. In many instances, it would be better to take the money required to start such a business and invest it in a certificate of deposit.

Oh, really? As of the time of printing, you'd be lucky to earn a minuscule 0.99% APY on a a CD for one year; for a $500 investment, you'd get back $4.95 in interest earnings. We don't know a cottage food business on the planet that couldn't beat that.

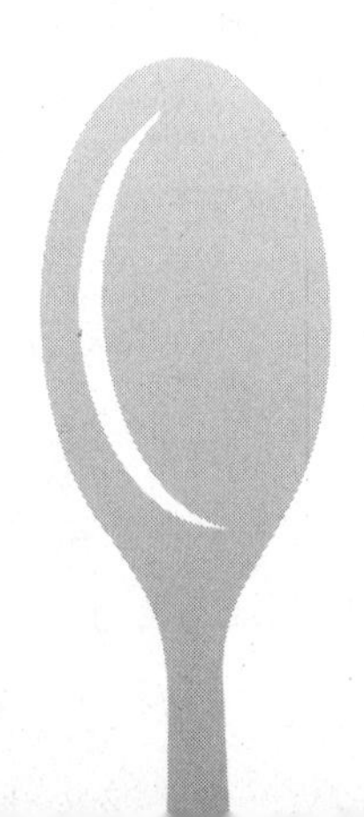

SECTION 4

Organizing, Planning, and Managing the Business

15

Ready, Set, Go: Organize Your Kitchen

IF YOU'RE LIKE most folks starting a cottage food business, you already know your way around a kitchen. It may very well be your favorite spot in the house, where you bake up your holiday cookie favorites or Sunday morning bagels.

The key next step, and what this chapter covers, is how to shift from being a homespun casual cook to viewing your kitchen as the base for a viable business enterprise. It's like your kitchen now has dual personalities. On one side, it's still the hub of your family meals and routines. On the flip side, it transforms into an efficient production facility where you pump out your pickles and pound cake like nobody's business.

Take your kitchen setup seriously and make the time to organize systems that ensure food safety. By keeping things under control and practicing proper procedures, you avoid stress, inefficiency, and food safety issues. This chapter offers five steps for setting up your home processing facility.

Five Steps for Setting up Your Home Processing Facility

By now you have figured out your recipe and developed your product and the marketing that goes with it. Next, set up your kitchen so you can make ten dozen brownies as easily as one dozen. If you're operating out of a tiny apartment or urban kitchen, this will take especially careful planning. Since you can feed your extended family a Thanksgiving turkey dinner, you can pull off making cases of strawberry-rhubarb jam, too.

As much as you can, separate personal use from business use for equipment, ingredients, and item storage; in some states, this is required by law. There will be overlap in your kitchen, particularly as it relates to use of space, from counters to mixers. The magic of a cottage food business is that you don't need to buy a lot of new equipment. However,

Lauren Cortesi's home kitchen, used for creating amazing custom cakes and other desserts for Bella's Desserts. *See page 142 for the story profile on Cortesi.*
CREDIT: LAUREN CORTESI

items that are clearly business-only, such as product ingredients, need to be stored, labeled clearly, and tracked separately.

Step 1: Assess Equipment

What recipes are you making? What equipment do you need to make them? Write out a list answering both these questions. Your answers will depend on the type of food products you make, but will include some of the typical items used for baked products and canned items that are described below.

For baked products:

- **Stand mixers**
  Stand mixers will be much more efficient than hand mixers for preparing batters and dough. They free up your hands for other tasks, and with their mighty motor, produce a batter that will have a smoother texture and bake more evenly. Most models have a wire beater attachment that adds air to keep batter light and fluffy. These heavy and clunky mixers, however, require more storage space, and they're not cheap either. The main difference between various models is how they handle dense dough; the more solid—and pricier—models tend to do this better.

  Stand mixers come with different bowl sizes, ranging from 3 to 7 quart. If you're looking to purchase a new mixer, bigger will always be better and more efficient for making multiple batches. If you have the funds for a larger mixer up to the 7-quart size, give it serious consideration. Extra mixing bowls allow you to prep one while another is mixing; extra small bowls mean less washing when you're only beating smaller amounts. Double-check that all additional bowls you order work with your make and model of stand mixer. KitchenAid mixer accessories have a reputation for being interchangeable.

  Another stand mixer add-on particularly helpful to cottage food baking enterprises is a pouring shield, a plastic edge that sits on top of your mixing bowl and keeps ingredients, particularly light ones like flour, inside the bowl where they belong. A range of other attachments can transform the motor into another appliance, including a food processor or a pasta roller.

  When you're ready to invest and upgrade, the commercial KitchenAid amps up both quantity and power behind your mixing.

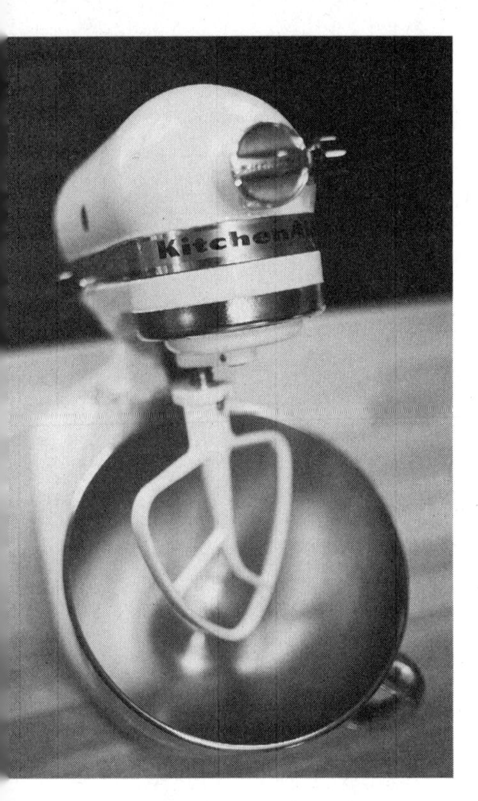

The KitchenAid stand mixer is a go-to appliance for author Lisa Kivirist in her home kitchen at Inn Serendipity.
CREDIT: JOHN D. IVANKO

Lisa loves her commercial KitchenAid, even though the weight of the unit gives her a workout every time she takes it out of the cabinet. She finds heavy bread doughs like her rye bread come out much smoother and easier to work with.

- **Hand mixers**
  A hand mixer is much lighter and better for small simple tasks, like whipping one egg white. Because it has less power than a stand mixer, avoid over-tasking it with denser dough or batter; otherwise, you'll burn out the motor.

- **Baking pans**
  Multiple baking pans help you operate efficiently by maximizing cooking time. While one set of cookies bake, you can prep another and keep rotating. Most home ovens have three racks that can accommodate three cookie sheets, so with six cookie sheets you will triple your output in half the time. Buying identical pans helps with storage since they stack together easily.

The most versatile pan in your baking setup will probably be the sheet pan, also called a cookie sheet. You'll be using this pan so much that it's worth the time to research one that will hold up to hundreds of uses. Cookie sheets come in various materials, sizes, thicknesses, and finishes, insulated or not, with rims or not. To bake items evenly without burning, thicker sheets work best and are less likely to warp over time than thinner or insulated sheets. Sheets with rims tend to be easier to handle, and the sides prevent anything from spilling in your oven. Of course, get as big a sheet as will fit in your oven to maximize baking space.

Some new products make baking easier. The COOKINA Cuisine Reusable Cooking Sheet (cookina.co) from Poirier Richard Inc. creates a non-stick, easy-to-clean alternative to aluminum foil, parchment, or wax paper. Place it on your sheet pan or baking tray to bake without oil. The sheet is easy to clean with soap and water afterwards and does not hold odors or flavors from previous uses. It is 100 percent non-stick and PFOA-free, reusable, and reversible. The company also makes a COOKINA Gard Oven Protector to catch spills and a COOKINA Grilling Sheet for barbecue grilling.

Beautiful Bread with Bannetons

A banneton adds an artistic crust to your bread which can increase the perceived value and price.
CREDIT: JOHN D. IVANKO PHOTOGRAPHY

Make your bread loaves look just like they came from a premium commercial bakery by using bannetons, lightweight baskets often made from rattan that shape the dough during its final rise. They come in different sizes and shapes and create patterns in rustic breads, including that spiral pattern you often see on sourdoughs. The most popular shape is circular, but you can find unique versions like triangular. Bannetons also absorb any extra moisture during that last rise. Experiment to see if you need to use the cloth liner that often comes with them; this will depend on the type of dough you use. Flip your bread out of the banneton when ready to bake and the loaf will hold the shape.

Other options are food-grade silicon bread or pastry liners and flexible molds from Sasa Demarle (sasademarle.com). They have a Silpat Workstation Roul'pat (silpat.com) that is coated with silicon on both sides, allowing you to roll out any kind of dough without using flour; it also allows for spreading nougat, cooked sugar, chocolate, or caramel. Their molds come in various shapes and sizes for pastries, specialty breads, and muffins, but you'll need to go to a restaurant supply store for these. Their Silpain non-stick baking mat for breads has perforated qualities. The water seeps through the mat, leaving a crusty finish for your homemade biscuits and breads.

COOKINA Cuisine Reusable Cooking Sheet holding two croissants, easily lifted off the non-stick surface.
CREDIT: COURTESY OF COOKINA/POIRIER RICHARD INC.

- **Cooling racks**
  Don't just let your baked items cool in the pan. Cooling racks are essential for the baking process. Unlike trivets or hot pads, they allow air to circulate underneath the rack, so the item in your baking pan cools down faster and doesn't over-bake or dry out.

Cooling racks can take up a lot of valuable counter space, so look for a stacked rack that uses your existing cookie sheets and lets you stack four one above the other with plenty of air space for circulation in between each. King Arthur Flour makes a stacked rack that hold four sheets and folds down for easy storage.

For canning:
Even if you're already a home canner, when you're making cases of products, you'll want to have the following canning items on hand.

- **Water bath canner and rack or pressure canner**
  If you've been getting by with a stock pot and a MacGyvered rack out of rolled foil, let your business launch be the reason to upgrade to an official water bath canner with a fitted metal rack. Designed

What Is Food-Grade Plastic?

Not all plastic is suitable for food preparation or storage. The US Food and Drug Administration (FDA) requires that plastics that come into contact with food are of a higher purity and not harmful to humans. If you're looking for storage buckets and bins — or a plastic container for proofing your bread dough — here are a few considerations.

- **Use recycled containers previously used for food.**
  Restaurants and other food service establishments can be good resources for free food-grade containers, such as 5-gallon buckets that were once filled with potato salad or soy sauce. Of course, you'll need to clean and sanitize them thoroughly before use.
- **Look for food safe symbols.**
  A wine glass and fork is the universal symbol for food-safe plastic.
- **Identify HDPE: Number 2 plastic.**
  The plastic recycling number "2" indicates "high-density polyethylene" (HDPE), one of the most inert and stable forms of plastic. All plastic food-grade buckets used at restaurants will be made from HDPE. Not all HDPE plastic is safe, however. Look for the stamped markings FDA, NSF, or the wine glass and fork symbol to confirm the plastic is food-safe HDPE.
- **Buy from a kitchen retailer.**
  Purchasing items specifically designed for the kitchen, such as food storage containers from the Container Store or Bed, Bath & Beyond, will ensure food-grade plastic is used. Restaurant supply stores that service caterers will have larger, more functional plastic food-service containers that are often cheaper than those available at chain retailers.

to fit perfectly into your water bath canner, these sturdy racks are easy to lift out and allow you to load and unload full batch of jars all at once.

Pressure canners went through a major redesign in the 1970s, resulting in today's modern devices that are much safer due to improved gauges for regulating pressure. While pressure canners are an approved method for sealing jars, they involve more steps and detail than water bath canners. The National Center of Home Preservation (nchfp.uga.edu/) has specific resources for the step-by-step process of safe pressure canning; be sure to check that pressure canning complies with your state's regulations.

- **Wide-mouth funnel**
  This keeps your product in the jar and off your counter. Norpro makes a stainless-steel version.

- **Jar lifter**
  This works better and safer than kitchen tongs for moving hot jars from the water bath.

- **Lid wand**
  This enables you to remove sanitized jar lids from the boiling water without burning your fingers or contaminating the lid.

- **Large cleaning brush**
  Typically made from a sponge material adhered to a handle, this helps scrub out any debris as you prepare your jars.

General Equipment

In addition to the key baking or canning equipment, consider the following equipment for your cottage food operation that, while shared with other people in your home, is still essential for your enterprise.

- **Refrigerator**
  You already have a refrigerator—now you need to sort out how to handle the increased storage needs your enterprise will bring. Be sure to cover, date, and label all ingredients used in your items. Use square food storage containers since they use space more efficiently than round ones. As required by many cottage food regulations,

Above: *Canning in a home kitchen requires attention to the recipe and the process, but it's not hard if you have the right tools.* Credit: John D. Ivanko

Below: *Carefully remove jars from the canner after processing with canning jar tongs.* Credit: Renee Pottle

place a thermometer designed for refrigerators in the back of your unit and make sure your unit maintains a temperature at or below 40° Fahrenheit (4° Celsius).

Depending on what you're making and your available space, you may need a second refrigerator to use exclusively for the business, which could be a capital business expense. It will both give you extra space and avoid confusion with your home items and what the kids know they can snack on. A second refrigerator will also minimize food odor issues, which could jeopardize the taste

Kitchen Considerations: Ovens and Cooktops

Before visions of a cottage food business danced in your head, your oven and cooktop probably served as the workhorses of your home kitchen. Whether you own a dual element with an oven built in underneath the cooktop or two separate units, you probably use them every day, for everything from baking birthday cakes to simmering soups. But now that you've stepped up production in your home kitchen, make sure these two pieces of equipment can handle the new workload. Do your research to ensure you invest in what's best for your needs.

Options and considerations vary, depending on if you use gas or electricity to power these two large appliances. For cooking, professional chefs and home foodies tend to be loyal to gas since you can better control the heat and the gas burners; both heat up and cool down fast. But electric appliances come with built-in safety features because they don't have pilot lights that can go out and cause gas leaks. Electric cooktops have different burner sizes to heat pots or pans efficiently. Flat-top electric cook surfaces are also easy to clean.

The other kitchen contemplation involves potentially investing in a commercial-grade oven or cooktop, akin to what is used in a restaurant kitchen. Here's some variables to think about when researching commercial equipment.

- **Determine space and setup requirements**
  Often double the size of a standard home unit, a commercial appliance generally requires more floor space. Additionally, because a commercial oven generates high heat, it needs to be at least six inches away from the wall, which may need to be tiled or covered in metal to protect from this heat. These units may also require more complicated, and therefore expensive, ventilation. Be sure your house can handle the gas or electric needs for such commercial units. Most ranges use gas.
- **Research heat output and insulation**
  Generally, home units are much better insulated than commercial units, meaning the latter will let off more heat into your home and often be hot to the touch. A commercial oven might then cause you to run—and pay for—more air-conditioning in the summer if you operate a baking business. ☛

of your products. Home refrigerators may hold a range of items, and the smells they bring with them, like a spicy curry, garlicky potatoes, or a fish dish. A second refrigerator stops such smells influencing the flavor of your dough or frosted cake.

- **Food processor**
  A real ninja in the kitchen: the food processor. It can slice, dice, chop, and puree, making a variety of prep tasks more efficient. Get a food processor with a large cup size for large batch processing; Cuisinart has bowl sizes that range from 7 to 14 cups. Food processors often come with a wide open tube at the top called a feed tube that allows you to push larger pieces in at one time. Look for a model designed for effective storage with retractable cords and specific compartments to store attachments like blades.

- **Timer**
  Don't lose track of time when you have multiple recipes baking, proofing, and mixing. Most smartphones come with timers. The good old wind-up versions are great standbys and can be carried around with you to different rooms. Avoid over-using the oven or microwave timers, prematurely frying the electrical

Do you have young kids in the kitchen at times you're not baking for the business—little hands that might touch the unit and burn themselves? Alternatives include commercial models specifically designed for the home. Higher-end appliance companies like Viking and Wolf offer such units that, while pricey (they run into the thousands of dollars), provide commercial quality and function but are well-insulated and designed for a home kitchen layout.

- **Check insurance requirements**
  Because of the high-heat nature of commercial equipment, your insurance policy may not allow such an oven or cooktop under your standard homeowner's policy.

Another home cooktop option to consider is induction. Induction instantly heats up a pan by using an electromagnetic field. This leaves the cooking surface cool to the touch as soon as the pan is removed and does not heat the air around the cooktop. While safer and more energy-efficient than either gas or electric, induction cooktops cost more than $1,000; they also require all pots and pans to be made out something with iron, like steel or cast iron, which may require an additional investment.

motherboard and losing your oven controls in the process. Happened to us!

Step 2: Inventory Ingredients

Since you're making larger batches than you typically would for home use, you'll need to take managing your ingredients up a notch. "Make do" or substitutes in a recipe are out. Having everything on hand before you start is essential.

To get a handle on your ingredients, list everything the recipes call for and their approximate quantities. As you scale up in quantity, consider converting your recipes to weight measurements. Changing "cups" to "ounces and pounds" makes calculating total amounts easier. Use a calibrated scale for weighing quantities.

Should you purchase larger quantities in a bulk bag, you'll need your own storage containers and a system to keep track of your ingredients and make sure they're fresh. Heavy-duty food-grade plastic bins can be found at the Container Store and restaurant supply stores. This one-time investment ensures that your ingredients remain fresh and safe while in storage.

Whether your ingredients are refrigerated, like milk or butter, or stored in the pantry, like chocolate chips, use the "first food in, first food out" inventory principle; use the oldest ingredient first to keep inventory fresh. If an item doesn't have an easy-to-read expiration or "purchase by" date, write the date of purchase directly on the package with a Sharpie permanent marker. Make sure everything is sealed and covered when stored. If you use glass jars, mark dates on them with the Sharpie. When the jars are empty, use rubbing alcohol to remove the permanent marker notations. Adhesive stickers can work, too, but they're more likely to fall off or get stained when wet; plus the labels may leave glue residue on the jar.

Some cottage food laws require that you keep ingredients for your business separate somehow from those for personal consumption. For refrigerated items, CFOs often dedicate a shelf to work ingredients. For dry ingredients, bins, cabinet shelves, and racks may be set aside for business-use-only ingredients.

Step 3: Organize the Kitchen

Now that you have a handle on your equipment and ingredients, how will you use your kitchen space most effectively to access and use these items

when you're in production flow? Organization improves your operation on many levels: efficiency, cleanliness, ease of use, food safety. Take the following actions to organize and streamline your production.

- **Clear clutter**
  You can never have enough workspace, so remove anything nonessential, especially anything decorative. Create as large and clear a workspace as you can. Potted plants, antiques, collectibles, and that random cookie jar need to go. Kitchen space may be limited, so pack up seasonal items like the Thanksgiving turkey roaster or summertime ice pop molds and store them far away. You probably have some dishes taking space in your cabinets that are only used intermittently or for larger dinner parties. Again, find space somewhere else.

- **Designate cabinets specifically for business inventory**
  This separation clearly distinguishes between your personal kitchen and cottage food business and may enable you to calculate and manage your expenses more clearly. If you just dip into your home inventory for ingredients, how will you figure out how much money you are making? Focus on high-volume dry goods that you use for your business, like flour and sugar for baking, and keep those separate. That teaspoon of salt or cinnamon might not matter so much to your bottom line, but some ingredients, like vanilla extract and saffron, are expensive. If your recipes regularly call for high-cost ingredients, keep a separate set of these for business use only. Always keep cleaning supplies stored separately and away from food products.

- **Add storage space**
  Are there any underutilized spots in your kitchen? Can you add shelves? Chrome wire shelving racks can hold up to 500 pounds. Mount some sturdy stainless steel S hooks on them to hang your large pots or bulky utensils. Likewise, add hooks to the inside of your pantry door for lighter items like kitchen towels or strainers.

  By keeping your key supplies where you can access them readily, you'll reduce preparation time. Consider adding a lazy Susan turntable inside cabinets to hold items like spices and flavorings

Keep a clear work space with only the ingredients and items you currently need.
CREDIT: JOHN D. IVANKO PHOTOGRAPHY

for easy access. If your cabinet runs deep, consider adding pull-out shelving so you don't always have to reach into the back and fumble around looking for items.

Don't forget, you may need storage space for your final products, depending on what they are. Canned items are easiest since they're shelf-stable and can go anywhere in the house that is cool and dark, like on basement shelving. Most baked goods not yet packaged can go in large food-grade containers, then be stacked. Items made close to the time of sale can go directly from the cooling rack to bakery boxes or bags for transport.

Step 4: Manage Time

Managing your time is integral to your cottage food business mix. To reduce stress, increase enjoyment, and ensure profits, keep the following considerations in mind.

- **Plan your schedule**

  How and when you work in the kitchen will depend on what you're making. Canned items like jams and jellies can be made weeks before a sale. Production schedules for those items will be based around when the ingredients are available. If you're using strawberries from your bountiful garden patch, you'll need to reserve time blocks for major canning sessions during that peak harvest. You can then label at your leisure and sell year-round.

  For baked and other fresh goods, time production closer to the actual sale. If you're making one key item, like a large order of cinnamon rolls for a breakfast meeting at an office, you can get everything organized the night before, bake the rolls that morning, and you're done. However, if you're preparing for a farmers' market or festival booth where you envision selling a range of baked items, plan your production schedule accordingly.

  See if there are some items, like cookies, that can be made a day or two in advance so as to free up the day before for baking items that need to be super fresh, like bread or muffins. Some high-volume cookie or cake bakers who do not promise "freshly baked" as a part of their marketing message have a carefully devised and tested system of baking, freezing, then defrosting their

products in order to meet demand. In this way, they can easily keep up with large or last-minute orders. Every item doesn't freeze the same, so it's important to test the process to insure you have the best quality product in the end.

- **Establish family boundaries**
  While cottage food laws open up a wealth of stay-at-home business opportunities, integrating your operations into established home routines isn't always easy, especially if everyone in the family is used to 24/7 kitchen access and snacks on demand.

  Carve out specific time blocks for your business kitchen work. While an older child may offer assistance, younger children likely to stick fingers in batter should be kept out of the kitchen when you're filling an order. Rearrange your refrigerator magnet

Parbaking

Consider parbaking when planning your baking schedule, especially when you need a lot of fresh items finished simultaneously for a market or event. Parbaking means baking bread or other dough-based items partially and then freezing them and finishing the baking at a later time. For bread, this initial phase both kills the yeast and cooks up the inside of the loaf, forming the internal structure of the proteins and starches that gives the loaf its spongy internal texture.

After this initial bake, cool and freeze the item. When you're ready for the final loaf, bake it a bit more to form the crust. This saves time during your final baking rush and typically won't diminish the taste or texture of your product.

Experiment with a few batches to determine exactly what parbaking procedures work for your specific recipe. Generally cut about 25 percent off your full cook time for the initial bake; for example, if your bread cooks for an hour, parbake it at the same temperature for 45 minutes. With parbaking, you want to bake the bread long enough to get it to an internal temperature of about 185°F (85°C) for softer crusts such as sandwich loaves and at least 205°F (96°C) for harder, more rustic crusts.

After the initial bake, let the item fully cool to room temperature. This can take up to 2 hours for a dense loaf of bread. Once completely cooled, tightly wrap the item in plastic wrap like Saran Wrap, add another layer of tightly wrapped foil for added preservation, and freeze.

Right before you need your final product, take the loaf out of the freezer and place it in an oven preheated to your regular baking temperature; bake it that remaining 25 percent of the full time, typically 10 to 15 minutes or until golden brown.

collection and post your production schedule for the week for all to see. When planning your day, avoid letting your business take over your life. Of course, you want to care for your customers. But this shouldn't come at the expense of your family or personal well-being.

Step 5: Practice Proper Food Safety

Proper food safety procedures form the foundation of your business, ensuring the quality and safety of your product. Make our cottage food industry proud by proving that a fully licensed commercial kitchen isn't a synonym for food safety; home-based operations can be as safe, if not safer. You wouldn't poison your own family, so why would feeding the public be any different? When cooking for the public, look at your kitchen from the eyes of a potential customer; make sure it sparkles and confidently communicates cleanliness so that anyone would feel safe eating what is prepared there. Making something in your home kitchen and sharing it exemplifies the ultimate in trust. Celebrate that fact by prioritizing safe procedures in your kitchen every day.

Having reviewed your state cottage food law, you'll have noticed the requirements related to sanitation and food safety. It may be as simple as reading and practicing a basic checklist of proper procedures. Or there may be a specific requirement list and a mandatory on-site inspection. Don't panic if your kitchen will be inspected; just make sure it is spotless and double-check any list of requirements. The morning of the inspection is not the time to do anything unusual, like unplugging the refrigerator to clean behind it. What if your refrigerator doesn't readily restart or the temperature isn't at the "safe" level on the thermometer? Don't jeopardize your inspection. Have everything ready and operational the day before and avoid the stress.

If you happen to live in a state that requires an on-site kitchen inspection, approach it as if you were checking off your shopping list, running down the inspector's list of items, and be able to demonstrate that you've done what's being expected. Due to the COVID-19 pandemic and limited staff, some states have moved to virtual inspections or walk-throughs. Some inspections are on FaceTime, Zoom, or Google Meet, while others are accomplished through emails with attached photographs that show that you've accomplished various requirements, like having separate bins for your business ingredients (if that's a necessity). If a kitchen inspection is mandatory, be

sure to get as much information and your questions answered before the actual inspection. See if you can connect with other CFOs in your state who have completed the process already and can give you insider tips and advice. This is another reason to join a cottage food-related Facebook group.

Many states require some form of food handler course and, upon completion, a license or card, similar to what restaurant employees would have. ServSafe, operated through the National Restaurant Association (servsafe.com), offers an annual online food handler certificate for a nominal fee that meets many states' requirements. ServSafe takes about an hour to complete and covers five areas: basic food safety, personal hygiene, cross-contamination and allergens, time and temperature, and cleaning and sanitation. Some states have also partnered with university extension to offer such a course.

Some considerations to keep in mind when setting up and operating a safe food business in your home kitchen include those below.

- **Wash those hands**
  Hand washing is the first line of defense to prevent the spread of illness-causing bacteria. Wet your hands and rub with soap for at least 20 seconds; sing "Happy Birthday" as a timer and make sure to scrub under your nails where bacteria often dwell. Repeat this before and after handling food, after handling uncooked eggs, or after blowing your nose, coughing, sneezing, eating, and using the bathroom. When in doubt, wash.
- **Sanitize the prep area**
  Your food preparation area needs to be spotless at all times. Scrub surfaces before and after they come into contact with food, including utensils and cutting boards, using hot soapy water. Then sanitize. A simple and inexpensive solution of one gallon of water mixed with one tablespoon of unscented household bleach (5.25% to 6%) will serve as a sanitizer for counters. Place in a well-labeled food-grade spray bottle and use on any surfaces that come into contact with food. Let the surfaces air-dry. Since most homes don't have a three-compartment sink like restaurants do, if your state specifies how to wash, have a bucket system that would accomplish the same thing. Some state inspectors are sticklers for keeping cleaning supplies separate from everything else you might use for the business; having only your cleaning supplies stored under your sink might suffice.

"None of this could have happened without you all. The biggest opposition that we hear about cottage foods is safety. And every time we go into a state and someone says, whoa, whoa, making food in a home kitchen…that sounds unsafe. We're able to come back and say, no. Actually, these foods are legally sold in every state, and foodborne illness from any of these foods is almost unheard of. In fact, statistically, they're even safer than foods that you have that are being sold in commercially licensed kitchens. Hats off to you for doing such a great job, being safe, staying clean, and keep up the good work."

— Erica Smith Ewing,
Institute for Justice

Simple steps, like separating cutting boards, ensures safety when making those pear and apple pies.
CREDIT: JOHN D. IVANKO PHOTOGRAPHY

Try some eco-friendly cleaning options and save money and the planet at the same time. Make your own by filling a spray bottle with equal parts vinegar and water and use this to clean the top of the stove and appliances. Don't worry about the vinegar smell. It disappears when dry.

- **Separate your cutting boards**
  Use separate cutting boards and plates for produce, meat, poultry, seafood, and eggs. Other than a few states with exemptions, nothing made under cottage food law can contain meat, poultry, or seafood, so it's best to keep any of these that you have in your home for personal use sealed and stored separately in the refrigerator.
- **Wash fruits and vegetables thoroughly**
  Run produce under cold water and scrub with a firm produce brush, a food-grade model with sturdy nylon bristles for removing any soil. Do not use soap on produce.
- **Keep children out of the kitchen at all times when you cook or bake for the business**
  Establish firm boundaries in your family between when you are "working" and when things are in "home mode" and the kitchen space reverts to family space. If your children are still young, you may need to work late at night or early in the morning when they're still sleeping. You could also make arrangements for childcare so you can focus in the kitchen.
- **No pets in the kitchen**
  Check your specific state regulations, as some states do not allow any pets in the home at all if you are operating a cottage food business.
- **Separate your personal items, from those used by the business**
  And for the pots and baking sheets, store them upside down or facing down so nothing can accidently fall or crawl into them during storage.
- **Keep insects out**
  Make sure all window and door screens remain in good repair and without any tears to ensure all insects keep out of your kitchen workspace.

- **Make sure your water is safe**
  If using a private well, make sure you annually test your water for coliform bacteria and, possibly, for other chemical contaminants if you live in an area with chemical agriculture.

- **Keep records of each of your product batches**
  Keeping records of your product batches is essential. You can use a simple notebook where you record the date, what and how much you made, and what ingredients you used. If any issue ever came up regarding your food handling procedures, you will have these logs to reference. We empathize: record keeping sounds dull and detailed. But records that document the proper procedures you took will show that you employed the highest standards possible should any question arise.

  Most cottage food producers are exempt from the sort of third-party inspections and regulations that pertain to large food producers. However, you're still responsible for every last item you make. A written log indicates you take this role seriously.

Don't agonize, organize. A place for everything and everything in its place makes an efficient and safe kitchen. In the next chapter, we'll turn to time management for your business and learn how to identify signs of burnout.

16

Business Time Management and Beating Burnout

IN THIS CHAPTER, we'll outline exactly what you need to do to keep a balance between your cottage food business and the rest of your life, including caring for your family or holding down that full-time job. We'll explain how to create a profitable business that you wake up every morning refreshed and excited to do, always with a robust smile on your face.

You laughing yet? Yes, we're joking. Unfortunately. If there was a simple, achievable, one-size-fits-all solution to the stress and craziness of running your own business, we would be first in line for that answer. But we each bring our unique situation, needs, and priorities to our entrepreneurial plate, from balancing work and kids or eldercare to squeezing our business in between another full-time job. It's an often overlooked but exceptionally important piece of our life pie that we craft a livelihood that reflects who we are and what lifestyle we envision.

Think of the topics we'll talk about in this chapter as your tool kit in what will undoubtedly be an ongoing journey as you evolve your cottage food business. Note our word choice of "evolve" versus "grow" is intentional. Our society gets so focused on bigger is better and that success is defined solely by size, growth, or money. Play by your own rules. You're the boss.

For most of us cottage food operators, we embrace the small. We love the idea of working from home, being near family, and having many of the perks of a commercial business with minimal investment and hassle. The main point for us is to not get caught up in those societal pressures of "more is better." Define your version of success, which should include staying in business as long as you decide you want to be in business.

Closing up shop shouldn't result from being overwhelmed, losing the fun factor, or getting burned out. Rather, moving on from a business should mean that those personal or financial goals you've set forth from the start have been achieved. And you're ready for the next chapter of your life, be

it retirement, RV-ing across America, or taking on a new career entirely and perhaps heading back to school.

A simple yet powerful theme here to keep top of mind: you are in charge. Your business, your rules. Celebrate the fact that you run your business out of your home kitchen and don't have rent due at the end of the month if you leased commercial space. Ultimately, it's you who decides to take another order or to work with a certain client. Turning one opportunity down because your plate is full does not mean that door is shut forever. You made a healthy decision for yourself and set needed boundaries.

Identifying Burnout

We're not alone in our cottage food community when it comes to experiencing burnout, a condition generally defined as a state of emotional, physical, and mental exhaustion triggered by excessive and extended stress. Burnout happens when you feel drained emotionally, overwhelmed, and unable to meet constant demands.

Identify and spot burnout in yourself or others in our industry, before we fall into a state of crisis. Here's some of the warning signs of burnout.

Always Feeling Dread

When you wake up knowing you have a big baking batch to work on today, do you feel positive excitement and anticipation or trepidation and anxiety? When orders give you angst, when that cookie decorating or truffle making that used to give you joy now stresses you out, take it as a sign to re-evaluate and adjust your business before life grows worse.

Perpetually Tired

Our bodies can only take so much before they start to shut down. Feeling exhausted, especially if you're tired right when you get up in the morning, add up to a physical toll that can lead to chronic physical and mental issues. Look at fatigue as a warning sign that could lead to a bigger issue.

Stressed and Irritable

Do activities that used to give you joy now put you in a bad mood? This funk can materialize in acting crabby and having a short fuse around others. Of course, we can from time to time get annoyed with our families and those closest to us, but living in this angry state takes its toll and can quickly

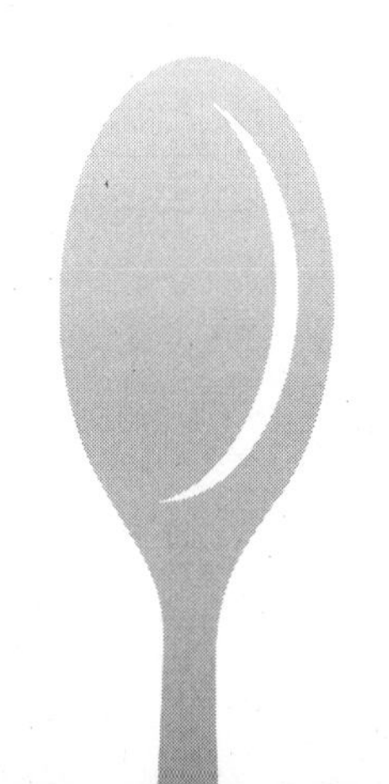

extend to customers. Snapping angrily at a client's inquiry should be recognized that there are other issues you need to address.

Friends and Family Notice

When someone who knows you well says, "Hey, you don't seem like yourself lately," take it as an open and loving door to objectively evaluate where you are right now. Take them up on their invitation for a conversation. Ask about what they specifically notice. Above all, don't take the easy and slippery route of becoming defensive, justifying how you've been acting, or claiming it's just temporary until you get past this month, order, whatever parameter.

Six Components of a Healthy CFO Lifestyle

Let's explore some fundamental elements of a well-balanced, healthy entrepreneurial lifestyle.

Identify Your Priorities

This question goes beyond the business plan and digs into your underlying motivations behind why you are doing this in the first place.

Let's start with the priority of earning a profit for the business. You moved on from cookie baking as a hobby and are now running a legitimate enterprise. Earning income off your venture can and we'd argue should be a priority, the question just remains how much and how does generating a profit affect other priorities.

Your business probably has other priorities above and beyond profit, including family. This is a big one for many cottage food entrepreneurs as a kitchen-based business means no need to leave your house and family. But blending business with raising kids can add its own strain and stress as you are now juggling multiple demands under one roof. An approach to consider when family is a priority is to directly involve your kids in the business. Yes, this may likely mean taking on less business because being a CFO in conjunction with especially young kids can be challenging. But what an inspiring example you are setting for your children who, as they grow and become teens, can even operate their own cottage food business.

Freedom ranks as another motivating priority. Are you tired of the corporate cubicle scene? Does the idea of entrepreneurial freedom and operating on your own schedule warm your heart? Independence can be a bit of an illusion for small business owners as it's easy to let the day-to-day to-dos

take over and tie you down. Going back to not taking on too much can be a vital factor here in usurping any feeling of freedom. You're in control of your schedule and how much, or how little, business you take on.

Cottage food entrepreneurs are artists at heart with creative expression a priority, just instead of paint and a canvas, we love to get our fingers in dough and other ingredients. That creative self-expression, from the actual process to the pride you feel in a job well-done, can be an essential priority for many of us. Several variables keep the creative priority positively flowing, such as charging enough for your time, expertise, and ingredients.

Value Your Time

Chapter 18 covers pricing and profit in detail, so consider this a philosophical reminder that the most important ingredient here is you, the cottage food entrepreneur. This can be a stretch when you've been giving away your treats for years to shift to a mindset of you are valuable, but consider today your invitation to start. Not valuing ourselves and our time quickly leads to burnout.

Establish Boundaries and Saying No

It's the shortest and simplest word that we cottage food entrepreneurs have the hardest time to say: no. You don't need to accept every order. You don't need to make crazy accommodations for out-of-line clients. Yes, it's completely okay to take the two weeks before Christmas off from any orders to spend time with your family. If a family member asks you to bring cookies to Christmas dinner, you can indeed say no. Sticking to the boundaries you set is as important as setting them.

Think of boundary-setting as a muscle, the more you practice it, the easier it will get. Draw on support from our cottage food community if you need backing in saying no. We've been there, saying yes when we should have said no.

Time Management

Create a time management system that works for you in operating your business to help keep you organized and avoid last-minute stress. You may find it helpful to track and cap the time spent on certain activities, particularly marketing and working with social media as these can get out of control and consume much time and life energy. No matter how hard you work, there's always more marketing that could be done, and there's no bottom to a social media feed. Apps and online programs may help manage your

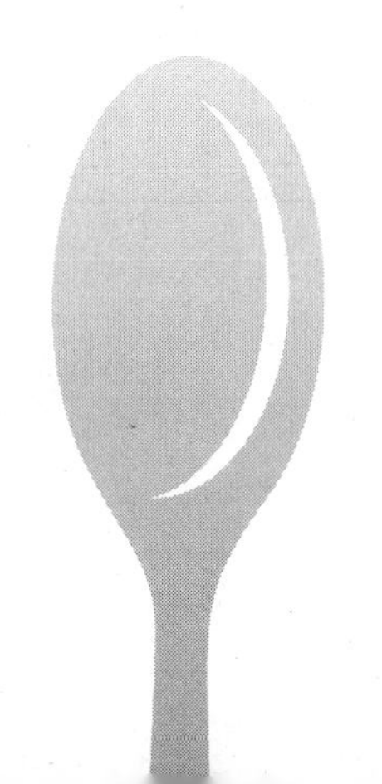

schedule, depending on your skill set and needs. Software tailored to food entrepreneurs can help manage numerous tasks, including orders, payment processing, customer correspondence, and bookkeeping. The Castiron platform, for example, was built to help independent cooks, bakers, and food artisans start, build, and grow their businesses.

Most CFOs find themselves, like most people, with a sense of time scarcity—of there never being enough time to get everything done. When you're operating a business, time equals money, in terms of how efficiently you can produce a beautiful, hand-decorated cake to make it worth your

A Permission Slip for Saying No

Saying no means you know your limits and can make healthy decisions. It's not easy, but it's essential to the long-term success of your business. It's vital to set boundaries and clearly communicate them.

It's okay to say no:

... when you had any issue with a customer before
... to any last-minute orders
... when you realize you've neglected your puppy
... when your calendar is overloaded with orders already
... to anyone you had to track down for a payment
... if a customer requests a product or design that is outside your normal scope
... when you have plans with your family
... when you want to reserve the two weeks before Christmas for your kids
... if you or someone in your family come down with a cold, the flu, or COVID-19
... when you simply are not excited about a customer custom cake request
... to friends or anyone wanting a discount
... to family requests to bring your treats to holiday gatherings
... when not saying it will affect your mental health
... to always taking on the new hot item for fear of missing out
... to cooking dinner, instead asking your kids or spouse to take care of it
... to simply say no for any reason

Remember "no" is itself a complete sentence. You don't need long explanations. Try a simple phrase like one of the following:

- Sounds like a fantastic opportunity, but I am not available.
- I am so very honored that you asked me, but I can't do it.
- Unfortunately, I am already booked but maybe next time.
- Sorry but I require orders a minimum of a month before the event.
- I really appreciate you asking me, but my calendar is full already.
- No, thank you.

time to do so. Quality, as most will agree, can't be rushed. Sometimes, however, we just need to discover short-cuts that make the process more cost effective. It's about working smarter, not harder. For example, one CFO who does DIY cookie kits devised a clever system for efficiently filling multiple frosting bags by placing all the bags in one big cup, then filling each bag, one after another. The process saves time and cuts down on wasted spilled frosting. Waste is lost profits. Time is money.

Maybe you want to incorporate a seasonality mentality to your time management. Instead of being open and producing year-round, focus on specific holidays. The upside is you'll have time off between the holidays. Christmas or Thanksgiving may pop to mind first, but think about other celebrations you can target, such as Mother's Day or the Fourth of July. After all, who wants to be short on time, prepping orders, when you'd rather be celebrating the Christmas holidays with your family?

Reflect

It's too easy to jump from order to order, never stopping to reflect, evaluate, or just sit back and bask in the satisfaction of what you created. Read the raves, faves, and comments from your happy customers. Take advantage of this opportunity to strategically process and tangibly improve. Make some time, even a short 15 minutes, to reflect on what you just did and write down notes on how to improve next time. This can be especially helpful if you do an annual event like a specific holiday market.

Celebrate

Take time to celebrate what you just accomplished. This is an especially important and overlooked opportunity to thank and involve your family, as they may or may not have been involved with or even witnessed what you created and accomplished.

Such celebratory gestures can be simple and small, such as saving some samples for your valued family. Take the time to gather and celebrate after a busy time like the holiday baking season. Take them out to dinner or have a special meal at home to thank everyone for their support. This ties back to your business priorities and, if both profit and family are important, how can you blend the two? We've known cottage food entrepreneurs, for example, whose profit goal is to earn enough money for a family vacation, a highlight to definitely share and celebrate together as a goal.

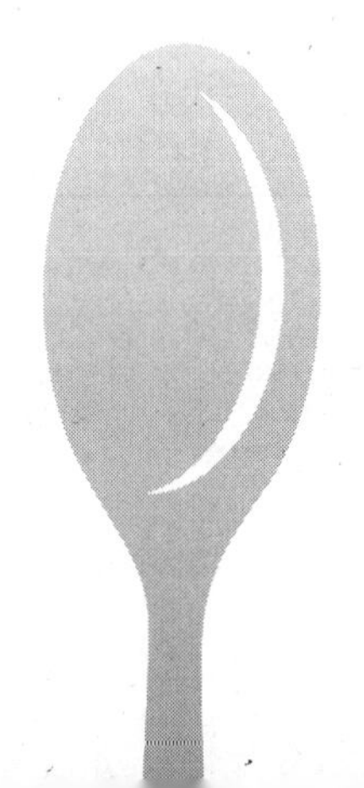

Dawn M. Belisle, Delights by Dawn, Atlanta, Georgia

Name: Dawn M. Belisle

Business: Delights by Dawn (Atlanta, GA)

Website: https://delightsbydawn.com

Products: alcohol-infused cupcakes and desserts

Sales Venues: website orders, farmers' markets, sports stadiums

Gross Revenues: $45,000/year

Don't Stress Out, Says Boozy Baker

"Entrepreneurship is a roller coaster. It goes up and down," admits Dawn M. Belisle, an attorney turned boozy baker with her home-based enterprise, Delights by Dawn. She should know. Since launching her business in 2014, her alcohol-infused cupcakes and desserts have been sold in the Georgia Dome stadium at Atlanta Falcon games and concerts, at the Atlanta Motor speedway hosting NASCAR races, and even featured in the Cupcake Showdown on The Cooking Channel.

"I have always loved baking and cooking and knew someday I would make it a business," recognizes Belisle. "After practicing law for many years, I no longer wanted to live a life of stress, and I was not happy doing traditional law anymore." She found the stress related to her baking business much easier to keep under control. Plus, it's her passion.

As a home-based baking company operating under Georgia's cottage food law, Delights by Dawn primarily markets through their website. Belisle offers eight flavors of her boozy cupcakes, plus seasonal flavor variations. While she adds flavors and introduces new infused products, Belisle remains focused on her unique marketing niche. Her desserts are well suited to events—corporate events, celebrations, birthdays, weddings, tailgating—or to satisfy a sweet tooth fix for those passing through a farmers' market when she has a stand.

Dawn Belisle and her cupcakes became famous when featured on the Sugar Showdown on The Cooking Channel.
Credit: Dawn M. Belisle/Cooking Channel's Sugar Showdown

"I grew up with infused cakes made by my mother," shares Belisle, remembering her alcohol-infused Caribbean fruit cakes her mom made. "I didn't want to make regular cupcakes or cakes, so I started with the original rum cake, then developed flavors based on what I liked to drink and what I felt others would like. Profit margins can be higher because the price point will be higher due to the alcohol." From the very start, she knew she wanted to bake something different, a product that would stand out from everything else on the market.

"Anyone can start a business, and it's pretty easy to do so," says Belisle, recognizing the proliferation of cottage food laws that have popped up around the country. "The point is you want to be able to sustain your business. You want to be in this business for the long haul." Among the reasons that Delights by Dawn continues to thrive include cultivating a unique product niche, clearly identifying viable and profitable markets for her products, and following various strategies to prevent burnout and manage stress. She also spent a lot of time early on researching the market potential for her products. She even hung out with people tailgating before sports games and gave out product samples, listening to their comments about her cupcakes—what they liked, and what they didn't.

"I started small to see if my business would be sustainable and grow," explains Belisle, on why she didn't rush into opening a bricks-and-mortar storefront. "I have also worked out of a rented commercial kitchen and then transitioned back to my home. Success for me is not having a store front. To stay in business, you must be smart and make sure your overhead doesn't exceed your profits, otherwise what's the point. Storefronts encompass a lot of overhead, and if it isn't necessary, why take on that debt.

Delights by Dawn booth set up for a pop-up stand at the Curb Market. Credit: Delights by Dawn

"I use social media a lot, both Facebook and Instagram, sometimes with some paid ads," says Belisle, related to her primary marketing efforts. "I also use Nextdoor because their system targets people in my community directly, based on my address. It's easier to get to those buyers than trying to target them on Facebook. Over the years, I've sold retail at the stadiums because I had a unique product. It's very difficult to get into those venues, but profitable when I did. I made about 300 cupcakes along with other baked goods for each home game." She was still able to bake these products at home. However, for the quantity produced and the time involved, Belisle concluded that some people would have found it easier and quicker to complete such orders in a rented commercial kitchen.

Dawn Belisle's Delights by Dawn food stand inside the Georgia Dome. Credit: Delights by Dawn

"My biggest sales came from special orders from alcohol companies themselves," admits Belisle, glad they

happened after she had refined her operations to be effective at producing a consistent, high-quality product efficiently. "The orders would average 1,500 to 2,500 cupcakes. I handled those by myself because I had a system down and was organized when I had to fulfill those orders."

Belisle understands her business, as any cottage food operator should. Her practiced elevator pitch goes a long way in helping land new customers: "My online baking business specializes in alcohol-infused cakes, cupcakes, and other desserts. Based in the Metro Atlanta area, we do pickups and deliveries, and they're great for birthdays, celebrations, or just something unique that you can have. You can order online on our website, delightsbydawn.com.

"There are legalities to baking with alcohol," admits Belisle. "Each state has their own legal rule, which is what I specialize in consulting through my law practice. People must be careful because not knowing the law can result in the Alcohol Tobacco and Firearms, or ATF, shutting the business down. It's best to research your options before jumping in." In addition to the following her state laws, Belisle has found it necessary or required to carry liability insurance, with $5 million in coverage, due to her products being sold in stadiums. That provides some piece of mind and protection. Her business is also structured as a limited liability company (LLC), which separates her personal assets from those of the business. Belisle continues to offer legal assistance for cottage food operators through her Law Office of Dawn Belisle Facebook page.

Delights by Dawn Jack Daniels "Whiskey Cease & Desist" alcohol-infused cupcakes.
CREDIT: DELIGHTS BY DAWN

"If you don't manage your time, if you don't manage your stress, you might experience burnout that may result in you deciding to give up on your production or your product," cautions Belisle. "We may get to some point where we get burned out because, for most of us, we are doing this by ourselves," says Belisle. "Technically and legally, you are the only person that can actually produce the products.

"One of the things to avoid the stress and the burnout is time management," advises Belisle. "With time management, you just really have to be a little bit more organized than you already are. What I've found helps me is having one or two days to organize the rest of the week. My suggestion would be to take off one to two days, if you can. Most baking businesses, even the ones that have storefronts, are not open on Mondays. I found pickups start on

Wednesdays and definitely run through the weekend. So, Mondays and Tuesdays were the best days for me to get organized and prepared for the orders later in the week.

"I call Mondays my administrative days," details Belisle. "That's when I sit down at my computer and send out any emails to anybody I need to respond to. That's when I email businesses that I'm trying to do some type of partnership or venture with, or talk to them about my products. It's also the day that I check my inventory for the week and get the supplies, if needed. While you love to bake and make treats, you might not like to deal with the business side. But you have to deal with the business side if your business is going to sustain itself.

Delights by Dawn alcohol-infused strawberry colada cupcakes.
CREDIT: DELIGHTS BY DAWN

"Tuesday, is often my prep day, especially for batter," continues Belisle. "Then Wednesday's the day that I take to make all the frostings and the decorations. Thursday is the day I'm going to take to bake the actual cake or cupcakes. If it's a big order or a big event, I split production between Thursday and Friday. You know what your schedule is like and what works best for you. But you must prep ahead. There is nothing wrong with you baking the layers of your cakes, two, three, or four days ahead of time, wrapping them correctly and putting them in a freezer. Many bakers will freeze their cakes in order to decorate them anyway, but without the icing or the frosting on it. Finally, Sunday is for self-care and rest.

"Find a mentor, someone that is in the business or knows the business," says Belisle, about another stress-reducing strategy. "You need someone that you can talk to, that can understand your struggles and who can give you some feedback to help you bring that stress level down. I have an advisory board, too, which can just be a few close and respected friends. They can be a lifeline and provide an objective opinion and ask me an important question, like 'That's a great idea, but let's take a look at the numbers.' It helps me avoid making bad decisions or costly mistakes. If you can't afford to pay them, throw them a cake or bake some cupcakes for their family as a way to show your appreciation for the information and the advice they're giving you.

"I also practice meditation," says Belisle, about another strategy to manage stress. "As a busy baker, we're doing drop-offs, we're doing pickups. Or we spend hours and hours on our feet baking. Meditation helps to put you

Profile

Delights by Dawn mini-rum bundt cake.
CREDIT: DELIGHTS BY DAWN

in that calm state, to relax. I do it before I go to bed at night to calm me down. It helps me sleep. I do it in the mornings before I start my day."

Belisle also makes time to go outside and exercise. "Being outside with nature is just fantastic. I usually take a relaxing walk, often in the morning before I start my day. I feel so great that I am even more motivated when I come back in to pump out some cupcakes or to pop out those cakes.

"Being an entrepreneur is twenty-four-seven business," concludes Belisle. "That's the problem. You have to know when to step away. If you have been bombarded with orders or a big event, and you have been going, going, going, take a day or two to step away."

While Belisle creates unique products, finds innovative ways to sell them, and is fortunate to attract customers who enjoy the alcohol-infused cupcakes and don't mind paying for them, ultimately, her success comes down to her ability to manage the daily stress that comes with running her own business as well as her talent in selling and telling her story, her narrative. "The passion for what I do is seen by my customers. It turns out that they are just as interested in the person making the products as the products themselves. I'm energetic and always try to change things up."

With an eye to the future, Belisle remains eager to learn or try something new for her business. "I went to the three-month pastry program at Gastronomicon in Cap d'Agde in Southern France," shares Belisle. "I've always loved the art of French pastries and wanted to learn how to create their beautiful desserts.

"With everything that was happening in the world, I was ready for a change and growth," adds Belisle. "That is what inspired me. It was a total business write-off as I plan to rebrand my business to incorporate what I learned, with my added twist. I learned so many new skills, like baking with less sugar and more fruit and nuts for flavor and using quality ingredients. I also picked up professional decorating skills that turn my products into a work of edible art." And it goes without saying, there's a lot to be said for a relaxing, stress-relieving stroll along the spectacular Mediterranean coast between classes.

Let Your Care for the Product Carry Over to You

Cottage food production can be hard physical work, especially if you have a larger order to get ready for pickup or drop-off, or when preparing for an important farmers' market or holiday bazaar. While most of us don't keep track, we might find ourselves on our feet for hours at a time. A small dose of strategic thought and preventative care goes a long way in supporting your health, both mental and physical, so your business remains fun and you avoid burnout.

"Ergonomics is a word you don't hear much in cottage food circles but is super important as it means making sure your movement through whatever task you're working on is suited for the situation you are in," shares Laura Gosewisch, owner of Vital Ground Farm in Minnesota. She is both a seasoned food entrepreneur and a Clinical Massage Therapist with a specialty in supporting farmers and food producers, empowering them to care for their bodies in order to do their job long-term. "Professional kitchens in restaurants, for example, are strategically designed with an eye toward ergonomics and creating safe movement to avoid injury. Your home kitchen wasn't designed with that in mind but there are things you can do to compensate."

Explore both your physical kitchen layout and your movement within it from a strategic lens. Gosewisch offers six expert perspectives:

Take Time to Be Aware

"Most of the time we act like the task is more important than the task do-er, and we quickly jump into a job without thinking, which is not what you want to do," observes Gosewisch. "Make it a habit before you start any longer kitchen project that you quickly think through what you need to do and what is the most efficient process while prioritizing caring for your body." Repeating the same movement too long can add strain, as cookie decorators well know. Break up the task, for example, by not doing all the cookie piping straight through. Mix it up with a less demanding task, like labeling or packing.

Aim for Symmetry

"Remember to use both sides of your body equally, as ergonomic problems can result when you consistently put too much strain and pressure on one side," Gosewisch advises. Center your body as much as possible and distribute weight evenly on both legs. After squeezing those piping bags for a

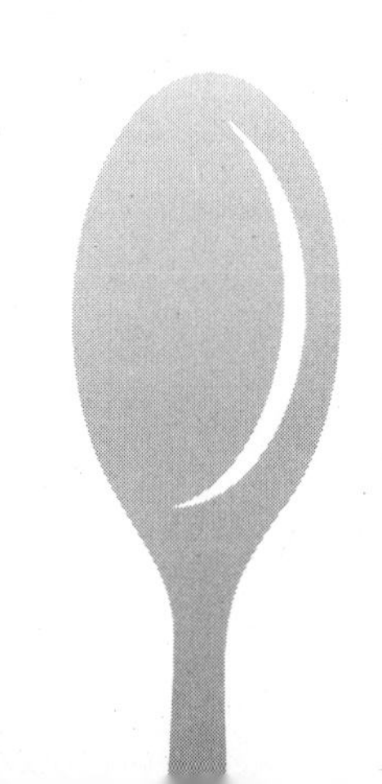

while, take a break and gently push your palms up against the wall, creating the opposite muscle motion to the piping movement. Your busy hands will crave the change, and that motion, even for a few minutes, should feel really good.

Take Care of Your Feet

Think of yourself more like a restaurant chef versus a stay-at-home mom baking bread. What would a chef use that could help you ergonomically in your own kitchen? Gel mats, sometimes called anti-fatigue mats, are those squishy mats you often see on restaurant floors that create a more cushioned base for standing on your feet for long periods. We've used GelPro Comfort Floor mats for years and were amazed at the immediate difference in comfort over standing on our hardwood farmhouse floor. Also, trade the slippers for supportive footwear when you're taking on a longer production cycle while standing.

Warm Up Your Body

Think of that cookie-baking marathon just as if you were going out jogging and take care of your body accordingly. Don't jump into that repetitive motion without warming up a little first. Try a couple of jumping jacks, stretches, or even a few yoga poses to get the blood flowing.

Keep Fueled

Be fed and hydrated when you work. For Lisa's cookie-making marathons, which usually happen in the evenings, she always has a healthy dinner before starting. Just because she's baking for three hours, doesn't mean she should make a tapas dinner out of them. Baking for Lisa is a way to relax, unwind, and have fun. She often puts on her noise-cancelling headset and listens to her favorite podcasts while working. If it's been a particularly long day, she might add in a cup of kava tea or glass of cabernet. We've found that having high-quality, nutrient- and protein-dense foods, and water on hand gets many CFOs through long days at a market, especially if there's inclement weather.

Know Your Limits

"If you're finding yourself needing to choose between your business and your life, it's too late," sums up Gosewisch. "As business owners, we often

feel timid to create what we truly envision for our business lifestyle and feel compelled to fit into what's expected. Charge what you are worth and make sure the economics of the time and physical effort you give add up to a profitable, sustainable business for you for the long term."

Bottom line, if you're starting to feel overly stressed and on the way to burnout, it's time to stop and take a breath. Reevaluate as needed, apply some of the sage strategies and advice in this chapter, and give yourself permission for whatever you need to keep baking, canning, candy-making, or whatever you do for as long as you want.

Mynhan Hoang working in her home kitchen. CREDIT: MYNHAN HOANG

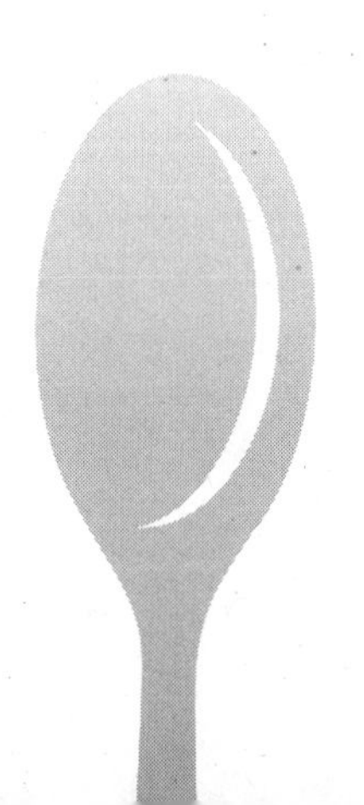

17

Make It Legal: Establish Your Business in 7 Easy Steps

DON'T LET THE GOVERNMENT, your health department, an insurance agent, a CPA, or a family member get in the way of you launching your food business from the kitchen. Avoid letting self-doubt creep in or pangs of fear overwhelm you. You can do it. Tens of thousands of other home cooks have.

We've broken this chapter into seven easy steps to get you going. While most states have start-up guides for a business, cottage food enterprises can avoid most of the red tape due to your size, lack of employees, and limitation on sales. Progressive states, eager to help CFOs get started, often have easy-to-follow checklists, specific to the state cottage food law as well as to other applicable business requirements on the state and local level.

But to run your business legally—which everyone should do—there are a few federal, state, and even local licenses you might need to get before you sell your first bagel. For a comprehensive list of the regulations, the Small Business Administration (sba.gov) provides an overview with detailed links to state-by-state requirements; go there only if you want to be overwhelmed.

Sure, the national statistic of failed businesses may be nine in ten, but as we pointed out previously, it's almost impossible to fail with a home-based cottage food business since you're starting it in your own kitchen with practically no start-up costs. Your only expenses may be a few licensing fees and the ingredients for the first batch of products you sell.

Step 1: Do a Local Zoning Check

Just because the state says you can operate a business from your kitchen doesn't mean your county, township, or municipality agrees, so check before you go to the next step. Zoning ordinances can be all over the board, vary from one county to the next, and sometimes leave a lot of discretionary interpretive control to the administrator in charge. There may be restrictions

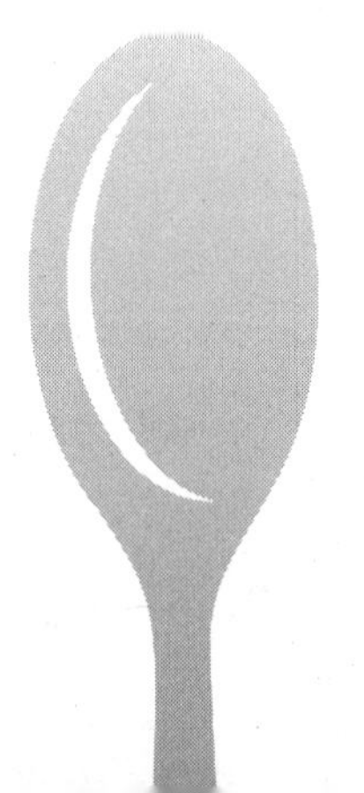

on everything from the appearance of your home, use of signage, or the volume of customer foot traffic. Signage limitations may be an issue if you offer pickups at your home; how will your customers know they're at the right place? A work-around might be a clever decoration that would not

Taking Exemptions

Here's the great news. Unless you strike a gold mine with your food product and want to go big, below are some of the many regulatory exemptions most cottage food enterprise owners can take, whether or not you're a political libertarian:

- All employee and new hire state regulations. This assumes that you don't hire employees and it's just you in the kitchen, plus your spouse, a family member, or kids pitching in from time to time.
- State unemployment insurance, especially in those states that restrict how much the business can gross, and therefore, how much an owner could earn and how often they might be in a position to actually pay themselves a salary.
- State worker's compensation insurance, especially in those states that restrict how much the business can gross.
- USDA's Food Safety Modernization Act, because of the products you're allowed to sell under cottage food laws.
- Food and Drug Administration's nutritional labeling, unless you explicitly make a health or nutrition claim or sell wholesale and/or in volumes that exceed their clearly defined exemptions. This exemption includes nutritional analysis and testing.

Specifically, per the US FDA Small Business Nutrition Labeling Exemption Guidance Document:

> One exemption, for low-volume products, applies if the person claiming the exemption employs fewer than an average of 100 full-time equivalent employees and fewer than 100;000 units of that product are sold in the United States in a 12-month period. To qualify for this exemption the person must file a notice annually with FDA.... If a person is not an importer, and has fewer than 10 full-time equivalent employees, that person does not have to file a notice for any food product with annual sales of fewer than 10,000 total units.... If any nutrient content claim (e.g., "sugar free"), health claim, or other nutrition information is provided on the label, or in labeling or advertising, the small business exemption is not applicable for a product.

If in doubt, consult their website (fda.gov).

Some of the above exemptions are based on gross revenues earned, whether you have employees or not, and other variables particular to your state. Be sure to double-check that each of these exemptions applies to your situation.

perceived as being out of place if your home is in the city or suburb, perhaps a lawn statue or birdfeeder.

In your conversations or research of the zoning codes in states with more restrictive laws, it's important to convey that you're not starting a huge wholesale enterprise, just a small direct-to-customer retail operation. If the concern is too much traffic at your house, offer to deliver products to your customers. You may find that you need to bring the zoning administrator up to speed on what a cottage food law even is. If you're in a state that allows wholesale and has no sales cap, just be open with respect to your plans and see what they say. If your local zoning laws are outdated—perhaps written before the ubiquitous and powerful home computers, versatility of mobile phones, and explosive growth of delivery services and Amazon Prime—and do not allow "businesses incidental to the home," it may be something you need to advocate to change. You would not be alone. The COVID-19 pandemic, in part, has forced many municipalities to revise their zoning requirements in order to allow home-based businesses, including cottage food operations, to operate legally.

We found it ironic, in our rural county despite our wide-open spaces dotted with an occasional farm or residence, that the zoning requirements explicated stated that "no retail sales on the premises" were allowed. Interestingly and rather arbitrarily, our county has allowed a robust bed and breakfast industry for decades, and numerous small businesses have been operated off rural residential properties, from construction enterprises to dried flower businesses. It took an active county board member, who also sat on the zoning committee, to tackle the problem head-on to get the language changed in our county, allowing home-based bakeries and other home-based businesses to operate. The zoning administrator was arbitrarily applying the rules to one type of business but not others. Not anymore. Our zoning code now allows businesses to be operated "incidental to the home."

If you rent an apartment, live in a condo with a condo association, or lease a home, you'll also need to read the fine print in your lease or agreement and see if there's anything explicitly preventing you from running a business out of your rented home. The same holds true if you happen to live in a planned residential neighborhood or complex; check with the homeowners' association before you proceed.

In each scenario above, based on your research and to cover your bases, make sure you write down the specifics of any conversations that give you

the green light, including the name of the person you talked with, when, and exactly what was said. Try to get as much information as possible in writing since you can call upon it later should issues arise. Email works great for documentation if you choose to use this method of correspondence. Take screen shots of text messages as backup evidence.

Step 2: Get Licensed

Contact the governmental office that deals with the cottage food law for your state, the department of agriculture, health, or whatever agency is responsible for the formulation and implementation of regulations or rules. Often, it's the department of agriculture, but the regulations vary a lot between states. The health department typically does not license and enforce cottage food law; they handle restaurants, catering operations, and other facilities where food is prepared and served.

What agency you need to contact may vary depending on expanded cottage food laws and new food freedom and microenterprise home kitchen operation laws. For example, a cottage food operator may not be licensed or permitted by the same department or agency as a MHKO or a food entrepreneur operating under a food freedom law, depending on the state.

In most cases, you'll need to file for a "cottage food license" or "home food processor license" or some similar designation. A nominal fee may be charged in some cases. Some states require an on-site inspection of your kitchen facilities while others call for some form of food-handling training. Due to the pandemic and staff shortages, some of the inspections are done on Facetime, Zoom, or alternative, non-face-to-face means. As covered previously, ServSafe Certification is an online or classroom-based nationally accredited program set up by the National Restaurant Association; it's often used by the restaurant industry to make sure their employees understand basic food safety practices for preparing and serving food.

Step 3: Set Up Your Business and Structure It Wisely

By now, you have a name for your company, plus another fictional name (i.e., doing business as or DBA). Next is setting up your business. There are several ways to do so. You'll need to evaluate your own situation, your tolerance for risk, and your business to determine which works best for you.

While cottage food entrepreneurs sell non-hazardous foods, there is a possibility that something might not be just right with your product, no

fault of your own. Maybe one of your ingredients was mislabeled; perhaps a sliver of a nutshell found its way into the bag of walnuts you used for your granola. It happens. If a customer breaks a tooth or chokes on this shell, you could be held liable for damages. By operating as a corporation or LLC, you may be shielded from possible issues on a personal level.

Depending on your comfort level, you may be best off leaving the specifics of setting up your business to a certified public accountant (CPA) or a business attorney. While all business structures require governmental record-keeping and forms to be filed, corporations and limited liability companies (LLCs) involve additional legal and accounting stipulations. That said, many cottage food operators we've interviewed have found the process straightforward enough that they did it themselves.

Below are several common business structures, broken down by the most recognized reason for choosing one over another: personal liability protection. This is a shield that prevents anyone with a court judgment or financial claims against the business to touch anything other than the assets of the corporation or LLC. In other words, certain business structures protect the personal assets of the company officers, stockholders, and employees, reducing the risk that your house, personal property, or bank accounts could be seized as a part of a court settlement.

No Personal Liability Protection

Sole Proprietorship

By far the most common, easiest, and least costly business structure is a self-employed sole owner or sole proprietorship. As covered in the research findings summary (see Appendix A) from the Cottage Food Operator Assessment conducted by the University of Wisconsin-Stout, 66 percent of current CFOs operate as a sole proprietorship. Income from the business is reported as a part of the owner's personal income using the IRS Schedule C or Schedule C-EZ; you may be subject to self-employment taxes of 15.3 percent. You are also responsible for the liabilities and debts of the business. If your business is sued, everything you own could be threatened by the lawsuit.

General Partnership

If you go into business with a sibling or other family member, you would do so as a partnership instead of as a sole proprietor. When there are two or more individuals who are owners of a for-profit business, typically operating

under a written partnership agreement, the business is a general partnership. All partners are responsible for the liabilities and debts of the business. Income is reported on the IRS Schedule K-1 and may be subject to 15.3 percent self-employment tax. The partnership must file an annual return, Form 1065, with the federal government and possibly a state return.

Distinct Legal Entity Offering Personal Liability Protection to Shareholders

S Corporation, or Subchapter S Corporation

Essentially a tax accounting classification, an S corporation is a common stock-issuing, legal entity, income from which is taxed only once when it passes through to the employees or shareholders of the corporation on their personal income tax return. Like C corporations, discussed below, S corporations must file articles of incorporation, hold director and shareholder meetings,

In addition to providing personal liability protection to its shareholders, an LLC or subchapter S corporation may offer potential federal tax savings, as illustrated in this example. CREDIT: JDI ENTERPRISES, INC.

	W-2 Wage Earner	Active Owner of LLC Taxed as Partnership	Active Owner of LLC (or S Corp) Taxed as S Corporation
Gross Earnings	$50,000 paid as W-2 income	$50,000 paid as an LLC distribution	$50,000, paid $20,000 as W-2 income and $30,000 as distribution
FICA Taxes	$7,650	$0	$3,060 (15.3% of $20,000)
Self-employment Taxes	$0	$7,650	$0
Federal Taxes (sample)	$5,000	$5,000	$5,000
Net Income	$37,350	$37,350	$41,940
Based on two-person household, filing jointly.			

Officers, Shareholders, and Taking Stock

Unlike a sole proprietorship, a corporation or LLC is a distinct legal entity, with a corporate formality that separates the owners of the company, the shareholders and its advisory body, the board of directors and its officers (president, secretary, treasurer) and managerial body, the chief executive officer (CEO) and the chief financial officer.

By law, a corporation must maintain a registered office and agent within the state where it is formed to respond to legal and official matters. If your corporation is in the same state as your residence, you can be your own resident agent. A one-person or family corporation must still follow the formality of corporate procedures related to decision-making and meetings. Document the "meeting" with corporate minutes, even if that means you write down your decisions if you're the only board member as well as the CEO, president, secretary, and treasurer in a one-person-owned corporation.

Ownership of the company is signified by receipt of stock certificates reflecting financial, property, or service contributions to the business; shares can be voting or non-voting, common or preferred; the latter acts similarly to a bond in terms of its value. Shareholders taking stock usually have voting rights, financial distributions rights to dividends if declared by the board of directors, and proportionate rights to assets should the corporation be dissolved.

file an annual corporation tax return, keep corporate minutes, and vote on corporate decisions. Most S corporations can use the more straightforward cash method of accounting whereby income is taxed when received and expenses are deductible when paid. Unlike C corporations, S corporations are limited in the number of shareholders they can have.

Limited Liability Company

The limited liability company (LLC) is a separate legal entity established by filing articles of LLC formulation or similar documents in the state where it is formed. The number of LLC members, various classes of stock, and tax accounting selection determine a diversity of avenues to properly meet tax liabilities, whether the LLC is treated as a partnership or a C or S corporation. Most CFOs who decide to form an LLC do so as a single-member LLC. Per the IRS: "If a single-member LLC does not elect to be treated as a corporation, the LLC is a 'disregarded entity,' and the LLC's activities should be reflected on its owner's federal tax return." Similar to a sole proprietorship, the CFO business structured as a single-member LLC would complete the Form 1040 Schedule C, plus other required schedules.

C Corporation

The most expensive and complex of business structures, the C corporation is a legal entity set up within a given state and owned by shareholders of its issued stock. It's unlikely, due to the scale of your operation, that you'd form a C corporation—unless, of course, you strike it rich and turn your products into a full-blown big-time business, a possibility we cover in the Business Expansion section of this book.

The corporation, not the shareholders or directors, is responsible for the debt and liabilities of the C corporation. It must file articles of incorporation, hold director and shareholder meetings, file an annual corporation tax return, keep corporate minutes, and

Affordable Legal Documents

Some states have very straightforward forms that must be completed to set up small businesses as a corporation or LLC; others, less so. Below are two low-cost options to consider if you want to structure your business as either. Of course, if you tend to be risk adverse and have the funds, you may feel most comfortable hiring an attorney licensed in your state who specializes in small business legal issues.

- Nolo Press
  nolo.com
  One of the Internet's leading websites offering free and easy-to-understand legal information and various do-it-yourself products.
- LegalZoom
  legalzoom.com
  For a nominal charge, plus state fees, this online company can help you set up your enterprise as an LLC or subchapter S corporation in most states. It could be a source for other legal documents, too.

NAICS Code (North American Industry Classification System)

The federal government likes to keep statistical data and classify businesses in the US. They do so by requiring businesses to select a NAICS code, or number, which is then used when completing an annual tax return. The Census Bureau (census.gov) has a listing of these self-assigned codes. For example, some common codes used by CFOs are 311811 for Retail Bakeries, 311352 for Confectionery Manufacturing from Purchased Chocolate, or 311421 for Fruit and Vegetable Canning. There are lots more. If you need help, call the Census Bureau, 888-756-2427.

Besides being needed to complete your tax return, these codes are often essential when applying for certain special funding from state or federal government. For example, in Wisconsin, you must have the correct NAICS classification and number to be able to receive a pandemic-related grant, since the grants were targeted to specific businesses or industries.

vote on corporate decisions. Income from a C corporation, after expenses have been deducted, is taxed both at the corporate level and at the individual level, on wages and dividends paid to shareholders.

Income Tax on Wages or Self-Employment Tax

Regardless of the structure of your business, you will need to file some form of annual state and federal income tax returns, using either the FEIN for your business or your social security number if you're a sole proprietor. CFOs may be liable for income taxes on your CFO wages (if you issue a W-2) or self-employment taxes if you're operating as a sole proprietor. Federal and state income tax is completely separate from state sales tax if your state requires you to collect it, covered in more detail in chapter 18.

As mentioned previously, if a CFO adopts a sole proprietorship business structure, the easiest of options, the CFO must complete an IRS Schedule C.

For the CFO who has an LLC business structure, the return that must be completed, either Form 1065 or Form

Federal Employer Identification Number (FEIN)

If you end up forming a corporation, LLC, or business partnership or find yourself hiring employees, you'll need to get a federal employer identification number (EIN) from the US Internal Revenue Service. You can apply for this number through the IRS on the Internet (irs.gov) or by filing the IRS form SS-4. The FEIN is sometimes referred to as an EIN, Employer Tax ID, or a tax identification number or TIN; they're the same thing.

SCHEDULE C (Form 1040)
Department of the Treasury Internal Revenue Service (99)

Profit or Loss From Business
(Sole Proprietorship)
▶ Go to www.irs.gov/ScheduleC for instructions and the latest information.
▶ Attach to Form 1040, 1040-SR, 1040-NR, or 1041; partnerships generally must file Form 1065.

OMB No. 1545-0074
2020
Attachment Sequence No. 09

DRAFT AS OF July 13, 2020 DO NOT FILE

Name of proprietor | Social security number (SSN)
A Principal business or profession, including product or service (see instructions) | B Enter code from instructions ▶
C Business name. If no separate business name, leave blank. | D Employer ID number (EIN) (see instr.)
E Business address (including suite or room no.) ▶
City, town or post office, state, and ZIP code
F Accounting method: (1) ☐ Cash (2) ☐ Accrual (3) ☐ Other (specify) ▶
G Did you "materially participate" in the operation of this business during 2020? If "No," see instructions for limit on losses ☐ Yes ☐ No
H If you started or acquired this business during 2020, check here ▶ ☐
I Did you make any payments in 2020 that would require you to file Form(s) 1099? See instructions ☐ Yes ☐ No
J If "Yes," did you or will you file required Form(s) 1099? ☐ Yes ☐ No

Part I Income

1	Gross receipts or sales. See instructions for line 1 and check the box if this income was reported to you on Form W-2 and the "Statutory employee" box on that form was checked ▶ ☐	1
2	Returns and allowances	2
3	Subtract line 2 from line 1	3
4	Cost of goods sold (from line 42)	4
5	**Gross profit.** Subtract line 4 from line 3	5
6	Other income, including federal and state gasoline or fuel tax credit or refund (see instructions)	6
7	**Gross income.** Add lines 5 and 6 ▶	7

Sample IRS Form 1040 Schedule C on the Federal income tax return. Additional schedules are also required. CREDIT: US INTERNAL REVENUE SERVICE

Form **1065**
Department of the Treasury Internal Revenue Service

U.S. Return of Partnership Income
For calendar year 2021, or tax year beginning , 2021, ending , 20 .
▶ Go to www.irs.gov/Form1065 for instructions and the latest information.

OMB No. 1545-0123
2021

A Principal business activity | Name of partnership | D Employer identification number
B Principal product or service | Type or Print | Number, street, and room or suite no. If a P.O. box, see instructions. | E Date business started
C Business code number | City or town, state or province, country, and ZIP or foreign postal code | F Total assets (see instructions) $
G Check applicable boxes: (1) ☐ Initial return (2) ☐ Final return (3) ☐ Name change (4) ☐ Address change (5) ☐ Amended return
H Check accounting method: (1) ☐ Cash (2) ☐ Accrual (3) ☐ Other (specify) ▶
I Number of Schedules K-1. Attach one for each person who was a partner at any time during the tax year ▶
J Check if Schedules C and M-3 are attached ▶ ☐
K Check if partnership: (1) ☐ Aggregated activities for section 465 at-risk purposes (2) ☐ Grouped activities for section 469 passive activity purposes
Caution: Include **only** trade or business income and expenses on lines 1a through 22 below. See instructions for more information.

Income	1a	Gross receipts or sales	1a	
	b	Returns and allowances	1b	
	c	Balance. Subtract line 1b from line 1a		1c
	2	Cost of goods sold (attach Form 1125-A)		2
	3	Gross profit. Subtract line 2 from line 1c		3
	4	Ordinary income (loss) from other partnerships, estates, and trusts (attach statement)		4
	5	Net farm profit (loss) (attach Schedule F (Form 1040))		5
	6	Net gain (loss) from Form 4797, Part II, line 17 (attach Form 4797)		6
	7	Other income (loss) (attach statement)		7
	8	**Total income (loss).** Combine lines 3 through 7		8
[illegible]	9	Salaries and wages (other than to partners) (less employment credits)		9
	10	Guaranteed payments to partners		10
	11	Repairs and maintenance		11

Sample IRS Form 1065.

CREDIT: US INTERNAL REVENUE SERVICE

Form **1120-S**
Department of the Treasury Internal Revenue Service

U.S. Income Tax Return for an S Corporation
▶ Do not file this form unless the corporation has filed or is attaching Form 2553 to elect to be an S corporation.
▶ Go to www.irs.gov/Form1120S for instructions and the latest information.

OMB No. 1545-0123
2019

For calendar year 2019 or tax year beginning , 2019, ending , 20
A S election effective date | TYPE OR PRINT | Name | D Employer identification number
B Business activity code number (see instructions) | Number, street, and room or suite no. If a P.O. box, see instructions. | E Date incorporated
C Check if Sch. M-3 attached ☐ | City or town, state or province, country, and ZIP or foreign postal code | F Total assets (see instructions) $
G Is the corporation electing to be an S corporation beginning with this tax year? ☐ Yes ☐ No If "Yes," attach Form 2553 if not already filed
H Check if: (1) ☐ Final return (2) ☐ Name change (3) ☐ Address change (4) ☐ Amended return (5) ☐ S election termination or revocation
I Enter the number of shareholders who were shareholders during any part of the tax year ▶
J Check if corporation: (1) ☐ Aggregated activities for section 465 at-risk purposes (2) ☐ Grouped activities for section 469 passive activity purposes
Caution: Include **only** trade or business income and expenses on lines 1a through 21. See the instructions for more information.

Income	1a	Gross receipts or sales	1a	
	b	Returns and allowances	1b	
	c	Balance. Subtract line 1b from line 1a		1c
	2	Cost of goods sold (attach Form 1125-A)		2
	3	Gross profit. Subtract line 2 from line 1c		3
	4	Net gain (loss) from Form 4797, line 17 (attach Form 4797)		4
	5	Other income (loss) (see instructions—attach statement)		5
	6	**Total income (loss).** Add lines 3 through 5 ▶		6

Sample IRS Form 1120-S business income tax return. Additional schedules are also required. CREDIT: US INTERNAL REVENUE SERVICE

1120, depending on the designation, or a Schedule C on Form 1040 if a Single-Member LLC. Consult with a tax professional or CPA for further details.

For the CFO who has a subchapter S corporation business structure, they must complete a business filing for the IRS using a Form 1120-S. The Form 1120-S is in addition to a personal tax return, Form 1040.

Step 4: Secure a State Business License

The state in which you live usually wants to know if someone is operating a business there. For those of you who are merely diversifying your already established business by selling products through the cottage food law, you should have already completed this step. For everyone else, you'll need to contact your state's department of revenue (or equivalent) to complete a simple application and pay a fee for the privilege of being in business for yourself. If your business is incorporated, an LLC, a partnership, or a sole proprietorship operated under a fictitious or trade name (i.e., DBA, doing business as), there is a specific fee for your business license. If you operate as a sole proprietorship under your own name, you may not need to get a license. Verify what your state requires.

Step 5: Get a State Sales Tax Permit

Now that you're selling something to the public, your state's department of revenue may require your business to collect sales tax on certain "value-added" products, like pickles, wedding cakes, or chocolate confections. To do so, you'll need to get a sales tax permit and understand the state and, possibly, county and city taxes associated with every gift tin of stollen that you sell at a Christkindlmarket in December.

If a CFO is required to collect sales tax for a particular product, this tax is usually collected on behalf of the government and added to its price. Most CFOs write this sales tax amount on a separate line on an invoice or receipt. Sales tax is not intended to be a tax on the business itself, but rather on each item sold to the customer.

Collecting and keeping track of sales tax can be onerous. Some states may tax chocolates but not muffins topped with chocolate shavings. In Texas, there's no sales tax on pretzels, but when you dip them in chocolate, they're taxed. Currently in North Carolina, sales tax is based on the county where the transaction takes place, adding more complexity. Most online credit card and third-party processors have systems that automatically collect the sales tax correctly, if required; make sure you have the sales tax feature set up in their system before you make your first sale.

Heads up. In the government's move to make everything electronic (except voting), many states are requiring Internet-based access and payment for related filings and fees. If you have little computer know-how, you may need to see if your local library can help you with this process.

LINE ITEMS	
Cookies × 21 Dozen (Decorated) *Candy bar*	$840.00
Pre-Order Payment Enter Payment *Delivery*	$50.00
Subtotal	**$890.00**
Sales Tax	$76.86
Tip	$194.00
Total	**$1,160.86**

Sales tax can be added, if needed, as a line item on third-party credit card processors for individual products.
Credit: John D. Ivanko

Step 6: Get a Local Business License (if needed)

Some cities or counties may require you to have a business license or tax certificate before you can operate. A call to your city or county's clerk's office will lay this one to rest.

Step 7: Manage Risk with Insurance

Living is risky business. Cars slide off the road after hitting a patch of ice, products stop working, and bones break. When you go into business selling a food product, you're accepting an additional amount of risk. You could be held liable for someone getting sick from eating your product, perhaps at no fault of your own. Today's headlines are filled with outbreaks of *E. coli*-tainted vegetables and salmonella-laced peanut butter, largely a result of an increasingly industrialized food system. Major product recalls are about as regular as oil changes on your car.

Generally speaking, the cottage food industry is the antithesis of our industrial food system. It's likely that you're the only person preparing the entire order of marmalade or macaroons. You personally select each and every ingredient, knead and mince as needed, then bake, simmer, or hot bath. You're the one packing your product. Delivering it, too. Most of what you sell may travel less than 20 miles.

What we find in our supposedly "safe" supermarket travels thousands of miles, can be highly processed, and is filled with artificial ingredients and preservatives thanks to the magic of modern chemistry. But the ingredients

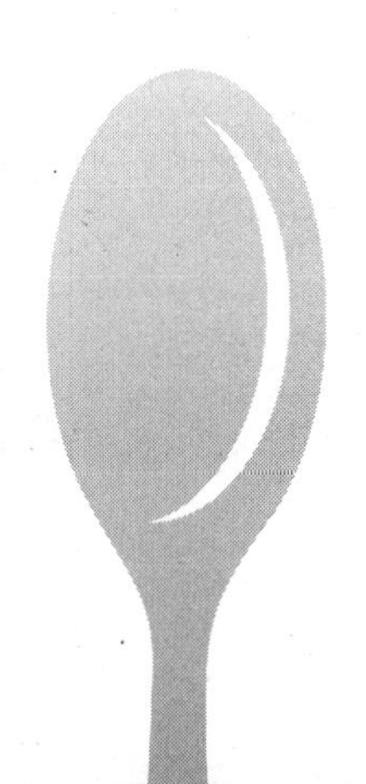

listed on your package can be pronounced; they're real, minimally processed, and made locally.

If you scale up and sell wholesale to regional grocery stores or a national specialty food chain, it's different, covered in greater detail in the Business Expansion section. You may even be required to have a recall plan in place for your product. Plus, once your product is out of your hands, you don't have control over how the distributor or retailer handles it, spawning the growth of tamper-proof packaging.

What if your product gets left in a distribution truck that breaks down in the desert for two days? What if a retailer decides to display your preserves in direct sunlight in a south-facing front window? Of course, you would want to avoid such extreme heat or sunlight conditions on your products. But what if? That's what insurance is for: covering you for accidents, the unknown or situations beyond our control.

Regardless of your approach to your ingredients, products, customers, and scale of operations, there's always a possibility something may not go exactly as planned. In response to our litigious society, insurance has become a necessary part of both living and doing business. Insurance, however, is a business decision, not a requirement of your state's cottage food law.

What you need to evaluate is your appetite for risk and the insurance requirements related to what you want to do with your business. You should start by checking if you are already covered in some way, through either your existing homeowner's insurance policy or your business structure (covered in Step 3 of this chapter). To manage risk, consider combining insurance with other strategies. Of course, your non-hazardous products themselves are another way you reduce your risk exposure.

If you're already in business, then you're probably covered at some level for food or personal

People Might Do the Craziest Things (With Your Products)

CFOs do everything they can to make the most delicious and safe products to be enjoyed by their customers. Right? But what you cannot control is what a customer might do with the product once it's in their possession and out of your hands. That's why you might package it the way you do or include an allergen statement on your labels.

But we've all seen TV shows and cartoons featuring a pie in the face or a smash cake. The last thing a CFO would want is their amazing products used in this way. But it's possible. For those cake-selling CFOs who sometimes use straws or sticks to hold their cakes together, they remind their customers in their written contract about this fact. Some CFOs even have dowel waivers, signed by clients. A good perspective to have is never assume anything, and buy insurance (or form an LLC) for additional peace of mind. Like *America's Funniest Home Videos* documents all too well, people do the craziest things.

liability issues. In most cases, it's nothing more than checking with your insurance company.

For example, for our small B&B (and cottage food enterprise), we have the business specifically listed on our homeowner's insurance policy as a rider; the annual premium is less than $100 and provides $300,000 of personal liability coverage. Our business is viewed as "incidental to the home" by our insurer, Cincinnati Insurance Company. Additionally, we have a $1 million umbrella insurance policy that covers anything we do on our property and in our car, above and beyond the $300,000 coverage. Everything changes should we decide to prepare food products in a rented commercial kitchen; at that point, we'd need to purchase a commercial business liability policy that may run, at minimum, over $500 per year.

If you're just hanging out your shingle, you should explore with an insurance company what level and type of coverage you might need to feel comfortable and sleep well at night. The annual premium for your business and product liability coverage will depend on the level of coverage, sales venue, gross sales volume, and, of course, your products themselves. In many cases, a commercial insurance policy will be required not for your state but for the venues where you sell your products. Many sales venues require a "Certificate of Insurance" for an amount ranging from $300,000 to $1 million; this certificate, generated by your agent based on your policy, explicitly refers to the venue by name.

ACORD — JDIEN-1 — OP ID: AS

CERTIFICATE OF LIABILITY INSURANCE — DATE (MM/DD/YYYY) 04/17/2018

THIS CERTIFICATE IS ISSUED AS A MATTER OF INFORMATION ONLY AND CONFERS NO RIGHTS UPON THE CERTIFICATE HOLDER. THIS CERTIFICATE DOES NOT AFFIRMATIVELY OR NEGATIVELY AMEND, EXTEND OR ALTER THE COVERAGE AFFORDED BY THE POLICIES BELOW. THIS CERTIFICATE OF INSURANCE DOES NOT CONSTITUTE A CONTRACT BETWEEN THE ISSUING INSURER(S), AUTHORIZED REPRESENTATIVE OR PRODUCER, AND THE CERTIFICATE HOLDER.

IMPORTANT: If the certificate holder is an ADDITIONAL INSURED, the policy(ies) must have ADDITIONAL INSURED provisions or be endorsed. If SUBROGATION IS WAIVED, subject to the terms and conditions of the policy, certain policies may require an endorsement. A statement on this certificate does not confer rights to the certificate holder in lieu of such endorsement(s).

PRODUCER 608-325-9126
Lanz & McArdle Agency Inc.
1022 17th Ave. PO Box 116
Monroe, WI 53566
Jeff McArdle

CONTACT NAME: Jeff McArdle
PHONE (A/C, No, Ext): 608-325-9126 FAX (A/C, No): 608-325-9128
E-MAIL ADDRESS:

INSURER(S) AFFORDING COVERAGE	NAIC #
INSURER A: Cincinnati Insurance Company	244106
INSURER B:	
INSURER C:	
INSURER D:	
INSURER E:	
INSURER F:	

INSURED JDI Enterprises Inc
W7843 County P
Monroe, WI 53566

COVERAGES CERTIFICATE NUMBER: REVISION NUMBER:

THIS IS TO CERTIFY THAT THE POLICIES OF INSURANCE LISTED BELOW HAVE BEEN ISSUED TO THE INSURED NAMED ABOVE FOR THE POLICY PERIOD INDICATED. NOTWITHSTANDING ANY REQUIREMENT, TERM OR CONDITION OF ANY CONTRACT OR OTHER DOCUMENT WITH RESPECT TO WHICH THIS CERTIFICATE MAY BE ISSUED OR MAY PERTAIN, THE INSURANCE AFFORDED BY THE POLICIES DESCRIBED HEREIN IS SUBJECT TO ALL THE TERMS, EXCLUSIONS AND CONDITIONS OF SUCH POLICIES. LIMITS SHOWN MAY HAVE BEEN REDUCED BY PAID CLAIMS.

INSR LTR	TYPE OF INSURANCE	ADDL INSD	SUBR WVD	POLICY NUMBER	POLICY EFF (MM/DD/YYYY)	POLICY EXP (MM/DD/YYYY)	LIMITS	
A	X COMMERCIAL GENERAL LIABILITY; CLAIMS-MADE [ ] X OCCUR; GEN'L AGGREGATE LIMIT APPLIES PER: X POLICY [ ] PRO-JECT [ ] LOC; OTHER:			ENP 0409784	10/31/2017	10/31/2018	EACH OCCURRENCE	$ 1 Million
							DAMAGE TO RENTED PREMISES (Ea occurrence)	$ 100,000
							MED EXP (Any one person)	$ 5,000
							PERSONAL & ADV INJURY	$ 1 Million
							GENERAL AGGREGATE	$ 2 Million
							PRODUCTS - COMP/OP AGG	$ 2 Million
								$
	AUTOMOBILE LIABILITY: ANY AUTO; OWNED AUTOS ONLY; SCHEDULED AUTOS; HIRED AUTOS ONLY; NON-OWNED AUTOS ONLY						COMBINED SINGLE LIMIT (Ea accident)	$
							BODILY INJURY (Per person)	$
							BODILY INJURY (Per accident)	$
							PROPERTY DAMAGE (Per accident)	$
								$
	UMBRELLA LIAB / OCCUR; EXCESS LIAB / CLAIMS-MADE; DED / RETENTION $						EACH OCCURRENCE	$
							AGGREGATE	$
								$
	WORKERS COMPENSATION AND EMPLOYERS' LIABILITY Y/N; ANY PROPRIETOR/PARTNER/EXECUTIVE OFFICER/MEMBER EXCLUDED? (Mandatory in NH) N/A; If yes, describe under DESCRIPTION OF OPERATIONS below						PER STATUTE / OTH-ER	
							E.L. EACH ACCIDENT	$
							E.L. DISEASE - EA EMPLOYEE	$
							E.L. DISEASE - POLICY LIMIT	$

DESCRIPTION OF OPERATIONS / LOCATIONS / VEHICLES (ACORD 101, Additional Remarks Schedule, may be attached if more space is required)

CERTIFICATE HOLDER BLANK00

CANCELLATION

SHOULD ANY OF THE ABOVE DESCRIBED POLICIES BE CANCELLED BEFORE THE EXPIRATION DATE THEREOF, NOTICE WILL BE DELIVERED IN ACCORDANCE WITH THE POLICY PROVISIONS.

AUTHORIZED REPRESENTATIVE
Jeff McArdle

ACORD 25 (2016/03)

The Certificate of Insurance for JDI Enterprises Inc. that provides up to $2 million in general liability coverage in cases where the delivered product or completed service cause damage or injury to a customer.

CREDIT: ACORD/CINCINNATI INSURANCE COMPANY

In response to the growing number of businesses and sole proprietorships in the food industry, Utah-based Veracity Insurance Solutions offers a Food Liability Insurance Program (fliprogram.com). The company offers a general liability policy limited to $2 million.

"Starting a cottage food operation has huge legal ramifications, and cottage food laws accidentally make people think they are shielded from rules and regulations. I have concerns about whether cottage foods actually increase potential liability and about the insurability of the operations. I've heard of folks getting dropped by insurance companies or having trouble finding an affordable quote. This has to do with insurance agents not fully understanding what these laws entail and the small scale that we're talking about. Many are going without insurance at all. The state laws authorize you to sell certain foods but do not cover nor exempt you from liability issues."

— Rachel Armstrong, an attorney and executive director of Farm Commons (farmcommons.org), providing legal education for the sustainable agriculture community. Check out the Farm Commons website for various free webinars and resources that dial deeper into legal issues related to value-added products.

As discussed previously, structuring your business from the start as a corporation or LLC offers a liability benefit but comes at a cost and with more complicated paperwork. Maintaining adequate insurance coverage would add to your protection.

The challenge remains finding a balance between the joy and financial benefits of operating a food-based enterprise and managing some of the risks associated with doing so. In the end, it's your decision. But keep in mind that, in nearly all cases, cottage food laws by their very definition apply to non-hazardous food products. Enough said.

18

Small Business Finances

WITHOUT BEING TOO CUMBERSOME, boring, or filled with pages of numbers, this chapter covers the day-to-day financial aspects of your enterprise. As a CFO, your success is practically guaranteed. You just need to load up the minivan with your cookies, keep track of your sales, and smile on the way to the bank at the end of the day to deposit your profits. But as a CFO, you also need to be a chief financial officer for your enterprise, and that means keeping track of the finances.

To be legitimately in business, you need to make some profit in at least three of the last five years, according to the IRS. As we'll cover next, business revenue minus expenses equals profit. For most cottage food enterprises, it's rarely a matter of if they'll be profitable; rather, by how much. Remember, you're starting with practically no overhead and few, if any, start-up expenses.

Day-to-Day Financial Management

Even if you think you hate numbers or dread balancing your checkbook, you can keep track of your revenues (sales) and any expenses related to your operation as a business. It's just a matter of coming up with an easy process that works for you.

Again, business revenue minus expenses equals profit. It's this profit that the IRS must see either on your personal tax return or that of your LLC or corporation during three of the last five years for your enterprise to be considered a for-profit business and not a hobby. According to the IRS, someone operating a hobby cannot deduct any losses at the end of the year.

Going right to the source, on the IRS website:

> An activity qualifies as a business if it is carried on with the reasonable expectation of earning a profit.... The IRS

presumes that an activity is carried on for profit if it makes a profit during at least three of the last five tax years, including the current year.

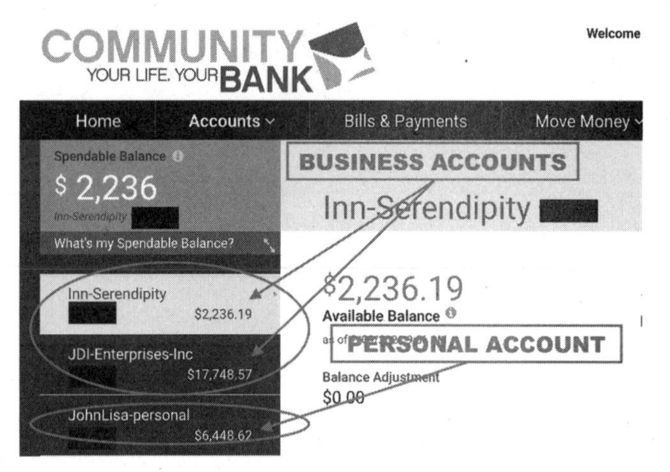

It's important to separate your personal assets from the revenue collected by your cottage food operation.
CREDIT: JOHN D. IVANKO

So, you don't need to make a profit every year. The business loss that results in a year where expenses exceed revenues can be claimed on your personal tax return and may end up reducing your income tax liability if you have other sources of income, say from your full-time job, interest income from savings accounts, or dividend income from stocks. For more clarification on this, consult with a CPA or other tax professional.

Making and Taking Money

Revenue is the money earned by your business, also called gross sales or income. Before your first sale is made, you must open a business checking account, separate from your personal checking account. Co-mingling business and personal money is the easiest way to lose track of what you're earning and draw the unnecessary and unwanted attention and scrutiny of the IRS.

When you sell a jar of pickles, just deposit the proceeds from that sale into your business account and you're good to go. When you have an expense, pay for it with a check from this account, creating a nice paper trail for the IRS to follow. If your business warrants it, consider acquiring a business credit card for purchases made for your enterprise; this allows you to track and account for your business expenses and avoid having to use your personal credit card for business purchases. The more transparent you can make it for the IRS, the better.

Before your first sale, figure out how to receive payment. Cash works great; it won't bounce, and it's simple to deposit. Depending on your community, personal checks can add additional flexibility since some people may not walk around with wads of cash. For those CFOs selling to corporate accounts or special events like weddings, not only will checks be the only way to go, you'll likely need to crunch a simple invoice for payment. Be prepared to generate a receipt as well.

These days, some of the customers eager to buy your products may not use cash or checks much. It's a decision you'll likely face: a customer who

How the Patriot Act Changed How We Bank

When the Patriot Act passed after the tragedy of 9/11, it transformed how banking is done in the US, in part to intercept and obstruct terrorism. Now more than ever, your banking business is government business.

As a result, to open a business checking account, you'll require the following if operating as a corporation or LLC:

- a copy of the articles of incorporation for your business
- Federal Employer Identification Number (FEIN) or Tax Identification Number (TIN)
- the minutes from a board meeting that explicitly state the representatives of the business who are authorized to access the bank account
- a resolution that states who is authorized on the account (a form to be completed, usually provided by the bank)

If your business is a sole proprietorship or partnership, you'll likely need the following:

- Social Security number (SSN)
- some form of statement or note, perhaps generated on your company letterhead, that explicitly states the person or persons associated with the business who are authorized to access the bank account
- a resolution that states who is authorized on the account (a blank form to be completed, usually provided by the bank)

The above requirements may vary slightly, so check with your local bank.

wants your products but can only buy them on credit. Credit and debit cards, thanks to their convenience and widespread use, have become the de facto way people pay for things. The question then becomes, are the additional sales made possible by accepting credit cards worth the fees you'll be charged for each transaction? Of course, these fees are legitimate business expenses, covered later in this chapter.

You don't need a full-blown merchant account with cumbersome contracts and expensive scanning machines to accept a credit card payment for a dozen donuts; these expensive, complicated, and ever-changing systems may be best left for larger companies with sales volume to support it.

Thanks to the proliferation of mobile devices, smartphones, and computers, plus Internet or cellular connections, processing credit cards and accepting payments via digital wallets has also become easier and more

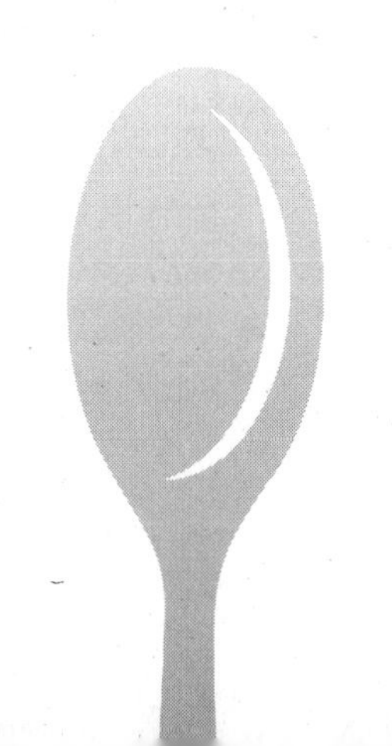

Tahnohn Hayes's NutFrusion, based in Chula Vista, California, uses the Square Register and Stand when selling at the North Park Thursday Farmers' Market in San Diego.

CREDIT: JOHN D. IVANKO PHOTOGRAPHY

widespread. Payments can be accepted online, within an app or in person. Most companies offering card readers, small devices that can read a swiped credit card, also provide an option to manually key in the credit card number, but charge a higher percentage fee and fixed transaction cost for this feature. When you use these third-party processors to invoice or take payments online, simply link your credit card or payment processor to your business checking account. Digital wallets provide a way for customers to pay with their mobile device instead of with a credit card or cash.

The following are some of the many credit card or digital wallet third-party processing options where you only pay a nominal fee based on a percentage of the charge:

- **Square (now called Block): squareup.com**
  Using a free Square device that plugs into the phone jack on your smartphone, tablet, or computer, you can swipe the card and complete your checkout from just about anywhere. Use this referral link—squareup.com/i/HOMEMADE22—and you'll receive free processing on up to $1,000 in sales for the first 180 days.
- **Venmo: Venmo.com**
  Owned by PayPal, Venmo is a mobile payment service to manage payments, within the app, online, or in person.
- **PayPal: PayPal.com**
  Among the most widely used, secure, and safe ways to receive payment via credit cards or through someone's PayPal account via the computer, tablet, or mobile device. No contracts or monthly service fees; just a percentage fee and a charge deducted for each transaction completed. PayPal offers a mobile app and card reader for payments on the go.
- **Cash App for Business: cash.app**
  Owned by Block, another way to receive payments for your business.

- **Other digital wallets options: Google Pay, Apple Pay, and Samsung Pay** Many online marketing platforms have created integration with digital wallets from these major tech companies.

FILER'S name, street address, city or town, state or province, country, ZIP or foreign postal code, and telephone no.
FILER'S TIN
PAYEE'S TIN
1a Gross amount of payment card/third party network transactions $
OMB No. 1545-2205
2021
Form 1099-K
Payment Card and Third Party Network Transactions
Check to indicate if FILER is a (an): Payment settlement entity (PSE) ☐ Electronic Payment Facilitator (EPF)/Other third party ☐
Check to indicate transactions reported are: Payment card ☐ Third party network ☐
1b Card Not Present transactions $
2 Merchant category code
Copy 1 For State Tax Department
3 Number of payment transactions
4 Federal income tax withheld $
PAYEE'S name
5a January $
5b February $
Street address (including apt. no.)
5c March $
5d April $
5e May $
5f June $
City or town, state or province, country, and ZIP or foreign postal code
5g July $
5h August $
5i September $
5j October $
PSE'S name and telephone number
5k November $
5l December $
Account number (see instructions)
6 State
7 State identification no.
8 State income tax withheld $ $
Form 1099-K www.irs.gov/Form1099K Department of the Treasury - Internal Revenue Service

If you use third-party processors, like PayPal, Square, or Venmo, to receive payments, you will receive a 1099-K from the IRS that totals your revenue from these services.

CREDIT: INTERNAL REVENUE SERVICE

PayPal, CashApp, and the growing list of other third-party and digital wallet processors have both business and personal accounts. For your CFO, you need to make sure it's set up as a business account. At the time of this book's printing, the digital payments network offered by Zelle is for friends and family, not for business use, and should be avoided by CFOs. As a CFO, it's essential to keep business and personal finances separate. You'll quickly notice that more than one of the services are, in fact, owned by the same company, so select the one that works best for your situation. We wouldn't be surprised if one day soon you'll be able to even accept cryptocurrency as payment through one of the digital wallets.

If you have an online store for your cottage food products and accept credit card payments or other forms of digital wallet payments over the Internet, you could be getting a 1099-K form from your third-party or credit card processor. The 1099-K form, reflecting income, is for your business account you should have set up, not a personal account that you might use to send money to your kids. Many CFOs, including ourselves, know that our customers like to use credit cards or third-party processors like PayPal or Venmo to collect payments for goods and services. Not included are the personal third-party processors used to transfer money sent as gifts, transfers of funds to kids at college, reimbursing a friend for dinner, selling personal items at a loss, or some other non-commercial transaction.

While the processor already collects fees associated with each transaction, as of 2022, the US government now wants to make sure they get their cut of your hard-earned revenues. The American Rescue Plan signed into law by President Biden on March 11, 2021, now requires that these credit card and third-party processors report the amount of revenue they processed to the IRS and you. This is really nothing new, since you should

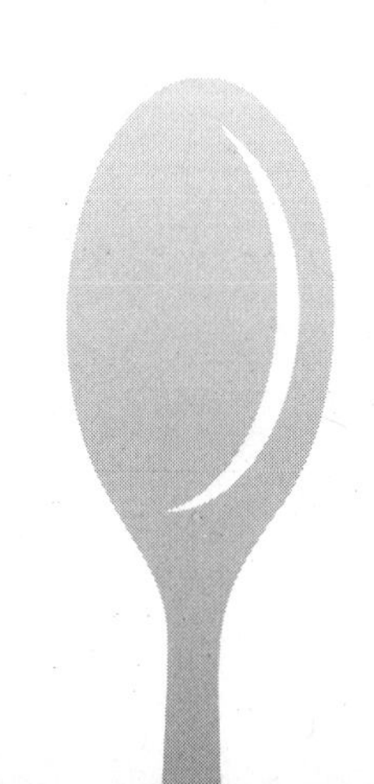

already report this as revenue on your tax return. What's new is that the IRS now has a way to cross-reference what you report.

Some states may have, by law, a lower threshold than the federal threshold for the issuance of the 1099-K. For example, at the time of printing, on the PayPal website it states:

> "PayPal tracks the total payment volume on your account to determine whether it meets the IRS threshold in a calendar year:
>
> - $20,000 USD in total payment volume from sales of goods or services in a single calendar year and,
> - 200 payments for goods or services in the same year.
>
> Some US states require merchant reporting at a lower threshold:
>
> - Vermont, Massachusetts, Virginia, Maryland: Have a $600 USD total payment volume threshold from sales of goods or services in a single calendar year. That's regardless of the number of transactions.
> - Illinois: Has a $1,000 USD total payment volume threshold of goods or services in a single calendar year. And at least 4 payment transactions."

PayPal website's Q&A section states: "For the 2022 tax year, you should consider the amounts shown on your Form 1099-K when calculating gross receipts for your income tax return." To accomplish this, the apps will require you to submit your Federal Employer Identification Number (FEIN or EIN) or your Social Security Number, if it wasn't already collected.

Fees charged by credit card or third-party processors are legitimate expenses. So are the miles you drive to deliver your products to market, the meal you have there when manning your booth, and every single item you invest in for your beautiful market booth. This is why you need to keep excellent records. Covered later in this chapter, this doesn't have to be hard or complicated.

Money Belt or Drawer

You'll discover few people can pay with the exact change. Depending on the venue, customers may arrive fresh from a cash station with twenties or fifties in their wallets or purses.

To cover your cash sales, you'll need to have a system for making change. A money belt or cash drawer, besides being convenient, helps avoid bills and change being placed in your pockets or coat jackets in the flurry of business transactions. A shoebox can be used in a pinch, but think about the mess of money that piles up in a shoebox and the message it conveys to customers about your level of professionalism.

For small-time operators, a system to manage your money when you're doing events helps keep you organized. If you're the type of person who needs to know exactly how many muffins and what flavors sold, keep a tally sheet at your booth and track each sale. For a less detailed summary, you can just add up what you didn't sell and subtract it from what you made to arrive at your sales total, then subtract the variable costs that went into your order to get your profit for the event. You'll miss some details about your volume discount doing it this way, but your profit at the end of the day will be the same.

Income Statement and Balance Sheet

Eventually, the financial activities of your business are organized into an income statement, also called a profit and loss statement (P&L), with revenues at the top and expenses at the bottom. Your business can also be summarized by a balance sheet reflecting the assets and liabilities (and equity) of the business. Come tax time, your CPA or tax preparation professional will help you sort out your balance sheet, with the difference between assets and liabilities being the net worth of your business. Bookkeeping refers to the recording of all financial transactions, both revenues earned off sales and expenses, documented with receipts. Accounting refers to the presentation and analysis of the records you keep on those revenues and expenses. Your bookkeeping records are what allow you to generate the profit and loss statement that indicates whether you made a profit or loss, and how much. This information is then used when you complete your annual tax return. Most small businesses are set up to have a calendar year rather than a fiscal year, that is, a period of 12 months starting at some date during the calendar year.

Chances are, due to your small scale, that you'll only need to tabulate these records once, at the end of your calendar year, when you prepare your state and federal tax returns. If you have to pay sales taxes, you may even be able to file these annually instead of quarterly, monthly, or weekly. When in

Reading a Sample Profit and Loss Statement

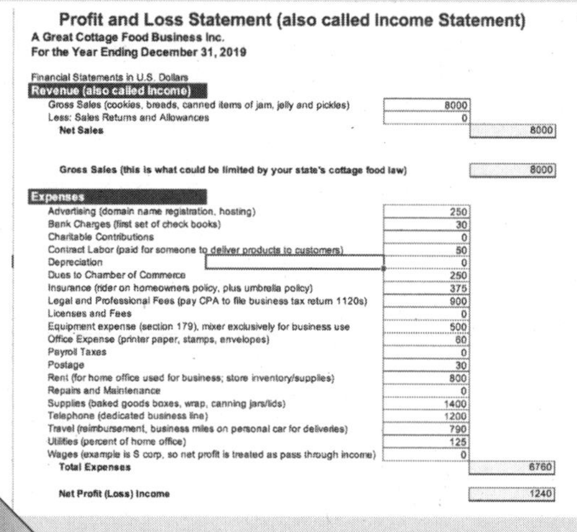

Profit and Loss Statement (also called Income Statement)
A Great Cottage Food Business Inc.
For the Year Ending December 31, 2019

Financial Statements in U.S. Dollars

Revenue (also called Income)		
Gross Sales (cookies, breads, canned items of jam, jelly and pickles)	8000	
Less: Sales Returns and Allowances	0	
Net Sales		8000
Gross Sales (this is what could be limited by your state's cottage food law)		8000
Expenses		
Advertising (domain name registration, hosting)	250	
Bank Charges (first set of check books)	30	
Charitable Contributions	0	
Contract Labor (paid for someone to deliver products to customers)	50	
Depreciation	0	
Dues to Chamber of Commerce	250	
Insurance (rider on homeowners policy, plus umbrella policy)	375	
Legal and Professional Fees (pay CPA to file business tax return 1120s)	900	
Licenses and Fees	0	
Equipment expense (section 179), mixer exclusively for business use	500	
Office Expense (printer paper, stamps, envelopes)	60	
Payroll Taxes	0	
Postage	30	
Rent (for home office used for business; store inventory/supplies)	800	
Repairs and Maintenance	0	
Supplies (baked goods boxes, wrap, canning jars/lids)	1400	
Telephone (dedicated business line)	1200	
Travel (reimbursement, business miles on personal car for deliveries)	790	
Utilities (percent of home office)	125	
Wages (example is S corp, so net profit is treated as pass through income)	0	
Total Expenses		6760
Net Profit (Loss) Income		1240

A sample profit and loss statement for a Great Cottage Food Business Inc.

CREDIT: JOHN D. IVANKO

You don't need to be a numbers person to read and understand a profit and loss statement for your business. In this example, the fictional Great Cottage Food Business Inc. generated $8,000 in revenue, selling cookies, breads, and other cottage food items. The business had various expenses, including business miles reimbursement for deliveries, a large mixer that was depreciated under IRS Section 179 in one year, and rent for a home office, totaling $6,760. Net income, after expenses was $1,240; this is also called profit. Since this is an S corporation, the profit would be reported on the individual's tax return. If this business had been structured as a sole proprietorship, a Schedule C would have been completed on a personal tax return, along with the associated required schedules.

doubt, request your state regulatory agency to be exempted or allowed to file annually to cut down on your (and their) paperwork.

Expenses Defined

There are many financial benefits of becoming a business, depending on how you structure it. Not only are businesses taxed after their expenses have been deducted, but many legitimate deductions are available to a small business that reduce its reported earnings. The IRS tax code specifies the following related to business expenses:

> **IRS Code Section 162(a), Trade or business expenses:**
>
> "There shall be allowed as a deduction all the ordinary and necessary expenses paid or incurred during the taxable year in carrying on any trade or business."

> IRS Code Section 212, Expenses for production of income: "In the case of an individual, there shall be allowed as a deduction all the ordinary and necessary expenses paid or incurred during the taxable year."

An ordinary expense is one that is common in our industry, like flour, butter, and sugar. A necessary expense is one that is helpful and appropriate, like a canopy tent for a farmers' market stand. Be "fair and reasonable" in your business expenses. You can't deduct a family trip to Hawaii. However, deducting a trip and related expenses to attend the Summer Fancy Food Show in New York City seems fair and reasonable, so long as the trip involves researching products, developing your marketing plan, reaching out to potential wholesalers, and so forth; document who you meet and what you accomplish.

Some of the more common deductible business expenses include the following items.

Supplies and Ingredients

From canning jars to product ingredients, any expenses associated with your product, its production, labeling, and packaging can be deducted.

Government Licenses and Fees

Any fees associated with compliance with governmental regulations and licenses are deductible, like an annual cottage food operator's registration if your state has one.

Credit Card Processing Fees

If you accept credit cards or other forms of payment beyond cash and checks, these fees can be deducted.

Advertising

From printing costs for flyers or a banner to website hosting plans, if you spend money on advertising to make money, it's deductible.

Use of Your Personal Vehicle for the Business

Owners of vehicles who use them for business purposes can deduct those miles associated with business use and be reimbursed for mileage by the business. For example, when you drive to sell your products at a local event,

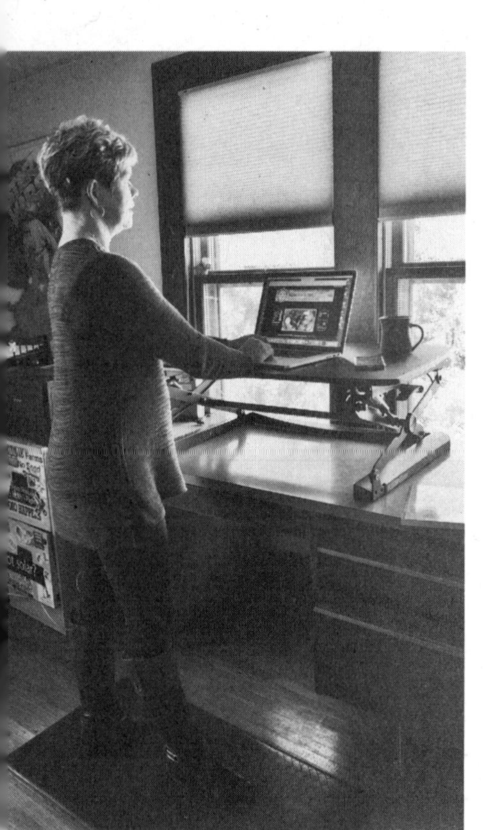

Author Lisa Kivirist using a standing desk in a home office to maintain the business website, share posts on social media, and correspond with customers. The office is also used to store packaging materials for the cottage food operation.
CREDIT: JOHN D. IVANKO PHOTOGRAPHY

you can reimburse yourself at the IRS-specified rate; if it's a 30-mile round trip, your business would reimburse you, as the owner of the car used for business purposes, 30 miles multiplied by the IRS mileage rate established for that year. Pay yourself by business check to create a paper trail for the IRS. Make sure to maintain a vehicle travel mileage log for each vehicle used for business purposes, recording the date, purpose of the business trip, and the starting and ending odometer reading. Note that when you take those business miles as a deduction, you cannot also deduct actual gas or diesel fuel purchases, or any car repairs or maintenance.

Employee Training

Direct expenses related to culinary training, educational programs, or workshops or other ways you might endeavor to improve your skills and receive technical information on managing your business are deductible. Be sure to document these expenses with a receipt for payment; file those class notes as backup, should the IRS want to know what you learned. A ServSafe Food Handler Program would fall under this expense category.

Use of Premise for Business Purposes Only

Here's the bad news: paying yourself, as the homeowner, rent for the use of your kitchen for business purposes is *not* acceptable because you also use this space for personal use. However, if you decide to use a home office exclusively for business, perhaps to fulfill orders, print out flyers, store packaging containers, or conduct other company activities, you can deduct the corresponding portion of the square footage of the property as a business rental expense, plus the corresponding portion of utilities, insurance, repairs, and taxes.

Based on the fair market value of a local office space, you can establish the rental rate for the use of your personal property (i.e., a room in your home for a home office) and pay yourself, as the homeowner, rent for such use by the business. Of course, you need to set up a simple rental agreement between yourself, as the homeowner or property owner, and the company to have on file as documentation for the IRS. A triple net lease requires the business to be responsible for paying its appropriate percentage of real estate taxes, insurance, and maintenance. Note that this rental payment, from the business to the homeowner, does not have any FICA (or self-employment taxes) deducted; for example, a $700 annual rent payment is a

$700 expense, from the business to the homeowner. The business would have to file a Form 1099-Misc with the IRS to reflect rent payment. Just for kicks, it wouldn't hurt to take a nice clear picture of your home office for documentation purposes.

Equipment and Capital Expenses

Some investments, like a brand-new mixer for your bakery business, are considered capital expenses and reflected as assets on your balance sheet. Rather than deducting them, you must capitalize them as long-term investments. These assets, however, can be depreciated, reducing reported earnings. There are options, like Section 179 in the IRS tax code, where businesses can opt to take accelerated depreciation for a 100 percent deduction of a big-ticket capital item in the year in which it was put into service instead of spreading this expense out over several years. This is one way some CFOs may have a loss in one year when they purchased a few pieces of expensive equipment or perhaps a refrigerator only used for business purposes, resulting in a reduction in income tax for that year.

Depreciation

Business assets wear out, break down, and become obsolete, especially with the rapid advancements in technology. The IRS allows a noncash deductible business expense of depreciation to account for the loss of value over time for assets it owned. Depreciation reduces the reported earnings of the business. The amount of depreciation and its duration varies by the type of asset.

For more details on deductions, review some of the Nolo Press books and their website (nolo.org). For an overwhelming headache, visit the IRS website (irs.gov) for the latest updates and changes to the tax code, then consider hiring a CPA who specializes in small business returns. As a bonus, their fee is a tax-deductible business expense; however, penalties resulting from you making an error on your tax return are not.

Payroll Income Tax or Self-Employment Tax

As discussed previously, if your business has more than $400 in net profit, you, as the owner, are required to pay income tax on those profits. Owners of CFOs cannot just keep the profit without paying any federal income tax on their net income. Per the IRS: "Self-employed individuals with a net

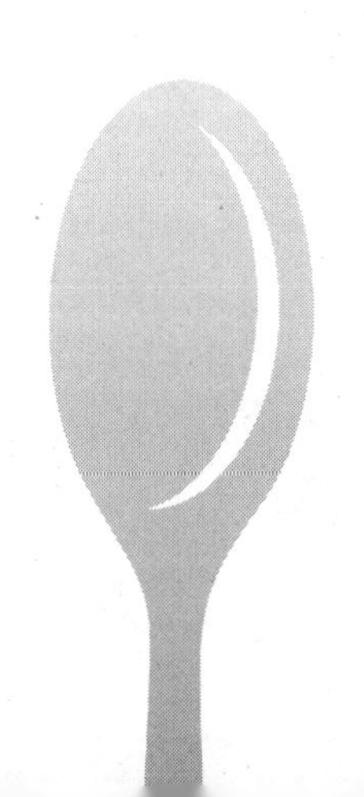

profit of $400 or more must file self-employment tax. If your net profit was less than $400, you do not need to file self-employment tax." The rate for self-employment tax is 15.3%, and consists of two parts: 12.4% for social security and 2.9% for Medicare. If you're generating large profits, you may have to pay quarterly self-employment taxes based on an estimate of annual net income from your business. The self-employment tax is reported on Form 1040 Schedule SE, used to calculate your tax liability.

For businesses structured as LLCs or subchapter S corporations, some CFOs opt to pay a salary and issue a wage statement, the IRS W-2, at the year-end. As a subchapter S corporation, that is what we have done over the years, paying ourselves a salary often on a quarterly basis. In our example, the employee, us, and employer, JDI Enterprises Inc., share in the payment of FICA taxes. Consult a tax professional or CPA for further details on this if you structured your business as an LLC or corporation since the specific tax laws keep changing and there may be particular nuances specific to your situation.

Retirement, in the Form of a SIMPLE IRA

As the owner of your CFO, you can create a Savings Incentive Match Plan for Employees Individual Retirement Account, commonly called a SIMPLE IRA. It's a deferred employer-provided retirement plan for the small business, allowing you to deposit revenues into the SIMPLE IRA for retirement, less the required withholdings for social security and Medicare (FICA), and defer income you might have earned, and be taxed on, in the current year. The business can also offer up to a 3 percent contribution match, independent of your contribution as the employee. Beyond the scope of this book, there are lots of ways to wisely use profits of the business to fund retirement, education, or healthcare needs in the future, worth exploring with a tax professional or CPA.

Bookkeeping Basics

We know you want to be in the kitchen, decorating cakes or simmering your pizza sauce—not adding up numbers or itemizing receipts. Since you're in business, however, you'll need to keep track of the money coming in and going out of the business. It's called bookkeeping, for short.

As a CFO, you can keep track of sales and expenses with a ledger, either electronically with a computer or tablet or the old-fashioned way by writing

them down by hand. You can also use your ledger to record transactions related to assets, liabilities, and owners' equity. There are numerous tablet-based bookkeeping apps. For the more computer-savvy crowd, Intuit's popular QuickBooks (quickbooks.com) may suffice, but you could find these too detailed and expensive for your needs, at least when you're just starting out. A free bookkeeping and accounting alternative is Wave (waveapps.com).

To keep records for your business, you can put your sales receipts in one folder, box, or cabinet drawer by month, quarter, or year, depending on the scale of your operations. If you don't have a receipt system, just create a simple paper receipt with the date, customer/event, and total sales. For expenses, hang onto every receipt, from your start-up costs to ingredient purchases, again, organized by month, quarter, or year. These receipts are proof that you're in business. You don't have to make it any harder than this.

Two methods can be used for accounting, the process by which financial information is recorded, summarized, and interpreted. The more commonly used and straightforward cash basis method of accounting establishes that income is taxable when received and expenses are deductible when paid. The more complex "accrual basis" method records payments or expenses when they're agreed upon, which may take place at some future date; cash may not have been received or spent by the business. Most CFOs opt for cash basis accounting due to its simplicity.

There's no cooking the books for CFOs, though. Keep everything on the up and up. Go out of your way to deposit every last cent of revenue you earn and document your fair and reasonable business expenses.

Cash Flow Is King

Cash flow is simply the cash received and spent by your business over a specific period of time, usually a year. Some cash is essential to getting your business up and going, though with cottage food enterprises, you don't need much.

It's essential that you don't run out of money while customers are still discovering your great-tasting products. It may take longer than you imagine for customers to discover your products. There may be a seasonality to your sales, meaning you could be rolling in the bucks around the holidays but light in the summer months when families often vacation. Many CFOs find that their sales drop off from January to March. Instead of stressing out over

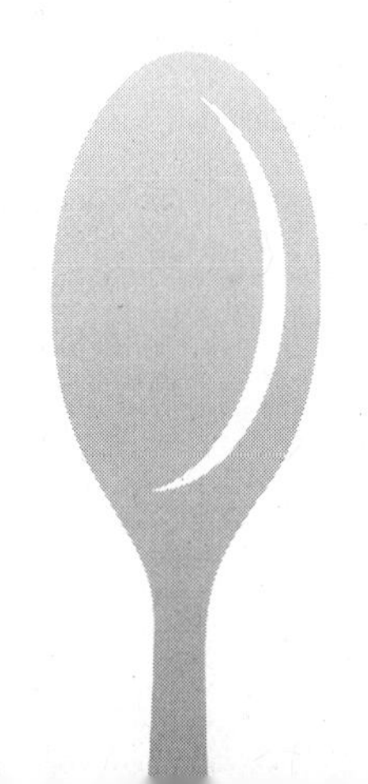

slower sales, these wise food entrepreneurs use this time to do their taxes, reorganize supplies, deep clean the kitchen, or take a well-deserved break after the holidays. Account for seasonality and allow some time to get your business established.

A cash flow projection includes both anticipated cash receipts from sales on a monthly or quarterly basis and cash disbursements for expenses, including direct costs related to your products, marketing, license fees, delivery costs, and equipment. The goal is to avoid or minimize any periods where you have a net negative cash balance.

Cash Flow Projections for Inn Serendipity Fresh Baked Homemade Bakery

Inn Serendipity® FRESH BAKED

Item	Jan	Feb	Mar	Apr	May	Jun	Jul	Aug	Sep	Oct	Nov	Dec	TOTALS
Sales (forecasted)													
- Special Orders			35	45	190	250	220	300	225	90	45	15	1,415
- Events				325						580		150	1,055
TOTAL SALES	**0**	**0**	**35**	**370**	**190**	**250**	**220**	**300**	**225**	**670**	**45**	**165**	**2,470**
Expenses													
- License Fees	10	25											35
- Ingredients		35	20	55	34	35	40	25	20	95	10	20	389
- Flyers Printing		20											20
- Booth Fees				25						200		35	260
- Business Miles	40	45	30	40	25	35	35	25	25	45	20	45	410
- Credit Card Fees				12		10		3		34	2	13	74
TOTAL EXPENSES	**50**	**125**	**50**	**132**	**59**	**80**	**75**	**53**	**45**	**374**	**32**	**113**	**1,188**
Starting Cash	**300**	**250**	**125**	**110**	**348**	**479**	**649**	**794**	**1,041**	**1,221**	**1,517**	**1,530**	
Ending Cash Balance	**250**	**125**	**110**	**348**	**479**	**649**	**794**	**1,041**	**1,221**	**1,517**	**1,530**	**1,582**	

Above serves as an example by month, starting with a $300 cash balance, of projected cash flow in year 1. Sales revenue minus expenses results in a net gain or loss in cash in any given month. By the year-end, based on the sales projections and expense estimates, our cash balance would increase to $1,582.

No Cakewalk: Be Prepared

Starting and operating your own business, even a small one, takes time, energy, perseverance, hard work, and a little money. As in life, your business may have ups and downs, recipe flops, and customers who may be challenging to work with or bounce a check. However, by following the advice and guidance offered throughout this book, you'll hopefully sidestep most of the trapdoors and find enough of the secret passageways to find your way along on your journey so that it's fun, satisfying, meaningful, and financially rewarding.

"The [cottage food] law allows entrepreneurs to start a business without going into great debt. It allowed them to try their hand, so to speak—and then if their business did well, they could know they had an idea that could be successful, and some profits to start their own company."

—Jeannie Nichols, Michigan State University Extension

Once you get going, you may find that some aspects of operating the business are less enjoyable. Making sales calls to solicit possible corporate events, invoicing a company for a delivery of cookies, preparing and signing a contract for an expensive decorated wedding cake, posting updates on Facebook, or following up an email campaign with potential customers may diminish some of the enjoyment of operating your food enterprise. Don't let it.

To cope, stick to your strengths. Focus on what you love about your business and explore ways to operate it that are true to your priorities and values. Just because "everyone" is on Instagram doesn't mean you have to be. Find what works for you. If you're fortunate to find people eager to help you with your enterprise, go with your instincts and invite them to do so; just be mindful of the legal requirements if you decide to take on bona fide employees.

One thing is for sure: expect the unexpected. Don't be shocked the day before your first big order that your reliable car suddenly has a flat tire—or your oven goes on the blink after an early morning thunderstorm. Even if disruptive events never happen, having a plan in place and anticipating setbacks or issues, like power outages, will allow you to weather most storms that come your way.

Consider having some contingency plans, like a backup option for a car—or a taxi number on file. While an extended service contract for a home oven may seem excessive, if you're a slightly

Laughter is a great way to manage any stress that may come from running your own business.

CREDIT: JOHN D. IVANKO PHOTOGRAPHY

risk-adverse home bakery owner, take one out for this heavily used appliance anyway. You may live to regret it if you don't.

In the end, you define the success of your business. No one else does. And don't lose sight of why you became a cottage food entrepreneur in the first place.

Business Expansion

SECTION 5

19

Scaling Up

PERHAPS YOU'RE HITTING your state's cottage food sales cap. Or discovered that your product is not just great, it's awesome. Maybe you're getting hounded by specialty food stores that can't wait to stock your mandel bread, as soon as you can sell wholesale. On a personal level, perhaps you want to scale up your operations because you're having so much fun and like the thrill and excitement of running your own enterprise. Maybe you increasingly find making scones more enjoyable than your current job that confines you to a cubicle; you desire a full-time food venture based in a commercial kitchen. Then this chapter is for you.

Part of the attraction to and purpose of cottage food laws is to give entrepreneurs a chance to test the market before sinking thousands, or hundreds of thousands, of dollars into an idea. It reduces the risk and jumpstarts innovation and small business. As we write in *ECOpreneuring* and throughout this book, we believe anyone can be a small business owner and make a living by following their passions and dreams rather than earning a living clocking in at a job. Life's too short not to do what you love and create a life worth living.

Whether you want to take it to the next level to see if you can hit the jackpot, or at least earn a full-time livelihood with your passion and talent for cooking, we'll begin this section by pressing a pause button to encourage some contemplation. Then we'll summarize the next steps if you decide to scale up your enterprise and point you in the direction of books, websites, and other resources that might help.

In most cases, scaling up takes place along a continuum, from the cottage food entry level with its various limitations all the way up to a multi-million-dollar company that could even, one day, be gobbled up by a multinational food conglomerate like Unilever.

Please note that this Scaling Up chapter will not, however, address food freedom and microenterprise home kitchen operation (MHKO) laws

sprouting up in various states; we'll cover these exciting opportunities in chapter 23. The food freedom and MHKO laws represent a nearly complete return to a time when neighbors could, in fact, sell just about any food product, including prepared meals, to neighbors with little regulatory oversight, sometimes not even involving a home inspection.

First, a Reality Check

Scaling up your operations can be as fulfilling as running your small cottage food enterprise, except the potential payout and profits could be much higher. With this financial freedom, however, comes the regulatory super storm, depending on where you rest on the continuum of expansion. Operating under a $10,000 sales cap is considerably different from wholesaling to a regional Whole Foods Market.

The challenges of expansion are hardly insurmountable—there are thousands of food businesses out there thriving, after all. You just need to be aware that much of what this book has covered about regulations, licenses, UPC codes, and nutritional labeling for food products may no longer apply, depending on how much you're scaling up.

Before jumping in with both feet, revisit your aspirations for the business—and your life. How much time do you want to spend cooking, cleaning, canning, or delivering product? How do you feel about hiring the employees you'll probably need to expand the business? Or will you subcontract some aspects of the business that you either find yourself avoiding or feel need more attention, like bookkeeping, website development, social media, or sales?

Many hired hands make light work for your stepped-up production. Now that you've moved beyond a cottage food enterprise, perhaps required to make hundreds of loaves of your Honey Hearth Bread for a regional grocery store, you're going to need some help. Instead of kneading the bread yourself, you'll now be managing other bakers and trying to make sure they do it as well as you do. Ditto for your new sales force and delivery person. You're an owner-manager now, no longer the cook in the kitchen.

This distinction between "bread baker" and "bread baking manager" is a big and important one to consider. Did you get into doing this because you love having your hands in the dough? Do you get a real kick out of talking to your loyal customers every week at the farmers' market? If so, think

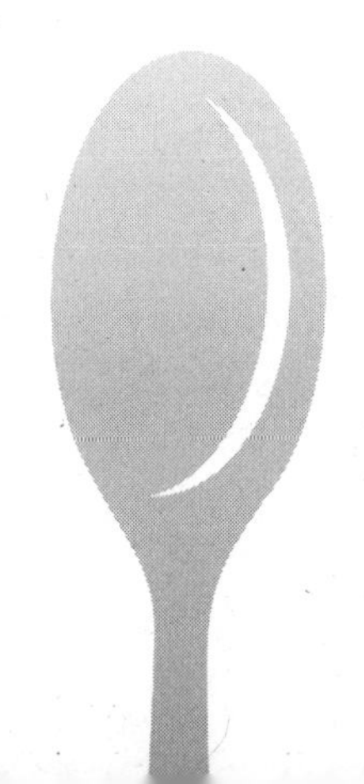

carefully about the expansion and its potential to separate you from the very process of baking or canning or other aspect of the business that you enjoy. Instead of keeping an eye on the oven, you may find your face in front of the computer screen managing orders, inventory, and payroll. As summarized in Appendix A, the Cottage Food Operator Assessment research study revealed that only about a third of aspiring CFOs are even thinking about a bricks-and-mortar storefront.

Outside of these business considerations, what does your family think? To take it the next level, are you giving notice at the company you've worked at for the last decade, and if so, do you have healthcare or retirement plans? Do you have enough emergency funds to cover the mortgage or car payments while you're expanding?

These can, and should, be heady questions, requiring some soul-searching. As you grow your enterprise, risk, failure, liability issues, employer responsibility, and complexity grow with it. You may find, too, that the expectations of your customers also change, becoming more demanding, requiring a higher level of service, even more exacting consistency. Depending on how much you expand, chances are you'll no longer be on a first-name basis with them either.

If you've never worked in the kitchen of a restaurant or catering company, you may find yourself staring at commercial equipment you have no idea how to operate. And your recipes, how do you prepare them in a 20-quart mixer, so big it sits on the floor and resembles an inverted R2D2?

Before proceeding, it's time to yank out that back-of-a-napkin business plan, punch a pot of coffee, and put onto paper a polished 50-page-plus business plan with sales projections, a more detailed marketing plan, and so forth. Now that you're investing some serious cash, time, and energy, make sure that you're pulling a salary (the government requires it!) and have some profits left over at the end of the day.

Casting off the Shackles of the Cottage Food Law

In a commercial kitchen, there's nothing you can't make. How about cakes with whipped cream frosting? Yep! Blueberry sour cream pies? Ditto. Both will require refrigeration and a host of other factors when you sell them to the public, but the point is, you can. You can even make chicken pot pies for the frozen counter or fresh-daily Tex-Mex burrito wraps for resale at the local convenience store.

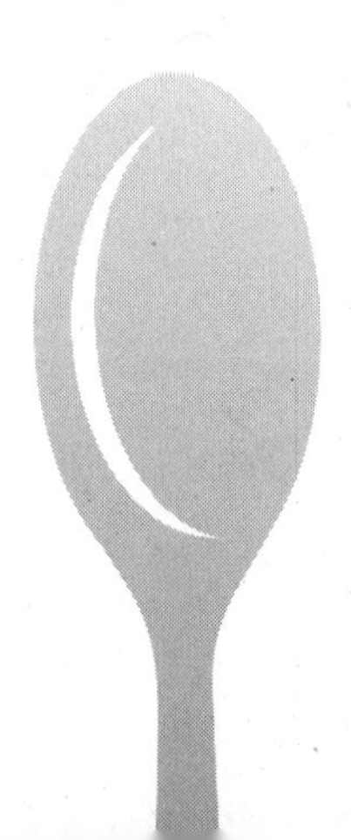

You can make anything you want in that commercial kitchen, depending on what it is authorized to make and the classification of your permit. And with the license comes the litany of regulations and product safety precautions you must implement before anyone even gets to take one bite.

Wholesale Expansion

So, the time has arrived to scale up. To be clear, your business is going to get more complicated and costly and demand a level of commitment far beyond what you put into your small cottage food enterprise.

While you may continue to sell directly to the public, the rules change at this stage for the various other sales venues open to you, including wholesale and mail order. As mentioned earlier, your production must take place in a licensed commercial kitchen appropriate for your type of product. Some states, however, are relaxing cottage food laws that used to restrict mail order within the state and, occasionally, selling wholesale; this is why CFOs must remain connected to any modifications of the law in their state.

So, You Want to Grow Big

Many aspects and options related to scaling up your enterprise, as summarized briefly in this chapter and the next, provide tools for you to consider as you contemplate your next phase.

Homemade for Sale was explicitly written for the small-scale, home kitchen-based food entrepreneur. While much of the marketing and business management chapters are as applicable to small operations as they are to large ones, the following resources will serve guides beyond the basics covered here.

- *From Kitchen to Market: Selling your Gourmet Food Specialty* by Stephen F. Hall
  The authoritative book on getting a specialty food product to as wide a market as possible is paired with a dynamic website (specialtyfoodresource.com) that picks up where Hall's book leaves off.
- *How to Start a Home-based Bakery Business* by Detra Denay Davis
  Focusing exclusively on a bakery business, Davis's book covers, in a little more detail, issues related to scaling up your operations.
- *Starting a Part-time Food Business:* Everything You *Need to Know to Turn Your Love of Food into a Successful Business Without Necessarily Quitting Your Day Job* by Jennifer Lewis
  This is a straightforward look at what you may need to do to take your business up another notch.

State Prerequisites for Wholesale and Mail Order

Other than those states with food freedom or MHKO laws, most have two prerequisites for producing your food items for wholesale, and possibly, for mail order.

Food Processor Permit or License

A food processor permit is the state-approved documentation and training that proves and legitimizes that you can safely produce a specified item with the intent to sell to the public. In other words, it's the necessary process to prove to your state that you can legally and safely produce your goods.

Generally speaking, the more foods are processed, the more tightly they're regulated. The more steps involved in making them and the longer the list of ingredients, the more complicated the regulations are. Note the exact license title varies by state; it may be called a "retail food license," "food processor permit," "processed food business license," or something similar, meaning basically the same thing. Additionally, there may be different layers of licenses depending on exactly what you are producing and to whom you are selling. States often distinguish wholesale in a separate licensing category with specific requirements and procedures.

Both emerging food freedom and microenterprise home kitchen operation laws, covered extensively in chapter 23, have created sweeping opportunities for home-based food entrepreneurs to make certain food products, even prepared foods, for sale through various channels, including wholesale and by mail. These new laws, in diverse ways, sidestep the previously restrictive laws, in essence reversing the regulatory environment associated with food production and sales.

There may also be federal requirements and additional labeling requirements, depending on your products. But once you receive your wholesale license, the doors of opportunity open wide. You can sell your products anywhere in the United States and to anyone, including larger retail outlets and via mail order across state lines. As mentioned previously, there seems to be an exception to every rule. For example, an inspected and registered "limited food establishment" in Pennsylvania permits a home-based baker to sell and mail their food product out of state, according to Suzanne Pyle, a food safety specialist with the Pennsylvania Department of Agriculture.

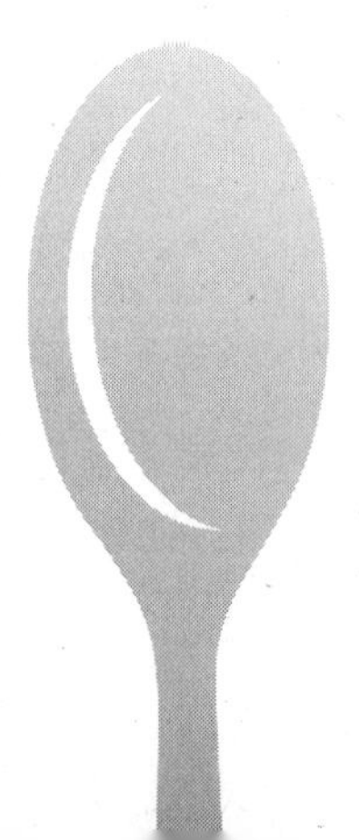

Licensed Food Production Facility

The type of food processor permit you receive will determine the type of commercial facility in which you must process your product. Commercial kitchens are not all treated the same by state regulators.

Three Options for a Licensed Food Production Facility

Thanks to the booming food industry, there are three main options for making food products legally: renting a licensed space, building a commercially approved kitchen in your home, or contracting with a co-packer. In all cases, these are licensed commercial production facilities. Some of these options provide an affordable way to scale up your product in modest ways without having to take on major debt.

Option 1: Renting a licensed food production facility

One of the more affordable ways to start selling wholesale quickly is renting an existing licensed facility. This could be an incubator kitchen, a restaurant, or a church kitchen.

Licensed incubator kitchens

Incubator kitchens, sometimes called cooperative or shared-use kitchens, are commercial kitchens that are run in a collaborative fashion. You simply rent it for a set time and use the space and equipment.

Incubator kitchens can be operated privately or, more often, by nonprofit organizations. Nonprofit incubators often provide resources and support in the expansion of your start-up, such as culinary and marketing training and shared office space. Some even have a video production lab that allow business owners to make educational or promotional materials. Many provide networking opportunities among other food entrepreneurs. When you succeed, these incubator kitchens succeed.

For example, Blue Ridge Food Ventures (blueridgefoodventures.org) in Asheville, North Carolina, offers 11,000 square feet of shared-use space to food venture start-ups ranging from value-added products to caterers and food-cart vendors. As a nonprofit initiative, it offers strong support to help fledgling businesses succeed, including everything from storage space and equipment use to label design advice.

The majority of incubator kitchens are located in urban areas, where they can serve a larger population, but rural incubator kitchens are increasing in

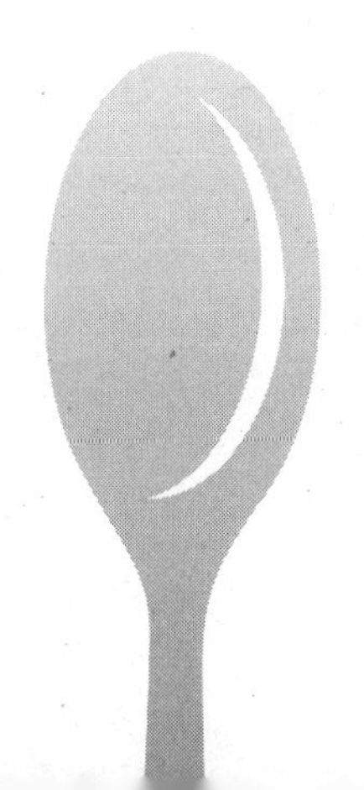

number as well. Locating a facility may be a challenge, depending on where you live. While incubator kitchens are created to serve small food enterprises, they're not free. Less expensive than building your own commercially licensed kitchen, they rent out their facility by the hour, from $10 to $60 an hour. A nonprofit facility is generally cheaper than one privately owned. They may require a minimum block of time and a lease contract; they may also require a detailed business plan, liability insurance, and ServSafe certification.

Since rural incubator kitchens rarely experience the same volume of use that urban ones do, they are often run by nonprofit organizations that draw on grant support for their operation, one reason they may be a more

Renting an Incubator, Restaurant, or Church Kitchen Checklist

Now that you're scaling up, what should you consider when selecting a commercial kitchen to rent? The following are a few essential questions or issues to consider, arranged as a checklist.

[] **Licensing:** Is the kitchen licensed properly for the food product you want to make there?

[] **Equipment:** Does the kitchen have, in proper working order, the equipment you need to make your item in the desired quantity?

[] **Storage:** Will you have access to storage space, either refrigerated or on shelves for dry goods? Is storage included in the rental fee or an additional charge? Is the storage area private and secured or shared and accessible to others who use the space?

[] **Hours of access:** When can you access the kitchen? Are there a minimum number of hours that you must commit to before being able to use the facility?

[] **Price:** Are there peak and non-peak rates for the use of the kitchen?

[] **Management:** How is the facility managed from the perspective of safety, theft prevention, and security? Are others using the facility required to complete ServSafe certification, which might ensure that health and food contamination issues are fully addressed? Generally, how clean and well maintained is the facility? What happens if the equipment you want to use is either inoperable or breaks down while you're using it?

[] **Other facility benefits:** What other features are included with the rental of the kitchen? Is telephone, fax, wireless Internet access, or business office space included or available for an additional charge?

[] **Insurance:** What type and how much insurance must you carry to cover your use of the facility?

[] **Miscellaneous fees:** Are there any hidden charges or requirements in the fine print of your lease for renting the facility?

[] **Deliveries and lock-outs:** How are food deliveries handled? Should you be receiving ingredients or supplies at the rented facility? What happens if you get locked out of the facility by accident?

affordable option. For example, Starting Block (startingblock.biz), in rural northwestern Michigan, showcases a partnership of economic development groups and nonprofits, who have collaborated to create this resource for food entrepreneurs residing in or near the small town of Hart.

Kitchen rental hours can add up, especially if you're making something like bread with a long rise time. Plus you'll need to account for your time commuting back and forth. If you're raising young children, you'll need to recognize possible daycare needs—and costs.

Storage space at an incubator kitchen may be limited or come at an additional cost. You may find yourself schlepping ingredients and packaging back and forth every time you work. While the equipment is shared, you'll need to coordinate schedules to avoid any conflicts with others using the space or equipment at the same time.

If you specialize in products for customers with food allergies, you'll need to work out the specifics to avoid possible health issues. That said, some incubators, like Prep (prepatl.com), in Atlanta, Georgia, include a commercial kitchen, a USDA-approved meat kitchen, and a gluten-free kitchen, each as separate licensed food preparation facilities.

Licensed kitchens in churches or restaurants

Unless you're operating in a remote unpopulated area, most food entrepreneurs will be within reach of restaurants or churches that might have licensed kitchen facilities available for rent. Some church kitchens, particularly larger ones that host a lot of public events with meals, go through state commercial inspection. Most of your work can easily be timed not to conflict with those events. To see if one exists near you, check out the website Commercial Kitchen for Rent, commercialkitchenforrent.com.

The same rental arrangement could be made at a local restaurant that, because it serves food to the public, must undertake extensive health inspections and adhere to all regulations related to the license they hold. Scheduling a mutually agreeable rental period may be your biggest challenge, however, depending on how many hours the restaurant is open every day.

Sample Kitchen Rental Contract

Whether you're renting an incubator, restaurant, or church kitchen, you'll need to negotiate terms and sign a contract that details your rental fee. The contract should also specify your responsibility for utility expenses and obligations related to cleanup and proper hygiene. The kitchen will likely require that your business have general and product liability coverage, ranging from $300,000 to $1,000,000, that extends specifically to the kitchen in use; they will request a "Certificate of Insurance" be issued by your insurance company explicitly naming the rented facility as an additional insured party.

A sample kitchen rental contract can be found on this book's website.

Dave "Poppy" Sanders, Poppy and Sweetpea's Cookies, Carmel, Indiana

Name: Dave "Poppy" Sanders

Business: Poppy and Sweetpea's Cookies (Carmel, IN)

Products: custom decorated cookies, undecorated cookies, pastries, and other baked desserts

Sales Venues: mail orders, custom orders delivered

Gross Revenues: $30,000/year

Starting a Commercially Licensed Bakery at Home

You might have heard Dave Sanders speak at a sold-out CookieCon Cookie Art Convention and Show in 2018 or 2020. Or sampled one of his hand-decorated sugar cookies, stroopwafel, or pecan cinnamon rolls if you live near Indianapolis, Indiana. Dave Sanders, who often goes by Poppy, has been operating Poppy and Sweetpea's Cookies since 2013. Decorating cookies since he was a 5-year-old as a part of his family's Christmas holiday tradition, Sanders decided it was only fitting that the Sweetpea half of his business name should come from his youngest daughter's nickname. Cookies are a family affair for him. Always have been.

Sanders launched his cookie business as a way to express himself artistically. Then he realized he could make money at it, too. It took off from there, first as a home kitchen-based cottage food operation under his state's cottage food law, then three years later as a full-blown licensed commercial bakery based in his home. Because he ended up moving, he actually started a commercially licensed home bakery, twice.

"Initially I thought I would limit myself to selling at farmers' markets," explains Sanders. "But I found the politics and restrictions unworkable. One time I worked for three days preparing for a farmers' market only for it to be cancelled. I lost over $1,000 in revenue." Because his baked goods were made in his home under the state's cottage food law, he could only sell them through farmers' markets or a roadside stand. So, he ended up donating his homemade products to a local Ronald McDonald House.

Dave "Poppy" Sanders mixing up frosting for a cookie order.
Credit: Poppy and Sweetpea's Cookies

His eureka moment to start a commercial bakery at home was born of his frustration with the limitations of the state's cottage food law, a feeling shared by many cottage food operators throughout the country. "When I looked at the cost of a commercial kitchen in my community, it would cost me more to rent that kitchen than what I would possibly be able to earn selling baked goods.

"So, I started to explore how I could build a commercial bakery in my home," says Sanders. "I knew that by having a commercial kitchen, I would be able to sell at roadside stands and farmers' markets as well as do pick-up orders, delivery, catering, and mail orders." While most of his business remains local, some of his cookies have been sold to customers with orders coming as far away as India and Japan for their families in the US.

"I did significant research with respect to state and county health codes as well as fire codes," admits Sanders, when considering the viability of building a commercial bakery in his home. "I explored the requirements from the building department and my homeowners' association. It turns out that my home-based commercial kitchen for baked goods would be no different than what I'd need to consider were I to open a restaurant. I had to look at the zoning laws and what would be allowed. I had to address all the concerns from the state health department and the city fire department. I even had to deal with my homeowner's association." He focused on building positive relationships with building inspectors and other governmental agencies and representatives so that his renovations, once started, would proceed smoothly and follow applicable codes or requirements.

"What are the laws regarding licensing for the contractor, for the plumber, for the electrician, what kind of permits were going to be needed?" asked Sanders when in the research phase. "What type of building inspections were going to be needed? Will the health department approve or disapprove what I've done? Currently, the inspectors come out twice a year and review my operation. It helped that I asked for their guidance in the beginning, to be aware of the things that they looked for." This helped in avoiding expensive complications or delays.

"In my state, and to meet the requirements of the health department, I had to have a three-compartment sink with wings," details Sanders. "One compartment is for washing, one for rinsing, and one for sanitizing. The three big compartments in the sink must be large enough to accommodate half of my largest item. For my 12.5-inch by 17.5-inch cookie tray, that means I must be able to put half of it into the sink. I also have to have a separate hand-washing sink and separate mop sink in the kitchen.

"Once I had completed the research, I developed the plans and estimated construction costs," says Sanders. "I contracted some of the work out, and some I did myself. Contracting the work out easily doubles or triples the cost of renovation." To save on costs, he networked with neighbors who pitched in ideas for design and space layouts. The second time around, the whole home-based commercial kitchen remodel took three weeks and cost about $5,000, including the inspection fees.

Poppy and Sweetpea's Cookies home-based commercial bakery in the basement of Sanders' home. The sinks required for a commercial kitchen are placed on the left side of the bakery, along with a work bench that also serves as his mixing station. Credit: Poppy and Sweetpea's Cookies

Poppy and Sweetpea's Cookies home-based commercial bakery in the basement of Sanders' home. The butcher block in the center is used for rolling out cookie dough. Another work bench is where the cookies are left to dry after icing. When not in production, the bench doubles as a shipping station.
Credit: Poppy and Sweetpea's Cookies

A "onesie" cookie, displayed on an easel. CREDIT: POPPY AND SWEETPEA'S COOKIES

A dump truck cookie, displayed on an easel. CREDIT: POPPY AND SWEETPEA'S COOKIES

From the very start of Poppy and Sweetpea's Cookies, Sanders has been focused on meeting his customers' needs. "I expand my offerings based on their needs," says Sanders, who can bake as many as 500 cookies in less than three hours in his efficiently designed commercial space. He's down to about three to five minutes decorating each cookie, depending on its complexity. "The majority of my sales are custom decorated cookies. Customers bring me their ideas and I try to make what they ask for.

"I have over 1,700 cookie cutters and have access to multiple suppliers," adds Sanders. "In a pinch for unique cutters, I make my own in my wood shop. Making decorated cookies is the most fun because I can use my artistic skills to create beautiful or cute options." Like many cookiers, he's perfected a variety of decorating techniques including airbrushing, wet-on-wet, and stenciling. He often displays his cookies on a crafty wood-framed easel—like painters would work on their canvases—except his canvases are often delicious sugar cookies in any number of shapes and sizes. They're edible art.

Despite having few sales limitations as a commercially licensed operation, Sanders avoids selling wholesale. "I have turned down opportunities to sell wholesale because I would be undercutting my own efforts by charging a wholesale price for my retail work efforts. It takes the same effort to decorate the cookie, regardless of whether it is retail or wholesale. Having more sales through wholesaling just undercuts my own efforts. I am better off to increase my marketing efforts if I want to make more sales."

While Sanders intentionally only operates his business as a part-time, roughly 25-hours-a-week, endeavor, his business revenues have consistently grown every year. "One of the keys to running a successful business is to control expenses," he advises. "I pay cash for equipment, ingredients, packing, and seminars. For example, I use a household convection oven. Having anything larger would be a waste. It takes nine minutes to bake two trays of cookies and about the same amount of time to roll out the same number and prepare them for baking. I get into a rhythm, so as I prepare two sheets, two other sheets are already in the oven. Having more capacity with larger equipment would do nothing for my business."

But Sanders keeps everything in balance and is open to evolving as his interests and passions change. "I am taking a break from large-scale production and focusing more on smaller, more detailed work," confides Sanders, even though he knows he could double or triple his revenues by working full-time in the bakery. "I want to keep in touch with the artistic side of my business. I have been offering workshops in my bakery, with private groups of five to 15 people setting up time with me to learn more about decorating. We cover the fundamentals of making royal icing, developing basic decorating skills, and then decorate a variety of cookies to practice."

He's also penned a workbook, *Building a Commercial Kitchen in Your Home*, for others interested in transforming part of their home like he did. "It has been very worthwhile for me to turn part of my home into a commercially licensed bakery. So worthwhile that I did it twice," laughs Sanders. "I earned a solid return on my investment. Plus, my business continues to grow as I become more experienced and known in my community."

"It's important for anyone considering a similar opportunity to decide for themselves what they want to get out of it personally and professionally," suggests Sanders. "For years I focused on production and less on my art. I found customers who liked beautiful cookies, but within price limitations. In the end, the sales from my business not only covered the investment in the home bakery but also paid for the renovations of my '57 Chevy and the home I moved into two and a half years ago."

A spectacular diversity of sweater cookies, using the zig-zag technique with royal icing.
CREDIT: POPPY AND SWEETPEA'S COOKIES

Poppy Sanders' Top Ten Steps to Building a Home Bakery

1. Do your homework
2. Have family support
3. Know the laws and rules for your area
4. Plan, plan, and plan
5. Talk with the inspectors
6. Find the right contractors
7. Develop a construction sequence
8. Research the right equipment before building
9. Follow the plan and adjust when necessary
10. Engage the inspectors along the way

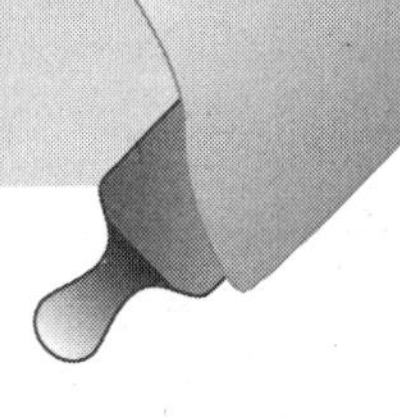

HeathGlen owner Dorothy Stainbrook in her commercially licensed home kitchen. CREDIT: COURTESY OF HEATHGLEN'S FARM & KITCHEN

Option 2: Building a commercial kitchen on your home property

If you thrive by operating a home-based business from your kitchen, perhaps while the young kids sleep in the other room, then building a state-approved commercial facility on your home property may be viable, providing you have both the space and funds. This facility could be in your house or possibly another structure located on your property.

While comparable, conceptually, to operating a cottage food enterprise, in that you're selling products made in your home, the similarities end there. For all practical purposes, this means you're turning your kitchen or separate facility on your property into a bona fide commercial kitchen that adheres to the required health code requirements for your food items.

Without a doubt, this is the most expensive option, costing $20,000 to over $80,000, depending on your plans and goals. What you'll need to renovate will depend on your state's regulations and what you plan on making.

The general requirements for building a commercial-grade kitchen include a hand-washing sink separate from the food preparation area, along with a three-compartment sink or approved dishwasher for washing equipment and utensils daily. Additionally, floors and walls must be smooth, nonabsorbent, and easily cleaned; you'll need to check on the specifics for your state. There may be aesthetic considerations, too, since you might have to replace that beautiful granite countertop with a stainless steel one. Shelving must adhere to strict floor elevation requirements.

When these commercial codes reference "approved" equipment, you want items that have "NSF" printed on them, indicating National Sanitation Foundation certification. This means the manufacturer adhered to strict commercial-food code guidelines. Most mainstream home appliances, such as the home kitchen refrigerator, neither bears the NSF initials nor adheres to the required standards.

Commercial kitchens in your state are not one-size-fits-all in terms of equipment or specifics; they depend on what items you'll be producing and in what quantity. Generally, the simpler and less processed the item, the less costly and complicated a commercial kitchen setup will be.

Want to simply grow your existing cottage food business? Because these operations focus on low-risk, low-hazardous food, creating a commercial kitchen to make your jam or bake your cookies will not be complicated. While not a cheap endeavor, a kitchen for these products will not require the same level of equipment or infrastructure as one for producing fried

meat pies or prepared meals. Many states provide a specific commercial kitchen classification, called "bakery," that outlines this simpler kitchen licensing and required setup.

When dealing with your state agency, if the inspector indicates that you need a costly piece of equipment that doesn't apply to what you are producing—say, an excessive stovetop venting system when all you are doing is making jam—speak up. Nicely, of course. Ask for an "exemption" to a specific requirement and give specific estimated usage data to validate your case. Or buy yourself some time and enquire if this issue could be revisited in a year to determine if it's really necessary based on your actual operational history.

Option 3: Working with a contract packer, or co-packer

A contract packer, or co-packer, is a company that processes food products, either using their surplus capacity or specializing in packing other businesses' food items. You turn over your recipe, perhaps some ingredients if you're growing them yourself, and any other marketing elements, and the co-packer takes it from there. What you get in return is a ready-to-sell product.

Depending on the co-packers, they might provide the following services:

- Production of the item
- Guidance on product formulation and development, including reformulating home recipes to large-scale production processes
- Packaging of the product
- Guidance on labeling, especially related to regulatory requirements
- Advice related to marketing and distribution

From a time and labor perspective, if you have customers lining up to place orders or a confirmed wholesale outlet, this service allows you to scale up without investing in or renting a commercial kitchen. You take your recipe and ingredient list to a co-packer that specializes in your food product and they make it for you. Due to the volume produced, this may afford greater consistency of your product, quality, and economies of scale realized through purchasing power, among other benefits. Additionally, co-packers can assist with the requirements that arise as you move from being a small cottage food enterprise to a wholesaler, including UPC codes, nutritional labeling, and any lab analysis that may be required, covered briefly in the next chapter.

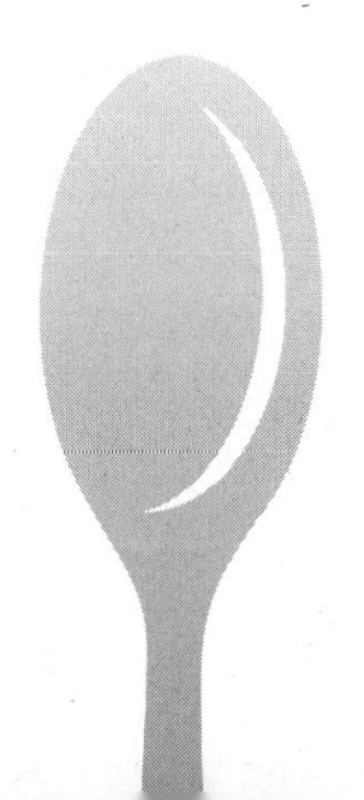

Going with a co-packer comes with a higher per unit cost. You should evaluate this increase in terms of time, labor, and the financial resources required to produce your items another way. If this streamlined and complete process of production seems too good to be true, don't forget the price and minimum order requirement.

Sandhill Family Farms' Organic Pureed Tomato made with the farm's organic tomatoes but processed by a local co-packer. CREDIT: COURTESY OF SANDHILL FAMILY FARMS

For example, Sandhill Family Farms in Brodhead, Wisconsin, used a local co-packer that specialized in items that are pumped, such as sauces, to turn their extra tomatoes into canned organic puree. While the final product they received is labeled and ready for wholesale, Matt and Peg Sheaffer, who ran the farm, chose to use most of the jars to add a little surprise to member share boxes of their CSA (community supported agriculture) in the early spring, when the boxes can sometimes run a bit lean as the harvest hasn't fully kicked in yet. The key with co-packers is that they typically require a large minimum produce volume with which to work. For the Sheaffers, their co-packer required a minimum of 5,000 pounds of tomatoes.

Loss of control over much of the process deters some food entrepreneurs from going in this direction. While appealing in its efficiency, the quality and flavor may not perfectly match what you feel you could do yourself. Your recipe will no longer be handmade, in your kitchen. Co-packers have very efficient means to produce items at significant economies of scale through factory-oriented processes. Therefore, you'll need to verify that your label goes on your product made with your recipe—and not just slapped on jars of "strawberry-rhubarb jam" made by the co-packer.

In the next chapter, we'll explore in more detail some of the marketing possibilities, changes in your operations, and sources of funding to make your culinary hit a reality.

20

Multiple Markets and Money Matters

As you ramp up your production along the continuum of scaling up your operations—perhaps moving from your home kitchen to a rented kitchen or renovated commercial space on your property—be particularly attentive to every aspect of your business. The scope of your operations, importance of marketing—especially packaging and pricing—and impact of competition will all be magnified.

At this point, profit is no longer a given, and the potential for financial failure can be devastating if you don't have a carefully devised and thorough plan in place. Once you head down the path of renting or building your own commercial kitchen or contracting production out to a co-packer, you may find that being the baker, canner, or granola bar-maker takes a back seat to running the business itself. This may be a great thing or take you away from what you love most: having your fingers in real dough.

There's also the opportunity to hit the specialty food Powerball with your product or create a viable and exciting full-time enterprise that makes a career in a cubicle obsolete. There's the possibility to pull in a six-figure salary or sell off your enterprise and retire a millionaire. You may be putting your cookies up against Famous Amos or Mrs. Fields. Markets are everywhere, and funds to fuel your expansion may be just a click away, thanks to new crowd-sourcing financing options available on the Internet.

This chapter delves into a few of the many market opportunities open to you. It explores some realities regarding how your operations must change due to your expansion plans and new regulatory environment. It also provides some financial avenues you might want to pursue, outside a commercial loan from a bank. At this stage, there's no such thing as a one-size-fits-all strategy.

As mentioned previously, we've written this book for entry-level home-based food entrepreneurs. We'll leave it to other books and resources for a more exhaustive examination of issues related to your expansion into a full-blown full-time food enterprise.

Markets, Markets Everywhere

In a licensed food production facility and with a food processor permit, you can sell wholesale, potentially to the world. As discussed earlier, some cottage food laws also permit sales via indirect or wholesale channels. Your markets could be specialty stores; institutions like schools, restaurants, hospitals, or supermarkets; or by mail order only. Your choice may be limited only by your financial means, access to capital, energy level, or perseverance.

In many cases, when CFOs grow big, they're selling products wholesale in the specialty food industry, defined by the Specialty Food Association as:

> "foods and beverages that exemplify quality, innovation and style in their category. Their specialty nature derives from some or all of the following characteristics: their originality, authenticity, ethnic or cultural origin, specific processing, ingredients, limited supply, distinctive use, extraordinary packaging or specific channel of distribution or sale. By virtue of their differentiation in their categories, such products maintain a high perceived value and often command a premium price."

Grocery Retailers

Your packaged products may line the shelves of grocery stores, gourmet food shops, and specialty food retailers, large and small. Regional specialty food stores, food cooperatives, and other retailers might focus on health foods, seasonal or year-round gifts, or items that are made locally or regionally.

Included among the list of retailers might be the following:

- Supermarkets, like Safeway, Kroger, and BI-LO
- Specialty natural foods grocers, like Whole Foods Market and The Fresh Market
- Big-box stores, like Costco and Sam's Club

To reach these retailers, one of the more effective ways to market your products will likely be through exhibiting at a trade show where you can take orders from retailers or distributors in the markets you wish to serve.

Direct-to-Customer Sales

When you scale up to a point where boxes of product become cases or pallets, you'll need a sales force to accomplish what you once did yourself. No one can be in more than one place at a time, so plan on hiring staff to work your booths or fulfill orders as they come in via telephone, text, or the Internet. When selling wholesale, many food entrepreneurs contract with brokers who take a commission on every order they secure on your behalf.

Mail Order

By producing in a licensed commercial kitchen facility, suddenly you can ship your product to customers anywhere they can receive a package within the US. Packaging your product for safe transport, plus the added cost and labor associated with such, will be important variables to consider when determining a viable and profitable business model. As mentioned previously, however, interstate sales may become more accessible with expanded cottage food and food freedom laws.

Mail-order specialty food catalogs are another way to reach out to potential first-time customers. Getting one or more of your products listed in these catalogs may be a relatively affordable way to build relationships with new customers.

Institutions Serving Patrons

Institutional sales may include supplying schools, restaurants, hotels, and even hospitals. Sales to these outlets are for consumption by the patrons they serve. For example, your individually packaged, specialty, gluten-free graham crackers could be the perfect item for an institution unwilling or unable to make them in-house.

From Handmade to Mechanized

If you found it challenging to put your peal-and-stick labels on 50 packages of biscuits, tidy and straight, try it with 1,000—or 10,000. Cutting attractive cloth tops and adding a nice ribbon for a box of 12 jelly jars becomes overwhelming when an order comes in for a case of 240 jars. When you scale up, you'll be forced to re-evaluate the systems and procedures you put into place for your once-small cottage food enterprise.

Depending on your degree of expansion, you might find that new equipment in the kitchen or office becomes a necessary part of delivering a consistent, professional-looking product. The $300 to $700 you end up

"One of the greatest strengths small food businesses have is the ability to think and quickly act outside of standard business models to meet customer needs in new and unique ways. This might include providing healthy snacks to corporations for their employees, creating subscriber-based food boxes based on a CSA-business model either alone or with other artisan food entrepreneurs … adding new flavor profiles to your product line, or hundreds of other ideas. Don't be afraid to mix business models like you mix ingredients, searching for the right combination that will catch consumers' interest."

— 2014 Plate of the Union Report, Small Food Business (smallfoodbiz.com)

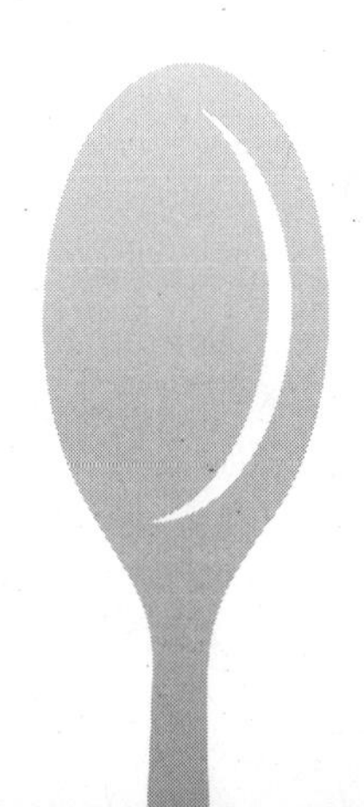

paying for various label machines, depending on your type of packaging, will improve the presentation of your product and save on labor costs. For example, a label machine designed for various styles of containers from Zap Labeler (zaplabeler.com) can pay for itself within the year, plus improve the consistency of the application of the label; avoid crooked or misplaced labels when serving any retail markets. Some machines can take self-adhesive roll labels and attach them to as many as 1,000 containers in one hour.

Labeling for the Big Leagues

Attaching a cute homemade label printed on your color laser-jet printer to your packet of dried seasonings mix may have worked just fine for most cottage food laws. But when you're selling wholesale, meticulously following the US Food and Drug Administration (FDA) label requirements is a must; download it from the FDA at fda.gov. The nutritional label must conform to Title 21 of the Code of Federal Regulations and include a nutritional fact analysis. Only food companies with "annual gross sales made or business done in sales to consumers that is not more than $500,000 or have annual gross sales made or business done in sales of food to consumers of not more than $50,000 are exempt," according to the FDA. As discussed earlier and related to specialty food production, the only other exemption, per the US FDA, is for products sold at a low volume. The exemption applies:

> "If the person claiming the exemption employs fewer than an average of 100 full-time equivalent employees and fewer than 100,000 units of that product are sold in the United States in a 12-month period. To qualify for this exemption the person must file a notice annually with FDA.... If a person is not an importer, and has fewer than 10 full-time equivalent employees, that person does not have to file a notice for any food product with annual sales of fewer than 10,000 total units.... If any nutrient content claim (e.g., "sugar free"), health claim, or other nutrition information is provided on the label, or in labeling or advertising, the small business exemption is not applicable for a product."

Securing the required labels need not cost a fortune, however. ReciPal (recipal.com) offers an affordable online label creator software option, providing FDA-compliant nutritional fact labels and ingredient lists. The

company also offers recipe costing by batch and package. Best of all, it was designed by food entrepreneurs for food entrepreneurs.

Those CFOs able and eager to sell via wholesale accounts will need a scannable UPC Code. You may also have to secure a SKU or stock keeping unit, an eight-digit alpha-numeric code unique to your product that's different than an UPC Code, a string of 12 numbers that's standardized for business use. A company could have different SKUs but the same UPC code for a particular product. Did we mention things get more complex at this stage?

In some cases, if you opt to use a co-packer, the work you did packaging, labeling, and ingredient sourcing may require revisions; you may need to completely redo your product based on licensing regulations or standards dictated to you by the industry, distribution channels, or markets you serve.

Pricing and Distribution Revisited: A Whole New Formula

Like many other facets of your business, when you scale up and sell wholesale, you change the dynamic of your profit margins since other businesses need to make money off selling your product. You may need to revise your pricing structures to incentivize initial orders.

While your product might retail for $8 (also referred to as the "suggested retail price"), you'll only receive a portion of that to allow the retailer and distributor to each make some money along the way. At this point, your profits are based largely on the volume you can move through your distribution and retail channels. You're forfeiting some profit per item when you sell through indirect channels.

When it comes to distribution, most CFOs evaluate their market in terms of a region, if not a city or neighborhood. When scaling up, they'll determine if they'll select a third-party distributor; ship via FedEx, UPS, or the US postal service; or deliver their products themselves. Third-party distributors often require a 15 to 30 percent markup over wholesale cost and may do their own ordering and invoicing with retailers they supply with your products.

In some cases, you may find retailers will only work through distributors. That means, to get your product to market, you have to entice distributors to stock and sell your items. As a result, many companies with specialty food products head to trade shows to prospect for companies willing to carry their items.

Keep in mind, just because you can sell your ginger snaps nationally to 500 specialty food stores doesn't mean you actually will or that the process

will be a fun ride. Beyond the scope of this book, you'll need to sort out shelf-life issues, sell-by dates, and have a product recall plan in place.

Margins, Markup, Warehousing Costs, and Freight

For food entrepreneurs selling wholesale, the distribution channels open up in ways that allow hundreds of thousands of potential customers to buy your products. Getting your items to market, however, may require the services of distributors, co-packers, food brokers, or a sales force. Commissions and fees vary based on your product, season, market, and a host of other variables.

Your business goal should always be to earn some profit after deducting expenses, both variable and fixed. In terms of your product cost, you'll also need to account for any freight expenses and commissions charged along the distribution channel, plus allow yourself a "fair" profit on each product sold at the end of the day. Of course, you must account for other expenses, including shrinkage from shoplifting or errors in shipping, any sales discounts you may offer, and changes in ingredient costs.

Your cost of goods sold, or COGS, refers to the variable and fixed costs that go into making your product. The details are beyond the scope of this book, but suffice it to say that if you're taking orders for 10,000 units, you'll need to have a very good handle on your COGS for each item you sell and your margins. Whatever amount you list as the suggested retail price, you allow for a 50 to 65 percent margin above your wholesale price so the different brokers, distributors, and retailers get their cut when they sell your product.

Some companies may be storing your products in warehouses, which will have an associated charge. To get your product to a distributor's warehouse, the freight cost may be included in the price, collected separately at the time of delivery or added to your original invoice. The "ex-warehouse cost" combines the cost of your product with the storage and handling costs.

While the market and your customers ultimately determine the retail price you're able to charge for your product, when determining this, you should analyze both your profit margin and markup to account for whatever distribution channel or channels you decide to pursue, each summarized below.

- Gross margin, or margin: An expression for a percentage of a selling price. It's the difference between total sales of an item and the costs associated with those sales.
  Example: One jar of jam sells for $6, but costs $2 to make; the gross margin is $4. Expressed as a percentage, the margin would be 67 percent. The math: ((6 – 2) / 6) x 100 = 67 percent.
- Markup: An expression for a percentage of the cost for a product. It's the selling price of the item minus the cost, then divided by the cost associated with those sales.
  Example: Using the same numbers, one jar of jam sells for $6, but costs $2 to make; the markup is $4. Expressed as a percentage, the markup would be 200 percent. The math: ((6 – 2) / 2) x 100 = 200 percent.

Again, beyond the scope of this book, careful analysis of this entire distribution chain and pricing in relation to your competition is essential to increasing your likelihood of financial success — profitability!

Magnifying Your Marketing

Much of what we've covered in this book related to marketing serves you well when scaling up your enterprise. However, if your sales forecast is $100,000, or 40,000 units, it's a good bet that you'll need to radically step up your marketing budget. At this phase, word-of-mouth remains essential, but boosting awareness with a PR campaign, setting up sampling demos at specialty food retailers, or exploring more traditional advertising outlets may be necessary to introduce potential customers to your products. This can cost big bucks. Depending on your product, prospecting for national distributors mean you'll be packing your bags and heading to a specialty food trade show.

Raising Some Dough

Any way you slice it, expanding your business will take more money than you needed to launch your business out of your home kitchen. There are numerous opportunities, however, to expand your production and marketing without going into major debt. If you decided to expand modestly, the profits from your cottage food enterprise may have stayed in your business checking account as retained earnings, providing some or all of the funds needed for reinvesting in your growth. Depending on your goals and ambitions, you may, or may not, need to refinance your home to secure funds to take your business up to the next notch along that continuum of scaling up.

If your business or personal sources for money aren't enough, you may consider a growing number of financial resources that have nothing to do with a commercial bank. Called crowd-funding, these mostly Internet-based sources of financing can provide small low-interest loans for thousands of dollars, depending on your needs and if you have the knack to create compelling, engaging fundraising campaigns and a customer base eager to support your dream with their open pocketbooks. The following summarizes a few of your financing options.

- **Kiva: kiva.org**
  More personal and accessible than a bank loan, Kiva taps the wealth of private individuals who fund small business with low-interest loans. You apply for a loan and share your story with prospective lenders who, through an online portal, decide if your venture is worth funding.

- **Kickstarter: kickstarter.com**
  The world's largest Internet-based, privately owned crowd-funding platform, Kickstarter supports a wide range of creative projects, including food products. Backers pledge various amounts of money in exchange for various incentives, called "backer rewards," associated with different levels of funding support. One bakery start-up launched a $10,000 campaign which, if funded, would pay for ingredients and manufacturing costs for their first major production run of three product items, initial packaging costs, FDA-approved database nutrition fact analysis, and SKUs for each flavor.
- **Indiegogo: indiegogo.com**
  Another Internet-based crowd-funding website that includes a food category. "Backers" receive "perks" with their financial contribution.
- **Kabbage: kabbage.com**
  Kabbage provides working capital online to currently operating businesses, based on the extension of a business line of credit.
- **Small Business Administration's MicroLoan Program: sba.gov**
  Government-backed loans to small businesses are made available through certain nonprofit, community-based organizations.

Keep Tabs

When scaling up, the volume and complexity of the business will expand exponentially—especially if you're juggling employees, various sub-contractors, relationships with multiple distributors and retailers, and the stepped-up governmental requirements that come with a business your size.

For bookkeeping, a software program like Intuit's QuickBooks will become indispensable. If you're a baker consider CakeCost (cakecost.net), a software program customized for a specialty baked goods business.

At this point, hiring a certified public accountant is a must. Retaining an attorney for legal matters is a wise decision, too. With your graduation from cottage food enterprise to food corporation, you've earned the right to hire professionals to steer you clear of possible financial or legal problems.

Additionally, that network of mentors who helped your business get off the ground will likely be reinforced by a board of directors and other managerial staff who you've invited aboard to help guide the growth of your business. Many hands helping to keep tabs will afford you the time you need to see your dream to fruition.

Future of Cottage Foods: Freedom!

SECTION 6

21

Importance of Cottage Food Advocacy

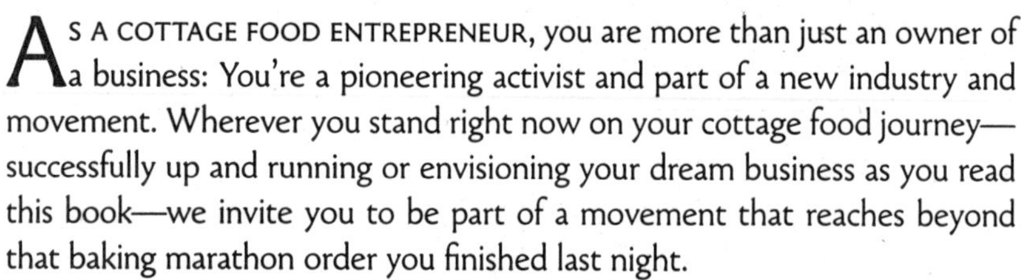

As a cottage food entrepreneur, you are more than just an owner of a business: You're a pioneering activist and part of a new industry and movement. Wherever you stand right now on your cottage food journey—successfully up and running or envisioning your dream business as you read this book—we invite you to be part of a movement that reaches beyond that baking marathon order you finished last night.

"I wish more people would realize the power they have when they work together to change the things they care about."

— Molly Pickering, Deputy Director of the Illinois Stewardship Alliance

Your passion for cottage food can impact so many others, people just like yourself who only a short time ago might never have envisioned in their wildest dreams being a food business owner headquartered right in their home kitchen. By sharing your story, supporting others in your community, our numbers, impact, and opportunities will grow. Just as the Founding Fathers who sparked the revolution that launched this country or suffragettes like Susan B. Anthony who fought for women's right to vote, together we share a responsibility to lead and advocate for improved laws and expanded opportunities out of our home kitchen.

A shout-out of gratitude to those early-day cottage food pioneers who introduced cottage food to their state legislature 10 or 20 years ago, processes that often took years and hundreds of cookies brought to countless meetings before a bill became law. Thanks to your efforts, we stand in a much stronger spot with tens of thousands of new businesses operating and percolating across all 50 states.

The initial hard work is done. The foundation built. We just need to continue to shepherd and protect this entrepreneurial vibrancy while pushing the envelope for what we, the bakers, canners, or home chefs, want. The power we have is in our numbers. along with our economic impact. The more organized we are, the more effective our actions will be.

In this last section, we'll share stories and strategies for how you can advocate for cottage food expansion. We will share three elements in your

advocacy tool kit that may improve your chances of success. We'll also share practical steps on organizing a state association in chapter 22.

Be Your Own Advocate

Maybe your state law prevents you from selling a product for which you know you have a market. Or perhaps doing a pop-up market on your driveway or front porch sounds ideal, but not permitted. Given the pandemic, more people than ever before have embraced e-commerce and mail order, but perhaps your state law hasn't caught up with the times. It's time to hang up that apron (temporarily) and advocate for a change to your law. Several of the CFOs featured in this book are among those who have.

For example, suppose the agency employee in charge of administering the cottage food law tells you, "No, roasted coffee is not allowed," but you know the product is perfectly non-hazardous and safe. What are your next steps and options? First off, take an informational gathering approach versus argumentative. Ask them the reasons why they believe that and what is their rationale, which ultimately falls back to interpretation of the existing law. Then connect with allies. We'll discuss this more in the next section. Your question—can you sell roasted coffee—may not require a full law change but rather simply clarity within the agency that can potentially resolve the matter.

Whatever your goals regarding changing the laws, make sure to have the following three elements in your advocacy toolkit before diving into the democracy pool.

"Strong state laws provide an important foundation for cottage food businesses to contribute to the local food economy. By engaging with policymakers at the state level, home-based food businesses can ensure cottage food laws are clear, risk-based, and supportive of the flourishing cottage food sector."

— Sophia Kruszewski, Center for Agriculture & Food Systems, Clinic Director, Vermont Law School

Partnerships

Consider collaboration the yeast that rises to the occasion and brings cottage food legislative change to life. We home cooks harbor business dreams and kitchen expertise, but we lack the deep pockets and big checkbooks others might have to influence politicians. Therefore, we need numbers. Numbers of people, people who vote. We need to demonstrate to our elected representatives the strong and widespread interest in cottage food law and the positive entrepreneurial impact it will have on our state's economy.

Contact the following potential partners.

State Representatives

Your first call should be to your own elected representatives, in most states, one from the state senate and one from the state house of representatives

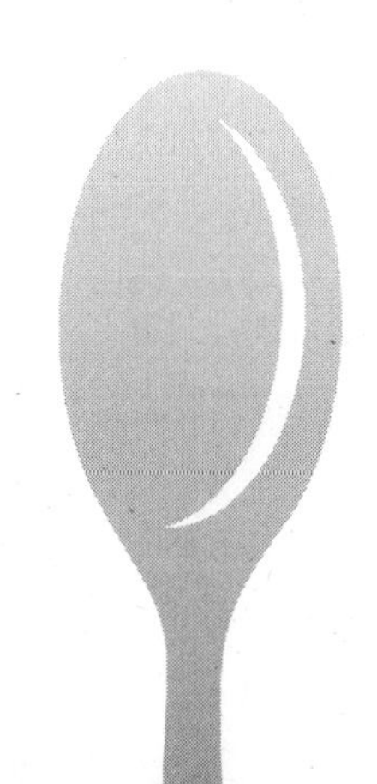

or assembly, just like on the federal level. Whether or not you voted for them is irrelevant. These elected officials should be your most loyal champions since you're their constituent.

When you contact your representative's office, you will most likely deal with the representative's aides and not her or him directly. Don't feel slighted. The legislator's staff forms the influential group that gets things done in that office. Staffers can also give you a snapshot of any pending cottage food legislation and other history, as well as make calls directly to an agency on your behalf, which can often be quite effective in facilitating and getting answers. They can also call your regulatory agency and act on your behalf if you're not getting the response you need.

If what you're advocating for does require a change in the law—perhaps legislation currently includes only baked goods but not all non-hazardous products like coffee—your representative's office can give you details on their legislative schedule and how a potential new proposed bill fits in. Most state governments operate under a fairly tight and specific schedule dictating when they meet for a vote and approximately how long it takes to shepherd a bill through the vetting process beforehand.

This vetting process often includes committee meetings where the bill is discussed and the public is invited to provide testimony. Of particular importance, these meetings provide an opportunity to rally cottage food advocates like yourself and provide oral and written testimony to influence the committee to support the bill. If the committee does vote in favor of it, the bill then moves to a full vote in the house that introduces the bill and then typically a vote in the other chamber and ultimately signed and approved by the governor.

Don't be intimidated by this process or feel unempowered. Democracy rises like that bread you have proofing when we all take action. Consider this chapter your constituent coaching session, blueprint, and cheering section rallying you on. As a citizen of your state and now entrepreneur, you have a voice in the cottage food law process.

Sure, dealing with bureaucratic agencies and legislation can feel daunting or intimidating. But remind yourself that these people represent you.

Like-minded organizations

Is there an existing statewide group that could adopt and champion your cause? This will help tremendously to provide organizational strength as well as legitimacy to your proposed legislation. The more you can prove

to representatives that the cottage food movement is a big deal with strong impact potential to your state's economy, the better your odds of success. Affiliating with a kindred-spirited nonprofit group will amplify your messaging.

A sustainable agriculture advocacy group might help since cottage food fits its mission of supporting family farms. Such an organization may also bring experience in the lobbying front and have a policy or government relation's person on staff to assist and advise. The Illinois Stewardship Alliance helped shepherd cottage food legislation in that state, and we've partnered with the Wisconsin Farmers Union in our efforts to expand cottage food law in our state.

Cottage food entrepreneurs like yourself

The pulse of your plan for cottage food law change comes from others just like you: fledgling food entrepreneurs who need this legislation to bring their kitchen business dreams to life. Do a thorough check to see if anyone is already organizing in your state and join forces. Start a Facebook page or webpage if one doesn't exist already to connect with others and keep an email contact list to get information out in a timely manner, especially when the bill is up for a vote and you need volumes of calls urging support to representatives across the state. If there isn't a cottage food association or group in your state, consider launching one. See chapter 22 for tips on getting started.

Planning

When you gather these partners, particularly your state representatives and kindred organizations savvy in the legislative process, you get an immediate sense of the legislative schedule and how your proposed bill fits in. Cue the Schoolhouse Rock song for a review of how your bill will become a law.

That said, depending on how your state's department of agriculture or health operates and sets regulations, you may not need a new or amended law but can work directly with the ag department on revised rules. This can potentially be an easier and faster route, so it's important to do your homework and plan first.

Patience

If you're aiming to get a new or amended law passed, realize your state legislature might only meet once or twice a year to vote on bills. If your bill doesn't make it through committee in time, it may have to wait a year, only to start the process all over again. The democratic system can really drag. Occasionally, however, bills are fast-tracked, usually (in our experience) because the process has been greased by political maneuvering, outside campaign donations, or other monetary influences.

The cottage food movement by its very nature does not have big lobbying bucks or deep pockets behind it, so it may creep along like a glacier. We can foster patience and determination while simultaneously advocating and championing the grassroots, people-driven story. Get your inspiring tales of food businesses that such legislation would jumpstart out to the media. Write an op-ed for your local or state newspaper.

Author Lisa Kivirist's Love Wisconsin cookies, baked fresh to share with legislators, fellow aspiring Wisconsin bakers, and the media.
CREDIT: JOHN D. IVANKO PHOTOGRAPHY

Even if you're working directly with your state's department in charge of the cottage food regulations, things may still take time. Let's just say government bureaucracy has never been known for fast efficiency! Identify some allies within the department who could be in a power position to make what you want happen. Also, these employees, who are probably already overworked and underpaid, have a long list of existing responsibilities, and your question just got added to the mix. Anything you can do to help, such as drafting up the proposed new rule, may work well as it would make their job easier and allow you to directly influence the process.

Wisconsin: Lessons in Lawsuits, Collaboration, and Patience

Let us share our own advocacy story here in Wisconsin, which wins the blue-ribbon prize as the weirdest in the country. We were left with no other course of action than to sue for the right to sell homemade non-hazardous products. Cookies! May our crazy saga encourage you that there is no cottage food barrier we can't together plow through with friends and legal allies.

Our cottage food story starts on our organic farm and bed and breakfast nestled in the rolling green hills of southern Wisconsin, which we opened in 1997. In most states including ours, you can start a bed and breakfast pretty easily with minimal regulations or expense. Many states want to help support small-scale lodging like ours to open. Someone from the health department did an annual on-site inspection with a checklist of basic items like working smoke detectors throughout the house. They confirmed our refrigerator temperature was safe at or below 40°F. Importantly, we did not need a commercial kitchen to serve breakfast.

With this health safety check out of the way for the B&B, we could serve whatever we wanted with no restrictions. With fresh produce from our

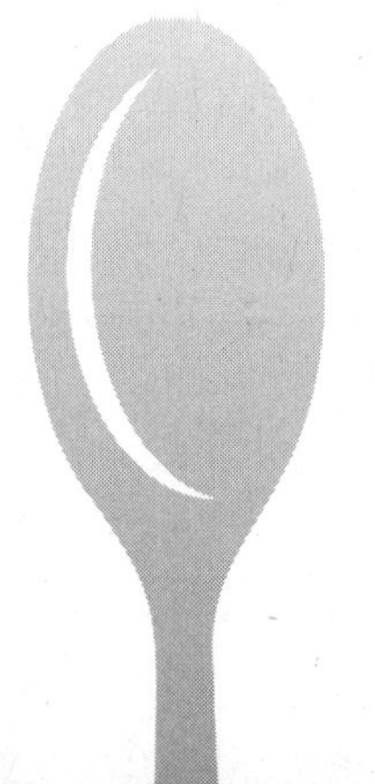

vegetable fields and ample award-winning Wisconsin cheese produced here in Green County, we quickly developed a reputation for creative breakfasts at what became an award-winning inn, with our favorite recipes showcased in our *Farmstead Chef* cookbook.

The health department made it crystal clear we couldn't do anything other than serve breakfast. The way the legislation is written, our breakfast is included as part of the overnight lodging fee. We could serve as many pumpkin spice chocolate chip muffins as we wanted, but we could not charge anything extra. If guests complimented Lisa on how much they loved those muffins, she'd often send a few back home with our guests. Legally we couldn't charge for them. It was a missed opportunity.

Climbing the Legislative Branch

Thirteen years after we opened the B&B, we learned about the concept of cottage food. Indeed, we could legally sell products made in a home kitchen. In 2010, Wisconsin passed into law what is still referred to in our state as the "Pickle Bill," legalizing the sale of only high-acid canned goods made in a home kitchen. The Pickle Bill has a gross sales cap of $5,000 and permitted sales only at farmers' markets or public events. Even with these restrictions, this new law—which exists in the same exact form today—opened up the possibility of directly selling food products made in our home kitchen.

The discovery of Wisconsin's Pickle Bill led us to research other states' cottage food laws. We quickly realized other states allowed home-baked goods, in addition to the high-acid canned goods. Both were considered non-hazardous. Adding baked goods would amplify opportunities for so many more people, including ourselves, given our situation running Inn Serendipity B&B where we could legally serve you muffins made in our home kitchen but couldn't sell you a dozen of the same muffins because of this existing ban on the sale of home-baked goods.

The next step appeared pretty straightforward, paralleling what other states successfully did. Partnering with the Wisconsin Farmers Union for navigation support to put these legislative pieces together, we helped introduce the "Cookie Bill" that would legalize the sale of home-baked goods. It passed our state Senate unanimously in the spring of 2015. Just about ready to turn on our

Wisconsin "Cookie Bill" cookie, baked and decorated by Shannon Heupel of Artfully Delicious Cookies. CREDIT: JOHN D. IVANKO

Author Lisa Kivirist and her friends, Dela Ends and Kriss Marion, successfully sued the state of Wisconsin over the right to sell cookies, cakes, bread, and other non-hazardous baked goods. CREDIT: INSTITUTE FOR JUSTICE

Author Lisa Kivirist shares her story of potentially going to jail over selling her B&B muffins during the lawsuit press conference in 2016 at the capitol in Madison, Wisconsin. CREDIT: JOHN D. IVANKO PHOTOGRAPHY

ovens, we found that the whole process of democracy came to a fiery halt because of one person with too much power.

The speaker of our Wisconsin Assembly, Robin Vos, did not put our Cookie Bill or any cottage food expansion bill on the agenda for a vote. As it turns out, he gets political contributions from industry groups like the Wisconsin Grocers Association, who are strongly opposed to any such bill. Bottom line, he just doesn't like the concept of cottage food. He owns a popcorn shop that, being a retail store, requires commercial regulations to pop and sell the popcorn. He has the mindset of one-size-fits-all regulations. If he needs to go through the commercial process to sell popcorn, everyone does, according to Vos.

Jumping on the Judicial Branch

Fortunately, we do have three branches of American democracy: legislative, executive, and judicial. We moved our issue over to the judicial side, thanks to the Institute for Justice, a nonprofit law firm that fights for underdogs like us, the cottage food expansion advocate we first mentioned in the introduction. They take on such cases of unjust laws that deny our constitutional rights. Erica Smith Ewing, senior attorney at the Institute, representing plaintiffs and championing cottage food rights across the country, fighting such barriers, took on our case. We couldn't have done any of this without her expertise and team at the Institute for Justice.

In January 2016, Lisa along with two close Wisconsin baker-farmer friends, Kriss Marion and Dela Ends, in partnership with the Institute for Justice, filed a lawsuit against the state of Wisconsin against this existing ban on the sale of baked goods. We launched the lawsuit with a press conference at our state capitol in Madison. The media quickly championed our underdog story calling us three the "muffin mafia" and "baking bad." Our quandary became national news as a full-story feature on CBS *Sunday Morning with Jane Pauley.*

"Sharing our story with the public gave us the opportunity to amplify how ridiculous this is as we're talking about non-hazardous food products," shares Dela Ends of Scotch Hill Farm. "No grandma ever killed her grandkids with cookies! Why would I ever put them at risk?"

Flash forward to October, 2017—after various legal hurdles—Judge Duane Jorgenson, circuit judge for Lafayette County, ruled strongly in our favor, agreeing with the Institute for Justice's argument that the existing ban was unconstitutional. We, as United States citizens, have the right to earn an honest livelihood, and the government does not have the right to make arbitrary restrictions, such as was the case with us being able to serve muffins to our guests but not sell them the same muffins if they wanted to take a dozen home. While we did not, and still don't, have a law, we could finally fire up the ovens and start baking and selling. Judge Jorgenson said so.

"The victory in Wisconsin reaches way beyond that state's border as it gave us strong legal precedent to quickly move legal change along in other states," adds Smith Ewing. "It's an example of the ripple effects of cottage food advocacy and how important it is to take a stand when you hit unjust barriers. The outcomes can have positive effects beyond your situation."

"I started my baking business after the Judge's ruling that legalized home bakery sales in Wisconsin, and it's been a life-changing opportunity for me to use my skills on my own terms and schedule while being home and raising my young kids," shares Jobea Murray. She brings both her pastry chef and technical skills to running her business, Jobea Bakes, in the Milwaukee area. "This supportive community of other cottage food entrepreneurs we've been growing positively fuels everything and inspires us to follow our home business dreams."

What's Baking Now in Wisconsin

Since 2017, hundreds of new home bakery businesses have popped up across the state. Lisa co-founded the Wisconsin Cottage Food Association (more on that in the next chapter), with over 800 members. We legally operate under this highly unusual situation where we technically don't have a law but it is perfectly legal to sell our non-hazardous baked goods. Because we don't have a law, we don't have any gross sales cap or burdensome regulations. That said, as a Wisconsin community of bakers, we've come together to foster collaborative education because we don't have a supportive state law.

Even with the judge's clear ruling, that doesn't mean its smooth sailing. Push-back from the Wisconsin Department of Consumer Trade and Protection (DATCP), the regulatory agency tasked with implementing the Wisconsin Pickle Bill law, kept creating new barriers. For example, DATCP stated that a "baked good" must contain flour, which was never part of the judge's original ruling and which is irrelevant to the safety of the product. Our attorneys needed to go another round with the judge to confirm that a baked good is not only one that contains flour: the baked good product can have any ingredients, as long as it comes out of the oven. This opened up opportunities for granola makers to gluten-free bakers who do not use flour.

Author Lisa Kivirist co-founded the Wisconsin Cottage Food Association to better represent the voice of home-based food entrepreneurs in her state.
CREDIT: WISCONSIN COTTAGE FOOD ASSOCIATION

New Lawsuit Offers Up More Opportunity

With no change in elected leadership in Wisconsin in the foreseeable future because of issues like gerrymandered districts, Robin Vos remains in control as Speaker of the Assembly. So the Institute for Justice filed another lawsuit in February 2021, one that would legalize the sale of all non-hazardous products made in a home kitchen. While the 2017 judge's ruling opened up tremendous opportunities for bakers, everyone making other non-hazardous products from candy to roasted coffee to dried herbs still couldn't legally sell out of home kitchens. The rapid popularity of cocoa bombs, the chocolate spheres filled with hot cocoa that you put in a cup and explode when hit with hot milk, made the need for this second lawsuit timely. Check the book's website for hopefully victory updates as this book will go to press before the final court date in 2022.

Work the System

While the Wisconsin cottage food saga sounds bizarre (and it is!), we've found a silver-sprinkled lining of positive insights that keeps Lisa going in this fight and might provide inspiration for you, should a battle erupt in your state.

The Power of Partnerships

Our Wisconsin story exemplifies that change happens through collaboration. When we first started noodling the idea of expanding our state's cottage food law to include baked goods in 2010, Lisa right away turned to others to start stirring up a grassroots coalition, like working with the Wisconsin Farmers Union on the original Cookie Bill legislation plan. This led to a long-standing partnership with the Institute for Justice and the lead attorney, Erica Smith Ewing.

Another benefit of our quirky Wisconsin situation is the super-strong and supportive community of cottage food entrepreneurs that we've built. Because we don't have state support for training or resources in cottage food baking, we've needed to create our own collaborative information sharing. As a result, we started the Wisconsin Cottage Food Association, which is among the plaintiffs in the new lawsuit. The Wisconsin Home Bakery Business Owners is currently one of the largest state-specific Facebook group communities in the country that is very active and vibrant. The next chapter will detail starting your own state group.

Practice Patience

If you do the math, Lisa has been working with many others to expand cottage food opportunities in Wisconsin for well over a decade. Changing the system takes time and therefore demands patience. Democracy drifts like

Don't Be the Self-appointed Cottage Food Police

As our cottage food movement continues to grow, we need to accept an issue that will not go away: there will always be people who don't follow the rules. We share the irritation you feel when you see someone selling their cheesecakes or charcuterie boards on Facebook. How can that be fair when you make such an effort to specifically follow every rule and regulation while others seem to just do what they please?

First, take a breath. Don't let anger lead your next action. Channel your passion and time to crafting your perfect cake or decorating that order for ten dozen cookies, not stewing over someone. Avoid being the drama queen or cottage food enforcer. Let it go.

If you feel compelled to act, then explore an educational avenue. It's possible that the person selling the empanadas or custard pies just didn't know. Most of us, after all, have parked our car somewhere we shouldn't have, unknowingly. Our cottage food movement is really just over a decade old, with a lot of work still needed on outreach and education. Try to connect this person with information and resources. Lecturing or guilt-tripping usually are not the best ways to go. These tactics rarely work when trying to persuade your kids to go to bed. Likewise, expounding to someone on why their custard-filled doughnuts are illegal may cause them to become defensive and not even listen to what you have to say. Instead, openly share your business story and what resources you found helpful, including direct links to your state's regulations. Add the personal, welcoming touch. Be there to answer questions and help them to navigate. Maybe they need a mentor.

Accept that you may receive a range of responses with the education approach. Best-case scenario: you are showered with warm gratitude and a reply of "I never knew that, thanks for telling me." However, be prepared for the opposite: the person gets defensive and questions you or point-blank tells you they don't care and will continue. Of course, they may just ignore you as well.

We suggest you not become the unofficial cottage food police. It's the job of the state's regulatory agency to monitor such vendors. It has Internet access and can see posts on Facebook too. Not only does turning in your neighbors who sell something illegally build negative feelings of mistrust in your community, you may directly foster the spread of mistrust and animosity.

By engaging the state regulatory agencies, calling out the problems resulting from a few bad actors, you add some evidence as to why cottage food operations may not be trusted. That's the opposite of what we need to highlight, especially as we want to expand into food freedom laws that may cover what they are doing anyway. Once you call the state, they are obligated to engage and act. You are responsible for whatever outcomes that may result.

an iceberg on a calm day. These lawsuits take years between when they are filed and actual hearings, with lots of legal detours along the way. They also take legal resources that require funding. Having a nonprofit legal gun like the Institute for Justice made this happen.

Frost with Fun

Given this long haul required for change, it's vital to keep it fun and rewarding for those involved. Collectively celebrate the impact by cheering cottage food entrepreneurs that go above and beyond. Share and showcase media covering the story of a local baker. Share the accomplishment around.

After the original judge's ruling, we set out baked goods and folding tables on the courthouse lawn and hosted an impromptu potluck with the aspiring bakers who came out for the hearing that provided the celebratory coming together after years of organizing. We planned this pop-up party ahead of time, of course not knowing the outcome of the hearing because either way, we knew we needed to come together as a community.

Go from Cookies to Candidate

Don't be surprised if putting your toes in advocating for cottage food rights in your state opens you up to a longer list of issues you want to see changed, inspiring you to take on a larger leadership role. You may see yourself first and foremost as a cupcake or fudge or strawberry jam maker, but does this experience embolden you to see a broader future?

That's Kriss Marion's story. She's a fellow Wisconsin lawsuit plaintiff with Lisa that led to a judge lifting the ban on baked goods. "Our experience fighting for the simple right to sell cookies in our state and the patriarchal barriers we encountered really hit me, that we wouldn't be dealing with any of this if we had elected officials who acted like true leaders, listening to their constituents and making change happen that isn't influenced by money," shares Kriss Marion, who currently serves as a supervisor on her county board. "We need more voices, particularly from women, around the decision-making table to truly shake things up. I realized I needed to stretch beyond my kitchen and figure out how I can support my broader community."

A crowd of happy bakers and supporters gather on the Lafayette County Courthouse steps after the victorious ruling in 2017 legalizing the sale of home-baked goods. CREDIT: LISA KIVIRIST

22

Organize Your State Cottage Food Association

MOST TRADITIONAL BUSINESS SCHOOLS still teach from a perspective of scarcity and competition. There are winners and losers. And that there is only so much of the profit pie to go around. Professors warn of rampant competition, fickle or too few customers to go around, and bemoan limited or too expensive resources. To succeed, you must build a better mousetrap and out-compete other enterprises.

As you already know, the cottage food industry is different. We help each other succeed. We share customers, recipes, and where to find the best price on butter. There's an abundance of collaboration under the umbrella idea that there are customers seeking quality, truly home- and handmade items, enough for every one of us. There's plenty in that profit pie. While this doesn't negate the need for you to still identify your customers' needs and develop a quality product at the right price, it's under a positive spirit of cooperation and support between other independent businesses. We operate by our own rules and don't fall victim to society's need to compete.

Cottage food entrepreneurs create an industry that defies traditional notions of cutthroat competition. We instead bring people together in trust and support to create something better. We grow stronger through relationships built on our mutual love of everything from perfecting that pie crust to sourcing cookie cutters to canning jar supplier recommendations. Baked into the cottage food movement is friendship. Not competition.

A first step in nurturing these relationships is knowing each other, connecting on a regular basis. While there are a growing number of fabulous national online cottage food communities that bring us together, this chapter focuses on gathering together cottage food entrepreneurs in your state, a topic that you can directly help lead. With cottage food laws initiated and managed on the state level, it is the laws specifically in the state where you live that are your priority. Your state's laws are what you want to see expanded.

An easy on-ramp to bring your state community together is to form a cottage food association. At the time of this book's printing, a handful of such formal groups operate in Minnesota, New Jersey, Utah, and Wisconsin, the one that Lisa helped found.

Why State Associations Rock

One thing to clarify is that we're talking about an entity more formal and with deeper strategic intention than say a Facebook private group for your state. Many of those exist and are ways to quickly share information and connect with your community. Lisa administers the Wisconsin Home Bakery Business Owners Facebook group, one of the largest and most active state-specific Facebook groups in the US. See the sidebar for ideas specific to administering Facebook groups.

If you already have a Facebook group, fabulous. But it can only go so far in accurately communicating and active organizing within your state. Important to keep top of mind: Facebook is a deeply for-profit corporate entity solely driven by money, data mining and selling what they know about you from your posts, likes, and groups. While these groups provide connection, exactly what members see in posts and how is controlled by algorithms, and you undoubtedly miss people along the way. Creating your own organizational structure, mailing list, and communication tools separate and distinct from these social media corporations gives you a much stronger base for coordination.

Let's start with five reasons why a state association can amplify the cottage food movement both in your state and nationally.

Establishes Legitimacy

"The vision for the Minnesota Cottage Food Producer's Association started when I began to feel that we were not being taken seriously by both our state legislature making the laws and the state agencies implementing the regulations," shares Shelley Erickson, president of the association and a Minnesota home-based baker. "In the early days it was mostly just my face representing cottage foods in my state, and the idea sparked that an association would bring together and more adequately represent the whole movement. It's not just my voice but many."

Many organizations use this strategy, including much larger entities ranging from the National Restaurant Association to the National Grocers Association, representing thousands of members when lobbying for amenable

laws. Understandably, state cottage food associations don't have the big funding pots these entities have but the organizing concept remains the same as we're showcasing and celebrating the cottage food industry. We are not just a bunch of stay-at-home moms baking cookies. We are a fast-growing movement of food business owners contributing to our state's economy, deserving of respectfully being heard.

Prepares for Change

As we've learned in our Wisconsin story in the last chapter, democracy and the process of advancing cottage food laws and opportunities run in often unpredictable spurts. Nothing happens, and then, all of a sudden, a state senator quickly introduces a new bill. While you think our elected officials would check with cottage food business owners themselves before writing a new law, that doesn't always happen. This is why having a current email list and other contact info for your cottage food community is essential. We'll talk more about how to establish those communication channels later in this chapter.

That state senator who just introduced that new bill may have a well-crafted proposal that expands product opportunity or increases the gross sales cap, at which point you want to rally support and communicate to everyone quickly to call their representatives to vote yes. Or the bill may be lacking or, for whatever misinformed reason, taking your state's cottage food laws back a step, requiring increased inspections or unnecessary hurdles. Whatever the need, it will be essential to be organized, active, and ready to do the required work, often quickly.

Shares Resources

While there is much to learn from cottage food entrepreneurs nationally, those local and more regional connections are invaluable. This can be anything from sharing when a supermarket chain has a fabulous sale on butter to finding someone nearby to do a cake print.

Likewise, if you run into a barrier where you live, the odds are someone else in your state has faced the same challenges and could provide direct, helpful insight. Local issues could be anything from dealing with a farmers' market manager not friendly to home-based food businesses to navigating township zoning issues. Connecting with others dealing with similar hurdles can prove super helpful.

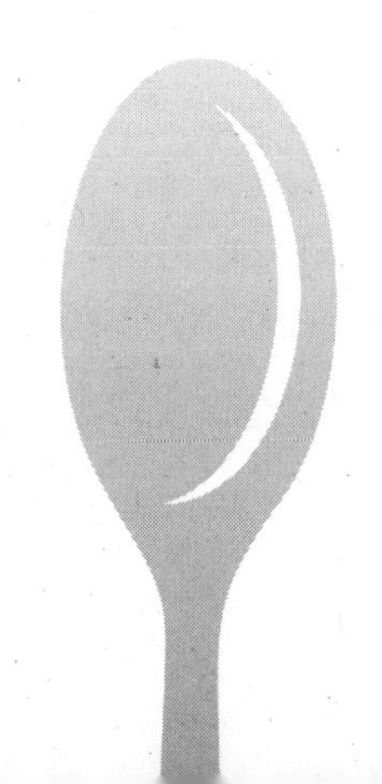

Facilitates Referrals

Again, defying the traditional competitive business model, we cottage food entrepreneurs often share an order inquiry with another fellow entrepreneur when we can't personally fill it. If you already have multiple cake orders for the weekend and realize you can't take one more and deliver the quality you are known for, you can turn to others in your area who might be able to take it on. Maybe you are the one giving someone their first order ever? With referrals, we grow our movement, but only if we know each other and have a means to communicate and connect.

Supports Newbies

If you already have your cottage food operation running, reminisce back to those days when you took the first steps to establish your business. Maybe you opened that business bank account and then started preparing for your first order. You probably felt starting up your enterprise was a combo pack of excitement and nervousness, which is another area where having a connected community goes a long way. Knowing you are not alone and that an association of established entrepreneurs has your back and wants you to succeed cooks up a huge mental boost.

Association Start-up in Four Steps

One important tip before we get into association organizing specifics is to keep it all as simple as possible. How can you best use your time to enhance cottage food in your state? Remember this effort is really intended to enhance your business vision, not suck time such that your own enterprise suffers.

We say that because it's an area Lisa especially finds herself entangled in—taking on too much. Obviously, she is one committed cookie when it comes to expanding cottage food opportunities in her state of Wisconsin. She's been leading this charge through years of grassroots organizing, and what is most rewarding for her is knowing she helped spur hundreds of business start-ups. That's what led her to co-found the Wisconsin Cottage Food Association, but essaying to keep it as simple and manageable as possible.

Step 1: Decide Organizational Structure and Mission

Under that umbrella idea of keeping things simple, a basic association structure is an entity to consider. On our Homemade for Sale website, you can

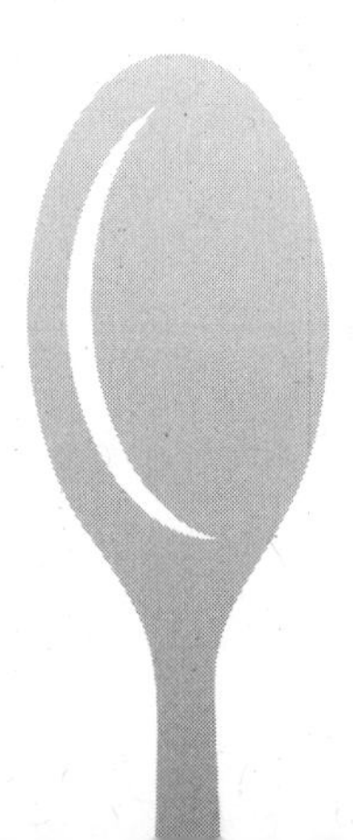

download a free sample of a State Association bylaw template that provides the basic organizational framework to launch your organization. The association gives your group the structure and legitimacy it wants as simply as possible to get up and running. This is only a starter template meant for you to tailor to your own situational needs.

There's a place in this bylaw template for your organizational purpose, why you are doing what you are doing. Again, this can be kept inclusive and straightforward. It's an important first step so the members are on the same page.

For example, the purpose statement for our Wisconsin Cottage Food Association is:

> This organization was formed for the purpose of educating, supporting, networking and galvanizing Wisconsin's collaborative cottage food community to champion home-based entrepreneurs who are producing and selling non-hazardous baked and high-acid canned items, currently legal in Wisconsin. We also support the effort to legalize the sale of all non-hazardous food products. Our inclusive and welcoming organization includes current home-based food entrepreneurs, those in the planning and research phase, customers and others who advocate for increasing food freedom access in Wisconsin.

Another piece of the organizational setup is determining leadership structure. You can, of course, have traditional officers such a president, vice-president, and so on. Or perhaps you are in the same situation Wisconsin and New Jersey were in when starting out. Both had a dedicated group of CFOs wanting to see this association happen, but everyone was already busy and no one wanting to step into a formal officer role.

In both states, these newbie groups launched with a more general committee of leadership, a designated group where the energy and input would be more fluid and collaborative. In Wisconsin, we called this our "founding leadership committee," made up of four individuals. For this to work, you need trust, knowing each other, and feeling confident in decisions made even if you aren't a part of it because you need to focus your energies on this week's big wedding order.

"For our New Jersey Home Bakers Association, we have a group of five women who serve as our leadership committee for the organization," explains Martha Rabello, one of these founding women who now runs Cherryspoon home-bakery since this group's advocacy efforts finally legalized the sale of non-hazardous products. "As many of us are stay-at-home moms with other jobs and responsibilities, this setup works well for us as our roles are fluid and we can help and support each other however we can to get the job done."

An association is different, and much simpler to start, than a 501c3 nonprofit organization. While being a nonprofit has its advantages, such as the ability to fundraise through grants or member donations, for simplicity's sake right now we'll focus on forming an association as a starting point. What often spurs an organization to become its own nonprofit, or potentially partner with an existing nonprofit, is liability. If you start doing regular events, particularly those open to the public, it may be time to consider incorporation.

"Any member of an unincorporated nonprofit association can become personally liable for the actions of the association as a whole," explains Rachel Armstrong, executive director of Farm Commons. "Now, if the association isn't exposed to potential liabilities like debt, injury of others, or the like, that risk may be minimal. The risk can also be mitigated by making sure the association carries its own insurance policy to cover liabilities. But at the same time, the potential for personal liability may be too much for some members. In that case, an incorporated nonprofit is the best route to take."

Step 2: Determine Membership

Next, determine what constitutes membership in your state cottage food association. Who qualifies to join? Who do you want to recruit that would represent your mission?

One membership approach focuses on established producers, those with up and running established businesses. This is the criteria to join the Minnesota Cottage Food Producer's Association. With members sharing the same status of business owners, this will inherently create a smaller but tighter group with everyone strongly vested in the cottage food movement by having their boots on the ground already.

Another approach, which the Wisconsin and New Jersey associations took, would be broader inclusivity with membership open to current producers as well as those considering starting businesses and even the more

general community who do not intend to sell but want to support and buy cottage food products. This more expansive direction does lead to larger numbers, with both these states attracting over 800 members at the time of this book printing. A perk of these larger association memberships is their stronger representation and influence when it comes to lobbying for expanded laws.

Your association will decide whether membership requires dues. The Minnesota Cottage Food Producer's Association charges dues and provides members with a broad array of resources, from training opportunities throughout the year to monthly Zoom happy hour meetings with the association leadership and other members to hear up-to-date information about the lobbying and consulting work being done at the state level and to discuss their impacts.

The cottage food associations in Wisconsin and New Jersey currently do not require dues since both wanted to attract as many members as possible without any financial barrier and also did not want the hassle of managing the funds. There are pros and cons to both approaches. A membership fee model generates a more dedicated membership base. When you pay something, you want to be engaged, yet at the same time, have higher expectations that the organization will deliver value. With free memberships, expectations can be lowered.

Keep in mind, your association might be up against very well-funded and powerful lobby or special interest groups. Since you don't have money, your power is in numbers. The more constituents, the more sway and power.

Step 3: Establish Communication Channels

The most valuable element of your state association is the members themselves. Databases allow for quick cost-effective communication with them via email. This list enables you to be much more inclusive than a flurry of social media that can be hit-or-miss at best for accurate messaging. It also amplifies your organization's legitimacy.

Yes, still have a state Facebook private group particularly as a means of exchanging information quickly and building community connections. See the sidebar for details on managing a cottage food state Facebook group. However, we advise you to not use this as a substitute for collecting contact information. With privacy concerns on Facebook already, doing so may prove very difficult.

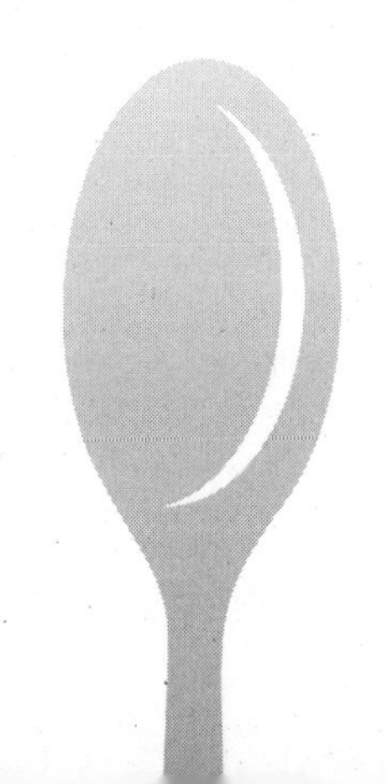

Start a Facebook Group for Your State

If your state currently does not have a state-specific cottage food Facebook group, here are some ideas to get it rolling.

Why use Facebook, when there are so many other social media tools and forums today? Instead of being a lone tree in the forest, the group is the forest bringing everyone together. What we've found in our work and research for this book is that most cottage food entrepreneurs have a Facebook presence, even running their whole enterprise only using a Facebook business page. A large proportion of your community is already on Facebook, so its Groups feature allows you to readily organize CFOs as a private group. Most of your target audience of CFOs or those who want to start a business are already familiar with the platform.

Here's some important things to do with your Facebook group.

Establish membership eligibility

Membership eligibility is determined via the membership criteria you set for someone who requests to join. Do you want this group to be broader and inclusive or smaller and more intimate for your producer community? In Wisconsin, our criteria for the Facebook group remains that you are already a home-based producer or are interested in becoming one. This keeps the community specific to business owners and topics related to non-hazardous Items. There are plenty of other resources for bakers looking for a cheesecake recipe, but we don't want to clutter our channels. Also, we define membership as those living in Wisconsin or looking to move to our state and start a cottage food business.

Set group rules

Facebook will offer you a set of group rules that involve standard practices of respect, no hate speech. Tailor these to your situation. One thing Lisa found important in Wisconsin is to specifically state the need for supportive collaboration. There were some negative situations where someone was calling out someone else for not doing it all perfectly, and it quickly festered into an unnecessary negative tone for the group. For example, folks selling cocoa bombs before candy was technically legal to sell in our state, even though the product was perfectly non-hazardous. As a result, a couple of members had to be banned, which immediately reset a more positive tone.

We now have the following first rule so everyone is in agreement: Support for all — no negativity. We are committed to collaboration, mutual education, and respect. Calling out or reporting those not doing everything exactly right hurts everyone and will not be tolerated in this group.

Add multiple administrators and moderators

Facebook has different terms for who can access and control what happens within the workings of the group. It helps to have multiple people in these roles to assure both continuity and engagement and to keep an eye out for any reported posts that violate group rules, which are rare but still important to nip. Also, multiple moderators can together more quickly approve new members and keep an eye out for timely questions needing answers.

On the public communication side, a basic website along with a means to capture member contact information may prove to be worth the effort in time and resources. Tap into the expertise of other cottage food producers in your state. Undoubtedly there are CFOs who have a technical background or even have a day job as a web designer. Such a basic site would fit under the free plan with providers like Wix, which is how we did our full Homemade for Sale site. You may still want a domain name, which would cost about $20 a year; a member might be willing to cover this cost.

A basic and free means to capture member information is through Google Forms, free survey administration software that enables you to create a form. Google then downloads the data into a CSV (comma-separated values) file to use via Excel or other spreadsheet software. You can import it into emails or, better yet, use the basic free plan of a newsletter distribution service. If this discussion of spreadsheets and databases causes your eyes to glaze over, tap into the expertise of your cottage food community for someone with tech expertise.

In Wisconsin, the Cottage Food Association connected with Jobea Murray. She's a trained pastry chef and has an engineering background. "I'm honestly self-taught in Google tools but with a tech background could pick them up pretty regularly," offers Murray. "While these tools are designed to be simple and user-friendly, it does help to have one-on-one support to get the organization up and running. I'm happy to be able to use my other skill sets outside of the kitchen to contribute to our state's community."

Step 4: Entertain Gatherings

Once up and running, your association can serve as the conduit for initiating direct connections and building relationships in your state. As home-based entrepreneurs, life can get a little lonely. While you love baking or canning or candy-making in your kitchen, most of us are solo entrepreneurs. State associations can help bridge those gaps by bringing producers together for direct connections, either in the virtual or in-person space.

One thing the pandemic taught us is embracing the virtual space. We've done state-wide Zoom meet-ups in Wisconsin that brought CFOs together from across hundreds of miles, attendance we would not have achieved in person. Google Meet can also serve the same purpose.

For these meet-ups, we spend some time with broader updates for the group and then have often a program of information sharing, such as a

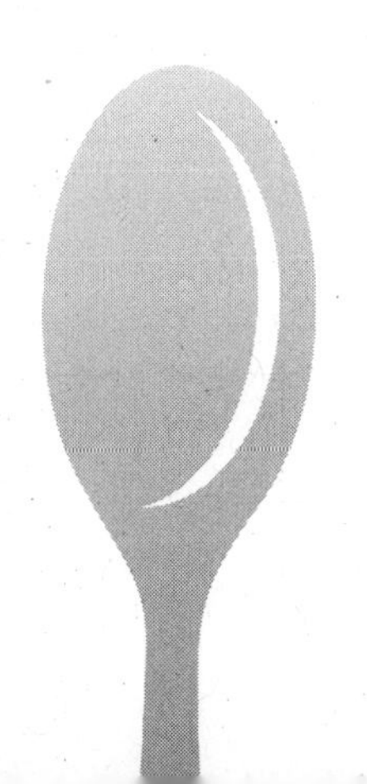

member discussing some business experience. The breakout room feature in platforms like Zoom and Google Meet easily enables attendees to connect deeper and be more specific on topics of interest, such as creating rooms based on what you are producing, such as one for cookie decorators, cake bakers, candy makers, and so on. Breaking out by geographic regions is also an easy means to stir up local connections. While in Wisconsin we aim to keep the official virtual meet-up to one hour to respect busy schedules, we've left these breakout rooms open for as long as people want to linger, often for another hour of good conversation and sharing.

These virtual spaces can be an effective and readily accessible means to kick off your state association and bring CFOs together across a wide geography. But eventually, there may be interest and opportunity to meet in person. Usually this happens more regionally, often building from connections planted in the virtual space, through someone saying we need to get together.

In-person gatherings amp up the connections and intimacy and, bonus, offer the opportunity to share and sample treats! Geography typically forces such meet-ups to be more localized, a gathering of bakers, canners, and candy makers from a specific region, perhaps at a park or member's home. For inspiration to gather on a state level, the Minnesota association leaders have organized several conferences, bringing together over 100 CFOs for a day of in-person workshops and networking.

Think of a state cottage food organization as you would a bullhorn. Loud. Clear. Focused. Not only will the association amplify your values and vision related to the CFO movement, it will help legitimize the hardworking bakers and canners and other producers and their role in the food system.

Having an association will enable you to more fully take on the state-organizing strategies outlined in the last chapter. Additionally, you will be ready to take on food freedom initiatives as opportunities rise in your state. We'll tempt your taste buds with these possible fortuitous changes on the horizon as we move to the next and final chapter.

23

Food Freedom

IF THE COTTAGE FOOD LAWS that you're currently operating under leave you hungry for more, then get ready for the next wave of home-based entrepreneurship: food freedom. Suddenly, cheesecakes, fermented foods, and other diverse food products that require refrigeration, or need to be frozen, may be possible. In fact, if you happen to live in a few states with laws recently passed, you can make entire ready-to-eat prepared meals for neighbors or even serve them on your converted backyard patio.

On the other hand, if you're completely content with operating under your state's current cottage food law, great. Why fix what's not broken with your $50,000 per year, custom-decorated sugar cookie enterprise. Those of you who are not satisfied or want to try something more, something new, keep reading for what might be in store for your dream-come-true home-based food business.

First, a heads-up: you might need to get involved to help make it happen. The secret sauce to getting food freedom laws passed is active and engaged home-based food entrepreneurs like you. Or, you could watch on the sidelines, simply keeping an eye on what's happening in your state, so you can pounce on baking those cheesecakes or tacos once the light turns green. Remember, Lisa sued the state of Wisconsin, twice, while John started honing his cookie-decorating skills until the Wisconsin judge declared the existing ban unconstitutional and removed the ban on selling homemade baked goods. We need food entrepreneurs active on both fronts: advocacy and advancing their food business once the law is passed.

These state-specific food freedom laws expand the cottage food law concept to cover other products, including homemade prepared food, sometimes without any cap on sales and often with minimal licensing, permitting, or kitchen inspection requirements. While some states may simply call them Home Kitchen Operations, many have named the law specific to selling prepared meals a Microenterprise Home Kitchen Operation, MHKO or MEHKO for short. While certain food freedom laws entail very little regulatory oversight or home inspections, MHKOs tend to involve a food-handling course and certification, home inspections, and more requirements.

For the purposes of this book, we have treated cottage food laws (applying to non-hazardous food products) separately from food freedom or MHKO laws that apply to the preparation and sale of "potentially hazardous" foods, including those products that require refrigeration, made in a home kitchen.

Whatever the states call these new laws is less important than what a home chef can do when cooking under them. Depending on the state where it was passed, the food freedom or MHKO law may allow you to sell just about anything you bake, process, grill, roast, dry, smoke, ferment, or sauté in your home kitchen, regardless of whether it needs to be refrigerated or frozen. Some of these laws may prohibit meat products, but sometimes the MHKO law does not since it essentially treats the home kitchen as a restaurant and its operator as a chef or cook. Interestingly, for MHKOs, operators are not required to purchase restaurant-grade stainless steel equipment or commercial ovens.

Thanks to MHKO and food freedom laws, residents in some states can operate a restaurant out of their home kitchen. Many MHKO operators focus on ethnic specialties, like tacos.
CREDIT: JOHN D. IVANKO PHOTOGRAPHY

Be advised, however, the food freedom movement is where cottage food law was back in 2008, when a wave of those laws started cropping up. Cottage foods was a new idea back then that required educational outreach and a degree of persuasion for its acceptance. The food freedom frontier means this new legislative territory will demand further study and research. It will also involve an ample amount of advocacy and education, just like home-based fledging entrepreneurs undertook in the early days of cottage food laws. We still recall the dirty glares from people passing by when we displayed our jars of pickles, made in our home kitchen, not in a licensed, certified kitchen inspected by the health department. Some, erroneously, advised us that what we were doing was "breaking the law."

Food safety remains paramount for food freedom laws being passed. But according to the state health departments with food freedom laws or MHKOs, there has yet to be a single outbreak of foodborne illness linked to a food freedom business.

Another reason for more emboldened state lawmaking related to foods might be a general loss of confidence in such decision-making and policies at the federal level. The COVID-19 pandemic revealed how unprepared and incapable the Centers for Disease Control and Prevention (CDC) actually was in terms of predicting, mitigating, and managing the aftermath of the

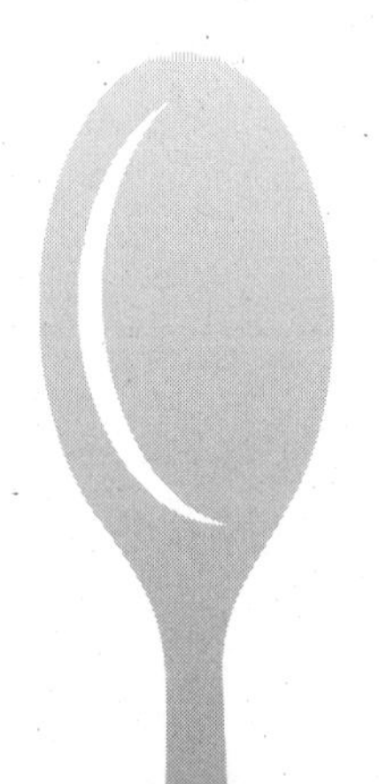

outbreak in the US. In many ways, managing the pandemic fell upon the governors of various states. States versus federal rights issues have cropped up in a host of other issues as well.

In part reflecting the times, state-initiated cottage food and new food freedom laws usurp the Food and Drug Administration's (FDA) control over food production. But given the massive consolidation in the food industry and unjust special interests and corporate influence on federal policies, bold moves like these seem both warranted and necessary. After all, state governors need to make sure their citizens can have a safe meal on the table.

In reality, the number of industrial foodborne disease outbreaks have grown so steadily and regularly that they've become a normalized part of the US food system. So, how safe are we, really, with the FDA in charge? The end result of the foodborne disease outbreaks, usually discovered after people have already become sick: millions of pounds of food products destroyed every year. And despite what we now know about climate change, the average ingredient used by a restaurant may travel upwards of 1,200 miles before being picked up in the drive-thru window. Hardly sustainable. Another bonus to localizing food production, there are fewer supply-chain problems when what's being served came from a producer or farmer nearby.

But competitive market forces and special interests may actually bear down more harshly on aspirational homestead cooks once they try to get going in these states. Corporations sway politicians. Some of the special interest groups, representing membership saddled with rent and expensive commercial kitchen equipment, want every last penny of the dining-out dollar. Bricks-and-mortar food service establishments feel the pain if the economy slows down or a pandemic temporarily shutters their doors. If food or labor costs are rising faster than what they can charge for their special of the day, this adds to the angst. Like Airbnb disrupted traditional hotels, and Lyft turned the taxi industry upside down, food freedom may very well disrupt the dining experience.

The Foundation of Food Freedom

One could say that the emerging food freedom movement draws its inspiration from the Declaration of Independence, giving meaning to the unalienable rights of "life, liberty and the pursuit of happiness."

For many of us home-based food producers, there is no greater joy than the satisfaction your product brings to family members, friends, or

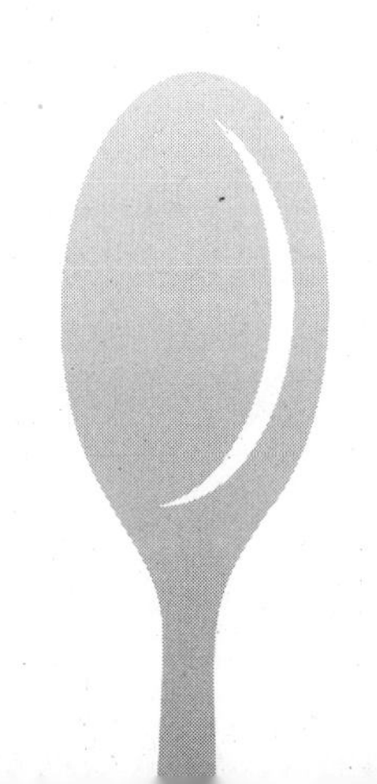

customers when they bite into your delicious cinnamon roll or spread some of your blueberry jam on a slice of toast. We want to be free from unnecessary, often times arbitrary or trite, governmental rules or regulations, and free to earn our daily bread by any way we deem fit. Sure, we need to be safe about what we make and sell, but as we've said before, it's practically impossible to harm someone with a chocolate-chip cookie. And for millions of Americans, food is the very essence of life: it nourishes us, brightens our day, brings a smile to a child's face, and gives us cultural meaning, especially during the holidays. It's one of those things that makes life worth living.

While the cottage food movement may have erupted from the bustling farmers' markets and economic fallout from the Great Recession, the food freedom movement emerging now harnesses the energy from the harsh realities of the COVID-19 pandemic, governmental lockdowns, and some more open-minded state legislatures eager to support the entrepreneurial spirit of Americans, not quash it by excessive red tape and counter-productive regulations. Successful, home-based start-up businesses are one way to keep those workers from bleeding further the state's underfunded unemployment compensation fund. They also encourage more robust local food systems and build community.

"States are already doing a great job expanding laws allowing people to sell homemade shelf-stable food," observes Erica Smith Ewing, lead attorney with the Institute for Justice, referring to many of legal battles fought over cottage food laws across the US. "There is such much momentum that it is inevitable these laws will keep expanding. The next frontier are laws allowing the sale of homemade meals and other foods requiring refrigeration." At the time of printing, six states—Wyoming, Utah, Oklahoma, North Dakota, Iowa, and Montana—allow the sale of homemade prepared foods with a minimum of red tape or regulatory oversight under some form of a food freedom law. Within a decade, Smith Ewing expects this number to double. Additionally, California was the first state to pass a microenterprise home kitchen operation law (MHKO), with other states passing or considering similar versions of this law.

"We know that customers desire to purchase value-added food from local producers, and regulations should assist, not hinder, the efforts of local producers," affirms Alexia Kulwiec, executive director of the Farm-to-Consumer Legal Defense Fund (FTCLDF). Through legal representation and policy work, the FTCLDF protects, defends, and broadens the rights and

viability of small farmers, artisanal food producers, and customers who support them.

"Customer interest seems driven in large part by their increased understanding of the vulnerability of our food system, and their wish to support the economic viability of smaller food producers and to purchase from sources they can trust," continues Kulwiec. "Interest in cottage foods and food freedom are also driven by increased attention to individual health. People are seeking food produced in a healthy and wholesome manner."

What is going on with respect to the restrictions placed on people selling homemade food products and especially prepared foods, entire meals, from their home kitchen? Why are these laws being passed right now?

"The pandemic generated huge interest in cottage food reform and the growth of food freedom," explains Meagan Forbes, legislative counsel for the Institute for Justice and active in food freedom initiatives. "Food freedom laws change lives for the better by opening up entrepreneurial opportunity simply by giving consumers the freedom to choose."

"The pandemic accelerated the trend toward deregulation of all kinds of homemade-food sales. Amid lockdowns, many people were out of work, particularly in the restaurant business, and looking for ways to make a little cash. And consumers, wary of supermarkets and restaurants, embraced delivery and takeout like never before."

— Emily Heil, *Washington Post* (October 13, 2021)

States Leading the Way

California

It comes as no surprise that the state of California, already among the leaders related to cottage food law options in the US, is the first to pass a brand-new and completely separate law permitting and licensing the Microenterprise Home Kitchen Operation (MHKO or MEHKO), allowing an individual to essentially operate a restaurant out of their private residence. This law permits a homeowner, after being inspected by the county health department and completing a course to receive Food Manager Certification, to prepare just about any foods they wanted and sell them directly to customers in their community.

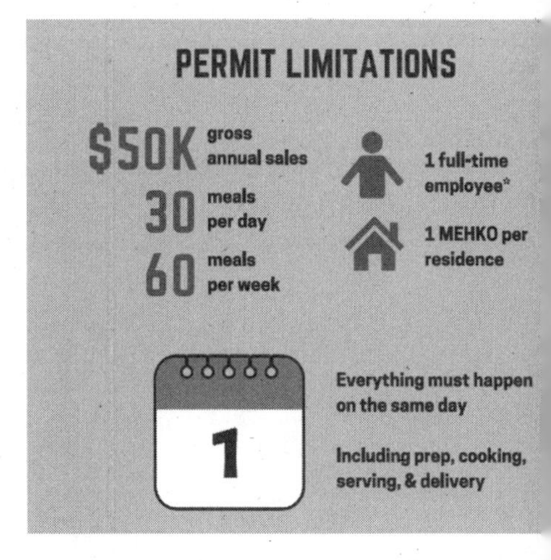

There are some limitations with the MEHKO permit in California.

CREDIT: COOK ALLIANCE/COOKALLIANCE.ORG

The foods offered have to be cooked, handled, stored, and served or delivered out of the private residence. Orders for food need to be secured through an Internet food service intermediary like Foodnome or ChefBnB. The only items not allowed for sale are raw oysters, raw milk products, homemade ice cream or dairy products, or products that involve food processes requiring a Hazard Analysis Critical Control Point Plan, like cured, smoked, pickled, or preserved foods.

At the time of this printing, the only kicker with California's MEHKO law is that individual counties needed to opt in to allow such MHKOs to

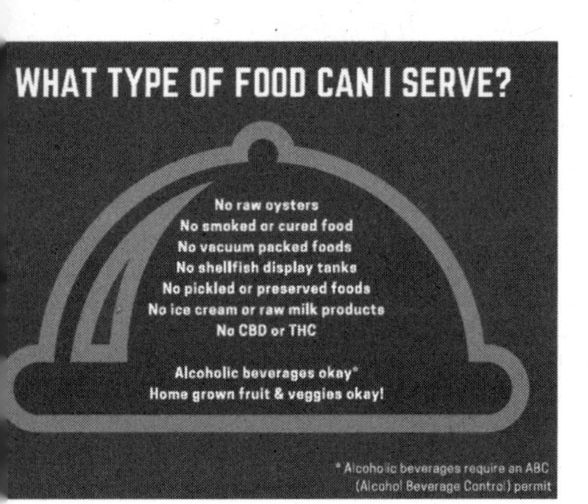

Home chefs can sell just about anything. In terms of what could actually be made or sold from a home kitchen permitted as a MEHKO, there were very few exceptions.
CREDIT: COOK ALLIANCE/COOKALLIANCE.ORG

operate. Translated: you had to live in the "right" county or aggressively campaign your county's political leaders and health department to opt in to the MHKO licensing. A home chef operating under a MHKO permit cannot sell wholesale, offer catering services, or use third-party delivery services to get their food to their customers. They could, however, offer in-home cooking classes.

The inability to use third-party delivery services such as Grubhub or DoorDash will hopefully change. "Ultimately, the limitations on California's MHKO's law are driven by the same things that limit all the other homemade food laws: unfounded fear and protectionism," adds Smith Ewing. "But there is only so long that legislators can hinder these businesses. Times are changing and progress is inevitable."

Cook Alliance has been at the forefront of the efforts to help legalize the country's first home restaurants through the passage of the MEHKO law. Since 2014, the nonprofit organization has been advocating for the recognition of home cooking as both dignified and socially invaluable. Cook Alliance has helped translate labor and social justice issues into equitable legislation while supporting the home cooks with a collective voice.

Online App Platforms Provide a Bridge to Your Customers

In response to the interest and growth in home-based prepared food operations, numerous online platforms have emerged to make it easier for customers to learn about and order prepared meals from neighbors in their community. In some cases, these online or app-based "Internet food service intermediaries" are required by law to facilitate orders for food operators, especially those offering prepared meals. Getting their start in California, Foodnome is one of the more popular intermediaries. Others include ChefBnB, Shef, and homemadefood.app. Castiron, having already established itself as a national commerce and small business management platform in the cottage food and commercially produced specialty food market, looks to naturally expand into the home-based prepared food niche.

Mynhan Hoang, My Fair Kitchen, Eastvale, California

Home-cooked prepared meals and custom cakes from My Fair Kitchen

Owner and home cook, Mynhan Hoang has found her passion while working out of her tidy kitchen in a Los Angeles suburb. Every week, she turns out tasty Vietnamese dishes like filet mignon and garlic noodles or beef or chicken pho noodles. One of her most popular dishes, Vietnamese spring rolls—gluten-free rice paper wraps with vermicelli, lettuce, shrimp, pork—is on the menu every week because her customers can't get enough. She also offers a variety of creative custom specialty cakes, including frozen cakes.

"I wanted to use all my talents and skills in the kitchen to share my unique and creative meals and baked goods with everyone," exclaims Hoang, a former software engineer turned home chef, launching My Fair Kitchen in 2020. While she decided to be a stay-at-home mom and raise her four school-age kids, she couldn't shake her entrepreneurial spirit, nor her inherent culinary talent and passion. She adeptly balances her business with the responsibilities of raising her children.

"California's cottage food laws are very limited for baked goods, nor could I make and sell prepared meals like I wanted to," says Hoang, on why she decided to get licensed as a Microenterprise Home Kitchen Operation (MEHKO). She was lucky that Riverside County where she lived was permitting such operations because not all counties do. As a licensed MEHKO, not only could Hoang sell cakes or other baked goods that might require refrigeration or be sold frozen, she could also sell prepared foods made in her home kitchen that are available for pickup or delivery. She can even offer her refreshing Thai milk tea with bobas or creamy Vietnamese iced coffee to thirsty customers.

"I welcome challenges," admits Hoang. "I like to do new cake designs whenever customers ask me. I experiment with new recipes all the time. Otherwise, I'd get very bored." The MEHKO license provided the greatest flexibility and freedom in terms of menu offerings.

Hoang's approach to Vietnamese cuisine reflects that it tastes like homemade because it is homemade. "I'm a very traditional person and always craved the authentic flavors of Vietnamese cuisine, like when I was growing up in Vietnam," explains Hoang, an immigrant to the US who was raised south of

Name: Mynhan Hoang

Business: My Fair Kitchen (Eastvale, CA)

Website: https://foodnome.com/My-Fair-Kitchen

Products: prepared meals and various custom cakes, including those that are frozen or require refrigeration, licensed as a Microenterprise Home Kitchen Operation (MEHKO)

Sales venues: home pickup or delivery

Gross Revenues: $26,000/year

Mynhan Hoang working in her home kitchen making prepared meals customers pick up at her suburban home.
CREDIT: MYNHAN HOANG

Ho Chi Minh City, in the Soc Trang province. "I want to give my customers these authentic tastes and a healthier version of the dishes whenever they want to eat out. That's how I set my food apart from the other Vietnamese restaurants around me." Besides avoiding monosodium glutamate (MSG), she cooks everything from scratch and with as many fresh ingredients as possible.

My Fair Kitchen's Vietnamese eggrolls. Credit: Mynhan Hoang

"Sometimes I receive messages from customers with special requests, like a vegan option—a completely animal-free version—for one of my dishes," says Hoang, about what inspired her vegan pho. Pho is often considered Vietnam's national dish, usually consisting of a broth, rice noodles, meat, and various herbs. "There were not many vegan options for Vietnamese foods in my area, so I came up with my own vegan variation of this popular soup. I enjoy making foods for everyone. I love to see people enjoying my food." She regularly accommodates vegetarians and those who prefer gluten-free alternatives.

"My best seller is lobster garlic noodles," smiles Hoang, recognizing her talent to create tasty Vietnamese fusion dishes. "I used Italian organic spaghetti and American butter in my special Vietnamese sauce for this dish."

Pho Bo Vietnamese beef noodle soup with filet mignon, back ribs, and homemade meatballs. Credit: Mynhan Hoang

Hoang had to pass her local Riverside County Health Department inspection to be legally permitted to operate as a MEHKO. As a part of the process, she obtained a Food Safety Manager Certification, the highest level of food safety training. "Before the inspection, I had the list of the inspection requirements and followed it carefully," says Hoang. "I gathered together the supplies or equipment needed. I followed the list of requirements. It was actually pretty simple, since most home cooks already have a good working sink, maintain the correct temperature of hot water, and have a freezer and refrigerator set at the proper temperature to ensure food safety.

"The hardest part of the permitting process was the Food Safety Manager Certification," admits Hoang. "Passing the test required some study since I had to learn a few new things, like better understanding food handling procedures to eliminate potentially harmful bacteria or viruses during preparation and the symptoms that might result from food poisoning." Her start-up costs included $800 for the Microenterprise Home Kitchen Operators permit, plus $400 that covered the Food Safety Manager Certification, test kits, and a refrigerator thermometer.

"I have all my time to care for my family," smiles Hoang, about the best part of operating her business out of her home kitchen. "And I don't have to wake up early to drive to work."

As a part of getting up and running, Hoang found she needed to expand her home kitchen slightly and figure out an efficient, safe, and cost-effective way to prepare and package take-out orders. Days when she takes orders are called "sell days."

"I bought more cabinets for my cake supplies and added a pantry for food container supplies. On sell days, I take out the to-go containers and set them up within reach on the counter so I can easily pack the orders. At the end of the sell day, I put all the packing boxes and other equipment back where they belong so my kitchen remains neat and organized." Like many cottage food operators and other cooks operating under similar MEHKO licenses, Hoang organized her home kitchen to separate various business aspects or uses from family uses.

Mynhan Hoang's braised pork baby ribs.
CREDIT: MYNHAN HOANG

To take and process prepared meal orders online, she turned exclusively to the Foodnome app, the first legal marketplace platform for home-cooked food in California that supports hundreds of home-based restaurant operations. She then cross-promotes weekly menu offerings on Facebook and Instagram. Her custom cake orders usually result from Facebook marketing efforts. Hoang makes her various prepared meals available Friday each week, from noon to 6:30 pm. Once the orders are placed, her customers simply pick them up at her home.

One of her more unique and popular regularly offered items is the Vietnamese Pandan honeycomb cake. It's gluten-free and loaded with protein, diary free and not overly sweet. Her specialty custom cakes, all made from scratch, often change throughout the year, based on the season or holiday. For her preorder 6-inch Mother's Day cakes, for example, she offered a custom cake topper, fresh flowers, and an edible image, either provided by her customer or another stock image. Cake fillings include strawberries, matcha, green tea, mocha, homemade pineapple jam, or cookies and cream. For dark or white chocolate, or fresh durian, a staple tropical fruit commonly found in Vietnam, were available for an extra charge.

Mynhan Hoang's Facebook engagement post for My Fair Kitchen, featuring a selection of her Vietnamese cuisine.
CREDIT: MYNHAN HOANG

"Custom specialty cakes are very important to the success of my business," says Hoang. "They require a high degree of skill and patience with details. If I didn't have the passion, I would not be able to deliver. Sometimes I stand 12 hours straight, overnight, to meet a cake delivery deadline." While most profits come from these cakes, the more consistent sales are individual meals ordered through the Foodnome app. Together, she averages about $500 in sales per week.

Banh khot, or Vietnamese mini meat pancakes. CREDIT: MYNHAN HOANG

Balancing her passion for cooking and motherly love for caring for her children, Hoang schedules the preparation of her meals via Foodnome and other preorders around the daily obligations of raising a family. With a click of a button, she can turn the Foodnome app ordering process on or off, based on time constraints that might exist.

"If you have a passion for cooking or just need an extra income while staying at home to raise your kids, go for it!" Hoang exclaims. She's eager to offer encouragement to others thinking about serving prepared meals out of their home. "With such a low start-up cost, it never hurts to try. The worst that could happen in terms of your business is not selling everything you make. In that case, your family will get to eat any delicious leftovers or unsold prepared food. So, you're never really wasting anything.

"I named My Fair Kitchen after *My Fair Lady*," says Hoang. "It also the same meaning of my name in Vietnamese 'Mynhan,' which translates to 'beauty lady' in Vietnamese. But for me, My Fair also means my price will be fair and reasonable to the customer, too." With hundreds of customers in her neighborhood who have placed thousands of orders, My Fair Kitchen is rebuilding community connections through shared food.

"Plenty of people want to be able to buy homemade meals from members of their community," says Smith Ewing, regarding the driving force behind the interest in food freedom legislation. "Many individuals and families have no time, ability, or even desire to cook, but they are having trouble finding freshly made, healthy food without additives and preservatives. The natural solution is to buy homemade. We just need the government to get out of the way."

Wyoming and Utah

"You can sell almost any food that you want!" exclaims Smith Ewing, about the groundbreaking food freedom law in Wyoming. Passed in 2015, it was the first food freedom law in the country. "You could sell shelf-stable foods, perishable foods, meals, macaroni and cheese lasagna. You could even, if you're a poultry farmer, take your own chickens and make them into a chicken sandwich. The only things that you can't sell are certain types of meat, unless you're a farmer and raised those meats directly on the farm."

Not far behind, was the state of Utah, passing MHKO legislation, inspired by the law in California but not requiring individual counties to opt in to allow MHKOs. They are statewide laws, with county health departments responsible for being the regulatory agency to complete the home kitchen inspection and issue the operator's permit.

"We knew there were people out there cooking for their neighbors, but there was no way to regulate or support these activities," says Utah Representative Christine Watkins, who was the main sponsor for the Microenterprise Home Kitchen Operation legislation. "Everyone likes to share in the delicious foods and culinary traditions brought into the state by many of the immigrants or refugees. It's one of groups we found to have the greatest interest in starting a home-based prepared foods or meals enterprise. We wanted to bring them out of the shadows and make it legal and safe."

North Dakota

Just because food freedom and MHKO laws are passed doesn't mean business is necessarily booming for home chefs. In some cases, regulatory agencies are tasked with how, exactly, to implement the laws passed. This takes time; it requires patience.

Passing in 2017, the Food Freedom Law in North Dakota reflects this ongoing conflict between legislators who pass the law and the state agency who have to set the rules and regulations under which the law operates. This is nothing new with food freedom initiatives as this happens time and time again. Sometimes, they might work against each other.

"After the legislature passed the fantastic North Dakota Food Freedom law, the department of health came in and tried to gut the law," explains Smith Ewing. "They didn't like it. They didn't want people to be able to sell perishable foods, chicken sandwiches, or lasagna. So, the health department said, 'You know what, we're going to just ignore the legislature and make our own rules.'" It took a legal case, led by the Institute for Justice and local North Dakota citizens, to secure a court decision that said what the agency did was wrong.

Montana

The state of Montana replaced their 2015 cottage food law with the Montana Local Food Choice Act in 2020. Per the new law: "'Homemade' means food or a food product that is prepared in a private home and that

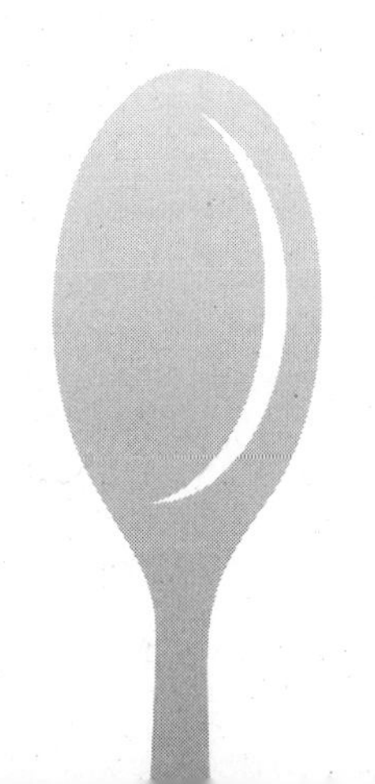

is not licensed, permitted, certified, packaged, labeled, or inspected per any official regulations." Unlike other states with MHKO laws or food freedom laws, the only requirement, really, is that the producer must inform potential customers that the homemade food or food product have not been licensed, permitted, certified, packaged, labeled, or inspected per any official regulations. Sales must, however, be direct, from producer to customer.

"While we have seen many states incrementally reform their cottage food laws for shelf-stable food, other states like Montana have fully embraced food freedom," explains Meagan Forbes, an attorney with the Institute for Justice. "There have been clear benefits for both producers and consumers in taking this more expansive approach without compromising food safety. Other states should follow suit and give home-based food entrepreneurs every opportunity to flourish."

According to the state of Montana SB 199, Montana Local Food Choice Act in 2020:

> The purpose of this act is to allow for the sale and consumption of homemade food and food products and to encourage the expansion of agricultural sales by ranches, farms, and home-based producers and the accessibility of homemade food and food products to informed end consumers by:
>
> (a) facilitating the purchase and consumption of fresh and local agricultural products;
> (b) enhancing the agricultural economy; and
> (c) providing Montana citizens with unimpeded access to healthy food from known sources.

What's striking about the language of Montana Local Food Choice Act is its emphasis on local, fresh, and healthy foods. In other words, not what you'd find at a fast-food drive-thru restaurant. Embedded in this law: an open invitation to any aspiring food entrepreneur. Start from home, test out your prepared food or food products, and support the farmers in your area.

"People understand that selling homemade foods is a good thing," says Smith Ewing. "It's good for customers who want to be able to buy local, buy fresh from their community. It's great for local economies. It's great for the environment. And when a customer bites into a freshly made chocolate chip cookie, right out of the oven, it's really good for that customer, too."

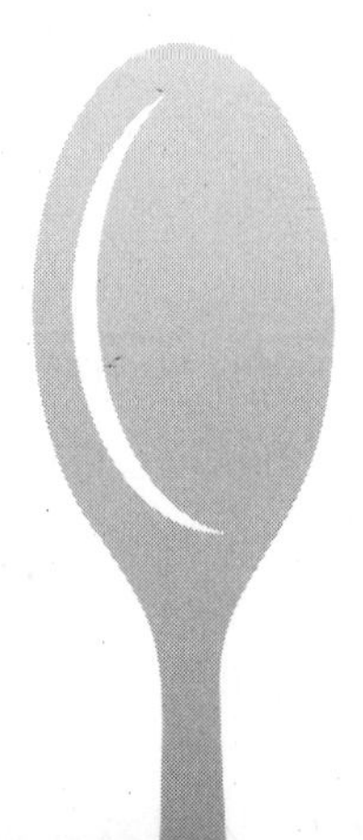

Oklahoma and Iowa

Oklahoma's Homemade Food Freedom Act, passed in 2021, boldly moved forward, allowing cottage food products to be sold wholesale to retail outlets or institutions, like restaurants. Additionally, it gave the green light to selling prepared meals, made in a home kitchen, as long as the ingredients didn't include meats, meat by-products, seafood, poultry, or poultry by-products. Alcohol, unpasteurized milk, and cannabis or marijuana products are also prohibited.

Oklahoma legislators used the acronym TCS, as mentioned in chapter 4, standing for "Time-or-temperature-controlled for safety." Sound appetizing? The term is right up there with "non-potentially hazardous." What we have been referring to as cottage foods in this book, low-moisture baked goods and high-acid canned goods, are classified in Oklahoma as non-TCS, meaning they don't require refrigeration. However, prepared meals and foods, because they require refrigeration, are TCS. Anyone selling these prepared meals, unlike cottage food products, must complete an Oklahoma Department of Agriculture, Food, and Forestry (ODAFF) approved food safety training course. This training helps ensure that the cheesecakes, cooked vegetables, and cooked noodles are safely prepared and delivered directly to the customers.

The Homemade Food Freedom law in Oklahoma creates two categories of homemade food for sale that use TCS classifications. The first is "non-time or temperature-controlled for safety" foods which are your non-hazardous foods typically found in cottage food laws like baked goods or candy. The bigger boost comes from the second category that includes some prepared foods and other foods that would be considered hazardous food that meet the TCS definition. Examples of prepared food items that are TCS include cheesecake, cooked vegetables, and cooked noodles. This law just doesn't allow homemade foods containing meats, seafood, or poultry, or any alcoholic drinks. In Oklahoma, the producer must meet certain other requirements, such as completing a food handler's certification course (just for people selling TCS foods) and a $75,000 sales cap.

"Allowing TCS foods open up lots of possibilities for cottage food producers and customers," adds Forbes, an attorney with the Institute for Justice who helped craft the law. "Cottage food producers can sell meals and other foods requiring refrigeration, like pastas, cooked vegetables, and cultural foods. This is a great option for customers who want to eat freshly made meals but either can't cook or don't have the time to."

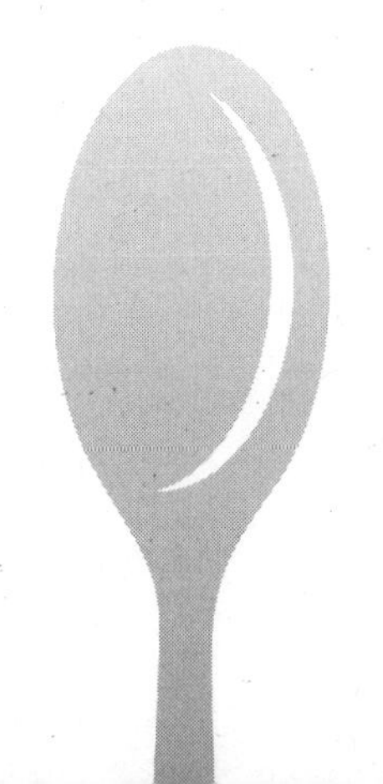

Food	Sold By	Sold To	Sales Location	Sales/Delivery Method	Public Notice	ODAFF approved food safety trainings
Non-TCS	Producer	Directly to the consumer	In person or by remote means such as phone or internet.	Any	Label or webpage	N
Non-TCS	Agent or 3rd party	Directly to the consumer	Retail sales venue. All marginal sales considerations of Chapter 257 apply.	Any	Labels and Placard	N
TCS	Producer	Directly to the consumer	In person or by remote means such as phone or internet.	By Producer directly to customer. No 3rd party sale or delivery,	Label or Webpage	Y

Oklahoma Homemade Food Freedom Act Guidance Chart for Time-or-temperature-controlled for safety (TCS).
CREDIT: OKLAHOMA STATE DEPARTMENT OF HEALTH

To help food safety risks, the *Risk Control Plan: Cooking TCS Foods* is a legal document released by the Oklahoma State Department of Health for home-based food entrepreneurs. We'd love to read all the Risk Control Plans generated daily by the diners, drive-ins, and dives in Oklahoma.

As we've written throughout this book, change is constant and usually expanding what cottage food operators can do in their state. A new cottage food law in Iowa (HF 2431) goes into effect and changes the state's license for "home bakeries" to "home food processing establishments." With this change, licensed home-based food operators can now sell products that contain meat or poultry, if the poultry was raised and slaughtered by the operator exempt under certain federal regulations and/or if the meat was secured from a local butcher or other approved source. This is in addition to home-based food operators being allowed to sell perishable baked goods like cream pies or cheesecakes that require refrigeration and other types of perishable foods like prepared meals, another rarity in the patchwork of state cottage food laws. Thanks to the elevated sales cap, ease of sales—both online and via mail—and nominal regulations, Iowa may have emerged as one of the best states in the country to launch a food business from home. In many states, cottage food laws are morphing into greatly expanded food freedom laws.

Food Fights

"Since 2013, with our first lawsuit brought against the state of Minnesota related to their restrictive cottage food law, we've been working on expanding cottage food and food freedom laws across the country," says Erica Smith Ewing with the Institute for Justice. "We do that by writing legislation and getting legislators to pass that legislation. And when that doesn't work, sometimes we just bring them to court. When the government says that you can't use your home kitchen to make food and sell it, we like to sue them." Technically, Smith Ewing is the attorney representing the bakers or canners, the plaintiffs in the cases, usually brought against the state.

"This is a constitutional right," explains Smith Ewing. This is the argument used in the successful Wisconsin lawsuit in which Lisa was a plaintiff.

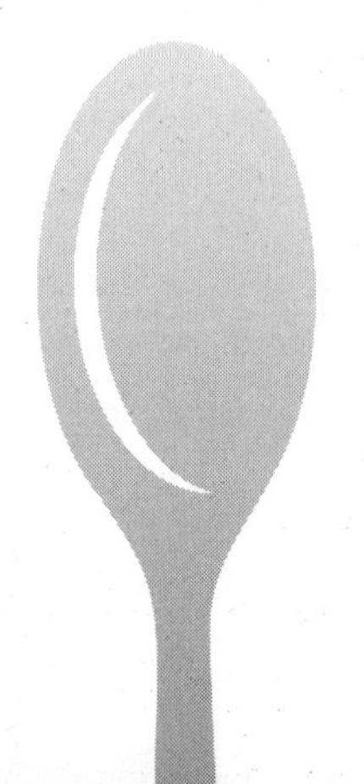

The judge ruled that the existing ban on the sale of home-baked goods was unconstitutional because the constitution gives us the right to earn an honest livelihood and for the government to not make arbitrary restrictions, which this was. Remember that before this ruling we could serve you muffins from our home kitchen for the B&B but we couldn't sell you the same muffins. Arbitrary. And ridiculous.

"The two biggest barriers are misinformation and protectionism," observes Smith Ewing, on what typically holds back the passage of food freedom or MHKO legislation. "First, many state agencies, like state health departments or agriculture departments, oppose food freedom legislation because they don't understand that homemade foods are extremely safe and rarely cause illness. In fact, there hasn't been a single illness in the food freedom states so far.

"Second, established commercial businesses fight these laws because they don't want the competition," continues Smith Ewing. "But this is America; competition makes us all better. And realistically, a single mom selling food on the weekend is not going to put any storefront out of business, at least not if that storefront is any good.

"The Institute for Justice is working with cottage food entrepreneurs in multiple states," says Smith Ewing, on the rapid pace of change related to these laws. "And there have been so many other groups that have made progress in other states."

Indeed, numerous battles on the state level have been undertaken by grassroots nonprofit organizations, working on behalf of their members. For example, the Illinois Stewardship Alliance had carried the torch since the very first steps were taken with the passage of the 2012 law, allowing for the sale of cottage food products. Today, they're moving forward on more expansive laws that support home-based food entrepreneurs with an eye to the future where home cooks can sell prepared foods in their community.

"Food freedom gives people greater power and responsibility over their food choices and decision-making for their own well-being," notes Molly Pickering, deputy director of the Illinois Stewardship Alliance, looking forward to the day when just about any food item, meal, or specialty food product will be available for neighbors and made by her neighbors. "Food freedom gives people greater power and opportunity to support their neighbors and keep food dollars local. Food freedom gives people more economic opportunity to start a business with the skills and equipment they

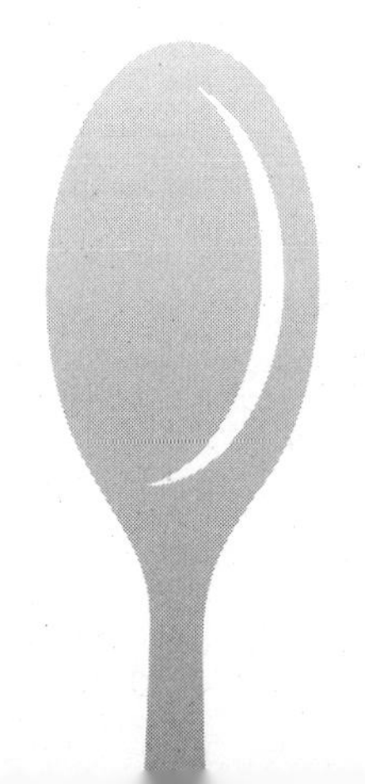

have on hand. Food freedom fosters the development of local supply chains and creates more resilient, food-secure, and self-sustaining communities.

"Supporting cottage food not only means supporting the growth of small businesses in Illinois. It also means supporting women-owned businesses," continues Pickering. "Ninety-percent of cottage food businesses are women-owned. It means supporting scale-appropriate regulations that enable people of all income-levels—but especially those of lower income—to start and grow a business. It means keeping food dollars local. It means reinvesting in Illinois communities. And it means laying the groundwork for a food secure Illinois, where Illinois farms and food businesses can feed Illinois."

Lemonade Law Loophole

Increasingly, some states are passing what have been dubbed "lemonade laws," publicly billed as taking down barriers for kids to sell lemonade. In most, selling lemonade is illegal. In a few states, the neighborhood kids were getting busted.

Interestingly, these lemonade laws are mostly not age-specific. So, there might be some opportunities for grown-ups too. Since lemonade needs to be refrigerated, it's excluded from state cottage food laws.

While worth researching and potentially tapping into if such a thing exists in your state, generally the full-scale, well thought-out food freedom law is what's preferred. Eventually a lemonade law would end up being amended as a food freedom law, perhaps expanded with various clarifications.

Ignite Your State's Food Freedom Law

"Check your state or local laws first, before jumping into a prepared food enterprise," counsels Smith Ewing, for potential prepared meal cooks not content with just making cookies, muffins, or crackers. "It's heartbreaking to see people put so much love and sweat into a business, only to have it shut down. And if the law doesn't allow what you want to do, don't be shy about contacting your representatives in government to ask them to change the law."

More than ever before, being in business also means being an advocate for what you believe in. This demands that you do more than just vote during an election. It may mean more involvement in the democratic process, talking with your representatives, and, in some cases, joining with the Institute for Justice to sue your state to overcome an obstacle or fight for greater economic justice.

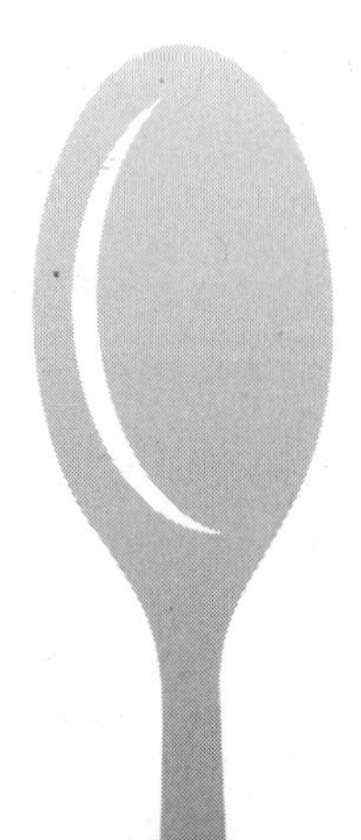

"The best way to get involved is to reach out to your state representatives and let them know the law needs to changed," continues Smith Ewing. "If your business has been shut down, don't be shy about reaching out to your local paper as well. You can always reach out to the Institute for Justice for help and legal guidance."

No one has a crystal ball to see the future or accurately predict the outcome resulting from the massive and disruptive changes underway, whether caused by climate change realities, evolving economy, untamed pandemic or future pandemics, or political power grabs. Regardless of what the future may bring, foods, especially locally made, will be an important part of that landscape, thanks to expanded food freedom and cottage food laws.

"I think that in future years, maybe ten years from now, food freedom will become the norm, and we will see that in a majority of states," predicts Smith Ewing. "I think we are going see a new website, a new software platform for cottage foods, that's going to be part Etsy and part Grubhub. We're going to see a service where you can order cottage foods and have them delivered maybe in a week, or even in a half hour. The next time you get a craving for cupcakes, you can order it and have it delivered to your home." In other words, the transaction of food service and food products will go full circle, just like they were exchanged a hundred years ago, from neighbors to neighbors in their community. Instead of drive-through fast food, we'll have homemade slow, delicious, and local food, prepared by neighbors.

Beyond the business entrepreneurship and economic development side, food freedom laws root in the heart of American democracy: the freedom to live our lives in a way we choose, providing we are transparent, authentic, and do not bring harm to others. Don't fence us in, federal, state, or local government. Be kind, fair, and neighborly.

The number of people losing faith in the government has been increasing for decades—through both Democratic and Republican administrations. In 2019, only 17 percent of Americans trusted the federal government to do the right thing "just about always" or "most of the time," according to the Pew Research Center. This has only taken a dive since the COVID-19 epidemic.

Many entrepreneurial Americans are increasingly fed up with business over-regulation and bureaucratic inefficiencies. Instead, they're eager to embrace the right to earn a living with a home-based food business under some form of food freedom or MHKO law. Some are willing to fight for it. We invite and welcome you.

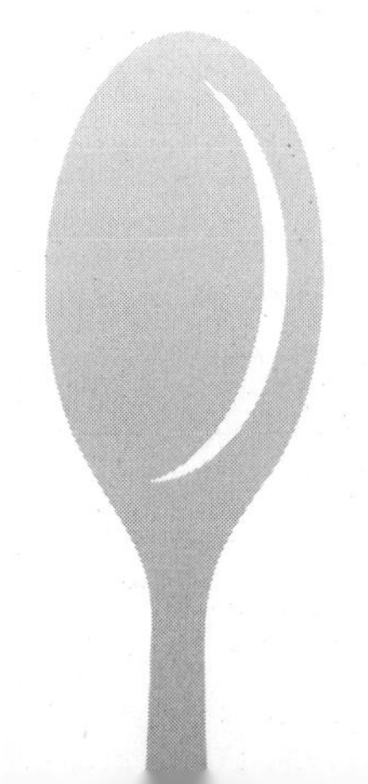

Epilogue: Icing on the Cake

HOMEMADE FOR SALE offers a snapshot of the growing cottage food and food freedom movements and the opportunities and the possibilities they offer. Tens of thousands of home cooks are embracing the idea of launching their own food enterprise. Many already have, captured by the inspiring story profiles found in this book. These cookiepreneurs, profitable picklers, and microenterprise home kitchen operators have made their dreams come true. Throughout these pages, we have also shared snippets of our own experiences at our home and business, Inn Serendipity Bed & Breakfast and farm in southwestern Wisconsin.

Our motivation to create a comprehensive start-up guide for cottage food operators stems from our interest in nurturing a nation of enterprising citizens. But our personal connection to the movement runs deeper than earning a little extra income by selling pickles and baked goods made in our home kitchen. We see food as a path to freedom and happiness in multiple ways. Back in our twenties, we did everything "right" according to our family, the media, and society. We commuted to corporate cubicles, received a bi-monthly paycheck, and bought shrink-wrapped groceries and take-out meals packed in Styrofoam containers. We lived tethered to the system, dependent on others for everything from our paycheck to our dinner menu.

We discovered early on, however, that this path wasn't for us. After we took the big leap in 1996 and moved to our five acres in Wisconsin, we planted our first zucchini seeds in the garden that following spring. Playing a joke that only Mother Nature can play, those initial zucchini seeds never sprouted. But we kept planting. And planting. The following seasons brought both bountiful garden harvests and increasing morning muffin baking as we learned, challenged ourselves, and grew in multiple ways.

We realized and embraced the independence that comes with connecting with both our food source and our entrepreneurial spirit. These two forces empowered us and peppered our lives with creativity, passion, and the satisfaction that comes with growing, preparing, and savoring our own meals, usually around the dining room table with our son, family, or friends. That intoxicating combination of food and self-employment transformed our lives and drives us to share this elixir with others, with you, through *Homemade for Sale.* The truth emerged from our jar of pickles and bread, still warm from the oven: we found our happiness in the foods we shared and the life we created around our passions for nourishing ourselves and sustaining the planet.

For more on our story, please see our other books: *Rural Renaissance, ECOpreneuring, Farmstead Chef,* and *Soil Sisters*. In the pages of *Homemade for Sale*, we aspired to provoke, inspire, and inform. We essayed to both provide a launching pad for your dream business built around your passions and offer a tool kit for you to start your own cottage food venture. Depending on where you call home, the passage of state laws related to cottage food, food freedom, and microenterprise home kitchen operations enables just about anyone, anywhere, to turn their home-cooked passion into some profits and revitalize their local economy.

While we can serve a delicious, locally sourced, hot breakfast at our Inn Serendipity B&B, we cannot sell that same breakfast to a neighbor down the road. We're excited about the food freedom and MHKO laws that are sweeping the nation, in part, because we've already completed most of the requirements as a result of operating the Inn. One day, we'd like to be able to invite everyone over to enjoy our amazing artisanal pizza, cooked in a 700-degree wood-fired outdoor oven, dining al fresco surrounded by rolling countryside. Our pizzas are made with our homegrown organic tomatoes, onions, garlic, spinach, zucchini, local Green County cheeses, and regionally sourced organic flour. In other words, our pizzas provide a taste of place. Home.

We invite you to share your story, idea, or inspiration on the website created for this book: homemadeforsale.com. And look for us in line at your holiday bazaar or farmers' market stand—or us clicking "Like" on your Facebook page.

Together, we can change the way America eats.

Author John Ivanko cooking artisanal pizza in a wood-fired pizza oven.
CREDIT: LIAM KIVIRIST

Appendix A

University of Wisconsin-Stout first-ever national Cottage Food Operator Assessment study completed by Rachael Miller, Principal Investigator and MS candidate, University of Wisconsin-Stout

CREDIT: RACHAEL MILLER, PRINCIPAL INVESTIGATOR AND MS CANDIDATE, UNIVERSITY OF WISCONSIN-STOUT

Who are Cottage Food Operators?

Most CFOs are married.

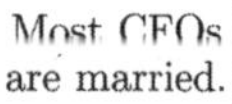

How much education have CFOs had?

- 34% bachelor's degree
- 20% master's degree
- 18% high school diploma
- 17% associate degree
- 7% trade school
- 4% other

CFOs live in a variety of places.

- 33% small town/rural
- 29% suburb
- 19% farm/rural
- 18% urban/city
- 1% other

Most CFOs are female.

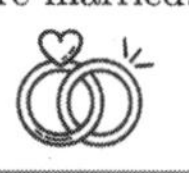

What are the annual household incomes of CFOs?

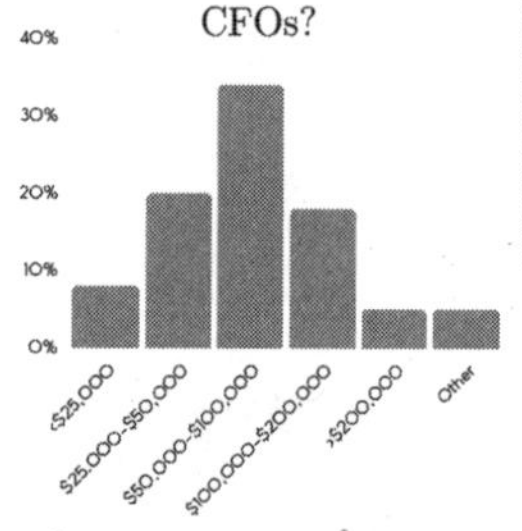

How old are CFOs?

- 2% 18-24
- 17% 25-34
- 22% 35-44
- 20% 45-54
- 25% 55-64
- 13% 65+
- 1% other

For CFOs currently operating... 34% have full time jobs, 16% are retired, 13% have a part time job, and 13% are stay-at-home parents.

29% of CFOs are caring for children under 18 years.

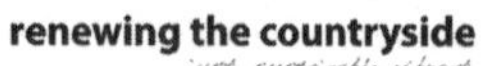

What are the business dreams of aspiring CFOs?

What products do aspiring CFOs want to sell?

- **11% bread**
- **11% undecorated cookies**
- 10% other baked goods
- 8% muffins, rolls, bagels, and scones
- 8% cupcakes
- 7% decorated cookies
- 7% undecorated cakes
- 7% high-acid canned goods
- 6% pastries
- 25% other

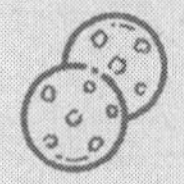

CFOs are divided on whether they want this to be their full time income.

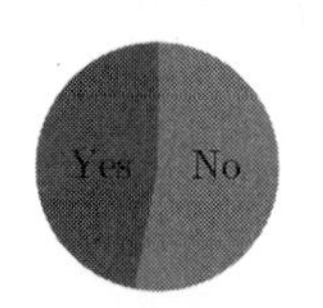

Only 32% of CFOs actually want a brick and mortar storefront.

Why do aspiring CFOs want to start?

17% said additional household income needed.

17% said to fulfill food entrepreneur and business owner dreams.

renewing the countryside
just. sustainable. vibrant.

Challenges & barriers of aspiring CFOs?

What barriers limit cottage food as their full time income source?

25% said lack of customers.

19% said lack of time or space.

16% feel restricted by cottage food laws.

10% said lack of support.

What challenges do aspiring CFOs experience?

23% said understanding state regulations.

17% said promoting and marketing products.

19% said managing the business aspects.

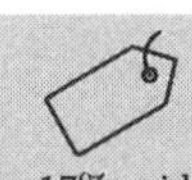

17% said pricing products.

14% feel state regulations are too limiting.

renewing the countryside 
just. sustainable. vibrant.

What do current CFOs sell? What's most profitable?

STOUT
Cottage Food Operator Assessment

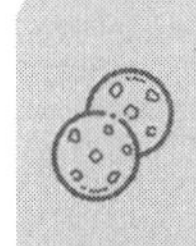

Undecorated cookies and cupcakes are the products sold by the most current CFOs.

What products generate the most sales annually for current CFOs?

- **18% decorated cookies**
- **17% high-acid canned goods**
- 12% custom decorated cakes
- 11% bread
- 10% undecorated cookies
- 7% other baked goods
- 6% cupcakes
- 5% pastries
- 4% undecorated cakes
- 10% other

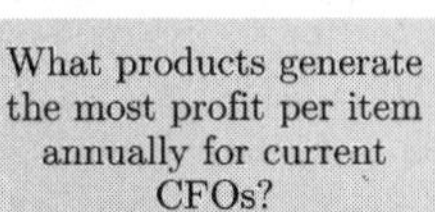

What products generate the most profit per item annually for current CFOs?

- **14% undecorated cookies**
- **14% high-acid canned goods**
- 13% decorated cookies
- 11% custom decorated cakes
- 11% bread
- 6% cupcakes
- 5% other baked goods
- 4% pastries
- 4% undecorated cakes
- 18% other

renewing the countryside 
just. sustainable. vibrant.

What does the current CFO's business look like?

CFOs are structured as... 66% sole proprietorship, 24% are single member LLCs, 10% other.

Only 40% of current CFOs reported having business insurance, with the largest barrier being the cost.

What percent of the year do current CFOs operate?

- 54% year-round
- 16% half year
- 14% only special events, birthdays, holidays
- 10% one big season
- 3% outdoor farmers' market
- 3% other

The most popular business insurance reported is business liability insurance specifically for the cottage food industry, with the most common annual insurance price being $300.

Taxes

Only 4% pay themselves a salary with a W-2 filing. 40% report paying self-employment taxes.

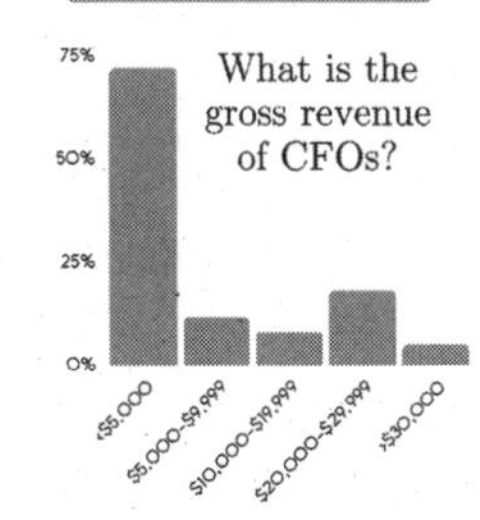

What is the gross revenue of CFOs?

For current CFOs: 47% have a home office/supply storage room; 91% use their personal vehicle for business.

renewing the countryside 
just. sustainable. vibrant.

Index

About the Authors

Lisa Kivirist and John D. Ivanko are nationally recognized speakers and writers, with 15 books between them, including the award-winning *ECOpreneuring, Homemade for Sale, Farmstead Chef,* and *Rural Renaissance.* Together, they spearheaded the first-ever Home-based Food Entrepreneur Virtual National Conference. They regularly offer hands-on workshops related to launching cottage food businesses as well as the best-selling online Udemy course: How to Start and Market a Food Business from Your Home Kitchen. Lisa and John also write extensively on topics related to homemade food products or on-farm food service, like farm-to-table dinners on the farm or "pizza farms." They work with Renewing the Countryside, an organization that offers on-farm food service training programs.

As recognized spokespeople for cottage food and food freedom laws, the national sustainable agriculture movement, and ecotourism, Lisa and John are regular presenters at national conferences and library, university, and community events. They've been featured in the *New York Times, USA Today, Conde Nast Traveler,* MSNBC, and on various radio programs countrywide, including Martha Stewart Radio, the Sirius Satellite Network, and *Good Food* on KCRW. As freelance journalists, they've contributed to *Mother Earth News, Reuters, Urban Farm, National Geographic Traveler, Hobby Farms,* and *Natural Awakenings,* among many others. They also contribute to MotherEarthNews.com.

A national advocate for women in sustainable agriculture, Lisa Kivirist leads the Soil Sisters project at Renewing the Countryside, providing training, resources, and networking for women in this area, the subject of her book *Soil Sisters: A Toolkit for Women Farmers.* She spearheads the largest women-farmer-led annual event of its kind in the country, Soil Sisters: A Celebration of Wisconsin Farms and Rural Life. She serves as a Senior Fellow, Endowed Chair in Agricultural Systems for the Minnesota Institute for Sustainable Agriculture at the University of Minnesota and served as a Kellogg Food and Community Fellow.

A leading advocate for cottage food entrepreneurs, Lisa acted as a plaintiff in the successful lawsuit against the State of Wisconsin that declared the ban on the sale of home-baked goods unconstitutional. As a result, she and her family launched Inn Serendipity Fresh Baked Homemade Bakery, offering truly homemade bakery items to the local community and throughout Wisconsin. Lisa co-founded the Wisconsin Cottage Food Association and is currently engaged in a new lawsuit to legalize all non-hazardous food products for sale from home kitchens.

John D. Ivanko co-authored, with Maya Ajmera, several award-winning children's multicultural photobooks, including *To Be a Kid, Back to School, Come Out and Play, Be My Neighbor, To Be an Artist,* and *Animal Friends*. As a professional photographer, John has had his work, some captured with his drone, featured in numerous international media as well as on ALAMY Stock Photo.

Lisa and John are also innkeepers of the award-winning Inn Serendipity Bed & Breakfast, completely powered by renewable energy. Their B&B features local seasonal vegetarian cuisine prepared with ingredients harvested from the Inn's organic gardens. Lisa and John share their organic farm in Browntown, Wisconsin, with their son and millions of ladybugs. You can connect with Lisa and John on Facebook.

Left: *Author Lisa Kivirist, baking in the home kitchen.* Credit: Institute for Justice

Right: *Author John Ivanko taking a break from growing organic vegetables used in many of the cottage food products sold by Inn Serendipity.* Credit: Lisa Kivirist

ABOUT NEW SOCIETY PUBLISHERS

New Society Publishers is an activist, solutions-oriented publisher focused on publishing books to build a more just and sustainable future. Our books offer tips, tools, and insights from leading experts in a wide range of areas.

We're proud to hold to the highest environmental and social standards of any publisher in North America. When you buy New Society books, you are part of the solution!

At New Society Publishers, we care deeply about *what* we publish — but also about *how* we do business.

- This book is printed on **100% post-consumer recycled paper,** processed chlorine-free, with low-VOC vegetable-based inks (since 2002).
- Our corporate structure is an innovative employee shareholder agreement, so we're one-third employee-owned (since 2015)
- We've created a Statement of Ethics (2021). The intent of this Statement is to act as a framework to guide our actions and facilitate feedback for continuous improvement of our work
- We're carbon-neutral (since 2006)
- We're certified as a B Corporation (since 2016)
- We're Signatories to the UN's Sustainable Development Goals (SDG) Publishers Compact (2020–2030, the Decade of Action)

To download our full catalog, sign up for our quarterly newsletter, and to learn more about New Society Publishers, please visit newsociety.com

ENVIRONMENTAL BENEFITS STATEMENT

New Society Publishers saved the following resources by printing the pages of this book on chlorine free paper made with 100% post-consumer waste.

TREES	WATER	ENERGY	SOLID WASTE	GREENHOUSE GASES
83 FULLY GROWN	6,600 GALLONS	35 MILLION BTUs	280 POUNDS	36,100 POUNDS

Environmental impact estimates were made using the Environmental Paper Network Paper Calculator 4.0. For more information visit www.papercalculator.org